THE EUROPEAN UNION SERIES

General Editors: Neill Nugent, William E. Pate

The European Union series provides an authoritative
from general introductory texts to definitive assessm   ~~.~ ~~..~~~, ~~.~~~~~,
policies and policy processes, and the role of member states.

Books in the series are written by leading scholars in their fields and reflect the most up-to-date
research and debate. Particular attention is paid to accessibility and clear presentation for a
wide audience of students, practitioners and interested general readers.

The series editors are **Neill Nugent**, Emeritus Professor of Politics at Manchester Metropolitan
University, UK, and **William E. Paterson**, Honorary Professor in German and European Studies,
University of Aston. Their co-editor until his death in July 1999, **Vincent Wright**, was a Fellow of
Nuffield College, Oxford University.

Feedback on the series and book proposals are always welcome and should be sent to
Stephen Wenham, Palgrave, 4 Crinan Street, London N1 9XW, or by e-mail to
s.wenham@palgrave.com

General textbooks

Published

Laurie Buonanno and Neill Nugent, **Policies
and Policy Processes of the European
Union**

Desmond Dinan, **Encyclopedia of the
European Union** [Rights: Europe only]

Desmond Dinan, **Europe Recast: A History
of the European Union (2nd edn)** [Rights:
Europe only]

Desmond Dinan, **Ever Closer Union: An
Introduction to European Integration (4th
edn)** [Rights: Europe only]

Mette Eilstrup Sangiovanni (ed.), **Debates on
European Integration: A Reader**

Simon Hix and Bjørn Høyland, **The Political
System of the European Union (3rd edn)**

Dirk Leuffen, Berthold Rittberger and Frank
Schimmelfennig, **Differentiated Integration**

Paul Magnette, **What Is the European Union?
Nature and Prospects**

John McCormick, **Understanding the
European Union: A Concise Introduction
(6th edn)**

Brent F. Nelsen and Alexander Stubb, **The
European Union: Readings on the Theory
and Practice of European Integration (4th
edn)** [Rights: Europe only]

Neill Nugent (ed.), **European Union
Enlargement**

Neill Nugent, **The Government and Politics
of the European Union (7th edn)**

John Peterson and Elizabeth Bomberg,
Decision-Making in the European Union

Ben Rosamond, **Theories of European
Integration**

Sabine Saurugger, **Theoretical Approaches to
European Integration**

Ingeborg Tömmel, **The European Union: What
It Is and How it Works**

Esther Versluis, Mendeltje van Keulen and Paul
Stephenson, **Analyzing the European Union
Policy Process**

Hubert Zimmermann and Andreas Dür (eds),
Key Controversies in European Integration

Forthcoming

Magnus Ryner and Alan Cafruny, **A Critical
Introduction to the European Union**

Also planned

The European Union and Global Politics
**The Political Economy of European
Integration**

Series Standing Order (outside North America only)
ISBN 978–0–333–71695–3 hardback
ISBN 978–0–333–69352–0 paperback
Full details from palgravehighered.com

The major institutions and actors

Published

Renaud Dehousse, **The European Court of Justice**

Justin Greenwood, **Interest Representation in the European Union (3rd edn)**

Fiona Hayes-Renshaw and Helen Wallace, **The Council of Ministers (2nd edn)**

Simon Hix and Christopher Lord, **Political Parties in the European Union**

David Judge and David Earnshaw, **The European Parliament (2nd edn)**

Neill Nugent and Mark Rhinard, **The European Commission (2nd edn)**

Anne Stevens with Handley Stevens, **Brussels Bureaucrats? The Administration of the European Union**

Wolfgang Wessels, **The European Council**

Forthcoming

Ariadna Ripoll Servent, **The European Parliament**

Sabine Saurugger and Fabien Terpan, **The European Court of Justice and the Politics of Law**

The main areas of policy

Published

Karen Anderson, **Social Policy in the European Union**

Michael Baun and Dan Marek, **Cohesion Policy in the European Union**

Michele Chang, **Monetary Integration in the European Union**

Michele Chang, **Economic and Monetary Union**

Michelle Cini and Lee McGowan, **Competition Policy in the European Union (2nd edn)**

Wyn Grant, **The Common Agricultural Policy**

Martin Holland and Mathew Doidge, **Development Policy of the European Union**

Jolyon Howorth, **Security and Defence Policy in the European Union (2nd edn)**

Johanna Kantola, **Gender and the European Union**

Stephan Keukeleire and Tom Delreux, **The Foreign Policy of the European Union (2nd edn)**

Brigid Laffan, **The Finances of the European Union**

Malcolm Levitt and Christopher Lord, **The Political Economy of Monetary Union**

Janne Haaland Matláry, **Energy Policy in the European Union**

John McCormick, **Environmental Policy in the European Union**

John Peterson and Margaret Sharp, **Technology Policy in the European Union**

Handley Stevens, **Transport Policy in the European Union**

Maren Kreutler, Johannes Pollak and Samuel Schubert, **Energy Policy in the European Union**

Tom Delreux and Sander Happaerts, **Environmental Policy and Politics in the European Union**

Forthcoming

Sieglinde Gstöhl and Dirk de Bievre, **The Trade Policy of the European Union**

Christian Kaunert and Sarah Leonard, **Justice and Home Affairs in the European Union**

Paul Stephenson, Esther Versluis and Mendeltje van Keulen, **Implementing and Evaluating Policy in the European Union**

Also planned

Political Union

The member states and the Union

Published

Carlos Closa and Paul Heywood, **Spain and the European Union**

Andrew Geddes, **Britain and the European Union**

Alain Guyomarch, Howard Machin and Ella Ritchie, **France in the European Union**

Brigid Laffan and Jane O'Mahoney, **Ireland and the European Union**

Forthcoming

Simon Bulmer and William E. Paterson, **Germany and the European Union**

Brigid Laffan, **The European Union and its Member States**

Issues

Published

Senem Aydın-Düzgit and Nathalie Tocci, **Turkey and the European Union**

Derek Beach, **The Dynamics of European Integration: Why and When EU Institutions Matter**

Christina Boswell and Andrew Geddes, **Migration and Mobility in the European Union**

Thomas Christiansen and Christine Reh, **Constitutionalizing the European Union**

Tuomas Forsberg and Hiski Haukkala, **The European Union and Russia**

Robert Ladrech, **Europeanization and National Politics**

Cécile Leconte, **Understanding Euroscepticism**

Steven McGuire and Michael Smith, **The European Union and the United States**

Wyn Rees, **The US–EU Security Relationship: The Tensions between a European and a Global Agenda**

Forthcoming

Graham Avery, **Enlarging the European Union**

Thomas Christiansen, Emil Kirchner and Uwe Wissenbach, **The European Union and China**

The European Union and Russia

Tuomas Forsberg

and

Hiski Haukkala

First published 2016 by
PALGRAVE

Palgrave in the UK is an imprint of Macmillan Publishers Limited, registered in England, company number 785998, of 4 Crinan Street, London, N1 9XW.

Palgrave Macmillan in the US is a division of St Martin's Press LLC, 175 Fifth Avenue, New York, NY 10010.

Palgrave is a global imprint of the above companies and is represented throughout the world.

Palgrave® and Macmillan® are registered trademarks in the United States, the United Kingdom, Europe and other countries.

ISBN 978–1–137–35534–8 hardback
ISBN 978–1–137–35533–1 paperback

This book is printed on paper suitable for recycling and made from fully managed and sustained forest sources. Logging, pulping and manufacturing processes are expected to conform to the environmental regulations of the country of origin.

A catalogue record for this book is available from the British Library.

A catalog record for this book is available from the Library of Congress.

Printed in China

Contents

List of Figures and Tables

Figures

Tables

List of Abbreviations

AA	Association Agreement
BRICS	Brazil, Russia, India, China and South Africa
CEECs	Central and Eastern European Countries
CES	Common Economic Space
CFSP	Common Foreign and Security Policy
CIS	Commonwealth of Independent States
CIUDAD	Cooperation In Urban Development and Dialogue
CMEA	Council for Mutual Economic Assistance
CoE	Council of Europe
COEST	Working Party on Eastern Europe and Central Asia
COPS	*Comité politique et de sécurité* (FR), Political and Security Committee (PSC)
COREPER II	Committee of Permanent Representatives to the EU
CSCE	Conference on Security and Cooperation in Europe
CSDP	Common Security and Defence Policy
CSTO	Collective Security Treaty Organization
DCFTA	Deep and Comprehensive Free Trade Area
DCI-HUM	Development Cooperation Instrument–Human and Social Development
DG	Commission Directorates-General
DG RELEX	Commission Directorate-General for External Relations
EaP	Eastern Partnership
EC	European Community
ECJ	Court of Justice of the EU
ECT	Energy Charter Treaty
ECTS	European Credit Transfer System
ECU	Eurasian Customs Union
EEAS	European External Action Service
EEC	European Economic Community
EEU	Eurasian Economic Union
EIA	U.S. Energy Information Administration

EIDHR	European Instrument for Democracy and Human Rights
ENI	European Neighbourhood Instrument
ENP	European Neighbourhood Policy
ENPI	European Neighbourhood and Partnership Instrument
ERPSC	Joint EU–Russia Committee on Security and Foreign Policy
ESA	European Space Agency
ESDP	European Security and Defence Policy
ESFRI	European Strategy Forum on Research Infrastructures
ESI	European Studies Institute in Moscow
EU	European Union
EUBAM	EU Border Assistance Mission
EUMM	EU Monitoring Mission
EUPM	European Union Police Mission
EWM	early warning mechanism
FAC	Foreign Affairs Council
FDI	foreign direct investment
FAE	fundamental attribution error
FPA	foreign policy analysis
FSB	Federal Security Service of the Russian Federation
FSU	Former Soviet Union
FTA	Free Trade Area
FTD	facilitated transit document
GAERC	General Affairs and External Relations Council
GATT	General Agreement on Tariffs and Trade
GMES	Global Monitoring for the Environment and Security
GRU	Russian military intelligence directorate
HELCOM	Baltic Marine Environment Protection Commission or Helsinki Commission
HR	High Representative of the Union for Foreign Affairs and Security Policy
IBPP	Institution Building Partnership Programme
IFI	International Financial Institutions Advisory Group (of the EU)
IMEMO	Institute of World Economy and International Relations
IR	international relations

IRT	EU–Russia Industrialists' Round Table
ISIS	Islamic State of Iraq and Syria
ITAR-TASS	Russian News Agency TASS
KFOR	Kosovo Force
KGB	*Komitet gosudarstvennoy bezopasnosti* [Committee for State Security]
LBT	local border traffic
LGBT	lesbian, gay, bisexual, transgender
LNG	liquefied natural gas
MGIMO	Moscow Institute of International Relations (University) of the Russian Ministry of Foreign Affairs
MID	The Ministry of Foreign Affairs of the Russian Federation
MNRE	Russian Ministry of Natural Resources and Ecology
NATO	North Atlantic Treaty Organization
ND	Northern Dimension
NDEP	Northern Dimension Environmental Partnership
NDPC	Northern Dimension Partnership on Culture
NDPHS	Northern Dimension Partnership in Public Health and Social Well-being
NDPTL	Northern Dimension Partnership on Transport and Logistics
NGOs	non-governmental organizations
ODIHR	Office for Democratic Institutions and Human Rights of the OSCE
OSCE	Organization for Security and Co-operation in Europe
P4M	Partnership for Modernization
PCA	Partnership and Cooperation Agreement
PMR	Pridnestrovian Moldavian Republic
PNR	passenger name record
PPC	Permanent Partnership Council
PR	public relations
PSC	Political and Security Committee (of the EU)
R2P	Responsibility to Protect
RELEX	DG External Relations
SCO	Shanghai Cooperation Organization
SFOR	NATO-led Stabilization Force (SFOR) in Bosnia and Herzegovina
SMEs	small and medium-sized enterprises

SVOP	Council on Foreign and Defence Policy
S&T	Science and Technology
TACIS	Technical Aid to the Commonwealth of Independent States
TCA	trade and cooperation agreements
TPA	third-party access
UEN	Union for Europe of the Nations, group of the European Parliament 1999–2009
UN	United Nations
UNMIK	United Nations Interim Administration Mission in Kosovo
UNSC	United Nations Security Council
USSR	Soviet Union
U.S./US	United States
WEU	Western European Union
WTO	World Trade Organization

Acknowledgements

This book deals with the evolution of EU–Russia relations since the end of the Cold War. During this period, our thinking about the topic has obviously evolved in lockstep with the development of relations between the two. We feel that the current crisis between the two 'strategic partners' is the right moment to try to tell the whole story of the relations, including their ups and downs and current failure. It is also a topic that calls for an explanation, as well as contemplation about what the future will hold. These are all things that this book seeks to provide. In fact, we had planned to write it in 2014, but the conflict in Ukraine and the consequent crisis in EU–Russia relations created such a tumult that we had to wait for the dust to settle somewhat. The rupture also posed new questions that had to be addressed, and now that a certain 'new normal' has set in, and although it will not last forever, it marks the end of one historical era in these relations and has enabled us to move forward with this book.

Originally, this was supposed to be a single-authored monograph, but luckily Tuomas joined as a riding shotgun early on. As a consequence, the book is based on intense and genuine collaboration between the two of us. Hiski has taken the lead in writing Chapters 2, 3, 4 and 8, and Tuomas Chapters 5, 6, 7 and 9. There has been plenty of interaction and mutual give and take in writing the chapters, and we feel confident about calling this a truly joint work.

This book is indeed the product and culmination of two decades of research on EU–Russia relations during which time our paths have crossed several times. We have lived in an academic environment where we have benefited from the richness of both university and think-tank traditions, and one of us has also acted as a practitioner (it goes without saying that none of what follows necessarily represents the official Finnish positions). Both of us have intensively followed the development of relations since the early years of our career, and along the way we have published a great deal of research related to the theme (Forsberg 2005, 2011, 2014, 2016; Forsberg and Herd 2005, 2015; Forsberg and Seppo 2009, 2011; Haukkala 2003, 2006, 2008, 2009, 2010, 2013a, 2013b, 2014, 2015; and David, Gower and Haukkala 2013; as well as Mäkinen, Smith and Forsberg 2016).

This earlier research has served as invaluable background material, but everything has been revised, rewritten and updated for the purposes of this book. We nevertheless thank the co-authors, publishers and others who made this earlier research possible. We have benefited from interaction with an intricate network of outstanding colleagues and friends over the years, most recently and concretely at the University of Tampere, but also at the Finnish Institute of International Affairs, Aleksanteri Institute, the Ministry for Foreign Affairs of Finland, College of Europe at Natolin in Warsaw as well as elsewhere abroad. A big thank you is due to all of you – you know who you are. We are also immensely grateful to the following individuals for their comments and/or assistance in preparing the book: Derek Averre, Magda Leichtova, Kari Liuhto, Graeme Herd, Michael Kofman, Sirke Mäkinen, Hanna Ojanen, Heikki Patomäki, Christer Pursiainen, Sinikukka Saari, Julia Simpanen, Hanna Smith and Laura Solanko; in particular, we would like to thank Pami Aalto, Jackie Gower, Tatiana Romanova and Petteri Vuorimäki, and the two anonymous referees provided by Palgrave for reading the whole manuscript and providing detailed comments on it. Draft chapters of the book have been presented at various international conferences (e.g. EISA Warsaw 2013, ISA Toronto 2014, EUIA Brussels 2014, EISA Giardini Naxos 2015) and we have also benefited from comments made by discussants and fellow panellists as well as the audience at large. We are furthermore grateful for background interviews and other discussions we have conducted for this book, either directly or indirectly, in Berlin; Brussels; Helsinki; London; Moscow; Warsaw; Washington, D.C.; and numerous other European capitals. We would also like to thank Matti Pesu and Ilmari Uljas for their excellent research assistance, flexibility and good humour in meeting our endless research needs. Finally, we would like to thank Lynn Nikkanen for making our English presentable once again, as well as the great team at Palgrave, including the Series Editors Neill Nugent and William E. Paterson, for their smooth cooperation and patience during a process that took much, much longer than initially expected.

Research for this book has been partially conducted in the framework of the Academy of Finland Centre of Excellence on Choices of Russian Modernisation at the Aleksanteri Institute and at the University of Helsinki together with the University of Tampere (grant nr 284664). This support is gratefully acknowledged.

Tuomas Forsberg and Hiski Haukkala

Chapter 1

Introduction: European Union–Russia Relations as the Partnership That Failed

March 2014 witnessed a dramatic rupture in European Union–Russia relations, and indeed even a collapse of the wider European security order, which had been in gestation for over 25 years. Russia's annexation of Crimea, and the destabilization of the eastern parts of Ukraine that followed, brought the European Union (EU) and Russia to the brink of a severe confrontation with each other as well. The EU imposed a series of restrictive measures; Russia retaliated with its own counter-sanctions; and most of the cooperation was halted. What is more, a military conflict between Russia and an EU member state was seen by many as likelier than at any time since the end of the Cold War. The prognosis for the future is dire, and there seems to be no easy way out of the vicious and antagonistic cycle.

The paradox is that neither the EU nor Russia aspired to this state of affairs. The EU favours cooperation with Russia, and vice versa, but the problem, and the story that will be recounted in full on the pages that follow, concerns on *whose* terms that cooperation should be carried out. The situation resembles a classical dilemma – a tragedy, in fact – where neither side wants the outcome it has obtained, but at the same time both have been unable to alter the policies that have contributed to the problem in the first place. At the end of the book, we will discuss some of the options for how this dilemma could be solved. In the meantime, it is important to probe how the parties ended up in these circumstances.

In this book the emphasis is put on the European Union and Russia, and the interaction between them, but essentially this is a book about the evolving and historical relationship between 'Russia' and 'Europe' (see Haukkala 2008; White and Feklyunina 2015). Both these terms are tricky and can easily mislead if they are taken literally. The EU, of course, is nothing more than the current incarnation and the latest institutional manifestation of a conglomeration of European nation-states that used to be, but are today not entirely, 'Western European'. In the process, it has reached a level of integration unprecedented in time and place. Twenty-five years ago, when our story was just beginning, the EU was still the European Community (EC). In the future it might be called something different yet again, or it may even cease to exist as we know it (Zielonka 2014). By the same token, Russia is officially called the Russian Federation today, but for most of the previous century it was the Soviet Union, and later in this century we may possibly end up talking more about the Eurasian Union than Russia.

Hence, on the pages that follow we should keep in mind that, on the one hand, we are dealing with a *longue durée* problem of Russia's place in (or with) Europe, both politically and institutionally (see Neumann 1996 and Hopf 2008). But on the other hand, we cannot avoid discussing the more technical present-day issues concerning the practical modalities of building those relations in the here and now. Therefore, a natural starting point for the narrative is not some sixteenth-century encounters (cf. Neumann 2011), although we will reflect upon some earlier relations too, but rather the end of the Cold War and the formation of relations between the European Union and Russia at that point in time and place.

Coincidentally, one day before the European Union was established by 12 member states of the European Communities at the Maastricht Summit in December 1991, President Boris Yeltsin of the Russian Soviet Federative Socialist Republic met with the leaders of the Ukrainian and Belorussian Soviet Republics in Belavezha Forest in Western Belarus and decided to dissolve the Soviet Union. The EU and the successor state of the Soviet Union, the Russian Federation, have been developing their relations ever since these historical events. In the initial stages, the relationship revealed certain asymmetries, because one union was integrating and the other disintegrating, and their economic welfare and living standards were at very different levels. These different starting points were reflected in the European Commission's Technical Aid to the Commonwealth of Independent States (TACIS) assistance programme in 1991. Before long, the two put their relations on a more stable and equal footing by concluding the Partnership and Cooperation Agreement (PCA) in 1994, which duly entered into force in 1997. Since then, they have made considerable efforts to develop the relations. They promoted the Northern Dimension as an interface between the EU and Russia to engage with each other at the regional level and created strategies to deal with each other in the early 2000s. They established the Four Common Spaces in economics, judicial matters, external security, and research and education in 2003; adopted a set of road maps for their implementation in 2005; and agreed on a Partnership for Modernisation in 2010. They also started to renegotiate the PCA. Yet, and all this hectic activity to enhance their relations and cooperation notwithstanding, the two 'strategic partners' ended up in a serious crisis in 2014 due to the conflict in Ukraine and, some would say, even *over* Ukraine.

The overall mood in EU–Russia relations had deteriorated long before the Ukraine crisis. The regular summits brought no major results, and the parties were not able to conclude a new basic treaty to replace the clearly outdated PCA. Even a decade ago some Russian analysts concluded that 'Russia has left the West' (Trenin 2006) and that it had little interest in seriously developing its relations with the EU. Many 'EUropeans' proposed that it was time to re-evaluate the relationship with Russia, get 'realistic' and stop pretending that EU–Russia relations constituted a functioning partnership (Barysch, Coker and Jesien 2011; Krastev and Leonard 2014). Deadlock, stagnation and fatigue were buzzwords often heard in the context of EU–Russia relations in the decade preceding the Ukraine conflict. Yet very few people expected a serious confrontation between the EU and Russia. When drafting the first version of this introduction a few years ago, in order to balance the predominantly negative view, we wanted to highlight many positive elements in the relationship, namely, that the parties were still cooperating closely over many issues; trade relations had flourished; increased interaction between citizens and civil societies existed; and no serious threat of a military confrontation between the parties seemed likely. Unfortunately, and although some forms of cooperation luckily still exist, not one of the above can be said with complete confidence anymore.

This is a bad outcome of the relations and an analytical puzzle to be solved in its own right. Arguably, EU–Russia relations are crucially important to both parties. As briefly highlighted, they have devoted a great deal of attention to nurturing them, but at the same time the actual interaction between the two has also often turned out to be mutually disappointing. That said, when seen from the perspective of Brussels, it is perhaps only the transatlantic relationship with the United States (US) that is more fundamental when it comes to the external positioning of the EU in world politics. In many ways, the EU's policy towards Russia can be seen as the hardest test of the credibility and nature of its external relations. The relationship with Russia exposes the EU's ability, or inability, to form a coherent policy and implement it. The received wisdom in the extant literature seems to be that the EU's track record in this respect has left a lot to be desired (see e.g. Haukkala 2009b; Forsberg 2013). Seen from the perspective of Moscow, the European Union is not only the primary trading partner but also a source of identity for, and a challenge to, Russia's domestic and foreign policy choices. Seen more generally, the relationship between the EU and Russia is one that has relevance in several key respects in the wider world politics as well. It is one of the key relations in the emerging new world order, or rather, if the relationship realized its full potential, it would be an important centre of gravity in global politics. By contrast, the problems and stagnation in the relationship have been part and parcel of the still ongoing shift in the global dynamics away from the Pan-European, or Eurasian, continent to the Pacific Area.

Moreover, the nature of EU–Russia relations is an important case study because it is often seen as a crucial test case for the existence of 'the West' as a meaningful entity in world politics, on the one hand, or indigenous European actorness to begin with, on the other (cf. Bull 1982). An often-heard complaint, particularly in conjunction with the Ukraine conflict, has been that the EU and its member states are not actors operating on their own volition, but merely a hapless collection of stooges operating at the behest of the US (Johnstone 2014; see also Sakwa 2015). Others, however, have detected in EU–Russia relations a challenge to the Cold War idea of 'the West'. Even during the Ukraine crisis, some pundits saw the United States and the EU diverging in their policies on Russia – with Germany in particular representing a soft approach and paving the way for a closer EU–Russia relationship that would sweep the transatlantic relationship aside (Szabo 2015).

In this book, we examine EU–Russia relations from three scholarly perspectives: European studies, Russian studies and international relations (IR), including foreign policy analysis (FPA). The European studies perspective prevails when we look at EU foreign and security policy and external relations at large; Russian studies predominate when we look at Russian foreign policy – both combined with insights from FPA; and finally, the theoretical vantage points of IR provide insights into the interaction between the two and their position in the global system. We outline the historical evolution of the relationship and consider in detail how it has functioned in the main issue areas, starting with economics and trade, political and security relations, and energy and environment, as well as justice and home affairs, and culture. We offer explanations for the overall evolution as well as the major successes and failures in the relationship.

Research on EU–Russia relations is plentiful, and works that cover either the overall evolution of relations or the key issues are in good supply (Pinder and Shishkov 2002; Prozorov 2006; Gower and Timmins 2008a; Haukkala 2010; Makarychev 2014; Maass 2016; Sergunin 2016; for a comprehensive overview of the field, see Schmidt-Felzmann 2015). Much of the extant research has, however, been policy oriented and has offered up-to-date analysis of the changing agendas in EU–Russia relations, either after or before major summits or other significant events such as the Russo-Georgian war of 2008. The need for a longer-term perspective and theoretical insights to balance the presentism is strongly in line with the general observations of works on EU foreign policy (Jørgensen 2015: 24). Although many theoretical perspectives have been applied to EU–Russia relations, there is no single paradigm that currently guides the analysis. Analysts have focused on the power struggle and economic interdependence as well as identities and worldviews as the key factors influencing and shaping the relationship. This book does not advance a single theoretical perspective, but attempts instead to amalgamate the existing literature and insights into a coherent overall narrative of relations while spelling out the relative strengths and weaknesses of different theoretical approaches and demonstrating where they have particular relevance as partial explanations. Nevertheless, we attempt to demonstrate the importance of the psychology of interaction and the negative dynamics that led to the spiral of deteriorating relations.

To this end, the book approaches EU–Russia relations in a comprehensive manner. We analyse the entirety of relations and examine both successes and failures, including the current rupture in relations, on their own merits. In terms of research design, this comprehensive approach also makes it easier to address the question of why cooperation or conflict has prevailed. Simply stated, if we find more cooperation in one issue-area than another, we can think that these areas are autonomous and that conflict depends more on the issues than the parties. By contrast, if cooperation and conflict vary similarly across issue-areas over time, or spread from one issue-area to another, we might conclude that the problem is not so much related to the issues at stake as such, but rather to the parties and their views of each other. We are also mindful of the fact that EU–Russia relations do not operate in a vacuum, but are indeed part and parcel of wider global developments and the ebb and flow of relations between Russia and the West.

Although we have covered all the traditional topics and tried to expand the analysis to those areas where little previous research exists, a fully complete appraisal is beyond the scope of this publication. For future students of EU–Russia relations, there are still plenty of issues that have been on the agenda but which have not yet received systematic empirical examination. Nor are our theory review and favoured applications comprehensive enough to cover more nuanced and original theoretical explorations. Finally, the analysis is lacking to the extent that access to the actual decision-making process both on the Russian as well as the EU side is rather restricted and likely to remain opaque for quite some time.

This book starts with an analysis of the political and institutional development of EU–Russia relations. Chapter 2 takes a tour d'horizon of relations from the beginning of the 1990s to the present. Special attention will be devoted to the formative phase of relations, namely, how and under what terms Russia was incorporated into the emerging post–Cold War order in Europe. The negotiation of the PCA features prominently here because it is one of the contested issues of present-day relations. The argument is that although the EU and Russia were not entirely equal partners during this period, the EU was ready to give in and negotiate with Russia on many issues. Following this formative period, we discuss the longer phase when the relations were repeatedly expanded but which also saw them being increasingly contested. During the 2000s, a growing mismatch emerged between the voiced and commonly agreed objectives and the underlying realities both in the EU and Russia. It became a partnership which, until the disruption caused by the conflict in Ukraine, endured but did not develop towards closer integration – an unfulfilled partnership in essence.

In Chapter 3, we look at the key actors in EU–Russia relations. The comprehensive nature of relations has entailed that the list of actors on both sides has been equally comprehensive. This situation has been further complicated by the fact that both the EU and Russia have, in effect, been moving targets in the sense that both have been consolidating their own actorness and policies during this period. Particular emphasis will be put on how the EU member states have interacted with Russia and how the varying web of bilateral relations affects the evolution of the wider partnership between the EU and Russia. In particular, we demonstrate how key national interests diverge and how this has affected the coherence of the EU's policy towards Russia.

Next we examine a host of issue-areas that demonstrate the broad scope of cooperation in general, but also the nature of some recurring problems in relations that have emerged across these diverse issues. In Chapter 4 we look at trade, energy and the environment as the genuine backbone of EU–Russia relations. Despite all the political wrangling between the two, the relationship is essentially an economic partnership based on some natural synergies and promises thereof. That said, the main puzzle discussed in Chapter 4 is why, despite the rather fortuitous beginnings at the turn of the 1990s, the economy and energy have also become negatively politicized and securitized, turning into a factor that increased mistrust and lessened the prospects of mutually satisfactory political ties in the process.

Another area where the partnership between the EU and Russia seemed promising at first, but which subsequently proved to be a source of increasing tension, is that of democracy, human rights and justice and home affairs, which is discussed in Chapter 5. Here we look at the evolution of these issues on the EU–Russia agenda, focusing particularly on the Chechen issue. The upshot of this problem is that although the EU and Russia initially agreed to foster common values, Russia went on to put more emphasis on material interests instead. The EU duly insisted on the role of values, only to later decide to lessen their emphasis in the relationship; but meanwhile Russia developed its own alternative set of values, which it started to propagate vis-à-vis the EU. Moreover, the chapter analyses cooperation in this Common Space, paying particular attention to the visa question.

Chapter 6 deals with foreign and security policy cooperation, the Common Space that is known as 'external security'. Although the EU and Russia were both willing to develop cooperation in this area in the early 2000s, the concrete results remained meagre. This chapter looks at the evolution of relations in this field, focusing particularly on the Yugoslav wars, frozen conflicts in the former Soviet Union and the Russo-Georgian war, as well as joint approaches to security issues and crisis management in the Middle East and Africa.

The negative effects of the conflict in Ukraine are also analysed in Chapter 6. Overall, most of the global and regional security problems that both parties have identified have not been resolved. The recent record with regard to Iran and Syria demonstrates a mixed package: cooperation is still possible, but difficult.

Chapter 7 is devoted to science, education and culture, an area of cooperation that was defined as the fourth Common Space in the relationship between the EU and Russia. Here again we can witness great promise at the beginning, some achievements along the way, such as Russia's participation in the Bologna process, but numerous disappointments and quarrels to boot, culminating in the stagnation and cessation of many projects and cooperation schemes due to the overall negative development in the relationship.

Chapter 8 moves on to examine the so-called 'common' – or shared – neighbourhood between the EU and Russia. The countries in between make up the key geographic area where the EU and Russia interact and which has had some unprecedented repercussions on the wider EU–Russia relations. It is argued in this chapter that due to lack of progress in other areas, the neighbourhood question has increasingly come to dominate the relations between the EU and Russia. Indeed, it can be argued that the 'common neighbourhood' became, first, a theatre for integration competition between the EU and Russia, whereby both parties tried to advance their own development models with a view to enticing the countries into their ranks. As a consequence, the current situation in the region is unsatisfactory for both parties, as each seems to be unable to realize its goals. On the contrary, it appears that the competition between the EU and Russia over the countries of Eastern Europe has only emboldened the countries in between, who have become adept at playing the two strategic partners against each other. Yet, as the war in Georgia in August 2008 and the conflict in Ukraine have both shown, the current dynamics entail significant risks that could spill over into much more negative and dangerous developments for the wider European security as well.

Chapter 9 revisits the historical narrative of the relationship and the development in the various issue areas in the light of key theoretical debates. First, it examines what the relations with Russia reveal about the EU as an international actor. The evolution of EU–Russia relations is discussed in terms of various explanations of what the aims of the EU have been and what has been its ability to have an impact on third powers in general. We also give Russia the same treatment. The tentative conclusion is that the EU has had relatively little impact on Russia, but that the lack of influence did not stem so much from the incoherence of its policies or the lack of military resources, but simply from the fact that many issues where the EU has tried to exercise influence have been matters that have belonged to Moscow's own remit as a fully sovereign decision-maker. The EU has been a 'normative power' only partially as far as its aims and means have been concerned, but even less so in terms of its actual influence. Russia, in turn, has been pursuing its economic interests and increasingly its wider geostrategic goals, including its status, in its relations with the EU. Finally, we take a look at explanations that deal with the overall evolution of the relationship. We start with realist theory that put emphasis on power relations, proceed with interest and value-based explanations, and finally discuss identity and interaction-based accounts for the conflict and cooperation between the EU and Russia. Our final objective in Chapter 9 is to outline our own analytical narrative stressing negative interaction dynamics to provide a better understanding of the failed partnership.

The final chapter of the book focuses on the future of EU–Russia relations. Based on the factors which – in the light of our empirical analysis – have influenced the relations, it also seeks to provide some policy-relevant guidance on how to improve the ties between the two. We argue that the situation in Ukraine is not the root cause of the problems, because these had emerged and persisted in practically all areas of cooperation well before the rupture of relations in 2014. Yet neither side can escape the continued interdependence and the eventual pull of partnership. The question to which we revisit at the end of the book is whether, and in what way, the two increasingly alienated partners can find the foresight and wisdom to reestablish their partnership. We argue that the conflict over Ukraine was not inevitable, but rather the result of the unintended effects of the choices made by both parties. The same applies to the improvement of ties: although there is no automatic guarantee that the parties will return to cooperation, moderation and reciprocity will be required to mend the fences. It is possible, although far from desirable, that the current conflict dynamics will prove to be too path dependent to be challenged and that EU–Russia relations will be stuck in a conflictual mode for the foreseeable future. But before we can draw these conclusions, we must recount the story of the relations between the two during the post–Cold War era in its entirety.

Chapter 2

The Political and Institutional Development of EU–Russia Relations

The development of relations between the European Union and Russia has taken place in fits and starts and has experienced several ups and downs. It is worth bearing in mind in the analytical narrative that follows that the pendulum swing between phases of optimism and even acute crises and pessimism can only be partially explained by the developments in the relations between the two. This is because the political and institutional development of their relations has not taken place in a vacuum. On the one hand, they have been built upon the legacy and tradition of interaction between the then European Community and the Soviet Union (see Pinder 1991). On the other hand, they have been predicated upon the wider and constantly evolving post–Cold War order both on the global and European levels. In fact, the analysis looks at how the EU has sought to lock Russia into highly institutionalized, indeed post-sovereign arrangements, with a view to creating an essentially unipolar Europe based on the EU's liberal norms and values (Aalto 2006; Haukkala 2010) and Russia's evolving responses to that project.

This chapter traces and discusses these themes by providing an overview of the political and institutional development of relations between the EU and Russia. The emphasis in the analysis is placed on the post–Cold War era, but a brief historical narrative of relations between the European Community and the Soviet Union is also provided, as it is useful in terms of setting the scene – and to a certain extent also the subsequent tone – for the developments that have followed. To complement the more detailed thematic analyses of key issues in the remainder of the book, a more chronological approach is adopted.

We argue that the development of EU–Russia relations after the Cold War can be divided into six phases roughly reflecting the presidential terms in Russia (for other periodizations, see Gower 2007: 119–25; Lo 2015: 22–6; Thorun 2009). The first, formative phase is the immediate aftermath of the Cold War, between 1992 and 1994, which was characterized by optimism. Then a much more strained era followed in the relationship between 1994 and 2000, which we have labelled 'the time of troubles'. The third period, from 2000 to 2004, is again more optimistic, and one that we call 'the Putin promise'. The promise, however, did not lead to a closer partnership, but rather turned into the fourth phase, 'mutual disappointment', between 2004 and 2008, which was not so much an era of sharpened conflict as yet, but instead one that was characterized by mutual frustration and a growing understanding that closer cooperation and even integration between the parties was not possible and that cooperation would remain selective and be based on common interests rather than on a strong vision of partnership, shared identity and common values. Yet, during the fifth phase, coinciding with the Medvedev era, especially after the Russo–Georgian war in August 2008 in which the previous period culminated, there was a renewed attempt to revitalize relations, this time under the heading of 'partnerships for modernisation'. This 'final push for partnership', however, came to an end in 2012 when President Putin returned to the presidency, marking the sixth and, for the time being, final phase, culminating in the eventual 'rupture of relations'. In stark contrast to his first presidency, this time Putin's agenda was even more determined to resist the growing presence of the European Union in the neighbourhood and the perceived danger of European values undermining the sovereignty and legitimacy of 'Putin's Russia'.

With the following analytical narrative, we add nuances and hopefully corrective interpretations to some of the common understandings concerning the grand narrative of the evolution of EU–Russia relations. The need for historical precision and rethinking applies most strongly to the early phase of the relationship. We argue that the usual image of relations during the immediate aftermath of the Cold War often relies on a flawed understanding of a 'romantic period' of problem-free relations. Once this period is analysed more closely, we get a picture that is much less 'romantic'. The period entailed much more contestation about the very nature of relations between the EU and Russia, not only because of the EU essentially telling and teaching Russia what to do (cf. Prozorov 2006) but also because Russia was equally eager to shape the nature of the relationship. As concerns more recent events, the big question seems to be who deceived whom in the prospect of building a strong partnership. This is a politically loaded question, with both the EU and Russia currently proposing diametrically opposing alternatives. However, when viewed against the actual evolution of relations, one is hard pressed to avoid the conclusion that the current unhappy outcome is more a result of unintended consequences than a premeditated political plan by either side to drive the relationship in a certain direction.

The background: relations between the EC and the Soviet Union

During the Cold War, relations between the EC and the Soviet Union were fully immersed in the bipolar East–West conflict. In this setting, the Soviet Union never viewed the budding EC as a fully autonomous entity. The initial Soviet reaction to the Schuman Declaration in May 1950 and its aftermath was hostile (Mueller 2009). For example, in March 1957 Moscow addressed diplomatic notes to all six countries that were engaged in negotiating the Treaty of Rome, warning against its conclusion (John 1975: 42). Yet the actual Soviet policy that followed the Treaty of Rome in 1957 was that of non-recognition and indifference, albeit with some negative undertones (Binns 1977).

By the early 1960s, when the Cold War had once again taken a frostier turn, the Soviet Union revised its policy from previous passivity to a more active agenda of seeking to contain the European Economic Community (EEC), 'to prevent its expansion to include additional members, and embrace large numbers of developing countries in one bloc' (John 1975: 44). This policy failed, as the EC's 1973 enlargement to include Denmark, Ireland and the United Kingdom testified. It was only in the early 1970s that the Soviet stance began to change towards a wary recognition of the perseverance and even success of Western European integration (Laird 1989: 222). A decisive moment came in March 1972 when Leonid Brezhnev, in a speech at the 15th Congress of Soviet Trade Unions, *de facto* – although not *de jure* – recognized the European Community (John 1975: 47). This act paved the way for rounds of intermittent talks between the EC and the Council for Mutual Economic Assistance (CMEA) on the issue of mutual recognition and establishment of official ties, which did not, however, yield any significant results. Interestingly, Brezhnev's change of tack towards Western European integration coincided with the first time that the Soviet Union had to come face-to-face with the European Community as an international actor. During the Conference on Security and Cooperation in Europe (CSCE) negotiations in the early 1970s, the European Community was the main engine in developing the Conference's agenda beyond questions of high politics and security towards 'respect for human rights and fundamental freedoms', which ended up in the so-called Basket Three of the Helsinki Final Act in 1975 (Thomas 2001).

It was against this background and into this normative landscape in Western Europe that Gorbachev's New Thinking and the concept of Common European Home (*obshchiy evropeiskiy dom*) emerged in the mid-1980s. It is, however, important to bear in mind that Gorbachev's European policy was largely driven by economic considerations (English 2000: 141, 194). The Soviet Union needed to ease the burden of the relentless arms race and to attract investments and technological know-how from the West – both feats that were unattainable in the frosty international climate of the early 1980s. The EC's drive for a single market, launched in 1986, gave the rapprochement increased impetus as the Soviet Union could hardly risk being excluded from what seemed to be perhaps the most dynamic upcoming economic area in the world (Wallander and Prokop 1993: 87–8). For this reason Gorbachev started his charm offensive by declaring 1987 the 'Year of Europe'. The Soviet initiative yielded swift results: by June 1988 the EC and the CMEA had already adopted a Common Declaration establishing diplomatic relations, followed by a host of bilateral trade and cooperation agreements (TCAs) with all members of the CMEA, the Soviet Union included.

In addition to economic gains, Gorbachev also saw other reasons for developing a relationship with the EC. The success of Western integration stood in stark contrast to the failures of the CMEA. On the one hand, Gorbachev hoped that some of the EC's economic successes could perhaps be replicated in the CMEA context (Stent 1991: 143; Timmermann 1991: 178). On the other hand, this very dynamism also posed a threat to the Soviet standing in Eastern Europe. The EC's success was seen as a potential magnet that could start ripping the Central and Eastern European satellites away from

Moscow's orbit (Wettig 1991: 93–4). For example, one Soviet diplomat noted, 'If the CMEA does not achieve a similar integration to the EC, then it is quite possible that the EC and with it NATO will suck in all European countries' – a process that would block the development of 'a constructive co-operation between the two systems enjoying equal rights' (*Pravda*, 3 July 1988, quoted in Timmermann 1990: 106).

But like all of Gorbachev's reforms, New Thinking also contained paradoxical and largely irreconcilable elements. One was that the voiced intention of improved ties with the West in general, and with Western Europe in particular, hinged upon the full recognition of human and civil rights as the key component of the international society that Moscow wanted to join in full (Timmermann 1990: 119–20; see also Thomas 2001: 231). Nevertheless, it is important to point out that Gorbachev's blueprint for Europe never entailed the total eradication of systemic and societal differences between the Soviet Union and Western Europe. For example, in a speech in July 1989, Gorbachev explicitly warned against thinking that 'the overcoming of the division of Europe is the overcoming of socialism. That is a course for confrontation' (quoted in Neumann 1996: 165). Instead, the idea behind a Common European Home – just like that of *perestroika* – was that of gradual convergence and cooperation between the two systems that would leave their basic differences in place (Malcolm 1991: 70–1). In a sense, they were defensive manoeuvres in the face of an economically dynamic and normatively consolidating Europe, the aim of which was to prevent the exclusion of the Soviet Union from that very Europe (Wæver 1990: 482; Malcolm 1991: 70–1).

Yet ending the Cold War without arriving at a shared normative basis was not what happened. In the aftermath of the fall of the Berlin Wall, Gorbachev started to embrace the idea of universal values. When he met with President George Bush in Malta in December 1989, he opposed the view that democracy and human rights were 'Western values', as Bush constantly characterized them, and quipped that 'these are our values too'. Thus the need to end the division of Europe was in accord with 'values that are becoming universal ideals' (Savranskaya, Blanton and Zubok 2010). This process then culminated in the adoption of the Charter of Paris for a New Europe in November 1990, which was endorsed by all members of the CSCE, including the already frail Soviet Union. The document emphasized the role of peace, democracy, human rights, the rule of law and economic liberty as the guiding principles in the building of a 'New Europe' (Charter of Paris 1990). It also erased the clear distinction between the internal and external – domestic and foreign policies – by obligating all European countries to develop not only their mutual relations but also, and primarily, their domestic policies in line with these principles. Even if one removes the pompous wording of the document, one is faced with the fact that the Paris Charter represented a drastic and final break in the bipolar normative constellation in Europe. In short, the Paris Charter discredited the socialist experiment as an alternative to Western modes of liberalism, the market economy and the democratic rights of individuals. Convergence was not to take place *between* the systems, as the convergence theorists and even Gorbachev had previously assumed, but by signing the Charter, Gorbachev signalled the end of a competing Soviet normative agenda in favour of a common Western one. Instead of reinvigorating Leninism, he had managed to undo it once and for all and paved the way for the dissolution of the Soviet Union.

The formative years

The dissolution of the Soviet Union in December 1991 and the emergence of the Russian Federation in its stead resulted in a radically different political setting in Europe, calling for new policies on the part of both the European Community/Union and Russia. For the Community, the most urgent challenge was to define an agenda of political rapprochement and economic integration that would ensure an orderly transition to a post-Soviet era (Höhmann, Meier and Timmermann 1993). For Russia, the main task was to secure a firm place in the new emerging architecture in post–Cold War Europe (Arbatov 1997: 136, 139). With its provisions on limited trade-related cooperation, the TCA that had been signed with the already frail Soviet Union in December 1989 was clearly inadequate for the tasks at hand. The Community acknowledged this as early as the end of 1990, when the European Council instructed the Commission to look for possibilities for a broader agreement with the Soviet Union that would include 'political dialogue and all aspects of a close economic as well as cultural co-operation' (Timmermann 1996: 200).

At the beginning of the 1990s, there was a clear asymmetry between the EC and Russia: The Community was consolidating its actorness, which we take to mean the gradual and still ongoing attempts at giving 'Brussels' an increased role and even autonomy in shaping its external environment, and relishing its role as one of the prime engines that set the pace for the emerging new European architecture. For its part, Russia was still smouldering in the ashes of the Soviet Union and was essentially a *demandeur* for economic assistance and political support, with clear expectations of being placated for having ended the Cold War (Utkin 1995: 18). It was in this frame of mind that the parties approached the negotiations concerning a new contractual basis for their relations in spring 1992. There is hardly any need to dwell at length on the actual negotiation process that began in November 1992 (for an analysis, see Haukkala 2010, Ch. 5). The expectation was that the negotiation process would be fairly short: initially, the EC was pushing for the PCA to be adopted by the end of 1992. But it soon became obvious to both parties that this would not be the case. Instead, the negotiation process continued for 19 months and included several rounds of official talks as well as sustained dialogue on the specific bones of contention at the expert level.

The difficulties in the negotiation process stemmed mainly from two sources. First, the Russians were driving a hard bargain, basically refusing to take any of the EC's proposals at face value. This was the case especially in the economic field, where Russia repeatedly pushed for more trade concessions and a more generous long-term perspective in the form of a free trade area than what was envisaged in the Commission's original mandate. Further, the EC's insistence on political conditionality was a source of concern for the Russians, resulting in additional difficulties in the negotiation process. Second, the EC was less than forthcoming in meeting the Russian demands. Some member states in particular were slow to respond to the Russian requests, and when they did so, it was usually in response to the domestic difficulties that the increasingly beleaguered President Yeltsin and his team of reformers were facing in Russia. In essence, the EC was constantly fearful of 'losing' Russia, which could have resulted in a rollback of Russian democracy and economic reforms in the country. As a consequence, the EC felt a compelling need to lock Russia into an institutional arrangement that would make the economic and political changes in the country irreversible – an argument that was at key junctures rather skilfully used by the Russians themselves (for a similar observation in the US–Russia context, see Stent 2014: Ch. 1). Moreover, encouraged by their successes, the Russians repeatedly pushed harder for new concessions from the EC.

The Partnership and Cooperation Agreement, signed on 24 June 1994, on the fringes of the Corfu European Council, represented a radical break from the previous forms of agreement that by now the EU had had with the countries of the former Soviet Union. Much like the TCA, the PCA too was primarily an economic agreement but much more wide-ranging and ambitious in its scope. Contrary to its predecessor, the PCA was not centred on trade and economic issues exclusively, but included other sectors of cooperation as well. In the agreement, the economic aspects of the relationship were complemented with a range of other sectors – including political dialogue; social and cultural cooperation; and education, science and technology – with a view to providing a 'framework for the gradual *integration* between Russia and a wider area of cooperation in Europe' (PCA, Article 1; [emphasis added]). This was indeed a much more ambitious agenda for rapprochement and convergence compared with mere trade and cooperation as envisaged by the TCA.

The PCA also included fairly robust obligations and mechanisms of political conditionality. To a large degree these stemmed from Russia's own negotiation tactics, as, in a sense, it was the Russian demands for greater trade access and the inclusion of a free trade area perspective in the agreement that resulted in the Union's decision to opt for a more integrationist approach. To be sure, the Union's emphasis on political conditionality was not unique, but part and parcel of wider trends towards 'good governance', or the 'second wave' of political conditionality that became prevalent during the post–Cold War era (see Weiss 2000; Stokke 1995). Taken together, the strong role afforded to norms and values in the PCA constituted what can be called the post-sovereign core of the EU–Russia relationship (Haukkala 2010). The relationship between the two can be summed up by saying that norms equalled the concrete 'rules of the game' *within* the game that was based on the (assumption of) shared values. This basic distinction was not confined to the PCA alone, but was, and still is, reflected in all of the EU external agreements (Youngs 2001; for comprehensive surveys of human rights in EU external agreements, see Miller 2004; Petiteville 2003).

In probing the post-sovereign nature of the PCA in more detail, two of its articles warrant closer examination. The main article in this respect is Article 2, which codifies the primacy of common values as the foundation of the partnership as follows:

> Respect for democratic principles and human rights as defined in particular in the Helsinki Final Act and the Charter of Paris for a New Europe, underpins the internal and external policies of the Parties and constitutes an essential element of partnership and of this Agreement.

This suspension clause proved to be a persistent source of problems during the negotiations. By insisting on establishing democracy and human rights as an 'essential' element of the PCA – as well as practically every other external agreement the EU has concluded since the end of the Cold War – the EU reserved itself a legal right to consider a breach of certain 'European values' as being sufficient to warrant the termination or suspension of the agreement (for the evolution of political conditionality and the suspension clause in EU external agreements, see Hillion 2009; Leino-Sandberg 2005: 239–301).

The Russian aversion towards a unilateral application of conditionality is acknowledged in Article 107, which states that although in the event of a breach of obligations either party may take 'appropriate measures', before so doing, except in cases of special urgency, they are required to consult each other in order to seek a solution that is mutually acceptable to the parties. Moreover, in the selection of possible retaliatory measures, 'priority must be given to those which least disturb the functioning of the Agreement' (PCA 1997: Article 107). The suspension clause is further clarified in the joint declaration appended to the PCA, which confirms that respect for human rights constitutes an essential element of the agreement and further qualifies the sources of this obligation on both sides, anchoring it most firmly into the CSCE commitments in the form of the Helsinki Final Act and the Charter of Paris for a new Europe (PCA, Joint Declaration in Relation to Articles 2 and 107). Christophe Hillion (1998: 416) – an international lawyer – has noted that by being included 'in the core of the PCAs', those references in effect became legally binding for the parties.

The idea of normative convergence as one of the central aims of the relationship is derived from Article 55. After taking note of the overall importance of the approximation of legislation in strengthening economic links between the Union and Russia, the article unambiguously states that 'Russia shall endeavour to ensure that its legislation will be gradually made compatible with that of the Community' (PCA, Article 55.1). The article then lists the areas to which the approximation of laws shall extend, including in particular company law; banking law; company accounts and taxes; protection of workers in the workplace; financial services; rules of competition; public procurement; protection of health and life of humans, animals and plants; the environment; consumer protection; indirect taxation; customs law; technical rules and standards; nuclear laws and regulations; and transport (PCA, Article 55.2). What is more, this overall obligation is further enhanced by several other articles in the agreement that further enumerate sectors where convergence towards and harmonization with the EU – or, when and where applicable, other international – norms and standards will be required. In short, the obligation, or in some other cases the expectation, of legal approximation deals with practically all walks of life even remotely connected with – but not exclusively confined to – the economy. In principle, however, the obligation is not confined to these issues alone, as the general obligation of Article 55 refers to Russia's legislation in general and even the list just enumerated is not exhaustive but only highlights those issues *in particular* where the process should move forward.

The PCA also put in place a regular political dialogue that the parties intended to develop and intensify further (Article 6). This was another innovation compared with the TCA, which only envisaged a 'joint committee' that would meet once a year (TCA, Article 22). By contrast, the PCA established a permanent and continuous multilevel dialogue between the EU and Russia that aimed at 'increasing convergence of positions on international issues of mutual concern' (PCA, Article 6): the biannual *EU–Russia Summits* between the EU troika (currently consisting of the Council president, the EU high representative and the Commission president) and the president of Russia, and the annual *Cooperation Councils* that meet at the ministerial level, *Cooperation Committees* (senior official level) that can meet as often as necessary and *Sub-Committees* (working level) below them to deal with more technical issues. And finally, a *Joint Parliamentary Committee* has also been established, where members of the European Parliament and the Russian Duma meet on a regular basis to discuss current issues (PCA Articles 6–9, 90–7).

In Russian circles in particular, an understanding exists that the PCA and the consequent post-sovereign institution were unilaterally imposed on Russia (see Prozorov 2006; Shemiatenkov 2002). To be fair, this is what IR theory would lead us to expect as well: especially in the aftermath of wars, economically (and one might add normatively) preponderant victors can be in a position to impose institutionalized arrangements on others (Ikenberry 2001). A parallel view, stressing the 'romanticism' of this era, is that Russian leaders were somehow blinded by the attractiveness of the Western partnership and were in effect lured by the Western wooing, and were not able to safeguard Russia's true national interests. Yet the empirical analysis above shows that instead of unilateral imposition or blind acceptance, the negotiations leading to the adoption of the PCA in June 1994 were mutual and tough – the scholars who have actually looked at the negotiation phase seem to be in consensus (see Timmermann 1996; Hillion 1998; Zagorski 1997). At the same time, it seemed that the hard bargain driven by the Russians themselves was the key factor that had some unexpected consequences for the very nature of subsequent EU–Russia interaction, resulting in the logic of post-sovereignty being injected into the relationship in a much more stringent form than even the EU ever originally intended.

The time of troubles

The mood of optimism following the signing of the PCA proved to be short-lived. Instead of swift ratification and implementation of the agreement, EU–Russia relations immediately slumped into a series of crises that froze them for years. One of the underlying reasons for this was because the adoption of the PCA and its ambitious integrationist agenda coincided with a major rethink in Russian foreign policy. The final stages of the PCA negotiations had already overlapped with the end of the 'romantic era' and the consequent sea change in Russian foreign policy, with the notions of spheres of influence, respect for sovereignty and overall equality between Russia and its Western partners replacing the ideas of universal values and joining the 'community of civilised states' at all costs (Arbatov 1997: 135, 142).

The domestic developments in Russia also had a negative effect on relations. The 1993 political crisis between President Yeltsin and the Russian Parliament had resulted in an armed showdown between the two. Although the conflict was followed by a process resulting in a new constitution, it also created a strong presidency and a precedent of settling political conflicts by resorting to the use of violence, both factors that have continued to affect Russia's subsequent development. The brief conflict between Yeltsin and the Parliament was, however, but a precursor to more substantial bloodletting to come. In December 1994, Moscow unleashed a military campaign to subdue the increasingly independent and belligerent Republic of Chechnya.

The conflict quickly engulfed the major urban centres of Chechnya, resulting in heavy civilian casualties and suffering. The events on the ground in Chechnya also resulted in the first major crisis in relations between the EU and Russia. From the EU's and indeed the wider international vantage point, Russia's handling of Chechnya highlighted the lack of heed paid to the 'European values' spelled out above. It also ruptured the ratification process of the PCA, which was put on hold indefinitely by the EU and was only fully resumed after the cessation of hostilities in Chechnya in 1996.

Meanwhile, Russia's foreign policy also started to change. Andrei Kozyrev, with whom the Western orientation had been associated, had become unpopular and was regarded as a culprit in the Russian foreign policy debate. Yeltsin decided that he had to go, and in January 1996 he appointed a new Foreign Minister, Yevgeni Primakov, who was an orientalist and the director of the Russian intelligence service. Primakov's appointment marked the definitive end of the Western orientation in Russia's foreign policy. In its stead, he developed a 'Primakov doctrine' based on the idea of a multi-vectoral foreign policy. This meant that Russia was an independent pole in the increasingly multipolar world and should therefore develop relations with all other centres and with the new emerging powers such as China and India in particular (M.A. Smith 2013). The profound nature of this change was later reaffirmed by Foreign Minister Sergey Lavrov, who paid tribute to Primakov's role: 'The moment he took over the Russian Foreign Ministry heralded a dramatic turn of Russia's foreign policy. Russia left the path our Western partners had tried to make it follow after the breakup of the Soviet Union and embarked on a track of its own' (TASS 2014).

When the PCA entered into force in December 1997, Russia had thus already started to question the very basis on which it was negotiated. In spite of this, cooperation with the EU was still seen as highly desirable. Even far-reaching objectives were not excluded at the time, as exemplified in the words of then Prime Minister Victor Chernomyrdin, who declared, 'I think that our work here, our entire scope of work, all issues and problems that we are discussing, are directed to one objective, that at a certain point Russia will become a member of the EU' (McEvoy 1997). Yet, in actual fact, the window to kick-start relations proved to be fleeting. In August 1998, the Russian economy was in free fall, forcing the Russian government to default on its debts and allowing the rouble to devalue uncontrolled. To all intents and purposes, this setback was seen as a mortal blow to Russia's successful transition to a working and growing market economy. As a consequence, instead of moving towards free trade and further integration, as was originally envisaged in the PCA, the EU found itself seriously questioning the feasibility of any form of economic partnership with Russia at all (Haukkala 2001).

In addition, the Kosovo war in 1999 – although not a particular crisis between the EU and Russia per se (see Maass 2016: Ch. 1), as it was a NATO operation, with the United States bearing the main responsibility of the military campaign against Serbia – was also important in the EU–Russia context. For Russia, the Kosovo case drove home at least two lessons that made a lasting impact on its subsequent relations with the West, the EU included (Averre 2009b). First, that the United States, together with some EU member states, uses military intervention to affect regime change in cases where it sees fit and, second, that unilateral military intervention can take place without an explicit mandate from the United Nations (UN) Security Council and against the voiced objection of the Russian Federation in particular. This is a pattern Russia has continuously perceived in other colour revolutions in the post-Soviet area and more recently in the Middle East and North Africa. Taken together, the Kosovo affair had the wider implication of distancing Russia from the West, the EU included, paving the way for the galvanization of a much more hard-nosed, realist foreign policy consensus during the Putin era (Trenin 2007).

Almost immediately after Kosovo, a fresh conflict in Chechnya resulted in another acute political crisis between the EU and Russia as Putin pursued a determined course of action to deal with the Chechen problem once and for all (Forsberg and Herd 2005; Haukkala 2010, Ch. 7). At first, the EU condemned the Russian actions, threatened the country with some sanctions and even imposed them in a limited manner (see Chapter 5). Unfazed, Putin successfully called the EU's bluff over Chechnya and insisted on pursuing the chosen course of action until the conflict was resolved on his terms – an approach that has come to characterize Putin's actions ever since (see Hill and Gaddy 2015). In the process, Putin managed to show that the EU had more bark than bite when it came to 'European values'. At the end of the day, key EU member states were eager to conduct interest-based interactions with Russia regardless of the malaise in relations. The case also showed Putin that by establishing direct links and seeking agreement with influential member states, the EU and its institutions in Brussels would eventually follow suit – another key modus operandi Russia has continued with varying success to this day.

The series of demoralizing setbacks in and with Russia resulted in a period of soul-searching in the EU. A reflection of this was a string of internal strategies and other stocktaking exercises the EU undertook at the end of the 1990s. The first stab at the topic was an internal strategy document prepared by the Commission in 1995. This was followed by the intergovernmental negotiation of a Common Strategy on Russia in 1999, the first Common Foreign and Security Policy (CFSP) instrument of its kind following the Treaty of Amsterdam two years earlier (for a detailed discussion of the strategy process, see Haukkala 2001). Politically, the strategies revealed the EU's belief in the importance of developing ties that would bind Russia closer to Europe. They also signalled the EU's insistence on the role of European values as the basis of any subsequent cooperation and possible integration with Russia. Scholars pondering EU–Russia relations concluded that although the relations had become much more conditional and fraught, the cooperative trend had not disappeared (Webber 2000: 17; Timmins 2002).

The Putin promise

The rapid ascent of a fairly obscure director of Russia's Federal Security Service (FSB), Vladimir Putin, first to prime minister and then to president of Russia in 1999, took many by surprise. The beginning of his tenure coincided with several contradictory tendencies in Russia, leaving several partners and analysts to feverishly ponder the question 'Who is Mr. Putin?' (Gevorkyan et al. 2001; Sakwa 2008; Gessen 2012). Strengthening the state both politically and economically was the key task that Putin set himself. Propelled by rising oil and other commodity prices as well as the positive effects of the 1998 rouble devaluation and the existence of spare industrial capacity, Putin's rule indeed witnessed a return to economic growth and increased – and welcomed – political stability in the country.

When it comes to EU–Russia relations, the initial years of Putin's tenure – after the acute problem with the second Chechen War was no longer determining the agenda – were a time of relative optimism. As Romano Prodi (2000) argued at the time, 'Europe must seize with both hands the extraordinary opportunity offered to open a comprehensive dialogue between the EU and Russia.' At first, Putin continued to talk of Russia's Europeanization. Putin, who was from the most European of Russian cities, St Petersburg, and had served as a *Komitet gosudarstvennoy bezopasnosti* [Committee for State Security] (KGB) officer in Eastern Germany, was seen as having a European calling. The foreign policy concept of the Russian Federation that was adopted in June 2000 underlined Russia's need to integrate into the world economy. Although the West was not the exclusive partner that Russia sought, indeed the concept did not depart too much from Primakov's doctrine of a multi-vectoral policy, it univocally signalled a cooperative attitude towards the EU and Europe in general, noting that these relations are of 'key importance' to Russia (Ivanov 2001a). Moreover, the adoption of Russia's own medium-term EU strategy (2000–10), a response to the EU's Common Strategy on Russia, was greeted rather optimistically and was seen as reflecting the view that the relationship with the EU was important to Russia, although a more careful reading of the document should have already revealed the clear differences between the Russian and EU visions concerning the future of relations (Haukkala 2001). Yet the prevailing mood at the time remained optimistic, captured by Vladimir Baranovsky (2000: 457), who insisted, 'Putin has unambiguously positioned himself as a Europeanist' (see also Timmins 2002: 87). Perhaps the clearest public manifestation of Putin's and Russia's warm-hearted attitude towards Europe was his speech, delivered in German in the Bundestag when visiting Germany in September 2001. In that speech, Putin (2001) underlined the unity of culture and declared, 'As for European integration, we not only support these processes, but we look upon them with hope.'

Russian foreign policy discourse in the early 2000s reflected these hopes of Russia consolidating its position in a dense network of relations with the EU. Foreign Minister Igor Ivanov (2000: 106) regarded 'all-round cooperation with the EU as one of the top priorities'. Partnership with the EU was Russia's 'European choice'. Although Putin's Westernism looked 'more radical than the overall mood in the country' (Baranovsky 2000: 457), a considerable majority of Russians in public opinion polls nevertheless favoured the idea of strengthening cooperation between Russia and the West in general, and the EU in particular. Vassily Likachev (2003), Russia's permanent representative to the European Communities, regarded Russia's European priorities as shaping the practice of, and forming a stable basis for, a comprehensive partnership. The extent to which the official policy relied on the idea of cooperation with the West at the time can be best pointed out by a reminder of how the nationalist critics of Russia's foreign policy feared that Putin was selling out Russia to the West (Baev 2003).

The EU was all too eager to reciprocate. During the 1990s the EU had already realized that it could not steer developments inside Russia, but when expanding its role as an international actor, it had to find a working relationship with 'its most important and valuable partner' in the field of economic cooperation and international politics. The goal was to enhance cooperation and strengthen the strategic partnership. Javier Solana (1999) argued, 'Building a partnership with Russia will not be easy, but I would argue most strongly that it is an opportunity we cannot afford to miss.' The partnership was 'of fundamental importance to us all but its full benefits have yet to be realised' (Solana 2000). Yet extending the EU enlargement to Russia was not considered seriously. As Romano Prodi is said to have explained to Putin in 2002: 'Well, yes, you are European, even if you are looking Eastwards, but you are too big for the EU' (Pihl 2002).

The EU–Russia Summits in 2000–02 were held in a constructive spirit witnessing an expanding agenda of relations. Forward-looking agendas were formed in a large range of diverse areas. The initiative of a Northern Dimension that was launched during the Finnish presidency of the EU in 1999 was actively fostered with the aim of strengthening stability, intensifying economic cooperation and promoting sustainable development in the region. In May 2002, the EU granted Russia the status of a full market economy.

The EU enlargement to the East that was to take place in May 2004 was creating a new reality for EU–Russia relations. The most difficult issue on the agenda at that time was related to this because the new members had to apply Schengen rules at their Russian border. This complicated the transit traffic between Kaliningrad and other parts of Russia in particular, but the issue was resolved as a satisfactory compromise in November 2002 by agreeing on a system of facilitated travel documents (see Chapter 7). Ahead of the planned enlargement, the EU also started to develop a new European Neighbourhood Policy (ENP) scheme that it initially offered to Russia as well. Russia, however, declined the invitation as it did not want to be treated like just another 'neighbour' in a group of smaller countries, but wanted a separate and more privileged 'Strategic Partnership' with the EU that would reflect and acknowledge its status as a great power (see Chapter 8).

Out of these concerns, the EU and Russia developed the idea of Four Common Spaces that became the landmark of this phase in the development of relations. The negotiations over the content of the document had already started in 2001, and it was finally accepted at the St Petersburg Summit in May 2003 (EU–Russia Summit 2003). The four 'common spaces' that were situated in the framework of the PCA were said to be based on common values and shared interests. They were elaborated at the Moscow Summit in May 2005 when the parties agreed on 'road maps' on how these common spaces were to be put into effect (EU–Russia Summit 2005; see also the subsequent thematic chapters in this book).

1. The Common Economic Space, covering economic issues and the environment
2. The Common Space of Freedom, Security and Justice
3. The Common Space of External Security, including crisis management and non-proliferation
4. The Common Space of Research and Education, including cultural aspects

The creation of the four spaces generated yet another burst of optimism, although no longer wholly without reservations. It was increasingly coming to the fore that both the EU and Russia were burdened by a diverse set of handicaps related to domestic politics and competing foreign policy priorities. Yet their mutual interests were nevertheless still seen as largely overlapping and complementary. The EU had learned the lesson that the normative agenda should give way to pragmatic cooperation as the best way to keep Russia on board and to benefit from the relationship (Flenley 2005). There was a 'growing consensus in the Western analytical community that Russia is on the right track, although it still has a long way to go on its painful path to normalisation' (Spiegeleire 2003: 83).

During this era the political dialogue between the parties also deepened. It was decided at the St Petersburg EU–Russia Summit in June 2003 that the Cooperation Council would be turned into a 'Permanent Partnership Council' with the aim of having a body that would meet more often and in various ministerial constellations. Political dialogue between the EU and Russia in the Permanent Partnership Councils takes place at the level of ministers (twice a year), political directors (four times a year) and experts (some 15 CFSP working group troikas meet with their Russian counterparts twice a year). In addition, the troika of the Political and Security Committee (COPS) was meeting with the Russian ambassador to the EU on a monthly basis to discuss CFSP issues.

The mutual disappointment

After the initial period of renewed optimism, the EU and Russia drifted into a period of continuous disappointments. Writing in 2008, Jackie Gower and Graham Timmins (2008b: 289) noted how a 'mutual disappointment' had set in with regards to the relations. Putin had consolidated his position as leader of the country through his re-election in 2004, after which he increasingly took steps that effectively steered Russia away from the idea of Russia and Europe sharing the same values (Shevtsova 2005; Fish 2005). There is no single overwhelming reason why Russia's, and President Putin's attitude to be more precise, towards the EU started to cool after the initial years of the European vocation and constructive search for partnership. Instead, there has been a series of overlapping and intersecting issues that were instrumental in inserting an increasingly negative momentum into the relations. First, there was a set of disappointments which, from the Kremlin's point of view, indicated that the EU does not fully understand or sincerely support Russia and was not showing any gratitude. The Chechen question remained a contested issue in the background, and European reactions to the school massacre in Beslan as well as the hostage crisis in the Nord-Ost theatre in Moscow were regarded more as a critique of the way in which the Kremlin had dealt with the crisis rather than condemnation of terrorism with support for the Kremlin in its fight against it.

Outside Russia's borders, the first sign of fomenting trouble related to the question of how best to resolve the conflict in Moldova. In late 2003, Putin's envoy, Dmitri Kozak, made an attempt to resolve the conflict by securing a Moldovan–Transnistrian agreement in the form of a so-called Kozak Memorandum that would have entailed a federal structure for the country. The EU, together with the US, however, torpedoed the agreement at the last minute, creating the impression in Moscow that it was done not because of some flaws in the Russian proposal, but precisely because it was a *Russian* proposal (Lynch 2005: 15; see also Chapter 5 for more).

Second, in Russia's domestic struggle for power there was a tectonic shift where the liberal group lost a great deal of their influence to the so-called *Siloviki* from the security organs. This was largely because internal consolidation and strengthening of the Russian state was seen as primary, with the diligent following of 'European values' relegated to a secondary status. These developments became evident in the case of Yukos, with the arrest and sentencing of its head, Mikhail Khodorkovsky, the wealthiest of the oligarchs at the time, in October 2003. The charges were based mainly on the allegedly illegal ways in which Khodorkovsky had acted in the privatization process when creating his economic empire during the 1990s, but the real reason, according to many observers, was his willingness to support alternative political forces in Russia and his lack of loyalty to the Kremlin in general. Khodorkovsky's fate was not an isolated case, but was linked to changes in the political appointments as Prime Minister Mikhail Kasyanov was dismissed in February 2004. Yet the biggest setback from the Kremlin's perspective was the Orange Revolution in Ukraine in the winter of 2004–5. The EU's role, in particular, in that context was perceived as negative because it had intervened in the electoral process and demanded new elections on the basis of election fraud, challenging the Russian blueprint for the future of Ukraine (see Chapter 8).

The progressive agenda that was created in the first years of the 2000s began to fade away. Timofei Bordachev and Arkady Moshes (2004) contended, 'The reality is that Russia and the EU represent different political and economic systems that are not integrable in principle.' Already, after the disappointing summits of 2004, the EU had prepared an internal memo in which it admitted that the attempts to manage relations with Russia had been ineffective and flawed and lacked an overall strategy. The conclusion was that the EU should speak with one voice and set out certain redline issues that it would not accept (Dempsey 2004). Similarly, some Russian commentators made complaints about the EU. For example, Sergei

Karaganov (2005: 27) argued that the rigidities of EU decision-making mechanisms 'reduce opportunities for external partners, as well as EU member states [sic], to influence the course of its common foreign and security policy'. Moreover, Karaganov found it hard to avoid the impression 'that the European Commission has started to revise its policy of rapprochement with Russia' (Karaganov 2005: 33).

These divergences with regard to the nature of the relationship were reflected in problems in implementing the jointly agreed agenda. For example, when the Road Maps for the Four Common Spaces were presented at the Moscow Summit in May 2005, it became rather plain that despite the investment in creating the new framework, not much progress had been achieved (see Chapter 4). Furthermore, the negotiations for a new PCA treaty, as the original was envisaged to expire in December 2007, did not progress. Bordachev (2006) argued that if Russia concluded a new PCA treaty with the EU, it 'would be voluntary admitting to its status as a "younger partner," thus becoming an object for inspection and instruction.' As Derek Averre (2005) wrote at the time, Brussels had to 'radically rethink the nature and extent of Russia's Europeanisation'.

The relations between the EU and Russia were further burdened by Russia's decision to impose an import ban on Polish meat in November 2005 because of a suspicion that Poland had exported meat to Russia from third countries, where the risk of animal diseases was high. The Commission responded by claiming that a ban on meat from the EU would be totally unjustified, as strict transitional measures to protect animal health and the food safety status of the EU had been adopted following the enlargement. Yet Russia did not accept these arguments and threatened to extend the embargo to all EU countries. Poland, for its part, suspected that the Russian ban was politically motivated. On the eve of the Helsinki EU–Russia Summit in November 2006, Poland vetoed the adoption of the negotiating directives for a new partnership agreement between the EU and Russia because of the Russian reluctance to lift the embargo. Moreover, Poland also threatened to veto Russia's World Trade Organization (WTO) membership on the same grounds. The EU–Russia Summits in 2006 were hence merely able to serve as face-savers for the seemingly frustrated leaders and to uphold the façade of a cooperative relationship. The subsequent Summit meetings in 2007 were also characterized more by disagreements over democracy development in Russia, energy questions and the status of Kosovo than by joint approaches and results. The increasing paralysis and the lack of concrete deliverables in EU–Russia relations resulted in some soul-searching concerning the potential trimming down of high-level summits to just one a year, a practice the EU has in place with all of its other major 'strategic partners' (Lukyanov 2013: 89). Yet both parties were reluctant to make the move, lest it be seen as an admission of defeat or a sign of downgrading relations.

Indeed, the developments after 2004 tempered the initial optimism on both sides, resulting in growing disillusionment concerning the prospects for a fully working 'strategic partnership'. Dmitry Trenin (2006) declared in his *Foreign Affairs* article, 'Russia's leaders have given up on becoming part of the West and have started creating their own Moscow-centered system.' Sergei Karaganov (2007) argued that Russia and the West had entered a 'New Epoch of Confrontation' that is perhaps less profound but could be more dangerous than the Cold War. In Russian foreign policy concepts, the EU was downgraded from being a partner 'of key importance' for Moscow in the 2000 concept to 'one of the main trade-economic and foreign policy partners' in the 2008 concept (Moshes 2009). The EU still paid lip service to 'strategic partnership', but very few people in Brussels believed in any rapid progress.

The most concrete evidence of the number of difficulties and frustrations was that the parties were unable to replace the PCA treaty when it was due to expire in 2007 (but as designated by its Article 106, the PCA is automatically renewed on an annual basis, unless either party denounces the agreement, something that has not transpired). Against this background, Sergei Medvedev (2008: 216) argued that stalemate – using the Brezhnev era concept of *zastoi* – 'may be the most appropriate definition of the present quality of EU–Russia relations'. Margot Light (2008: 25), in turn, summed up the situation in a keynote article for the *Journal of Common Market Studies*: 'It has been increasingly difficult to understand exactly what they mean by the term [strategic partnership]. As we have seen, there have been so many tensions during the recent years that, arguably, "strategic rivalry" is the more appropriate term to use to depict some aspects of the relationship.'

Thus, Putin's second term as president revealed a growing rift between the EU and Russia. At least three reasons can be detected behind this shift. First, the years of intense interaction between the two brought to the fore and perhaps even accentuated the differences in underlying worldviews between the EU and Russia (Haukkala 2010). In a sense, the two decades of EU–Russia relations can be likened to a three-cornered learning process where both the EU and Russia have learned about themselves, about each other and about their mutual relationship. On the whole, however, the balance sheet seemed to be edging towards the negative with increasingly sceptical stances about the relationship being put forward both in the EU and in Russia. Second, and partly following on from the first, the EU and Russia had, in fact, largely incompatible interests. To cut a long story short, what the EU offered and demanded were all things that Putin's Russia did not think it needed. Third, the effects of the EU's own enlargements had some deleterious effects on EU–Russia relations. On the one hand, the accession of Central and Eastern European member states in particular accentuated the critical caucus towards Russia within the EU. On the other hand, the countries that reside between the EU and Russia in Eastern Europe – the so-called 'common neighbourhood' – have increasingly become an object of contention and even competition between the two strategic partners (see Chapter 8).

The final push for partnership

Despite, and perhaps because of, these growing disagreements the EU and Russia did continue their dogged attempts to take the relations forward. By 2008 the EU had decided to change tack, shifting the emphasis from common values to putting the accent on the international legal commitments Russia had assumed during the previous two decades. According to the then External Relations Commissioner Benita Ferrero-Waldner (2008a), the EU should 'lose no opportunity to remind Russia of the need to respect the commitments she has entered into – but in a constructive tone, without "megaphone diplomacy".'

The decision by the Kremlin that the key candidate to run for president after Putin's constitutionally limited two terms were over was Dmitry Medvedev was interpreted as a signal that it indeed preferred cooperation over conflict in its relations with the West, although, as many suspected, Putin would remain in the top steering position of the new 'tandem' (Black 2015). Yet the expectations that some were harbouring of a complete overhaul in EU–Russia relations were always overblown. For example, during one of his first visits to the EU countries, Medvedev cautioned against expecting too much, arguing that:

> It is highly symptomatic that current differences with Russia are interpreted by many in the West as a need to simply bring Russia's policies closer into line with those of the West. But we do not want to be 'embraced' in this way. We need to look for common solutions.

Within half a year of the inauguration of Medvedev as president, Russia's relations with the West were seriously challenged by Russia's war in Georgia. The background to the war was years of simmering tensions between Moscow and Tbilisi that were aggravated by NATO's open-ended invitation for Georgia, as well as Ukraine, to eventually join the Alliance (Asmus 2010). The conflict came as a shock to the West, the EU included, but it was quickly resolved, in large part through successful EU mediation (see Chapter 5). Relations between Russia and the West were quickly restored, mainly due to new US President Barack Obama's decision to pursue a 'reset' in US–Russia relations in order to foster limited and pragmatic cooperation, especially in the field of international security (see Stent 2014: Ch. 9; Lo 2015: 168–77).

Signs of a more constructive mood were soon detected in the relationship between the EU and Russia as well. Medvedev's key policy agenda was modernization, which would be a response to Russia's persistent problems of economic backwardness, corruption and paternalistic attitudes, as Medvedev (2009) listed them in his agenda-setting *Go Russia!* article. Although Russia would not follow any model, the EU was 'in all respects Russia's most important partner for the purpose of modernisation' (Trenin 2011b: 20). The EU leaders returned to their belief that when it came to Russia an approach of constructive engagement was the way forward.

The Medvedev era's addition to the growing body of policy platforms was the Partnership for Modernisation (P4M), launched at the EU–Russia Summit in Rostov-on-Don on 31 May–1 June 2010. Parallel to the EU-level initiative, Russia and practically every EU member state concluded bilateral modernization partnerships with detailed agendas (see Chapter 4). The agendas were practical, focusing on economic and legal cooperation, pushing the wider debate on values to the sidelines, despite Medvedev's views that human rights are 'most basic and fundamental values' and 'a calm and honest discussion on a mutual basis' even of these issues would be welcome.

Although the Russian elite was increasingly unwilling to be socialized into the values promoted by the EU (Kratochvil 2008), the public opinion polls showed that the population in Russia still perceived the EU as a strategic partner of the highest priority (Tumanov, Gasparishvili and Romanova 2011). Another key item on the agenda was the possible abolition of visas, particularly ahead of the Sochi Winter Olympics (see Chapter 7).

All these positives notwithstanding, the Medvedev era turned out to be merely an interlude in the evolution of EU–Russia relations without managing to bring the relationship to a new progressive trajectory. On the contrary, the P4M was the final attempt at creating a semblance of cooperative and even expanding partnership between the two. The reality concerning the relations was, however, increasingly negative on the whole. The negotiations for a new post-PCA agreement resulted in a standstill and the understanding that the partnership was hollow started to be widespread. Russia felt that it had not been given the status it deserved and its interests were being systematically disregarded, while the EU was increasingly frustrated with the lack of concrete results and Russia's reliability as a 'strategic partner'. The attempts at deepening dialogue in the diverse fields of trade, energy or security came to a halt. Moshes (2012: 20) contended that 'by the end of 2011 it had become clear that the Partnership had essentially failed to make a difference' (see also Larionova 2015). Although both parties still attached great importance and even saw vast potential in their relations, at least rhetorically (see Lavrov 2013, Van Rompuy 2013), the continuous mushrooming of fresh instruments did little to conceal the lack of actual progress and concrete deliverables. On the contrary, it merely masked the negative trajectory on which the EU and Russia were traversing, which came to a head in the form of a drastic rupture of relations during and over the conflict in Ukraine.

The rupture: the conflict in Ukraine as the culmination of a long-term crisis in relations

The crisis over Ukraine can be seen as the culmination of the negative trends discussed above. Although Putin's return to the Kremlin as president in 2012 did not immediately cause a deepening crisis in the relations with the West, it was in many ways the point in time when the irrevocable countdown towards a rupture began. The popular protests over the fraudulent Duma elections in

December 2011 overshadowed Putin's return to the official pinnacle of power in Russia. They were also instrumental in changing Putin's tack concerning the West, the EU included. In the eyes of the Kremlin, the fears over the 'Orange virus' potentially spreading to Russia too were clearly confirmed. Initially, Putin reacted to the protests calmly, avoiding antagonizing them needlessly, but once the streets had cleared of marches, internal control and even selective forms of repression in Russia were quickly initiated (Finkel and Brudny 2012). Putin's agenda was clearly becoming more assertive externally as well. This was visible at the otherwise rather amicable EU–Russia Summit in St Petersburg in June 2012 where Putin demanded that the EU should recognize the Eurasian Customs Union, and explained that it was now actually the right counterpart for the formal treaty negotiations between Russia and the EU (Gotev 2012). However, before the Ukraine crisis the parties seemed to oscillate between cooperation and conflict in their mutual relations, as before. The expectations were kept rather low on both sides. Some positive achievements such as Russia's accession to the WTO in August 2012 were celebrated, although it soon turned out to be a mixed success at best (see Chapter 4). Russia's policy towards the West seemed to be on two tracks: there was a short 'charm offensive' before the Sochi Winter Olympic Games in 2014 that consisted of releasing Khodorkovsky from prison and allowing him to move to Switzerland, but at the same time Putin started to propagate Russia's own 'traditional' and conservative values as being superior to those prevalent in the liberal and increasingly decadent West (Putin 2013a).

The problems in EU–Russia relations started to be aggravated in earnest during 2013. The June 2013 EU–Russia Summit in Yekaterinburg revealed the rift between the two, the list of contentious issues ranging from the Russian anti-gay propaganda law to the conflict in Syria and beyond (Nechepurenko 2013). Writing at the time, the Russian analyst Andrei Zagorski (2013: 17) painted a pretty grim picture of relations:

> The hopes placed in the EU–Russia strategic partnership never in fact materialised. Russia and the European Union are now further apart than they were 10 years ago, especially when it comes to defining the purpose of their partnership. Instead of achieving greater convergence in the most contentious areas, the EU and Russia persistently have disagreed on a number of issues which

they believed were crucial to the nature of their relationship in the long run.

But worse was yet to come during the run-up to the Vilnius Eastern Partnership Summit that took place in November 2013. At the Summit, the EU expected to sign or initial a series of Association Agreements (AAs) that would have included the perspective of an eventual deep and comprehensive free trade area (DCFTA) with four partner countries, Armenia, Georgia, Moldova and Ukraine. Earlier that year Russia, which until then had remained fairly nonchalant about the EU's policies in the East, started to argue that these partnership agreements should be negotiated trilaterally or at least Russia's interests should be honoured when they were being concluded. According to the then Finnish Foreign Minister Erkki Tuomioja during a joint luncheon with EU foreign ministers in October 2013, Foreign Minister Lavrov complained about how Russia's earlier wishes of being granted observer status in the Eastern Partnership (EaP) had been turned down by the EU (Tuomioja 2015: 41). Granting such a role to Russia had indeed been mooted early on in the development of the initiative, but it was never carried out due to widespread fears that in the post-Georgian war situation Russia would abuse such a status and act as a spoiler.

Instead of granting Russia a privileged role in its policies, the EU regarded the negotiation of AAs as a bilateral deal between itself and the neighbouring countries. In response, Russia ramped up severe political and economic pressure to prevent the signing of the documents (for a discussion, see Wiegand and Schulz 2014; Wierzbowska-Miazga 2013). The first target was Armenia, which was quickly dissuaded from moving ahead with the AA and opted to join the Eurasian Customs Union instead during Putin's visit to Yerevan in September 2013. Moldova was also sent a strong message in early autumn when Moscow declared an embargo on Moldovan wine, citing health reasons, and sent the outspoken Vice-Prime Minister Dmitri Rogozin to Chisinau to warn the Moldovans that he sincerely hoped they would not freeze during the winter, making a less than veiled threat concerning the county's unilateral reliance on Russian natural gas.

But the real target and prize of Russia's actions was Ukraine. By late summer, Russia had already started to apply economic sanctions in anticipation of the negative economic consequences that Kiev's 'European choice' would entail for Russia. The measures included a ban on Ukrainian chocolate as well as the wholesale disruption of customs operations on the busy Ukrainian–Russian border. In addition to applying the stick Russia also dangled enticing carrots in front of Ukraine. In exchange for deferring the signing of the AA indefinitely, Moscow offered the Ukrainian President, Victor Yanukovych, a significant discount on the price of natural gas as well as preferential loans and other trade concessions to the overall tune of US$ 17 billion (Wierzbowska-Miazga and Sarna 2013). Sergey Glazyev, Putin's advisor on economic integration in the post-Soviet area, was sent to Kiev to speak about the negative consequences for Ukraine if it signed the treaty with the EU. In September 2013, he warned the Ukrainian authorities that they would 'make a huge mistake if they think that the Russian reaction will become neutral in a few years from now. This will not happen.' Moreover, 'Moscow would not offer any helping hand', but further sanctions could not be ruled out if the agreement was signed. Furthermore, in a rather ominous way, he warned of the possibility of separatist movements springing up in the Russian-speaking east and south of Ukraine and suggested that if Ukraine signed the agreement, 'Russia would consider the bilateral treaty that delineates the countries' borders to be void' (Walker 2013):

> 'We don't want to use any kind of blackmail. This is a question for the Ukrainian people,' said Glazyev. 'But legally, signing this agreement about association with EU, the Ukrainian government violates the treaty on strategic partnership and friendship with Russia.' When this happened, he said, Russia could no longer guarantee Ukraine's status as a state and could possibly intervene if pro-Russian regions of the country appealed directly to Moscow. 'Signing this treaty will lead to political and social unrest,' said the Kremlin aide. 'The living standard will decline dramatically . . . there will be chaos.'

The combination of threats and economic prospects swayed the Ukrainian government. After having met with Putin in early November, Yanukovych decided that he was not going to be able to sign the AA with the EU. The EU representatives were astonished when they learned of Yanukovych's decision only one week before the Vilnius Summit. Initially, it seemed clear that the EU had resigned itself to 'losing' Ukraine to Russia. Yanukovych's decision was, in the words of High Representative Catherine Ashton (2013), greeted as 'a disappointment not just for the EU but, we believe, for the people of Ukraine'. Although Barroso signalled 'our political readiness to sign sooner or later this association agreement', it was nevertheless accepted as a fait accompli. Despite some internal pressures to the contrary, the EU did not engage itself in a last-minute bidding war to try to win Ukraine over other than abandoning its demand that Yulia Timoshenko should be released. Before the summit, Yanukovych had started to talk about the need for €160 billion assistance for a transition period of five years, but the EU representatives announced that there would be no new benchmarks for the treaty. 'I feel like I'm at a wedding where the groom has suddenly issued new, last minute stipulations', Chancellor Merkel said at the Vilnius Summit (Spiegel Staff 2014) without thinking that the failure to achieve an agreement had any wider geopolitical ramifications. EU officials started to blame Mr Yanukovich directly for the failure rather than Russia, as he was seen as just wanting free money and playing Moscow off against Brussels (Buckley and Olearchyk 2013). Yet at the same time, the EU representatives made it clear that they would not accept a Russian veto in their ties with third nations: 'When you make a bilateral deal, we don't need a trilateral agreement', Barroso told journalists in a press conference (Marszal 2013).

As a consequence, instead of signing four AAs, the EU had to settle for just two, Georgia and Moldova. It is possible that this could have marked the end of all the drama over Ukraine, at least in the short term. Yet this was not to be, as the domestic unrest under the slogan of 'EuroMaidan' that started to gather pace in Ukraine from November 2013 onwards resulted not only in the collapse of the Yanukovych regime in February 2014, but also in a steadily escalating conflict between Ukraine and Russia that plunged EU–Russia relations increasingly into a crisis as well. The EU leaders empathetically supported the protest movement, which they saw as reflecting a genuine European calling for the Ukrainian people. Catherine Ashton, for example, visited the square in Kiev and sent a message to the protesters: 'I was among you on Maidan in the evening and was impressed by the determination of Ukrainians demonstrating for the European perspective of their country.'

The Russian response to the downfall of the Yanukovych regime was as swift as it was powerful and surprising. In less than a week, the so-called 'little green men' – soldiers without any identifying insignia that were later hailed as representatives of the Russian special forces and military intelligence directorate (GRU), even by Putin himself (see Lally 2014) – appeared on the Crimean peninsula, taking full military control of the area in a matter of days. After a hastily organized referendum on 16 March, Crimea was quickly incorporated into the Russian Federation, and the loss of the territory became an irreversible fact. The loss of Crimea was quickly coupled with a series of 'popular' uprisings in eastern parts of Ukraine that resulted in the destabilization of the country. Although the direct military role that Russia played in Eastern Ukraine remains somewhat contested, it seems clear that such a role did indeed exist (Granholm, Malminen and Persson 2014; Menkiszak, Sadowski and Zochowski 2014). Furthermore, Russia engaged in a powerful international information campaign against Ukraine, and indeed the West in general, a capability that also took the Western actors by surprise and one which, while drawing on well-established Soviet practices, had been evolving for years in Putin's Russia (Darczewska 2014; for the background, see Saari 2014). These activities were complemented with different forms of military intimidation directed at both Ukraine and the West, ranging from repeated airspace violations along Russia's western perimeter to nearly continuous and at times even massive war games and other exercises, including the country's vast strategic nuclear forces (see Chapter 5).

It seemed clear that Russia was operating on the basis of several different motivations in Ukraine. To begin with, it was clearly defending its perceived sphere of interests, perhaps even of influence from undesirable Western encroachments (Sergunin 2014; MacFarlane and Menon 2014). In addition, it was seeking to cordon off the spread of the 'Orange virus' from Ukraine to Russia proper. It was also probable that the situation reflected mounting personal frustrations, even resentment felt towards the US, but also the EU, by the Russian elites and perhaps in particular by President Putin. For example, in his 'victory speech' after the successful annexation of Crimea, Putin noted how 'they have lied to us many times, made decisions behind our backs, placed us before an accomplished fact. . . . But there is a limit to everything. And with Ukraine, our Western partners have crossed the line, playing the bear [sic] and acting irresponsibly and unprofessionally' (Putin 2014). In a similar vein, in an interview granted to the Russian news agency ITAR-TASS, Foreign Minister Sergey Lavrov (2014a) laid the blame for the crisis squarely on the EU with the following claim:

> Brussels told Ukraine to choose between the West and Russia. Everybody knows the root causes of the crisis: we were not being

listened to, Kiev was forced into signing arrangements with the European Union, which had been drafted behind the scene and, as it eventually turned out, were undermining Ukraine's obligations on the CIS free trade area. When Viktor Yanukovich took a pause for a closer look at the situation, the Maidan protests were staged. Then there followed the burning tires, the first casualties and an escalation of the conflict . . . (Lavrov 2014a)

But the EU remained far from convinced by this version of the crisis, and the Russian actions vis-à-vis Ukraine were met with sharp criticism. The extraordinary meeting of the Council on 3 March 2014 condemned the 'clear violation of Ukrainian sovereignty and territorial integrity by acts of aggression by the Russian armed forces'. Although the US was leading the drive for sanctions, the EU quickly followed suit. Yet due to the existence of serious misgivings concerning the chosen policy line of sanctioning Russia (see e.g. M. B. Kelley 2014), the onus especially for the EU was on preserving internal unity, not devising an optimal response to Russia's actions. As a consequence, the EU employed a three-tier strategy of sanctions against Russia. Interestingly, the EU did not resort to invoking Article 2 of the PCA and suspending the agreement – a sign of the growing irrelevance of the agreement and its increasingly outdated provisions – but to unilateral political decisions instead. The first and immediate response was to freeze Russia out of international meetings. Tier 2 sanctions that were applied after the annexation of Crimea were calculated to target people responsible for misdeeds and/or close to President Putin, while minimizing the damage to European economies. It was not until the shooting down of Malaysian Airlines passenger flight MH-17 on 17 July 2014, however, that the EU took a tougher stand. At the end of the month, the EU agreed to impose Tier 3 sanctions, a shift from a focus on sanctioning individuals to sanctioning key sectors in the economy. This restricted Russia's access to capital markets in the EU, prohibiting the buying or selling of bonds and equity as well as services. Imports and exports of arms were prohibited and, addressing previous criticisms of the EU, sanctions also prohibited the export of dual-use goods. The steady tightening of sanctions clearly managed to ruffle some feathers in Moscow. For example, during his visit to Finland in June 2014, Foreign Minister Sergey Lavrov was very outspoken in his criticism of the EU, calling the EU's position in the crisis 'dishonest and vindictive' (Rossi 2014). Russia also embarked on targeted retaliatory countermeasures, including the ban on food imports from the EU in August 2014, as well as threatening more substantive measures should the EU increase the pressure against Russia.

Another facet of the EU response was the decision to embrace the new Ukrainian government and President Petro Poroshenko wholeheartedly and to speed up the signing of the Association Agreement (AA) with the country. As early as 21 March, only a few days after the annexation of Crimea, the political chapters of the AA were signed, indicating in van Rompuy's words the EU's 'steadfast support for the course the people of Ukraine have courageously pursued'. This was followed by the conclusion of economic parts four months later on 27 June. A powerful symbol of the mutual determination to bring Ukraine closer to the EU was the mutual ratification of the AA at the Verhovna Rada and the European Parliament on 16 September 2014. The ratification process by the EU member states has not yet been completed, but the EU unilaterally removed tariffs and decided to 'provisionally' apply the treaty as of 1 January 2016. All of these acts can be seen as attempts to show support and solidarity towards Ukraine, as well as to signal that the EU found Russia's actions in Ukraine unacceptable and would not be deterred from moving forward with its own policies.

In addition to these measures, the EU also tried to allay Russian misgivings concerning the AA. To this end, and to facilitate dialogue between Poroshenko and Putin, the EU representatives took part in the Eurasian Customs Union (ECU) meeting in Minsk on 26 August 2014, de facto recognizing both the Belarusian president, Alexander Lukashenko, as well as the ECU in the process. The accords negotiated in Minsk – the so-called Minsk I – constituted the first attempt to create a road map to end the conflict. Moreover, the EU also took practically unprecedented steps, allowing Russia to take part in trilateral consultations with the EU and Ukraine concerning the possible negative effects of the deep and comprehensive free trade area (DCFTA) (Dragneva and Wolczuk 2014). Symbolism aside, Russia did not spare any effort to use these occasions to thwart the rapprochement between the EU and Ukraine. As early as 12 September 2014, in a tripartite meeting of the EU, Ukraine and Russia in Brussels, the parties agreed to postpone the provisional implementation of the DCFTA in Ukraine until the end of 2015. This was done at Kiev's behest, but only after Russia, in line with Glazyev's earlier warnings, had threatened it with devastating economic retaliatory measures should Ukraine move forward with the implementation of the DCFTA in any shape or form (Sadowski and Wierzbowska-Miazga 2014). The threat was repeated in autumn 2015, as the beginning of 2016 and hence the beginning of the provisional implementation of the AA was approaching. All in all, it was hard to avoid the conclusion that Russia was seeking, and to a degree also succeeding in its efforts, first, to derail and consequently overturn the AA and its DCFTA, and second, to eventually force Ukraine back into the fold of joining Russia-led economic and political projects in the former Soviet space. This success was reflected in the so-called Minsk II accords, negotiated in February 2015 once again in the Belarus capital, but this time under the stewardship of German Chancellor Angela Merkel and French President François Hollande, with Presidents Poroshenko and Putin clinching the deal. The Minsk II accords codified the Russian objectives in the conflict by obligating Kiev to amend its constitution to establish a special status for the rebellious republics, in effect auguring a frozen conflict scenario in Eastern Ukraine, hindering the country's European drive for the foreseeable future.

Although the events in Ukraine and consequently between the EU and Russia were evolving with potentially highly unpredictable consequences, the situation resulted in a dramatic disruption not only of EU–Russia relations but in the post–Cold War security order as well. The EU had imposed sanctions or frozen its cooperation with Russia three times before, during both Chechen wars and the Georgian war, but on all of these occasions the EU response had been half-hearted and short-lived, leaving the impression that the EU was not really willing and able to confront Russia. Many people expected this to be the case again in 2014, but within a year the conflict turned out to be a new normal from which a return to cooperation between the parties was anything but certain.

Conclusions

The analytical narrative above has discerned six periods or phases in EU–Russia relations. In the first phase (1992–94), the EU and Russia negotiated and finally agreed the contractual foundations of relations in the form of the PCA. In the second phase (1994–2000), the EU and Russia faced serious problems in putting the agreed mechanisms in place. The ratification of the PCA was delayed by three years due to the First Chechen War, and a renewed break in the relations was caused by the Second Chechen War in 1999. The strains, however, soon dissipated, and the third phase in relations, coinciding with Putin's first term as president of Russia (2000–4), was generally marked by optimism and progress in developing relations, particularly in the beginning. Discord started to increase again during Putin's second presidency (2004–8), a period that can be seen as the fourth phase in the relations. The problems manifested in trade disputes and clashes over values; the relations stagnated; and the parties were not able to renegotiate the PCA. The negative trends culminated in the Russo–Georgian war in 2008, but the war also marked the EU's success as a mediator of conflicts in the post-Soviet space. The Medvedev presidency (2008–12) – the fifth phase in the relations – was not as strained as the previous period, but to a degree this had less to do with substance and more with the style of Medvedev himself as president. A sign of things to come was the fact that the Partnership for Modernisation that the EU and Russia concluded in 2010 was no longer greeted with great enthusiasm on either side. Putin's return to the presidency in 2012 started the sixth and the most conflict-prone phase in EU–Russia relations, culminating in the rupture of relations over the Ukraine crisis.

There is a temptation to read history backwards, unidirectionally, and as inadvertently pointing towards the current conflict and rupture in relations. We revisit these narratives in Chapter 9, but at this point it is important to sum up our interpretation of the contested phases in the relationship. First, as far as the formative period is concerned, it is worth re-emphasizing that Russia was effectively not steamrolled in the process. Nothing was imposed on the country; on the contrary, Russia bargained hard and successfully in the process and perhaps unwittingly demanded a relationship that resulted in deeper forms of post-sovereign principles and the consequent expectation of political conditionality than it probably realized. Second, the relations have constantly evolved between more optimistic and more strained periods, rather than having been a steady linear story from a cooperative relationship towards conflict. There is probably no single overriding cause or culprit that would explain why the relative optimism of the early 2000s turned, first, into stagnation and then confrontation. One underlying reason could reside in what was *not* in fact achieved during the more optimistic times. The accumulation of unresolved issues and a growing list of mutual irritants and frustrations have all resulted in a steady erosion of trust and consequent growing mutual suspicion towards the objectives of each party. For the most part, the acute crises before the Ukrainian conflict – the Chechen wars, the Kosovo war, and the Russo–Georgian war – were all relatively brief, after which the parties rather quickly returned to cooperation. In that sense, the Ukrainian crisis is different from these past episodes and marks a much deeper rupture in the relationship. As Council President Donald Tusk explained in December 2014: 'This is maybe not a never-ending story but we need a long-perspective strategy. It will need . . . plans for years, not only for weeks or for months' (*Telegraph* 2014).

Chapter 3

Actors in EU–Russia Relations

The question of who or what the key actors are, and what consequently constitutes the EU's own actorness, is vexing, indeed perennial, in the study of EU foreign policy (Allen and Smith 1990). Another question concerns to what extent the EU can be seen as representing a much more metaphysical civilizational entity called 'Europe' or 'the West'. These questions must be tackled in the context of EU–Russia relations. At the same time, it is equally important to ask what kind of actor Russia is. Although as a sovereign nation-state it is a more traditional kind of entity, it nevertheless has, like all countries, its own idiosyncrasies that need to be examined.

There is a thick philosophical and conceptual debate over the nature of agency, actorness and the role of collective actors in social sciences in general, and in the study of international relations in particular (Wight 2006). Drawing on the work of Barry Hindess (1989: 132), an actor can be conceptualized as 'a locus of decision' that has the 'means of reaching decisions and of acting on some of them'. According to this view, not only humans but also more aggregate entities, even as multifaceted and complex as the European Union, or the Russian Federation for that matter, can be accorded with the ontological status of an actor. The fact that certain individuals have been empowered to make decisions and speak and act on behalf of such entities gives us reasonable grounds to use the shorthand 'Russia' and 'the EU' in the following.

The issues of agency and various levels of action are, of course, more complicated than this. Tatiana Romanova (2011) has distinguished between three levels of EU–Russia relations, namely the intergovernmental level of EU institutions and policies, the transgovernmental middle level of member states' institutions and policies and the transnational level of subnational institutions. Figure 3.1 presents these levels as well as the decision-making structures on

FIGURE 3.1 *Levels and decision-making structures in EU–Russia relations.*

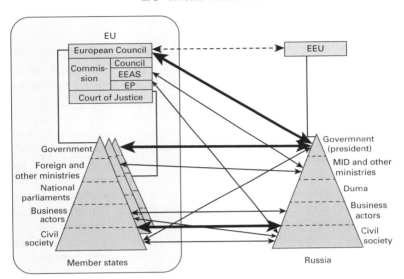

both sides. Although we do not follow these levels or terminology below, they are a useful reminder of the complexities involved if one wants to make sense of the entirety of EU–Russia relations (see also Bastian 2006). At the same time, and as is argued below, different levels of actorness and analysis are not equal in their heft and importance. On the contrary, there seems to be a trend towards increasing intergovernmentalism in relations over the years, with the conflict in Ukraine particularly accentuating the role of member states in EU decision-making.

In this chapter, we deal with the two actors in turn, starting with the more demanding case to be tackled – the European Union. We look at the institutional structures of the EU and discuss in which way they take part in the formation and implementation of policies towards Russia and the role of the member states in as well as outside of this process. We then move on to examine Russia and its nature as a foreign policy actor, where the key questions are whether all the relevant power is increasingly concentrated in the Kremlin and what kind consequences this has for Russia's policy towards the EU. Before concluding, we also touch upon the role of individuals, transnational groups and public opinion in the context of EU–Russia relations.

The European Union

Arguably, the European Union must be one of the most amorphous international actors in the world. In early 2000s, Brian White (2001: 3–4) noted how

> [d]epending upon the issue, references are variously and confusingly made . . . to the EU, or the EC, or the institutions of the EU such as the European Commission, or to one or more of the [at the time] 15 member states of the EU. Sometimes commentators seem to assume that Europe is a single integrated entity in world politics, acting internationally, rather like the United States, as another global "superpower" perhaps. But, at other times, references suggest that the whole (Europe) is little more than the sum of its parts (the member states), which are rarely united on anything!

Not only is the EU complex, but the rapid change in the nature of the EU as an international actor has made it difficult to 'keep track of what has become a very fast-moving target' (Carlsnaes 2004: 3). The Maastricht Treaty of 1992 established the Common Foreign and Security Policy. Since then, the key changes in the foreign policy system were made in the Amsterdam Treaty 1997, which created the post of a High Representative (HR) for the Common Foreign and Security Policy, and in the Lisbon Treaty 2007, which scrapped the old pillar structure and replaced the rotating nationally held presidency of the Council with the post of the President of the European Council and created the European External Action Service led by the HR. The Lisbon Treaty also included a mutual defence clause and a separate solidarity clause for natural and human-created emergencies.

Often in works dealing with the issues of 'European foreign policy' clarity has been sought – and to a certain extent also achieved – by reducing the internal complexity of the European Union to more manageable levels. In most cases, this has largely been done by sidelining the multifaceted nature of the EU and its institutions and by concentrating on the former Pillar II of the Common Foreign and

Security Policy (CFSP) alone (Stetter 2004: 723; Wessel 2000: 1135; Gegout 2010: Ch. 2). In other cases, clarity has been sought by brushing these problems entirely aside. For example, Hazel Smith, after discussing – and dismissing – the main objections to the idea of a European Union foreign policy, then goes on to assert that there are no conceptual difficulties and few practical ones in the idea of the European Union possessing a foreign policy much the same as that of any nation-state. But surely things are not as straightforward as this? In fact, it can be argued that the move Smith makes is a textbook case of a prevalent problem in the literature concerning the question of the European Union as an international actor. In most cases, the debate has departed from fairly state-centric notions that have resulted in a situation where the capabilities and institutions the Union possesses have been compared with those of unitary state actors (see Keukeleire 2003; Manners 2002). Asle Toje (2008), for example, has claimed that the strategic actorness of the EU resembles that of a small power. That kind of comparison has, for reasons that should become obvious below, cast a rather unfavourable light on the Union, which, in most cases – and this is where Hazel Smith's work is perhaps a rare exception – has been found seriously wanting (see C. Hill 1993: esp. 114). Most of the time the conclusion seems to have been that in order to have an effective foreign policy, the EU would have to evolve into some kind of a federal state (Forster and Wallace 2000: 462).

Another avenue for conceptualizing the EU's actorness has been to embrace its very multifacetedness. For example, James Caporaso (1996: 45) has captured these 'postmodern' characteristics of the Union by defining it as 'abstract, disjointed, increasingly fragmented, not based on stable and coherent coalitions of issues or constituencies, and lacking in a clear public space within which competitive visions of the good life and pursuit of self-interested legislation are discussed and debated'. But from the viewpoint of conducting actual research on such a beast, this conceptualization is not very helpful. Caporaso admits as much himself when saying that such a postmodern polity 'is not easy to describe' (Caporaso 1996). But in standard social science, description is the first step on the path towards theorizing, which should be the aim of our collective scientific endeavour to begin with. Therefore, one should perhaps be cautioned against developing too messy definitions and frameworks that, though perhaps doing some justice to the phenomenon in question, do not necessarily yield any clarity over the subject.

For the purposes of this work, pursuing any of these polar oppositions is unwarranted. Envisaging the EU as a postmodern entity would pose insurmountable challenges to the analysis that follows: how can one possibly discern actorness from such a maelstrom of overlapping players and processes? The path of straightforward reduction of complexity is not feasible in either of the forms discussed: concentrating solely on CFSP/former Pillar II activities does not suffice, as many of the most pressing issues in EU–Russia relations stem from policy areas that go well beyond its remit or which, at times, even fall wholly within the EU competence; whereas Smith's simplicity – although tempting – is clearly expecting too much from the conduct of European foreign policy. Instead, we have to depart from a middle-ground position that acknowledges that even within the EU, the institutionalization of the EU–Russia relationship falls equally, if not more so, within the remit of exclusive EU competence (the former Pillar I) rather than intergovernmentalism (the former Pillars II and III). This requires a more multifaceted understanding of the European Union as a unique, non-unitary international actor (B. White 2001: 24). Keukeleire and Delreux (2014: 61) have captured the essence of what they call the EU's foreign policy by arguing that it is 'single in name, dual in policymaking method, [and] multiple in nature', a foreign policy system defined precisely by the at times uneasy co-existence of two different and at times clashing policymaking modes of intergovernmentalism and community method.

Following Brian White (2001: 24, 40–1), the EU can be envisaged as an interacting 'foreign policy system' that is constituted of three different layers of foreign policymaking: the EU external relations (the former Community foreign policy, or foreign economic policy), the Union foreign policy (the CFSP and to a certain extent the CSDP) and the national (member state) foreign policies. The sometimes paradoxical entity called 'European foreign policy' is therefore an amalgamation forged in the interaction between these three layers of foreign policymaking. To a certain extent, the different layers can be expected to have competing, or at least inconsistent, objectives and agendas. What is more, it should not be taken for granted that any of the layers in their own right would be internally consistent and coherent either. For example, national foreign policies are vulnerable to different and competing bureaucratic pressures that often result in suboptimal policies (the classic text in this respect is G. Allison 1971). We should not expect that a multifaceted international bureaucracy like the Commission would be an exception to this rule either. The reverse is, of course, the case, as the Commission cannot be seen as a monolithic unitary actor but one with overlapping and competing agendas between the different DGs and Commissioners (B. White 2001: 55). In fact, it can be argued that at least some of the time, the European foreign policy can be envisaged as an internal crisis-management mechanism for the Union through which the competing agendas and (national) interests are managed (see Keukeleire 2003: 34–6; Zielonka 2011: 289).

It is easy to see how such a multifaceted system is hardly conducive to effective and coherent policies. In fact, the way the system has been built *practically ensures* the suboptimal and non-strategic nature of European foreign policy. Although the work at hand does not involve probing the consistency and coherence of the CFSP (Gebhard 2011), it nevertheless cannot avoid grappling with the issue to a certain extent. But this is done only and to such a degree as is necessary in order to shed light on the main problematique of the present work: the development of relations between the European Union and Russia and the problems the two have faced in the development of mutually acceptable forms of cooperation and a relationship.

The existence of manifold cleavages within the Union raises the admittedly tricky question of whether such an amorphous entity can have a policy in the singular worth talking about and studying in the first place. For the purposes of the work at hand, however, we need not be overly ambitious concerning this notion. Christopher Hill and William Wallace (1996: 1) have argued how, under the rubric of the CFSP, there is a process of *engrenage*, where 'habits of working together have gradually upgraded perceptions of common interest' (see also M. E. Smith 2000). These 'habits of cooperation, accepted advantages of shared information, responses to common threats, cost saving through increased collaboration, have all significantly altered patterns of national policymaking [into an] intensive system of external relations, in which the cooperating actors which constitute the system intertwine' (Hill and Wallace 1996: 12). Similarly, Dimitris Chryssochoou (2001: 13, 15) has called this the emergence of a 'cooperative culture' within the European Union where there is a sharing of experience among the participants in developing a transnational cooperative culture as a learning process of peaceful social and political change . . . [which] should not be confused with a certain type of diplomatic accommodation based solely on *quid pro quo* practices of interstate bargaining, but rather should be understood as stemming from *participation in a purposive forum that is capable of impinging upon the behaviour of the participating units* [emphasis added].

Quoting Laffan, O'Donnell and Smith (1999: 39), he concludes that 'the EU is more than an expression of modified interstate politics: it is the focus for processes that bring together new varieties of identity and need'. Indeed, the intense day-to-day interaction within the CFSP machinery produces 'transformationalist' effects on the member states as its very operation helps to foster a sense of shared identity, in essence a shared – although not necessarily a single – worldview based on creating 'a collective memory, based on shared myths' of working, succeeding and, more often than not, failing together under the banner of European foreign policy (Hill and Wallace 1996: 6, 8–9). This theme of trial and error is one that is revisited in the subsequent chapters.

But although such a thing may exist in principle, we are nevertheless faced with the problem of how to locate the actorness and the consequent policy at the EU level. It is argued here that the two can be found in two different avenues. First, we can distinguish what can be termed the negotiated actorness and consequent policy from the mainly intergovernmental exchanges between the member states. As Michael Smith (2000) has shown, the EU external policymaking can be envisaged as a negotiated order that produces policy positions and international policy outcomes. The other way of gauging the EU's actorness is through the set of actors that have been explicitly empowered to act on behalf of the European Union itself: the Commission, the Council and the European External Action Service (EEAS), as well as the individuals attached to these institutions. These are key actors in the sense that they frame the issues from an EU-centric perspective, looking at them through a wider 'European' lens while also keeping a constant eye on the member state interaction within the Union as well.

But a caveat is in order here, as it must be admitted that the end result of such aggregation should not be taken to imply a belief on the part of the present study in the existence of a *single* 'European' policy (see also Keukeleire and Delreux 2014). This is obviously not the case, as there is no unequivocally single culture on the basis of which such an understanding could rest and develop. In this respect, Brian White (2001: 100) has been perhaps overly optimistic when arguing that the creation of new institutions and actors since Maastricht has resulted in a certain 'Brusselization' of the foreign policy process in the European Union where the Brussels-based players are increasingly dominating both foreign policymaking and implementation. Surely this cannot be the whole picture, as one of the lowest points in common European foreign policymaking during the run-up to the war in Iraq in 2003 alone showed. Therefore, and as the pages that follow amply testify, 'Brussels' domination' is clearly not an apt characterization for capturing the essence of the EU's policy on Russia. Instead, White's argument has to be qualified by pointing out that if that is indeed the case, then it is not an all-pervasive phenomenon, but one that is confined to certain subjects where a relatively great degree of commonality – or exclusive EU competence – already exists. The depth and breadth of that commonality is not, however, a static given, but a dynamic by-product of European-level coordination, cooperation and integration which in its own right can be seen to result in feeding and strengthening the level of commonality between the member states on which European foreign policy, for its part, rests as the recent substantial literature on the Europeanization of national foreign policies suggests (Wong and Hill 2011). Instead, it is argued that – within reasonable limits – we can talk of a common set of shared understandings concerning EU foreign policy and its relations with Russia that are forged in the political and bureaucratic exchanges within the EU foreign policy decision-making machinery. Therefore, in the case of the European Union, instead of a single shared policy, it might make more sense to talk about an aggregated policy on Russia.

Yet to speak about 'the EU's Russia policy' on these pages is more than a convenient shorthand for the processes just discussed. In fact, the member states themselves have lent some credence to granting the European Union a subjectivity of its own: quite soon after the adoption of the CFSP, the member states agreed that any declarations made under the CFSP would be made not 'on behalf of the EU and its member states' but on behalf of the 'EU only' (Spence 1999: 266). This conclusion is further supported by the fact that in cases where the CFSP has worked effectively in reaching common positions, they have not been on the level of lowest common denominator, but often represent a median position and thus betray the formation of EU-wide consensus and understanding about the nature of the issues at stake and of the position that the EU as an entity will adopt on them (Keukeleire and Delreuz 2014; M. E. Smith 2004; Manners and Whitman 2000; Tonra 1997). In this respect, the different EU institutions, which have been entrusted with the power and authority to act and speak on the Union's behalf, are the key – but not the sole – actors in developing and articulating the EU views on Russia.

Turning to these actors, in the extant literature a division between intergovernmental and supranational entities is often made (for a fuller discussion of different EU institutions and actors, see e.g. Jones, Menon and Weatherill 2012: Part V; Richardson and Mazey 2015: Part 2). This approach pits the member states and the Council against the more communitarian players such as the Commission and the European Parliament. However, and as Stephan Stetter (2004) has argued, this usual division stems from taking the Union's (now defunct) treaty-based pillar structure at face value, which nevertheless underplays the significance of functional ties and the overlap between and across the pillars. According to him:

> behind the pillar structure looms a complex system which is characterized by multiple linkages between the pillars . . . Within these institutional regimes, a complex distribution of capabilities of different actors can be detected which not only discloses the existence of many cross-pillar linkages but also casts some general doubts over the allegedly sharp demarcation brought about by the pillar structure . . . Consequently, the Commission – but also the Council Secretariat – have emerged as central actors in all institutional regimes alongside member states, which continue to hold the key political resources within the double EU executive. (Stetter 2004: 733–4)

In this work, a different division suggested by Stetter is entertained, one between what could be labelled as the double 'EU executive' (the member states and the Council on the one hand, the EEAS and the Commission on the other), and the actors controlling the executive (especially the European Parliament, but also the Court of Justice and the Court of Auditors) (Stetter 2004: 721–2). The main emphasis is put on the executive arm of the Union due to the severe imbalance in the EU foreign policymaking process, which is in effect dominated by executive players (Stetter 2004). This notion also qualifies the idea of EU foreign policy as one dominated by the member states into one dominated by the executive actors, alleviating the problem of locating the policy at the EU level only by providing multiple channels for its identification. At the same time, it is important to point out that this division does not necessarily entail juxtaposition in substance between the two 'arms' of the Union. Nor should it be taken to imply that the arms would always see eye to eye among themselves.

The European Council

Of special significance is the gathering of member states in the form of the European Council which has, since the Treaty of Amsterdam (1997), been tasked with devising the strategic guidelines for European foreign policy. Although relatively little research exists on the actual decision-making at the European Council (but see Wessels 2016), it appears that there is seldom much actual deliberation on foreign policy and that the three biggest member states – France, Germany and Great Britain – play a crucial role in terms of determining the outcomes (Tallberg 2008; Debaere and Haesebrouck 2015). The Treaty of Lisbon asserted the primacy of the Council in terms of strategic agenda setting as well as designated a permanent president with a term of two and a half years to the European Council to chair its meetings, coordinate activities and represent the Council externally. The first holder of the post was Belgian Herman van Rompuy (2009–14), who was succeeded by the former Polish premier, Donald Tusk. Despite the fairly wide-ranging responsibilities, the role of president has remained rather minor in the EU's relations with Russia as both office holders have confined themselves mainly to occasionally issued statements or have given speeches on the topic, but with fairly little systematic impact on policies. This could be due in part to the fact that their terms have coincided with the euro and other crises in the EU that have perhaps consumed most of their energies.

The council of the European Union

In effect, the Council is the main intergovernmental decision-making forum in the EU, especially in foreign affairs. Here one must highlight the role of the Foreign Affairs Council (FAC, previously General Affairs and External Relations Council [GAERC]), which is a gathering of member state foreign ministers. It is in the FAC where items already discussed and developed either by the Commission or within the EEAS (see more below) will be largely decided and where the main CFSP instruments – the EU joint actions and common positions – are adopted. The Council is chaired by the HR of the Union for Foreign Affairs and Security Policy (henceforth referred to as the HR), a post that since its inception in 2000 has been held by three individuals: Javier Solana, Catherine Ashton and Federica Mogherini. Appointed by the European Council, this person is responsible for the conduct and consistency of European foreign policy. Since Lisbon, the HR heads the FAC and is also a vice-president of the Commission, thus having a foot in both the Council and the Commission. He or she can submit joint proposals with the Commission for the CFSP for external actions–related matters.

The HR is assisted in its work by the EEAS, an institutional innovation created by the Treaty of Lisbon. The EEAS is a hybrid organization combining heterogeneous institutional and organizational forms together in the EU (Henökl 2015). It gathers the external relations features of both the Council and the Commission under one roof, enhancing, at least on paper, the internal coordination and coherence of the EU's external action significantly. It is also worth noting that a third of the EEAS staff is seconded from member states, increasing mutual understanding and interaction between member states and Brussels, and enabling improved coordination between EU and member state foreign policies. The operation of the EEAS has drawn a great deal of criticism (see Balfour, Carta and Raik 2015). At the same time, it is possible that the benefits of the EEAS do not necessarily flow from the formation of an increasingly state-like foreign policy for the EU, but from creating novel means of external action for the EU and its member states (Bátora 2013).

The roles that the HRs have played in Russia relations have varied significantly over time. Due to their different institutional remits, a simple comparison is not feasible, but it seems that the efficacy of office holders depends not only on formal powers but on the personalities and situations at hand. Of the three office holders, it was perhaps surprisingly Solana who, while having formally the most limited mandate, nevertheless managed to have the biggest impact on policy. By contrast, Ashton never seemed to gain a strong foothold in the Russia portfolio (Helwig and Rüger 2014). Mogherini was elected to the post despite the voiced criticism that she was too inexperienced and 'soft' to deal effectively, particularly with Russia (see T. Wright 2014). To date, it seems that she has indeed been sidelined in the Russia portfolio by member states, and German Chancellor Angela Merkel in particular, and she has concentrated her energies on other international issues, such as the Iran nuclear agreement and the drafting of the revamped EU Global (Security) Strategy.

The commission

Although the Commission works as a collegium, not all the directorate generals (DGs) are equally important in relations with Russia. In this context, we should highlight three of them: Competition, Energy and Trade. Before the Lisbon Treaty, DG External Relations (RELEX) and the External Relations Commissioner were also naturally of particular importance. The president of the Commission has also shown consistent interest towards, and at times even played a key role in, the Union's relations with Russia. José Manuel Barroso's role grew, for example, in the run-up to the Ukraine crisis. As individuals, many Commissioners have played a visible role in Russia relations as well. Primus inter pares in this respect was probably Chris Patten who, as the External Relations Commissioner between 1999 and 2004, played a key role in steering and representing the EU policy on Russia. In the Commission, the role of the General Secretariat should also be noted as the primary seat of coordination.

The European Parliament

Turning to the actors controlling the executive, the European Parliament warrants close attention. It wields influence often through informal decision-making channels but sometimes also by taking concrete decisions, for example in budgetary matters (van Hecke and Wolfs 2015: 303). In particular, its Committee on Foreign Affairs has been very active, tabling several reports over the years on the Union's relations with Russia. In addition, the Plenary Sessions of the Parliament have been keenly following the developments in Russia, often inviting individual Commissioners and member state representatives to appear before it and conducting heated debates as well as accepting resolutions on Russia and the Union's relations with it. The Parliament is often seen as a more hawkish entity in its foreign policy standpoints than the Commission or the Council – and this image particularly applies to Russia. Often this has more to do with principled attitudes concerning human rights issues and the symbolic political effect of expressing them, whereas the other actors are much more clearly bound by the practical repercussions of their actions. It is also worth noting that in issues concerning Russia, the party affiliations determine the vote more often than nationality (Braghiroli 2015).

Court of Justice of the EU

The Court of Justice of the EU (ECJ) should also be mentioned in this context. One famous example of the significance of the Court in EU–Russia relations was the Simutenkov Case in April 2005, which dealt with the Russian footballer's right to play in the Spanish league outside the quota of non-European players (Schuilenburg 2005). Although it has no jurisdiction to review the legality of the intergovernmental CFSP acts, the ECJ nevertheless has a role to play in reviewing the economic and financial sanctions adopted by the Council, a role the Court has on previous occasions used to challenge and even overturn some decisions (Keukeleire and Delreux 2014: 89–90). This role has acquired increased relevance in light of the legal contestation of the EU's sanctions against certain Russian companies and individuals in conjunction with the conflict in Ukraine (Hille and Oliver 2014; see Chapter 4 for more).

Member states and their bilateral relations with Russia

Before the Treaty of Lisbon, member states were able to shape EU foreign policy most concretely when they held the rotating presidency of the Council. The presidency was responsible for statements and stances in the name of the Union. During every six-month period, there was an EU–Russia Summit, the agenda of which the country holding the presidency often actively fostered. For example, Finland used its first presidency in 1999 to insert the Northern Dimension onto the EU–Russia agenda and organized a dedicated foreign ministers' conference on the topic (see Chapter 8). One reason why the rotating presidency was abandoned was that the short cycle of presidencies was seen as being too brief for a consistent foreign policy. On the contrary, it seemed that the need to organize events and produce some symbolic results during each presidency overrode the long-term planning and strategic thinking in EU–Russia relations as well. Under the Lisbon Treaty, the member states still have the rotating presidency of Councils other than foreign affairs, and therefore their role in foreign policy is clearly diminished, although not entirely negligible, with some remaining marginal and symbolic functions (Duke 2015). This applies to EU–Russia relations as well.

The meeting and consequent enmeshing of member state perspectives and policies on Russia with the EU level takes place largely in Brussels. Here the key political fora for debate and decision-making are the gatherings of the European Council and the FAC, but it is the intricate bureaucratic machinery operating under the political overlay that is perhaps of greater significance. The actual details of common policies are debated and prepared especially in the Working Party on Eastern Europe and Central Asia (COEST), which convenes under the Chairmanship of the EEAS. In the COEST, the national diplomats prepare and agree issues and policies – in most cases the wording of documents and declarations – to be further debated and eventually decided in the Political and Security Committee (PSC) or the Committee of Permanent Representatives to the EU (COREPER II) that meet at an ambassadorial level. It is the deliverables flowing from this multifaceted machinery that prepare the EU's policy on Russia, and they are often approved without much further political or strategic debate at the FAC or in the European Councils. That said, under Mogherini, the FAC has undertaken a new initiative to ponder the state of play and the strategic direction of EU–Russia relations at the ministerial level as well.

As already noted, one of the key tensions in the development of a 'European foreign policy' is the interplay between national foreign policies of member states and the ambitions for a common policy line agreed at the EU level. Usually, Russia has been seen as a particularly sensitive and divisive subject for the EU and its member states (Haukkala 2006; Schmidt-Felzmann 2008). At first sight, this juxtaposition would seem to be somewhat artificial as almost by definition there can be no 'common' line at the EU level without the prior existence of national foreign policies from which this commonality should spring. Yet there is no denying that the existence of several – at the time of the writing 28, to be precise – 'national perspectives' on

Russia is a factor that affects, and at times even conditions, the EU's ability to come up with a coherent narrative and set of policies about its relationship with Russia (David, Gower and Haukkala 2013). Perceptions that there are distinct national traditions towards Russia are prevalent. In their famous 'A Power Audit of EU–Russia Relations', Mark Leonard and Nicu Popescu (2007) identified five groups of countries on the basis of their approach to Russia. The 'Trojan Horses' (Cyprus and Greece) often defend Russian interests in the EU system, and are willing to veto common EU positions; 'Strategic Partners' (France, Germany, Italy and Spain) cherish a 'special relationship' with Russia; 'Friendly Pragmatists' (Austria, Belgium, Bulgaria, Finland, Hungary, Luxembourg, Malta, Portugal, Slovakia and Slovenia) also maintain a close relationship with Russia and tend to put their business interests above political goals; 'Frosty Pragmatists' (Czech Republic, Denmark, Estonia, Ireland, Latvia, the Netherlands, Romania, Sweden and the United Kingdom) focus on business interests but are less afraid to criticize Russia in human rights issues; and 'New Cold Warriors' (Lithuania and Poland) have an overtly hostile relationship with Moscow and are willing to use the veto to block EU negotiations with Russia. Yet such a categorization is often misleading because the national positions tend to change and differ from the established image. Moreover, national positions also depend on the issue at stake. Nevertheless, images are also part of the reality in EU–Russia relations, and they are often more enduring than the actual policies.

To better understand why this is the case, we should turn our gaze to the structural reasons behind this variance. Summing up all the different national stakes the EU member states have with Russia is a task that is fraught with methodological pitfalls, and any attempt to arrive at a comprehensive picture would be a fool's errand. Yet the vastness of differing national stakes and consequent perspectives on Russia is important for both the theory and practice of EU–Russia relations, and indeed EU foreign policy. One way of illustrating this variance is to identify a single key variable, the relative individual economic importance that Russia has for the member states, to see what kind of a 'universe' of national perspectives that single variable would form. As a proxy, we use here what is often cited as the decisive factor in economic relations, namely the question of energy and the role that Russian natural gas plays for the individual member states. Following from this, we can envisage an axis whereon we plot the positions (in significance terms) of the member states' energy relations with Russia in the field of natural gas by looking at two variables: the share of natural gas in the overall energy mix of the member states (horizontal axis) and the share of gas imported from Russia to meet that demand (vertical axis). The size of the circles shows the volume of imported Russian natural gas by country. The image is striking in revealing the variance in this key issue. Yet vulgar interpretations should be resisted. Admittedly, Figure 3.2 is merely a snapshot based on a single issue. The point is not to argue that there is no commonality between the member states when it comes to Russia; as we shall see in the remainder of this book, there is. But the figure does capture in a graphic way that this commonality is not self-evident, but something that needs to be consciously identified and cultivated. Nor is it all pervasive. We could probably

FIGURE 3.2   *Universe of national perspectives on Russia in the field of natural gas.*

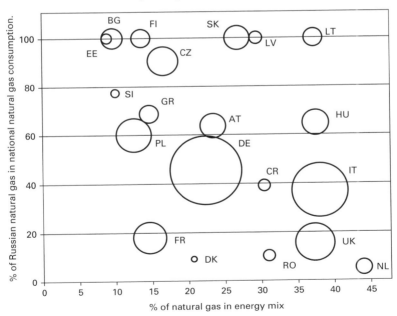

Source: The European Commission (2014a, Annex 1).

Note: Size of circles: volume of imported Russian national gas. Estimates based on preliminary industry data for 2013 and including natural gas volumes traded by Russian companies not necessarily produced in Russia.

think of other proxies that would reveal different dispersions of national perspectives on Russia. We should also bear in mind that none of these takes would be fixed and permanent, but changing over time in response to national and bilateral Russia-related reasons, and the process of Europeanization undoubtedly plays a role as well. In short, the matrix forming out of the national perspectives and their coming together on the EU level results in an almost bewildering complexity.

That said, one should remain cognizant that these proxies on their own do not say anything about the nature of the interaction, positive or negative, malign or benign, between the member states and Russia. In essence, the sum total of any member state Russia policies cannot be collapsed into any variable, be it energy dependence or the question of security. It is simply misleading to try to read the member state relations with Russia solely through the prism of any single variable, no matter how important it may be. Although the cases of, for example, Austria and Italy show energy is far from insignificant, we also have other cases, such as the Baltic states and Finland, where even a relatively high energy dependence on Russia does not necessarily play the leading role in framing their very different relations with Moscow. Or in other words, the national perspectives on Russia are not a function, or solely the outcome, of levels of differing energy dependence on Russia in the member states.

To understand why this is the case, a host of intervening variables need to be taken into consideration. This is not the place to discuss these issues at length and in detail (for a systematic attempt, see the contributions in David, Gower and Haukkala 2013), but this variance in national perspectives goes a long way towards explaining the persistent problems in generating a single coherent policy on Russia at the EU level. That said, the received wisdom of drastically differing national takes on Russia, and on the EU's overall strategic objectives when it comes to the member state as the root cause of the EU's problems, is to a degree also erroneous. In fact, there exists a surprising element of commonality between the member states concerning the overall analysis of Russia's current trajectory: This has been highlighted – probably to Russia's growing chagrin – in the EU's concerted response to the role Russia has played in the conflict in Ukraine (see Chapter 2).

We should also strive for a nuanced understanding of the differences between the member states. To take an example dealing with the role that Cyprus and Greece played in the EU's Russia policy during the Ukraine conflict, much has been made of their potential role as spoilers. Yet to understand the policy positions of these two countries, one must have a fine-grained understanding of history, economics, politics and even cultural and identity-related factors (Christou 2011; Karagiannis 2015). The point is not to argue away the fact that, at times, these countries do see eye to eye with Russia. On the contrary, they do, but the real issue is that they do not do so in order to blindly do Russia's bidding, but rather because they see it as being in their own interests sometimes to do so. Therefore, castigating these countries as 'Trojan Horses' (Leonard and Popescu 2007) is an oversimplification and misses the real issue. The same applies domestically where Russia has been busily cultivating links with various political actors (see more below).

This raises the question of leadership. Officially, EU foreign policy and the interactions between member states in the Council are based on the mutual recognition of the full sovereign equality between the member states reflected in the principle of unanimity. It is no exaggeration to claim that formal equality and unanimity are the *grundnorm* of EU foreign policy. Although possibilities for qualified majority voting have been gradually injected into the CFSP procedures, they have never been activated (Keukeleire and Delreux 2014: 101–4). Neither have the various proposals for establishing a great power '*directoire*' for European foreign and security policy materialized, although such an institution has been seen by some as an 'ideal forum for discussing western policy towards Russia' (Hill 2006: 2). That said, severe crises, both internal and international, have revealed a tendency whereby smaller informal groupings have assumed a leading position with the more or less tacit acceptance of other member states. At times, even single member states have taken almost sole leadership, as the French role during the war in Georgia in 2008 and the German stewardship of the Ukraine conflict during 2014–15 testified (Seibel 2015). This has raised the tricky question concerning the legitimacy of such informal groupings, especially when they are engaged in delicate negotiations with third parties with scant time for consultations among the 28. This has often also resulted in the sidelining of EU institutions and key players, to the detriment of the HR in particular. Indeed, the propensity of member states to brush the HR aside has become a recurring feature in EU foreign policy, and not only when it comes to the Eastern portfolio.

Russia

Compared with the EU, the Russian Federation is a much more straightforward actor to examine. As a more or less unitary state actor, it has the capacity and autonomy to conduct foreign policy in the manner in which it has traditionally been understood (see e.g. Holsti 1992). Yet the Russian case is not entirely devoid of anomalies or specific features either (see e.g. Sakwa 1996; Mendras 2013). In part, they stem from the beginning of the 1990s when Russia was seeking to take the place of the former Soviet Union on the international stage. This process was complicated by two factors: the lack of a clear formulation of what Russian foreign policy goals should be (often framed in terms of Russia's uncertain identity) and the lack of sophisticated machinery in terms of established working habits and a clear division of labour between the different actors. Since then, the Russian foreign policy system has evolved over time: not only was there the constitutional change in 1993 that granted foreign policy leadership to the president, but the real foreign policy leadership has vacillated between the president, prime minister and foreign minister, depending on the person in office.

The early months of the new Russia were a period of hectic diplomatic activity as new connections needed to be established with the rest of the world. This was also a period of tense infighting between the radical reformers gathering around President Yeltsin and the increasingly belligerent Supreme Soviet, the popularly elected parliament of Russia. The initial phase of a new Russian foreign policy revealed that the understaffed foreign ministry was unable to rise to the occasion and become the focal point of foreign policy – a role that was quickly usurped by the Supreme Soviet, which started to formulate a more nationalistic foreign policy in competition with Yeltsin, Kozyrev and the rest of the reformers (Checkel 1997: 110). There were also internal tensions between liberals and career diplomats at the Ministry of Foreign Affairs of the Russian Federation (MID). The key criticism in the early years was that Kozyrev neglected the 'near abroad' and the rights of the Russian speakers there and was overly eager to please the West and the European partners.

After the violent dissolution of the Supreme Soviet in October 1993, one of the key questions was how Russia's new foreign policy would be organized; who would be the main players be in this respect? The answer was the super-presidential system that was put in place in Russia (S. White 2006: 30). This stemmed partly from the lack of reliable structures and institutions, and partly from Yeltsin's own personality. Formally – institutionally and constitutionally – this was codified in the new 1993 Constitution that granted the holder of the presidency vast powers and autonomy in foreign and security policy: in a sharp reversal of the old Constitution, the president has the powers to govern the foreign policy of the Russian Federation (Art. 86), is the commander-in-chief of the armed forces (Art. 87), enjoys direct control over the foreign and other so-called power ministries (especially defence) and is the head and the sole appointer of the Security Council (Art. 83) – a key body for debating foreign and security policies in Russia (all of the articles are references to the *Constitution of the Russian Federation*, Chapter 4). In his tasks, the president is assisted by the government and its ministers and ministries. Of special importance in this respect is the foreign ministry, which has the formal responsibility of coordination and implementation of policies.

In actual fact, the making of Russian foreign policy has not been as neat as the above would seem to suggest. This was so especially during the Yeltsin presidency (1991–9), which was characterized more by zigzags and other abrupt changes in policy than a clear and coordinated approach to foreign affairs. In part, this was due to the legacy of the Soviet era and the fact that the new presidential administration was simply ill-equipped to deal with the full range of issues dealing with foreign policy (Webber 2002: 153). These problems were, however, accentuated by deep-seated rivalries within the Russian elites, resulting in a situation where different powerful actors, such as the president, foreign minister and defence minister, were all pursuing different foreign policy lines simultaneously (Arbatov 1994: 12; Sergunin 2008). These rivalries stemmed from the fact that – and unlike in many of the former Soviet satellites in Central and Eastern Europe – there were no systematic purges of former Soviet *nomenklatura* from positions of power and privilege. Instead, the new Russia was built on haphazard attempts at using, and at times modifying, the Soviet establishment, with the old mindsets and working habits still largely in place. In the words of Rurikov (1994: 125–6), 'a new Russian diplomacy . . . on the one hand, reflects the principles and approaches of Russian democrats, on the other, has inherited the problems, methods of work, and apparatus of Soviet diplomacy' (for a further discussion of the issue, see Kryshtanovskaya and White 1996). Writing in the mid-2000s, former External Relations Commissioner Chris Patten (2005: 205) noted how the Russian Foreign Ministry was the place where one could see the Soviet Union still in existence.

The role of the Soviet legacy is perhaps the key to understanding the subsequent development of Russian policies, both domestic and foreign. That said, a qualitative change in the making of Russian foreign policy nevertheless took place during the Putin era. Four main characteristics can be deciphered from the developments that are associated with Putin. First of all, the at times chaotic unpredictability of the Yeltsin era was replaced with a much more businesslike approach to Russia's foreign relations (Lo 2003a). Second, a consensus was reached concerning the key tenets of Russian policy. This included the waning of the influence of the liberal intelligentsia and its replacement with initially a more pragmatic, but over time increasingly belligerent, nationalistic position promoted by Putin and his circle (Gel'man 2015; Myers 2014; Laqueur 2015). Third, and perhaps as the most visible manifestation of the two previous characteristics, the locus of decision-making concerning foreign policy decidedly shifted towards the Kremlin and the presidential administration, giving grounds to increasing talk of genuinely 'presidential' foreign policy conduct (Lo 2003b: 4; Lynch 2003: 22). The role of the president has also been highlighted by the fact that, under Putin, the Security Council was elevated into the key forum for formulating foreign policy, eclipsing the foreign ministry and other institutional players in the process (Vendil 2001: 86). Finally, to a large degree, the Putin era witnessed a return to old Soviet thinking and habits. This particular homogenization of key elites was reflected in the rehabilitation of certain key Soviet figures, events and characteristics, as well as in the rise of the so-called *siloviki* – persons with a KGB and other security services background – to positions of political and economic power in Russia (for more about the role of *siloviki* in the present-day Russia, see Dawisha 2014).

As already mentioned, under Putin a political re-centralization has been the order of the day. This has made life easier for the analysts in certain respects as it has narrowed down the number of players that can be deemed as being of significance in shaping Russia's foreign policy. Bobo Lo (2015: 5) has suggested that the key functions in Russian foreign policy consist of decision-making, ideational inspiration, implementation and rationalization. The scholarly community seems to be in agreement that it is increasingly President Putin and a narrow circle of his colleagues in the Kremlin that take the key decisions (see Kryshtanovskaya and White 2005; Lo 2015; Polikanov and Timmins 2004: 228; S. White 2006). Dmitri Trenin and Bobo Lo (2005: 10) have gone as far as to argue that Putin is the sole decision-maker in all important foreign policy matters: 'Tellingly, Putin does not seem to need a real foreign policy advisor, only an aide to help him with the daily routine and flow of information. Evidently, the president believes he knows it all himself.' Obviously, this is an oversimplification that does not bear serious scrutiny, but it does point to Putin's role as the ultimate decider in Russia. In addition, it also alludes to the fact that, at least to a certain extent, we need to factor the biography, psychological dispositions and even personal idiosyncrasies of Gospodin President into our analysis (see Hill and Gaddy 2015; Forsberg and Pursiainen 2016).

Be that as it may, we may nevertheless proceed from a fairly hierarchical understanding of the key players in Russian foreign policy decision-making that stands in stark contrast to the institutional cacophony so evident in the case of the European Union. There is also some evidence that suggests that the Ukraine conflict has resulted in further reduction of the inner circle where Putin and a very small group of trusted confidants make the essential decisions concerning Russian foreign policy, at times even outside the formal decision-making structures and mechanisms. This has the unfortunate side effect of making it harder to gain reliable information about the workings of such closed and often very informal groupings, not to mention the dangers it brings in terms of accentuating group think and other forms of pathologies in group decision-making in Russia (Myers 2014).

Indeed, Putin's growing reliance on a small number of close confidants needs to be explicitly addressed. These people, mainly from security service backgrounds and/or from Putin's home town of Leningrad/St Petersburg, have assumed the commanding heights of both politics and economy during the past 15 years. This group – often called the *Pitertsy*, a Russian word referring to their town of origin – are both the main lever for using power in Putin's Russia and also the best guarantee of systemic stability in the country (Dawisha 2014). To a degree, the depth of personal ties and patronal linkages (see Hale 2015) makes the group more reminiscent of an ice hockey team – Putin's favourite sport – than a traditional political elite. This entails, in the words of Igor Torbakov (2011: 9), that 'the line between what is generally understood as national interests and the group interests is completely blurred in Russia'. Following from this, a word of caution is in order. Although the identification of key players in Putin's Russia is fairly straightforward, deciphering their 'true' views on the issues at stake might be more complicated. This is because the domestic processes of consolidation traced above have had the unwanted (from the vantage point of an analyst, that is) side effect of increasing secrecy around the Kremlin. Unlike during the Yeltsin era, when the presidential administration was still accessible and information was on offer, the Putin era has witnessed a much more closed and secretive atmosphere in the Kremlin and Moscow. This has, at times, had the effect of heralding the return of 'Kremlinology', but now under the heading of 'Putinology', to the debate on Russian foreign policy (Trenin and Lo 2005: 6; Aron 2015). Yet this need not pose an insurmountable obstacle in terms of our present task. The official Russia today produces an unprecedented wealth of material that will help us to build a case for Russian thinking and its evolution over time. At the same time, a note of caution is in order, as the conflict in Ukraine in particular has revealed the wanton use of misinformation to be part of the Kremlin's toolbox. Indeed, Lo (2015: 4–5) has talked about two policy milieus in Russian foreign policy, the real and the virtual. According to him, it is the virtual world of policy concepts, declarations and speeches that we see, and that the Kremlin wants us to see. The real milieu resides in small informal groupings shrouded in secrecy and is consequently almost invisible to outside observers.

The president and the presidential administration

The president has been the key individual in Russian foreign policy decision-making. This was already the case in the latter part of Boris Yeltsin's presidency, although his health problems diminished his ability to lead effectively – but the trend was only strengthened during Vladimir Putin's first tenure (2000–8). It is important to note that, increasingly, the political power has been concentrated not in the institution of the president, but in the persona of Vladimir Putin, as reflected in the fact that under President Dmitri Medvedev (2008–12), the locus of decision-making and the consequent political power largely moved away from the president towards the government headed by Putin as the prime minister (see Lo 2009).

Medvedev, however, had a notable role in the European policy that reflected his image as a more liberal leader. With the return of Putin to the presidency in 2012, the role of the president is again central in foreign policy, including relations with the EU.

The presidential administration – incidentally housed in the former offices of the Communist Party Central Committee on *Staraya Ploschad* – is, in the words of Trenin and Lo (2005: 10), 'the true national government', ultimately responsible for the strategic guidance of Russian policies, both domestic and foreign, and answerable only directly to the president. During the Putin era, the presidential administration has grown in both importance and size, becoming in the process a 'government within the government' and increasingly taking the leading role when it comes to several issues of both domestic and foreign concern. The problem for an analyst is that, of all the institutions of power in present-day Russia, the presidential administration is perhaps the most secretive of all.

The security council

The Security Council is a weekly meeting of the key Russian figures dealing with foreign affairs and national security. It is an exclusive tool for the president, who enjoys the privilege of appointing its members. Although originally intended to act as a politburo of sorts in foreign and security matters, the Security Council has practically never played a key role in Russian foreign policy (Mankoff 2009: 55). During Putin's tenure, however, the profile of the Security Council has been significantly upgraded. But once again we are faced with the rather secretive and closed nature of decision-making in Russian foreign policy, as Putin in particular has clearly preferred to conduct the real business of the Security Council within a more intimate circle of advisors, which has met outside the formal meetings of the Council itself (for an attempt at deciphering the people who attend these unofficial meetings, see Kryshtanovskaya and White 2005).

The foreign minister and ministry

Officially entrusted with the implementation of presidential foreign policy, foreign ministers have, at times, become powerful figures in their own right. This was the case especially when Andrei Kozyrev and Yevgeny Primakov were foreign ministers. Whereas

Kozyrev was associated with the Western orientation in Russian foreign policy, Primakov's doctrine was 'multi-vectoral'. Sergey Lavrov has been serving as foreign minister since 2004, but despite his popularity at home and prominence abroad, he has not been associated with a specific orientation of Russian foreign policy. By contrast, it seems that the foreign minister and his ministry have been sidelined in some of the key decision-making processes by the more influential actors already discussed above (Galeotti 2016). Although Lavrov's professional background is strong, he lacks the credentials of a *Pitertsy* and is therefore often not counted among the insiders in Putin's Russia. Yet the foreign ministry and its officials can be seen as influential figures, especially when it comes to Russia's relations with the EU: the foreign ministry tends to have specialists that have the kind of detailed knowledge about the Union that is often, and rather surprisingly, lacking in the highest echelons of Russian decision-making. The Mission of the Russian Federation to the European Union plays a key role here, and its head, Ambassador Vladimir Chizhov, has occupied a very visible position in EU–Russia relations during his ten-year tenure. That said, although the Russian foreign ministry coordinates, it must also compete with the other sectoral ministries (discussed below). In any case, the fact that the foreign minister often acts as the official spokesperson for the Russian government in foreign affairs makes the minister and the ministry serving under him an important actor to be analysed.

Other governmental figures

Traditionally, prime ministers in Russia have been fairly insignificant implementers of presidential directives. As mentioned above, during Putin's tenure as prime minister, the authority and power of this office grew immensely, assuming a leading role in Russian politics, only to lose that position once Putin moved back to the Kremlin. Other sectoral ministers also have relevance for relations with the Union, such as economic development and trade and finance. This is due to the multisectoral nature of EU–Russia interaction itself, which has strongly emphasized economic issues and cooperation, giving the specialists in these ministries added significance compared with some other bread-and-butter issues of foreign and security policies. The Ministry of Economic Development, for example, is a very important actor in EU–Russia relations, with its own mission responsible for trade in Brussels, and often represents a more liberal attitude than the MID.

The federal assembly and its two chambers; the council of the federation and the state duma

Officially, the Federal Assembly enjoys a respected role in constructing foreign policy as well. This is highlighted in its powers of 'ratification and denunciation of international treaties and agreements of the Russian Federation' (*The Constitution of the Russian Federation*, Chapter 5, Art. 106). In actual fact, however, the parliament and its deputies have become increasingly marginalized in the actual making of the policy (Mankoff 2009: 54). Yet they still have an important role as the official talking shop of the country. In fact, Trenin and Lo (2005: 13) have noted that their role is 'not so much to help make policy as to explain it to the outside world', in effect engaging in the 'rationalizing' function mentioned above.

Federal subjects

A number of federal subjects – most of them being regions, some of them cities – constitute the Russian federation. According to the Russian constitution, they have some formal powers to influence foreign policy decision within the federal system as well as to establish and carry out external policies of their own. They can conclude treaties, establish representative offices, make statements, attract foreign investments and tourism, and cooperate in many other ways with international bodies (Busygina 2007; Sergunin 2008). The actual foreign policy influence of the regions and other federal subjects, however, varies depending on the region, and it has also changed a lot in time. In the period before and after the dissolution of the Soviet Union, some of the regions grabbed a lot power – and Chechnya and Tatarstan even declared their independence. Other regions that were relevant, especially with regard to relations with the EU, were the regions adjacent to EU members states, in particular, Kaliningrad, Karelia and Pskov, which have participated in the so-called Euroregion schemes, such as Euregion Karelia across the Finnish–Russian border, Euregion Pskov-Livonia including the Lake Peipsi project across the Estonian–Russian border or Euroregion Baltic around Kaliningrad (see Roll, Maximova and Mikenberg 2001; Aalto 2002; Huisman 2002; Browning and Joenniemi 2004).

Some regions have had a high political profile because of their leader: for example, Alexander Lebed was the governor of Krasnoyarsk Krai and Boris Nemtsov of Nizhny Novgorod Oblast in the 1990s and Roman Abramovich the governor of Chukotka in the 2000s. The most active period of the involvement of the federal subjects in the external relations was in the 1990s and the early 2000s, after which such activities were curbed down rather effectively by the Kremlin. The regions nevertheless concluded hundreds of international agreements, and many of them sought tighter contacts with their foreign partners. Although the federal authorities have contested many of these agreements and replaced regional leaders who have been perceived as too independent, some forms of cross-border cooperation have continued. Crimea and Sevastopol are special cases in the list of the federal subjects because they have not been recognized by the EU as being part of Russia.

Other actors, factors and arenas

As already mentioned in the Introduction to this chapter, EU–Russia relations are not solely the remit of the EU, its institutions and member states, and Russia. The neat division between the EU and Russia is affected by other actors, factors and arenas that play a role and deserve a brief introduction. To begin with, international institutions are important arenas for interaction between the EU and Russia. In this field, the United Nations – and its Security Council (UNSC) in particular – is of importance, and several crises that have affected EU–Russia relations have been played out under its auspices. In Russian foreign policy, the UNSC enjoys pride of place as the symbol of Russia's great power status, and the veto Moscow has over its deliberations is the key ingredient of Russia's formal equality with other leading powers of the world (Panagiotou 2011). In a similar manner, the Organization for Security and Co-operation in Europe (OSCE) has been an important forum for discussions concerning European security (Kropatcheva 2012a; see Chapter 5 for more) and the Council of Europe (CoE) for discussing human rights (Saari 2010a). In addition, NATO has obviously been a factor affecting relations between the EU and Russia, especially its enlargement(s) and international missions, particularly in the Western Balkans (Forsberg and Herd 2015). Finally, G8 and G20 Summits have provided an important venue where the leaders of the major European states as well as EU representatives have engaged the Russian leaders.

In the economic field, the Eurasian Economic Union (EEU), established in January 2015, is an important factor and also a potential actor in EU–Russia relations. Potential, because the EU has not, due to serious misgivings about the legitimacy and durability of the institution, formally recognized the EEU as a negotiating partner (see Chapter 8). At the same time, Russia insists that the EEU and not Moscow is the correct counterpart to the EU in trade-related issues and that in the future the format of relations should be based on a wide-ranging common economic area from 'Lisbon to Vladivostok' (see Chapter 2).

Another important level of interaction concerns the businesses and enterprises that have taken the lead particularly when it comes to forging energy relations between the EU and Russia (Abdelal 2013). The EU–Russia Industrialists' Round Table (IRT) is a business platform that brings leaders of companies from the EU and Russia together. Established in 1997, it facilitates business dialogue and has evolved into a full-fledged organization that gives business recommendations to policymakers in the EU and Russia (see EU–Russia Industrialists' Round Table 2015). During the Ukraine conflict, Russia tried to use business ties with Western companies to undermine the unity and effectiveness of the Western sanctions regime. For example, in a clear attempt to underline the feeble nature of the sanctions, the St Petersburg Economic Forum, an annual gathering of international investors, was turned into a showcase for Western companies' continued commitment to engage Russia despite the conflict in Ukraine.

Lobbying also plays into this, and Russia is particularly active in this field in Brussels. For example, Gazprom has frequently used the PR company G-Plus to make its views heard in the European capital (Rettman 2015). Many EU businesses also engage in lobbying in Moscow. Perhaps the most important actor in this respect is the German Committee on Eastern European Economic Relations (Ost-Ausschuss), which has promoted business links between Germany and the East since the early 1950s. Other member states have also followed suit with similar organizations. Russia uses lobbying in several member states as well. To be sure, there is nothing wrong with relying on personal and business links, even lobbying, to promote interests. At the same time, however, some aspects of Russia's conduct in this field also have a more problematic side, as Russians use business ties and other financial incentives, not to mention outright corruption, to promote their interests (Hill and Gaddy 2015; Kupchinsky 2009).

Attitudes at the level of public opinion are a factor that shapes relations, although their exact significance is debated. It would be an exaggeration to claim that Russian or EU public opinion would determine relations, but it is still worth examining as it constitutes both constraining and enabling forces. The Ukrainian crisis has increased attempts on both sides to reach out to the public and has elevated the importance of thinking how sympathies and antipathies are formed and upheld.

Traditionally, Russians have held very positive views of the EU (Tumanov, Gasparishvili and Romanova 2011: 141). At the same time, it is doubtful whether they have ever really had a very detailed understanding of what the European Union entails, or whether the positive responses rather reflect the positive connotations connected with 'Europe' in general. Attitudes towards 'the West', towards 'Europe' and towards the EU are overlapping and not always differentiated (Semenenko 2013: 108). The popular support in Russia for EU membership – even if the question can be regarded as hypothetical – nevertheless declined from 50 per cent to under 30 in the early 2000s. People were not, however, passionate about the EU per se, and public opinion was shaped by negative events and media reporting (Semenenko 2013: 115). Yet, according to the polls conducted by Pew Research Center (2015), in 2013 nearly two-thirds of Russians still felt favourably disposed towards the EU. The EU's image has been on a consistently higher level than that of the United States, not to mention NATO. Of the member states, Germany in particular deserves to be mentioned as it has traditionally been seen as a 'business card' of the EU (Tumanov et al. 2011: 141). During the conflict in Ukraine, however, the perception of the EU, along with that of Germany and the US, took a marked turn for the worse: in 2015, only about one-third of Russians (still) regarded the EU favourably. The dramatic reversal in the EU's image in 2014 is captured in Figure 3.3. As a result, the image of the European Union is now almost on a par with the traditional adversaries, the United States and NATO, whereas China is now regarded as Russia's closest friend (see also VCIOM 2014 and Levada Center 2015). The negative trend has also impacted Germany's image, which is increasingly perceived as being under the tutelage of the US rather than being an autonomous actor (VCIOM 2015).

The same evolution in public opinion also applies in reverse: Russia's image has plummeted in the majority of EU member states. In the early 2000s, Russia's image in Europe was fairly positive, and

FIGURE 3.3 *The image of the EU in Russia 2003–15.*

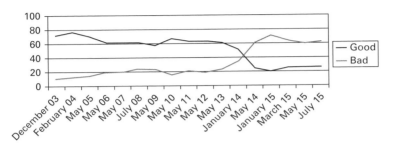

In general, what is your attitude toward the European Union?

Source: Levada Center, taken from Lipman 2016.

Putin was more popular than the US President George W. Bush. For example in Germany 75 per cent of the population had confidence in Putin and even in Britain the figure was 53 per cent in 2003 (Pew Research Center 2007: 63). The change in perception of Russia and Putin took place in the mid-2000s, for example in Germany confidence in Putin had sunken to 32 per cent by 2007 (Pew Research Center 2007: 63). Although the image of Russia slightly improved in the EU and elsewhere in the West during the Medvedev era, during the conflict in Ukraine it took a major battering. The proportion of EU citizens that hold a positive view of Russia varies from country to country but is generally around the 30 per cent mark (BBC 2014). These trends in public opinion are hardly without consequences for the future relations between the EU and Russia, particularly because the negative views have become rather prevalent among younger generations.

Finally, there is ample evidence that individuals also play an important role. This is hardly surprising as in international politics personalities and their interactions do matter (Mintz and DeRouen 2010: 18–19). At the same time, the personal level is also a source of tensions. Relying on individual links is indeed the preferred modus operandi of Vladimir Putin. According to Hill and Gaddy (2015: Ch. 11), Putin cultivates personal ties with prominent people in the West, the EU included, with a view to gaining important insights into partners as well as promoting Russian interests by using these people as intermediaries and spokespersons vis-à-vis the West. Perhaps the most prominent example of this was Gerhard Schröder, who, during his tenure as German chancellor (1998–2005), adopted a strongly pro-Russian stance, actively promoting, among other things, the Nord Stream gas pipeline between Russia and Germany. Another example was Italian Prime Minister Silvio Berlusconi. In both instances, the connections have endured beyond the officials' periods in office. After leaving the Federal Chancellery, Schröder quickly took up a lucrative position as chairman of the board of Nord Stream, creating at least the impression of being rewarded for his services to Russia. Berlusconi has also remained personal friends with Putin. Indeed, there seems to be a wider propensity in Moscow for thinking that 'every person has their price', as exemplified by a lucrative offer made to the departing Italian Prime Minister Romano Prodi to join the SouthStream gas pipeline project as chairman of the board in 2008, which he nonetheless declined.

Conclusions

One general conclusion that can be drawn from the preceding discussion is that both the EU and Russia have been moving targets during the period of building their relations. For one, the EU has been in a constant process of internal transformation (see Herrberg 1998, who already makes the same point). It has built up its actorness in international relations by creating formal policies and corresponding bureaucratic structures and policy instruments. Although in the 1990s the EU was intent on conducting policies towards third parties from two structural perspectives, that of the Commission and that of the Council, or supranational and intergovernmental, more recently it has tried to create coherence and unity through establishing 'a foreign minister' and diplomatic machinery in the European External Action Service. In the process, the EU has also been amassing new policy areas and increased competences in external action.

The EU, however, does not exhaust the notion of European foreign policy because it also includes the national foreign policies of the member states. It is widely understood that, particularly vis-à-vis Russia, the EU has demonstrated a structural weakness where it has suffered from a strategic gap between the member states and the EU and their corresponding policies towards Russia. In crisis situations, however, the role of some member states has been indispensable and positive. France played a key role as the president of the EU during the Russo–Georgian war in 2008, and Germany occupied a central position during the Ukraine conflict. Yet, while taking the lead, these member states have also sought to coordinate their policies with other member states as well as with the European institutions without which they would not have been able to act successfully.

For its part, Russia has also been in a process of transformation since the dissolution of the Soviet Union, but its nature as a foreign policy actor was clearer. During the 1990s, Russia was searching for its role and position in the world, but foreign policy, when the institutional structures had been created, was nevertheless formed in the Kremlin by the president and shaped and carried out by the distinguished foreign ministers Kozyrev and Primakov. This trend has continued unabated during the Putin era, to the point where Russia has become diametrically opposed to the EU, in the sense that power is concentrated in the Kremlin and all important decisions are either made by the president single-handedly or together with a very exclusive group of trusted people.

These differences between the EU and Russia have become increasingly manifest during their interaction. On their own they do not explain the problems the two have faced in developing their relations, but they are definitely a factor that has affected the process.

Chapter 4

Economy, Energy and Environment

Despite its political and institutionalized nature, the true foundation of EU–Russia relations is economic. This was already reflected in the PCA, which is largely an economic agreement aiming at the eventual development of a free trade area (FTA) between the EU and Russia (see Chapter 2 for a discussion). The history of EU–Russia relations since then can be read as a series of attempts by both parties to kick-start the ailing process of economic convergence and integration with a view to arriving at a common economic space 'from Lisbon to Vladivostok'.

This chapter provides an overview of the economic relations between the EU and Russia, starting from trade and investments and moving on to the repeated attempts at solidifying and institutionalizing these relations with a view to arriving at an eventual free trade area. This is followed by a discussion of energy relations, which highlights the dual problems of close interdependence and the growing contestation concerning the 'rules of the road' for managing those relations and consequent interdependence. The chapter also briefly touches upon environmental cooperation, including attempts to halt climate change. The chapter concludes by discussing the impact of the sanctions imposed on Russia over the Ukrainian conflict, and the economic relations between the two increasingly alienated strategic partners.

The development and structure of trade

The question of trade flows and investments between the EU and Russia is far from insignificant. Russia is the third largest trading partner of the EU, with an impressive annual turnover of €285 billion in 2014, totalling 8 per cent of the EU's external merchandise trade. To put this figure into perspective, it is, however, worth noting that over half of EU trade is internal, taking place between the member states. The variance in this respect is significant, ranging in 2013 from almost 83 per cent of Slovakia's total exports of goods going to other EU member states to under 43 per cent of Malta's (European Commission 2015a). Furthermore, if one excludes the mineral fuel imports, Russia's share would drop below 3 per cent, less than, for example, Turkey (European Commission 2015b). The EU runs a significant trade deficit with Russia.

By contrast, the EU is by far the largest trading partner for Russia, consisting of almost half of Russia's trade. This dominance is further accentuated by the fact that the EU and its member states are the most important source of foreign direct investments (FDIs) into the country, with up to 75 per cent of stocks in Russia coming from the EU, including the lion's share from Cyprus, which represents a good deal of repatriated Russian money. Here we see an interesting symmetry with some 68 per cent of Russia's outward FDI stock going into the EU (Liuhto and Majuri 2014: 200). That said, it is worth pointing out that Russia's share of the EU's inward FDI stock is meagre, representing less than one per cent of all FDI received outside the EU. Some member states are, however, significantly more exposed, including Austria, Bulgaria and the Baltic states with close to 5 per cent, and with Cyprus topping the bill with nearly 15 per cent of the FDI stock (Liuhto 2015: 81–2).

After the lost decade in the 1990s, the trade between the EU and Russia showed steep growth until 2008, when the positive trend was interrupted by the global financial and economic crisis, which also had a negative impact on EU–Russia trade. In 2010, mutual trade once again resumed growth, reaching record levels in 2012 (key trade figures have been captured in Tables 4.1 and 4.2). To illustrate the robust growth in trade between the EU and Russia, it is worth noting that the volume essentially tripled between 2003 and 2013. Since then, the weakening of Russia's economy and the decline in oil prices, together with the negative effects of the sanctions imposed by the EU and its Western partners over the conflict in Ukraine, have reduced the volume and value of trade, while casting the long-term prospects of Russia's economy as well as the future development of EU–Russia economic relations into doubt (see more below).

The structure of trade between the EU and Russia reveals natural complementarities, suggesting a good match between the economies. EU exports to Russia have been dominated by machinery

TABLE 4.1 *Evolution of EU-28 Trade with Russia 2005–14*

Year	2005	2006	2007	2008	2009	2010	2011	2012	2013	2014
Russia's share of imports (%)	9.6	10.5	10.2	11.4	9.7	10.6	11.6	12	12.3	10.8
Imports from RUS in millions of ECU/EUR	113.981	142.691	146.857	180.446	119.569	162.075	201.327	215.119	206.967	181.269
Russia's share of exports (%)	5.4	6.3	7.2	8	6	6.4	7	7.3	6.9	6.1
Exports to RUS in millions of ECU/EUR	56.690	72.399	89.196	104.970	65.697	86.308	108.587	123.442	119.451	103.311
EU's trade ballance with Russia in millions of ECU/EUR	−57.291	−70.292	−57.66	−75.476	−53.872	−75.767	−92.74	−91.677	−87.516	−77.958

Source: Eurostat (2015), 'Extra-EU28 Trade, by Main Partners, Total Product', http://ec.europa.eu/eurostat/en/data/database.

TABLE 4.2 *Evolution of Russia's Trade with Key EU Member States 2000–14 in Millions of US Dollars*

Exports from Russia in Millions of US Dollars

EU20	2000	2005	2009	2010	2011	2012	2013	2014
Austria	758	2353	1625	1022	1758	1500	1280	769
Belgium	757	2464	4045	4927	7480	6803	7726	9226
Bulgaria	585	1900	2190	3416	3493	4262	2217	1463
Cyprus	1722	5095	792	1641	1424	2067	1923	610
Czech Republic	1745	3817	4438	5500	5449	4925	5983	5162
Denmark	424	725	1796	1564	1896	1842	1480	2902
Finland	3104	7651	9162	12170	13197	12009	13308	11381
France	1903	6111	8726	12420	14859	10527	9203	7578
Germany	9232	19736	18710	25662	34158	34995	37027	37124
Greece	1273	1930	2338	2852	4684	5948	6245	3670
Hungary	2406	5004	3899	5355	7775	6733	6352	5140
Ireland	288	771	161	161	154	283	329	336
Italy	7254	19053	25100	27476	32658	32301	39314	35746
Netherlands	4349	24614	36407	53974	62695	76886	70126	67962
Poland	4452	8623	12503	14936	21367	19892	19582	15932
Romania	921	3041	1559	2025	1828	1877	1616	1461
Slovakia	2122	3190	2971	4576	7065	6153	5960	5196
Spain	1068	2823	2892	4048	6165	5721	6027	4579
Sweden	1733	2320	3200	3589	5127	6187	4476	4794
United Kingdom	4670	8280	9074	11309	14003	15028	16449	11505

TABLE 4.2 (Continued)

EU20	Imports to Russia in Millions of US Dollars							
	2000	2005	2009	2010	2011	2012	2013	2014
Austria	419	1211	2060	2463	3120	3393	3846	3438
Belgium	481	1476	2538	3265	4122	4491	4034	3573
Bulgaria	116	241	425	540	689	694	702	652
Cyprus	35.5	47.5	22.8	27	37.9	32.7	42.7	43.6
Czech Republic	367	989	2319	2918	4504	5354	5318	4898
Denmark	346	921	1373	1703	2053	2043	2178	1605
Finland	958	3100	3955	4584	5672	5004	5396	4571
France	1187	3673	8431	10043	13276	13804	13012	10743
Germany	3898	13272	21229	26699	37683	38305	37917	32963
Greece	125	188	342	423	586	634	611	498
Hungary	404	1100	2631	3141	3333	3103	3007	2739
Ireland	106	290	669	998	1237	1366	1372	1302
Italy	1212	4416	7891	10043	13402	13432	14554	12723
Netherlands	740	1941	3589	4442	5925	5978	5837	5248
Poland	716	2747	4214	5826	6651	7474	8326	7075
Romania	79.4	255	876	1345	1725	1736	2047	2210
Slovakia	105	503	1810	2492	2958	3715	3534	2864
Spain	313	1227	2274	3042	4306	4913	4915	4344
Sweden	465	1861	2039	2854	4038	3941	3917	3240
United Kingdom	861	2776	3544	4576	7180	8192	8106	7810

Source: Federal State Statistics of Russia (2015) 'External Trade of the Russian Federation with Other Countries'

and transport equipment, chemicals, medicines and agricultural products. EU imports from Russia are almost exclusively made up of raw materials, in particular oil (crude and refined) and natural gas (European Commission 2015b). In 2014, the share of primary products in Russian exports to the EU amounted to 80 per cent, a figure that reveals important trends in Russia's own economic landscape. First, it highlights the almost unidimensional, and growing, reliance on oil and gas as key export commodities (Movchan 2015). The resource sector has been the main engine of growth in Russia, and the increasing state control of key resources and companies has been an essential part of Putin's economic policy. The change in the ownership of Russian energy companies has been significant during the Putin era. This has been the case particularly in oil, where the privatization of the 1990s resulted in a situation whereby the state retained control of only about 10 per cent by the time Putin entered into office. Since then, the restructuring of the Russian energy sector, with the spectacular dismantling and expropriation of Yukos being the most drastic example, has resulted in the state acquiring a 40 per cent share of the Russian oil sector, with natural gas remaining virtually state controlled. This process of consolidation has also sent a strong signal to the rest of the private oil sector that they should take heed of the Kremlin's prerogatives and refrain from meddling with politics in the country in particular (Gustafson 2012; Newnham 2011: 136–38).

It is easy to see why Russia would guard the use of its energy resources and infrastructure jealously. The profits gained from oil and gas and the rents distributed domestically have enabled the relative stability and success of 'Putin's Russia' (Orttung 2009). Russia's international importance and clout is, by and large, also predicated on its vast energy resources and untapped potential (Goldman 2008; Tkachenko 2008). This has been acknowledged by the Russians themselves. For example, even in his doctoral dissertation, Putin envisaged the use of natural resources as an obvious springboard for Russia's domestic consolidation and international role (Tkachenko 2008: 171).

At the same time, Russia succeeded in establishing prudent macroeconomic policies to manage the oil and gas windfall in ways that, generally speaking, were able to rein in inflation while building currency and other reserves for a rainy day. The embodiment of this policy was reform-minded Alexei Kudrin, who served as Minister of Finance between 2000 and 2011. Indeed, Putin's first presidential term (2000–04) started with a series of domestic reforms that resulted in many observers, the EU included, viewing him as a liberal reformer. The most important reforms included adopting a flat income tax rate of 13 per cent and reducing corporate tax from 35 to 24 per cent. These reforms changed the Western view of Russia and made it look like an attractive business partner. For example, British Prime Minister Tony Blair's 'private visit' to St Petersburg in early March 2000, ahead of the Russian presidential elections and at a time when the EU was still imposing sanctions on Russia over Chechnya (Traynor and White 2000; for more about Chechnya, see Chapter 6), was seen as a starting gun for an intra-European race for the economic fortunes and investment opportunities in Russia, which was recovering from its economic crisis and buoyed by rising oil prices.

At the same time, however, a strong consensus emerged in Russia that across-the-board liberalization emulating Western templates should not, in fact, be the way forward for Russia. Instead, a combination of 'managed' democracy and state capitalism was increasingly seen as the order of the day (Zweynert 2010: 563). The impressive economic results of the 2000s seemed to overwhelmingly validate Putin's search for a specific 'Russian economic way'. That said, Putin and Russia under him were also exceptionally lucky, as almost the entire 2000s witnessed near-continuous and rapid growth in the price of oil and other commodities on the world market, boosting the Russian economy and consumption along the way (Hill and Gaddy 2015: 134). It also enabled the Russian state to rid itself of foreign debt almost entirely and amass significant currency reserves and a sizeable sovereign wealth fund that have proved invaluable in weathering the 2008–09 economic storm as well as the negative impact of sanctions over Ukraine. At the same time, the combined effect of the strong resource base and Putin's policies has resulted in a situation where Russia is more reliant on the primary sector today than what was the case during the Soviet era.

Also, and second, this pattern of economic growth reveals how dependent the Russian state was, as it still is, on these revenues – as well as the associated rents – to keep both the private consumption and the public economy afloat. The dominant role the primary sector plays in Russia is reflected in the share of oil and gas in the state's budgetary revenues, being approximately 60 per cent, but much more if one accounts for the knock-on effects of these financial flows in the wider Russian economy (Movchan 2015). This means that the Russian economy is highly vulnerable to external shocks. For example, and despite Putin's initial professions to the contrary, Russia was hit very hard by the global financial and economic crisis of 2008 and saw its economy contract by 7.8 per cent between 2008 and 2009 (P. Hanson 2013: 34).

But Russia's economic system was not only a source of vulnerability. Paradoxically, it was also a key enabling factor for the continued stability of 'Putin's Russia'. His personal popularity can be attributed in large part to the rapid growth in public and private incomes and the stability and even legitimacy of the political system created under his stewardship. An interesting question that follows is what will happen to Putin's popularity and the consequent stability of Russia should it experience a protracted period of sluggish economic growth at best, as now seems likely. At the same time, the economic structure and the rents it affords are a factor shaping the domestic structures in their own right in several ways. The so-called *Sistema* – informal networks of power and governance – are the key to how Russia is governed (Ledeneva 2013). This economic structure – combined with a set of neo-patrimonial, clientelistic and corrupt practices – is, in the words of Gaddy and Ickes (2013), one of the most crucial 'bear traps' – factors that constrain and even inhibit any attempts at reforming that very system. Other such traps are the Soviet legacy of central planning and inefficient economic structures, including the misallocation of people and physical and financial assets in faraway and climatically hostile places (Hill and Gaddy 2003). Coupled with the continued resource abundance, these factors lessen the urgency, and even the likelihood, of any meaningful economic reforms in Russia. We return to this topic when turning to the question of Russia's possible modernization below.

Moreover, the system and the consequent understanding of how the economy and politics operate are also the basis for how Putin and the Russian elite perceive the external world, and are a source of beliefs concerning the operational practices they wield in order to affect change in Russia's immediate neighbourhood and beyond, as the debate about the subversive and 'hybrid' tactics of influence in Europe and the wider West testify. This is not the place to discuss these tactics in full (see Jonsson and Seely 2015). Suffice it to say that the phenomenon is not new, as they were already part and parcel of Soviet tactics towards the West. What is more, writing a decade ago, the US scholar Celeste Wallander (2007) already warned how Russia's 'trans-imperial' tactics were taking advantage of global financial structures to corrupt, carve out and consequently influence Western political and economic systems and key actors, a practice that has been brought to the fore during and over the Ukraine conflict.

The institutionalization of economic relations

EU–Russia relations have revolved, in large part, around the question of the depth and breadth of economic integration and the eventual terms of reference for that process. As already mentioned in Chapter 2, the PCA does spell out the objective of an eventual FTA between the two and puts Russia under a broad-ranging yet somewhat abstract obligation to harmonize its laws, rules and regulations with the Community *acquis*. This is how the EU operates in general when granting third parties open access to its Single Market, but for the Russians in particular, this has entailed certain sovereignty-challenging dimensions that Moscow has, over the years, become increasingly uncomfortable with (Haukkala 2010).

As a consequence, one sub-theme of relations ever since the adoption of the PCA has dealt with how to 'operationalize' and eventually realize the ambition of an FTA, and through what mechanisms. The initiative for establishing a Common European Economic Space in the EU–Russia Summit in Paris in October 2000 must be viewed against this background. On the one hand, it was an attempt on the part of the EU to steer the ailing EU–Russia relations on a more constructive track after the freezing of relations during the Second Chechen War (see Chapters 2 and 6 for more). On the other hand, it can be seen as an attempt at 'operationalizing' the rather monolithic and abstract obligation for Russia to harmonize its trade-related laws and rules with those of the EU *acquis* (see Haukkala 2003: 75; Maresceau 2004: 210). In essence, it aimed at generating a forward momentum in a process which, from the vantage point of the Union, had remained disappointing, to say the least. Speaking in 2005, the commissioner for Enterprise and Industry, Günter Verheugen (2005), noted how 'to be honest, not much has happened [in legislative approximation between the EU and Russia]' (see also Barysch 2006: 13). Therefore, for the Union, the rationale for the process was clear: it was about creating a unified economic area that would be built on the EU's own achievements and experiences, especially in terms of legislative harmonization and regulatory synchronization

(R. Wright 2002: 180–81). In short, this was the original PCA agenda of 1994/97 revisited.

There is hardly any need to dwell at length on the development of the Common Economic Space (CES) as it became known in the context of the Four Common Spaces that followed (see Haukkala 2010, Ch. 8). Once again, the process proved to be drawn out and difficult, even 'bitterly contested' (Averre 2005: 183; see also Frellesen and Rontoyanni 2008). The CES document reveals significant tensions between EU and Russian readings concerning the way forward in their economic relations. The issue boiled down to the level and quality of the sovereignty-challenging adoption of EU norms by Russia. The creation of a genuine single economic space would, in effect, require the integration of all aspects of economic activities between the EU and Russia. In essence, such integration can only take place on the basis of commonly agreed norms and standards, which for the EU always entail its own normative basis (for a discussion, see Pursiainen 2008; Vahl 2004). Keeping this in mind, it is hardly surprising that the key issue at stake in the CES was the question of normative convergence, as originally codified in Article 55 of the PCA.

The CES road map envisioned a broad-ranging and intensive process of normative convergence between the parties. The development of cooperation and integration embraced nearly all facets of economic interaction – industrial products, public procurement, property rights, competition, investment, enterprise policy, financial services, accounting and statistics, agriculture, forestry, sanitary and phyto-sanitary measures, customs, transport and the environment – and it was made conditional upon 'approximation of regulatory systems' or the development of 'harmonised and compatible standards and regulations' (see the *Road Map for the Common Economic Space*: 1.1–1.6). But things are not as straightforward as the above would seem to suggest. Article 55 of the PCA explicitly obligated Russia to bring its norms, standards and regulations into line with the European ones. By contrast, it is highly significant that the CES refrains from mentioning explicitly from whom convergence is to be expected and according to whose standards it should take place (R. Allison 2006: 167–8; Emerson 2005; Van Elsuwege 2008). The muddying of waters in this respect was one of Russia's key aims in the negotiating process. The reason for this stems from the Russian view according to which legal approximation will represent a threat to Russia's sovereignty and that Russia should do its utmost to ensure a maximum degree of autonomy and 'liberty of action' in the process (Bordachev and Romanova 2003; Romanova 2004). Underlying this line of reasoning is the key Russian theme during the Putin era, namely that relations with the EU should be a reciprocal process whereby the partners would be 'meeting each other halfway, harmonizing the rules and regulations on either side' (Chizhov 2003a: 14; see also Likhachev 2006: 107). Keeping this discussion in mind, it should come as no surprise that Russia increasingly started to question the very feasibility and legitimacy of normative convergence with the Union (Karaganov 2005: 32; Bordachev 2003; Borko 2004: 172; Danilov 2005a).

A curious flip side to this stance seemed to be the constant concern in Russia that European integration is progressing without Russia and that it might result in new dividing lines detrimental to the country's economic and social development (for a short chronological sample of this thinking, see Gorski and Chebotareva 1993: 51; Shustov 1998; Chizhov 2006). Often, the issue was framed in the way in which the EU decisions, policies, norms and standards that affect Russia were prepared and made without Russia's participation (Chizhov 2005: 137). For example, the former Ambassador to Russia's Permanent Representation to the EU, Vassily Likhachev (2004: 104), noted how 'cooperation between Russia and the EU can be effective only when it is governed by international law rather than the whims or rules of one of the negotiating sides'. More often than not, the Russian reasoning seemed to be that the European norms were highly detrimental and that Russia remained committed to mutually beneficial cooperation only on a strictly equal basis (Lavrov 2007; Putin 2006; Putin 2015b).

These wishes, even demands, were entirely incompatible with the Union's views, which emphasized the mutually beneficial win–win logic of its aims and actions (at the level of rhetoric) and the post-sovereign projection, even imposition, of its norms and values (at the level of actual policies), while preserving its own decision-making autonomy. This is not to say that the EU was disingenuous in its professions of benign intentions. On the contrary, in the words of the head of the European Commission Delegation in Russia, Richard Wright, the EU wholeheartedly believed that the harmonization of norms and standards was singularly beneficial for Russia:

EU laws facilitate business effectiveness, and here unified approaches to standards would give Russia easy access to a potential single market. The advantages of harmonizing customs laws are obvious insofar as this removes trade barriers. . . . The application of EU rules and regulations would secure an effective functioning of any future free trade zone or unified economic area. Harmonization of regulations in the financial services sphere would help create a stable market in Russia, which would provide an incentive to attracting capital and stabilizing the capital flow. In conclusion, I would like to say that economic integration, accompanied by regulatory reform, would expedite Russia's economic growth. . . . I am sure that Russia and Russian business cannot afford not to adopt the same rules as are applied in all EU countries. (R. Wright 2002: 181–2)

Western economists agreed with this analysis by and large (see Broadman 2004; Chowdhury 2003; S. Hanson 2007; Hare 2002; Sutela 2005: esp. 28). Yet the Russians themselves were far from convinced. Russian economists pointed out that as the bulk of Russian exports to the EU consisted of energy and other raw materials that were already traded toll-free, the actual short-term benefits of economic integration would be meagre, while the potential costs for the domestic manufacturers could be prohibitively high (Pankov 2007; Shemiatenkov 2002; Volchkova 2007). Moreover, European norms and standards were not only seen as a source of dilution of Russia's sovereignty, they were also increasingly seen as incompatible with and even harmful to Russia's own economic trajectory, and as a source of double standards used to discriminate against Russian companies (Putin 2008: 13–14; for a discussion, see Pleines 2005: 275).

Especially at the height of the oil- and gas-led economic boom, Russians started to view their country as more dynamic and economically successful than the EU (Karaganov 2004: 180). In this respect, an interesting document is *The World Around Russia: 2017* scenario prepared at the influential Council on Foreign and Defence Policy (SVOP). In this document, the group of distinguished Russian scholars wrote how the 'stagnant model of Europe's political development is not beneficial for Russia' (SVOP 2007: 112; see also Gutnik 2006: esp. 122). The euro crisis and the associated economic woes in the EU have only accentuated this line of reasoning in Russia. To begin with, the EU's internal governance problems have cast a shadow over Brussels' insistence that it can offer a successful model that others should follow, while opening up space for competing powers to challenge the EU's international role (Keukeleire and Delreux 2014: 59; Howorth and Menon 2015: 14). This has increased the scepticism towards the EU among the Russian elites but has also impacted Russian society, which sees the EU less and less as a model to be followed (Fischer 2013: 31). The Cyprus bailout episode in 2013 was particularly disruptive as it was seen by many in Moscow as a cynical ploy pursued by the Europeans to punish Russian money and investors in Cyprus by confiscating parts of the deposits. The Russians were particularly angry because Moscow was not consulted by the EU in the process (Karaganov 2013). The EU Ambassador, Vladimir Chizhov, argued that the bailout scheme, known as a 'haircut' for larger depositors, was tantamount to a 'scalping'. The whole case had shown him the EU's 'lack of values' (Fleming 2013). Indeed, criticism of the EU's own lack of values and morals has become a mainstay of Russian rhetoric, as exemplified by Putin's words before the Valdai Discussion Club, in September 2013, where he accused Western Europe of rejecting 'their roots, including the Christian values that constitute the basis of Western civilisation' (Putin 2013a).

Russia's WTO accession and the partnership for modernization

The road maps for the Four Common Spaces presented in May 2005 received a highly critical treatment from scholars and commentators. In the Russian debate, they have been called 'road maps to nowhere' (Kononenko 2005) and criticized for their lack of concrete substance (see also Tyazhov 2006). Specialists on the EU side were not much kinder, branding the whole exercise as politically flawed (Barysch 2006: 14), or as the 'proliferation of the fuzzy' (Emerson 2005) with very little practical relevance. Yet, in actual fact, it is important to note that at the time it was neither the CES nor the EU that played the central role in the attempts at integrating Russia into the system of free trade and global norms and regulations. It was in fact Russia's accession into the WTO that took centre stage. The EU also made this clear by arguing that the marching order was WTO membership first, and only then would other arrangements in the field of economy be possible (Verheugen 2005). This stance is understandable as Russia's WTO membership obligated Russia to bring its trade laws and practices into compliance with WTO rules which, if implemented, would automatically make Russia more compatible with EU rules and regulations as well, thus facilitating the creation of a possible FTA with the EU too (Jones and Fallon 2003).

The WTO accession process began in 1994 and lasted for a gruelling 18 years, culminating in accession on 22 August 2012. The long and drawn-out process became a source of chronic irritation to Russia, which viewed it as a series of 'unjustifiably tough demands which virtually block Russia's entry' into the organization (Putin 2003; see also Chizhov 2006: 97–8). Indeed, there is some merit in Stephen Hanson's (2007: 9) claim that Russia was treated rather unfairly, with the country repeatedly trying to meet the demands of the WTO members only to see the rules of the game change and the entry bar raised in the process. Although true, the remark nevertheless misses the most important point: global rules and norms do not stand still, but are dynamically evolving, imposing a rather heavy toll in terms of unilateral adaptation on those who either fail to show up on time or who are, for one reason or another, unable or unwilling to become full members of the key global and, in the case of the EU, regional institutions. The then EU external trade commissioner, Pascal Lamy (2002: 31), noted the same when admitting that the WTO negotiations may seem 'like a one-way street with no end in sight' (see also Verheugen 2005, who basically conveyed the same idea). The Russians agreed with this analysis, but the conclusions diverged. Some, mainly scholars, regarded it as natural that there would be an entry price to be paid and that Russia should get a seat at the table to be able to decide on the content of those norms as soon as possible (Yasin 2002: 23). But others, the Russian president and government included, argued that eventual accession could only take place on equitable and fair grounds, which also take the Russian economic interests fully into account (Medvedkov 2002; Putin 2007b). In a speech at the 11th St Petersburg International Economic Forum in June 2007, President Putin turned the tables and criticized the WTO for lack of progress and accountability. According to Putin, the WTO and its predecessor, the General Agreement on Tariffs and Trade (GATT), were

> originally designed with only a small number of active players in mind [that] sometimes look archaic, undemocratic and unwieldy in today's conditions. They are far from taking into consideration the balance of power that has emerged in the world today. This means that the old decision-making methods do not always work. (Putin 2007)

The global financial and economic crisis resulted in Russia calling for a stronger role for itself in setting the new global agenda. As early as 2008, the new president, Dmitri Medvedev (2008b), labelled the main global institutions, such as the WTO and IMF, as 'discredited'. Speaking in his role as prime minister, Putin outlined the Russian alternative vision at the World Economic Forum in Davos in January 2009, calling for 'a more equitable and efficient global economic system' with a major role reserved for Russia in the process (Putin 2009). The following summer saw Russia moving from words to action: the June 2009 decision to establish a customs union with Belarus and Kazakhstan foreshadowed Russia's ambitions to build its own economic and political power bloc in the Eastern part of the continent while practically putting, as it seemed at the time, Russia's own WTO bid on hold indefinitely (Bovt 2010; see Chapter 8 for further discussion).

Be that as it may, Russia did finally accede. The entry spurred expectations and even a short-lived period of optimism concerning the prospects of the Russian economy (Connolly and Hanson 2012: 480). For example, writing in the immediate aftermath of Russia's accession, a group of Spanish economists mused enthusiastically how '[f]ull implementation of Russia's WTO accession is on the horizon' and how 'WTO accession not only will benefit the overall performance of enterprises and competitiveness of the economy, but also will contribute to developing technological sectors in which the position of Russia is weak' (Camacho, Melikhova and Rodriguez 2013: 337–8). Yet, to the European Commission's consternation, the reality pointed in the other direction, towards maximal use of protective measures afforded by the WTO and the creative adoption of novel ways to circumvent the WTO regulations and obligations (Connolly 2015a). This resulted in a host of complaints against Russia in the WTO dispute settlement procedure. Russia, for its part, remained brazen about this fact. For example, in a news conference in December 2013, President Putin highlighted the protectionist intentions of Russia, arguing that one of the motivations for joining the world trading body was precisely the opportunities it afforded for protection, adding how Russia had 'not yet begun to fully use all these options, but we intend to do so'. What is more, Putin turned the guns towards the EU, suggesting that it was, in fact, the EU itself that was engaging in unfair discrimination against Russia and that it would be taken to task by Russia in due course in the WTO dispute settlement mechanism (Kremlin 2013).

For some, Russia's WTO process nevertheless raised hopes for the diversification and eventual modernization of the Russian economy, as well as for joint rules on the basis of which trade disputes could be resolved. These themes have also played a prominent part in the EU–Russia agenda, as exemplified by the Partnership for Modernisation (P4M), adopted in 2010. The background to this innovation was the presidency of Dmitri Medvedev (2008–12) and the global economic crisis of 2008, which brought the question of the sustainability of Russia's economic system and the consequent need for modernization and the quality of innovation in the Russian economy to the fore (Fischer 2013: 27). This was reflected most starkly in Medvedev's (2009a) article Go Russia, a call to arms to radically restructure the Russian economy away from the resource sectors towards high tech and innovations. The EU, and Germany in particular, saw a political opening here and quickly took the initiative to adopt a wide-ranging Partnership for Modernisation with Russia (Makarychev and Meister 2015). The first such partnership had already been launched between Germany and Russia in 2008, but it was turned into an EU-level initiative at the EU–Russia Summit in Rostov-on-Don on 31 May–1 June 2010. In certain respects, the P4M formed an instance of 'constructive bilateralism', where a member state–level initiative eventually spilled over onto the EU agenda, creating positive dynamism in the process (David, Gower and Haukkala 2013). An indication of initial enthusiasm concerning the topic is that in addition to the EU-level partnership, a total of 24 bilateral P4Ms were signed between Russia and EU member states (for a full list and discussion, see Romanova and Pavlova 2014).

But the positive momentum of the P4M proved to be short-lived. The previous pattern of relations once again became quickly visible, with the initial enthusiasm concerning a fresh beginning soon getting bogged down due to differences concerning the meaning of modernization and the consequent way forward in its implementation (Larionova 2015). The key problem lay in the different understandings concerning what modernization entailed. For the EU, at stake was a democratic modernization of Russia, the key issues being good governance, fighting corruption and encouraging improvements in civil society and the business environment in Russia, including the development of small and medium-sized enterprises (SMEs). For Russia, the partnership boiled down to a much more conservative and technocratic approach, implying technology transfers and multibillion euro projects between major companies, essentially improving but not challenging or reforming Russia's current model (Romanova and Pavlova 2014; Makarychev and Meister 2015). What is more, after Putin's return to the presidency in 2012, it soon became clear that 'modernization' had been a Medvedev-era project. Clearly, the mass demonstrations following the contested Duma elections in December 2011 showed Putin the danger of creating expectations for reforms in Russia. Moreover, it seemed that Medvedev's reform-minded rhetoric had in fact been instrumental in creating an opening for a growing number of Russians to express their discontent with the political system and the elite as well (Fischer 2013: 29). Instead of modernization, stability became the new catchphrase in Russia. The end result was the P4M turning out to be yet another false start, a process only managing to feed the mutual frustrations and irritations in both the EU and Russia, and a concept that has now fallen completely by the wayside during the Ukraine conflict.

It would, however, be erroneous to claim that Russia's problems in modernization and competitiveness were of recent origin or that they related primarily to the lack of innovation. On the contrary, in an interesting study Graham (2013) has reconstructed a history of brilliant innovations in and by Russia from the fifteenth century onwards that have failed to bring about a lasting economic and societal change for the better in the country. In most cases, the innovators themselves have died poor and forgotten, or have perished in the purges launched by the suspicious rulers of Russia. According to Graham, the reason for this disappointing outcome is the fact that these fantastic innovations have remained 'lonely ideas', unmoored and unrelated to the wider economic and societal structures in the country which have, in fact, been and to a large extent remain hostile to those very innovations and the changes that their successful adoption would entail. In this respect, the failed attempt at modernization is simply the latest chapter in a longer saga of Russia's failed attempts at reforms.

None of this should be taken to mean that in order to fare better economically, Russia would necessarily require a radical diversification and restructuring of its economy. Gaddy and Ickes (2013: 24) have suggested that the reverse is the case, as the oil and gas and other natural resource sectors *are* in fact the natural competitive advantage of Russia (see also Cooper 2006: 409). That said, the challenge of modernizing the production, transportation and usage of these resources remains, as does the challenge of improving the overall business environment in Russia, currently and once again increasingly plagued by strong state intervention and management from the top (Gustafson 2012). These challenges are reinforced by the fact that the vast, internationally non-competitive sector in Russia consists of Soviet-era heavy industries, such as motor, civil aviation, and shipbuilding, and light industries like textiles, clothing and footwear (Cooper 2006: 413), which are nevertheless the primary source of domestic employment and income, and consequently a key factor in ensuring social and political stability in the country. When one also takes into consideration the fact that the radical economic and political reforms in Russia would entail the dual effect of disenfranchising and alienating the vast majority of blue-collar workers and pensioners – who form the backbone of Putin's political base – and encourage the political empowerment of the urban middle class which, at least until the hurrah nationalism spurred by the Ukraine conflict, remained critical of Putin, it is little wonder that Putin is unwilling to experiment with continued reforms (Gaddy and Ickes 2013: 97–8).

Yet reform Russia must, if it wants to return to a pattern of stable growth (Kudrin and Gurvich 2015). But the task is made harder by the fact that almost regardless of reforms – which, it is worth repeating, are not in sight – Russia's economy is set to face years of sluggish growth, if that (Connolly 2015a). The reasons for this malaise are rooted in the deep structures of the Russian economy: its declining demography and workforce, its eroding infrastructure and industrial capacity, and its suboptimally utilized and partially mismanaged oil and gas sector (P. Hanson 2015: 17). These are all factors that cannot be rectified with a presidential *ukaz*, but which require a drastic increase in the rate of investments and a host of reforms, both of which seem increasingly unattainable (Connolly 2011; 2015a). On top of this, Russia also faces conjunctural and geopolitical impediments to growth, ranging from the end of quantitative easing in the United States and the slowing down of economic growth in China to the rise of shale oil and gas on world markets, to the negative effects of the conflict in Ukraine on Russia (P. Hanson 2015: 17). As a consequence, Russia's economic prospects look very dim, as is the case with the future of EU–Russian economic relations, not to mention further integration, which itself has turned into a battleground between the two, as exemplified by the mounting problems in their energy relations.

Energy as the foundation and a bone of contention

If the nucleus of EU–Russia relations is economic, then its very hard centre is the trade and consequent interdependence in natural resources, particularly in energy. At first sight, the EU and Russia were a match made in heaven. Russia boasts one of the largest reserves of energy in the world, with some 80 billion barrels of proven oil reserves and a quarter – a leading share – of the world's proven natural gas (U.S. Energy Information Administration [EIA] 2014). By contrast, the EU is crucially dependent on energy imports, with 53.4 per cent of its energy consumption in 2012 being serviced by imported energy and with a third of its oil and gas coming from Russia, making it the EU's most important energy partner (European Parliament 2014; Eurostat 2014). This makes the EU Russia's largest customer by far. The EU is also the largest source of investments and an important source of technology and know-how concerning the Russian energy sector. Both the basic characteristics and the consequent economic structures and needs of the EU and Russia are inherently complementary.

Having established this, underlying this promise serious differences and problems abound. To begin with, the two share entirely different and irreconcilable understandings concerning energy security. For the EU, the issue boils down to the security of supply at affordable prices. For Russia, the emphasis has been put on achieving security of demand combined with the highest possible price (Kaveshnikov 2010: 586–7). This is the natural distinction between a buyer and a seller. But to achieve these contrasting aims, the two have also adopted diametrically opposed approaches. The EU has sought liberalization of the energy markets both within and around the EU. For Russia, the main issue has been increasing state control over key resources and industries while tying its main European customers into a dense network of bilateral and differentiated long-term energy deals and attempts at offsetting the possible losses on the European markets by diversifying away from Europe towards Asia and China in particular (Kaveshnikov 2010: 601–2; Krickovic 2015: 19).

The question of pricing has been a vexing one. Oil is, of course, a freely traded commodity on world markets, and its price fluctuates according to the supply and demand on the spot, but natural gas has been a different matter. In Europe, the bulk of the shipping of natural gas is tied to cumbersome pipeline infrastructure, which entails numerous fixed investments. As a consequence, Russia's preferred business model has been based on long contracts with a fixed price, including take-or-pay clauses. In recent years, the unconventional or shale gas revolution, however, has entailed changes in this respect, and the opening of new liquefied natural gas (LNG) terminals in several EU member states altered the picture further (Aalto 2011). This has resulted in a situation whereby the EU has been able to put pressure on Russia to renegotiate the terms, in particular the pricing, of long-term gas contracts. Although the situation is far from achieving the liquidity of oil markets, the preference of some member states for more flexible spot pricing is evident. Russia has retorted that this is not possible, taking into consideration the huge amounts of fixed investments required to make the business economically feasible.

There are also some concerns about Russia's ability to maintain its role as the main supplier of energy to the EU. Under Putin in particular, Russia has been very effective and successful in ramping up production of oil and gas, increasing the total volume of exports in the process. This magnificent result has, however, been based on tapping existing fields and infrastructure more effectively while so-called green field investments have been largely neglected (Henderson 2015). According to the leading expert on Russian energy, without significant improvements in the Russian business climate and subsequent investments in the Russian energy sector, Russia's energy production, particularly oil, may soon begin to decline (Gustafson 2012; see also Henderson 2015).

But EU–Russian energy relations are not shaped by pure market forces alone. On the contrary, once again the two strategic partners have found themselves at loggerheads concerning the very foundation of their relations. Over time, the EU and Russia have intensified their wrangling over what constitutes the legitimate rules of the game for the sale and transit of energy in Europe, consequently challenging its role as the wellspring of 'positive mutual interdependence' between the two. This is a long-standing debate that goes back to the beginning of the 1990s, but one that has intimate connections with the more recent conflicts concerning the future of the European security order as well. To cut a long story short (for more, see Haukkala 2014), since the beginning of the 1990s, the EU has sought to use energy as one of the key instruments to mould the post–Cold War economic setting throughout the continent. The first attempt at this was the negotiation of the Energy Charter in February 1991, followed by the adoption of a fully-fledged Energy Charter Treaty

(ECT) in December 1994. Here, an interesting parallel can be drawn with the PCA, which was negotiated largely in sync with the ECT. Here too, Russia drew a hard line, insisting on its needs being taken fully into consideration. Once again, the EU, and especially the European Commission, took several steps to accommodate the Russian concerns. As a consequence, the ECT, like the PCA, was never imposed on Russia, but was the end result of a mutual give and take (for a discussion of different aspects of the ECT, see Axelrod 1996).

In this respect, it is somewhat surprising that despite having signed the Treaty in December 1994, Russia failed to ratify the ECT and decided to withdraw from it entirely in 2009. Russia's decisions become less ominous, however, when one takes note that another important source of gas to the EU, Norway, has not ratified the ECT either. Despite the problems in getting Russia to sign up, the ECT has been the cornerstone of the EU's attempts at cementing a liberal energy order in Europe. In short, the EU's vision concerning a desirable energy order in Europe has had three main characteristics that have remained fairly stable over time. First, it is essentially pan-European in scope, encompassing not only the EU but the whole wider Europe from the Atlantic to Vladivostok, including the FSU. Second, it is based on unhindered market principles: the EU has also been promoting free competition in the field of energy and has viewed the traditional building blocks of energy security, such as national sovereignty, national energy champions and natural monopolies based, for example, on key infrastructure such as oil and gas pipelines, as detrimental to the effective functioning of a Single Market. Third, and finally, it is based on the assumption of the primacy of Western – and in the final instance EU – norms and standards as 'best practices' that should be adopted by all parties in the wider European space.

All in all, the energy order promoted by the EU during the post–Cold War era can be seen as part and parcel of the Union's wider attempts at projecting its 'normative hegemony' as the basis of an EU-centric order in wider Europe, and inviting Russia to liberalize its energy market (see Haukkala 2010; Bozhilova and Hashimoto 2010: 634). Once again, Russia has been less than enthusiastic to simply get on with the programme. In April 2004, the ECT was removed from the State Duma's agenda as 'flatly contradicting national interests of Russia' and 'being imposed on Russia from the outside' (Morozov 2008: 47). Yet, as a signatory, Russia remained bound by the principles of the Treaty. To cancel this effect, in 2009

Russia took a further step, deciding to withdraw from the ECT completely, citing its basic incompatibility and especially its so-called Transit Protocol with Russian commercial interests. The crux of the issue is the so-called third-party access (TPA) promoted by the ECT, which would obligate Russia to allow the countries of the former Soviet Union (FSU) to gain access to the pipeline infrastructure currently dominated by Russian companies. Although it is far from clear whether the ECT would, in fact, obligate Russia to open its networks at equal tariffs to all interested parties (see Talus 2011), the state-owned gas monopoly Gazprom and consequently the Russian government have decided to frame the issue in this manner and renege on the obligations assumed by signing the ECT. From a purely commercial point of view, the Russian policy makes some sense, as any company will have a strong self-interest in defending its dominant market position (Andrews-Speed 1999: 127). Moreover, the ECT would challenge the current Russian business model, whereby it has been using control over commodity streams to Europe to buttress its own economic and political position (Finon and Locatelli 2008: 425; Nowak 2010: 60–2). A cultural worldview element seems to be at play as well, where Russia clearly prefers bilateral, state-centric and sovereignty-bound practices in the field of energy and beyond. This is in stark contrast to the preferred solutions promoted by the EU and explicated above.

Frustrated by its futile attempts to induce Russia to join the ECT, the EU has since 2000 promoted a bilateral EU–Russia energy dialogue. The dialogue is co-coordinated by the Commissioner for Energy in the European Commission and the Minister of Energy of Russia. The day-to-day business between the annual meetings of the Energy Permanent Partnership Council is conducted under the auspices of four thematic groups dealing with different aspects of energy relations. For the EU, the objective of the dialogue is to provide reliable, secure and predictable energy relations based on market principles, as well as increase confidence and transparency between the EU and Russia. To this end, the 2009 gas crisis between Russia and Ukraine resulted in a major innovation as an early warning mechanism (EWM) was introduced between the EU and Russia. The objective of the EWM is to facilitate an early evaluation of potential risks and problems related to energy supply, as well as to ensure rapid reaction in the event of emergencies.

Although some useful inroads in developing mutually beneficial cooperation have been made in the dialogue, no radical breakthrough concerning the nature of a wider energy order in Europe has materialized between the EU and Russia (Romanova 2008). On the contrary, and as Pami Aalto (2012: 6–7) has suggested, the energy dialogue has become a process whereby two fully sovereign powers have sought to identify common interests and efforts without tackling or questioning the differences concerning underlying preferences and visions between the parties. Aalto notes that, as a consequence, Europe has witnessed an emergence of two sets of different energy policies: the EU's 'decarbonizing' long-term policy based on mixed competencies between the EU and its member states, and Russia's more traditional fossil-fuel and sovereignty-based intergovernmental policy. In a nutshell, where the EU, at least until recently, saw mutual interdependence that it sought to optimize through market principles, Russia envisaged varying layers of segmentation and dependence that it wants to cultivate, control and use to its own advantage (Boussena and Locatelli 2013).

At this juncture, we must once again confront the question of 'what *is* the EU' (see Chapter 3). Thus far, the chapter has implicitly assumed that the EU has acted as a more or less unified and intentional actor in seeking to develop the pan-European energy order. This is true to the extent that we examine the 'common' EU-level policies, and the role of the European Commission in the process in particular. But we must also acknowledge the fact that energy, its production, exporting and end use, does not in fact belong to the exclusive competence of the Union. On the contrary, the EU has relatively little supranational competence in the field of energy, as the majority of the member states, especially the large ones, have preferred to keep the issue under shared sovereignty (Maltby 2013: 7–8), entailing that the totality of EU–Russia energy relations stems from EU-level policies combined with a host of interrelated, yet significantly variegated and separate bilateral relations (Bozhilova and Hashimoto 2010: 628). In certain respects, this means that the EU cannot be considered a unitary actor in this field either, but one that contains internal tensions and even cleavages, also entailing important allies for Russia inside the Union.

The role of Germany is worthy of mention in this context, as it exemplifies the at times schizophrenic attitude that the member states have adopted in the field of energy. On the one hand, Germany has taken the lead in developing common multilateral and liberal approaches to energy. For example, Germany actively pushed for the ECT at the beginning of the 1990s and has advocated the liberalization of energy markets at the domestic level during the 2000s. On the other hand, Berlin has been one of the main culprits in cultivating a strong bilateral energy relationship with Russia to the detriment of common EU-level policies. Here, the clumsy adoption of the Nord Stream gas pipeline between Germany and Russia, as well as the overall role of German energy companies as close strategic partners and at times even as spokespersons for Russian commercial interests, are a case in point that has managed to undermine, or in the very least weaken, the Commission's attempts to extend the EU energy order beyond its own borders (Westphal 2008). To be sure, Germany has not been alone in these actions, as other major member states – Italy, France and the Netherlands in particular – have also portrayed similar tendencies in their dealings with Russia in the field of energy (for more on the role of national perspectives in the EU's Russia policy, see David, Gower and Haukkala 2013).

The internal divergences and cleavages *within* the EU have assisted Russia in resisting the EU's attempts at creating an energy order in Europe (Nowak 2010: 63). Indeed, on the EU side, the picture is mixed at best, with the Commission and some member states pushing for market liberalization and a Europe-wide market while many European companies as well as their host governments act in collusion with Russia and its companies, preserving the current contracts and at times engaging in shady business practices that have some potential to threaten not only EU solidarity but to corrode the rule of law both in Russia and in the EU (Finon and Locatelli 2008: 426; Kazantsev 2012; Wallander 2007). In a sense, the EU is and will in all likelihood remain a mosaic of different and overlapping interests and competences in the field of energy, although movement towards slow integration will nevertheless occur (Aalto and Korkmaz Temel 2014). For the time being, this favours Russia, which has built its own energy policy on a more tightly integrated vertical of government and key companies.

These developments have caused some concern in the Commission. For example, in the communication published in December 2012, the Commission noted how – despite important progress in creating a Single Market in the field of energy – the whole process remained fragile and in danger of 'unravelling' due to member state reluctance to implement its provisions in full (2012b: 2). That said, the European Commission has been very skilful in strengthening its position in the field of energy and pushing for more highly institutionalized and robust policies on the EU level. One of the main reasons for the EU's growing emphasis on its internal market has been Russia's own antics in the 2006 and 2009 gas crises with Ukraine, which brought the EU's own internal vulnerabilities into sharp relief. Because of the gas crises, the onus for the EU has increasingly turned to the security of supply, shielding itself from disruptions as well as the unwanted use of energy for political leverage and blackmail. These concerns have been further highlighted by the crisis in Ukraine in 2014 and have given the Commission's attempts at building EU-wide energy policies increased clout and urgency, resulting in a situation where several key member states were also willing to support more concerted common policies at the EU level (Maltby 2013; Westphal 2008: 113). The Polish initiative for an Energy Union that would entail new competences and widely shared solidarity between the member states is a case in point (Helm 2015).

It is possible, although not at all inevitable, that a push for a more common EU-level energy policy has now been given. To a degree, these prospects were contrasted with the decisions by Germany, Austria, France and the Netherlands to allow their energy companies to proceed with two large gas projects with Gazprom in September 2015. The first dealt with Nord Stream 2 project, the construction of two additional offshore pipelines alongside the original one, entailing the eventual removal of Ukraine as well as many Central European member states from the transit equation between Russia and its key customers in Europe (Gazprom 2015). The second deal complemented the first and included a lucrative asset swap between Gazprom and German BASF and Austrian OMV, giving the Europeans access to upstream reserves in Russia in exchange for downstream assets for Gazprom in Central Europe (BASF 2015; OMV Group 2015).

The announcement of the signing of the Nord Stream 2 deal in particular drew indignation from Central European EU partners, demonstrating that when it comes to large energy interests, internal EU solidarity does not always hold the primary position. For example, Slovak Prime Minister Robert Fico was quick to call the deal 'a betrayal' and say that 'they [western EU member states] are making idiots of us' by undoing commitments towards reducing dependence on Russian gas jointly agreed in the European Council (*Moscow Times* 2015). At the same time, if one wants to put forward a charitable interpretation of these decisions, one could argue that they can be seen as an attempt to preserve economic ties and interdependence in an otherwise fraught period between the EU and Russia. Yet the way the deal was conducted unilaterally without proper EU-level consultations reveals the thin veneer of EU internal solidarity in the field of energy, while indicating to Russia that the recourse to bilateralism, its favourite mode of operation when it comes to the EU, is still a viable option.

Yet not everything depends on the will of the member states anymore. Here, a clear change in the EU-level tactics can be discerned. As already explicated, the EU originally envisaged a treaty-based hard law pan-European order that would have included every major actor from the Atlantic to Vladivostok. As these hopes have been frustrated, largely by Russia's resistance, in the more recent period the EU has changed its tack to developing its own internal market and authority. Whether the Commission is in the right in pushing for a fully liberalized and integrated energy market in Europe is not the issue on this occasion (for dissenting views, see Konoplyanik 2012; Mané-Estrada 2006). Rather, the important point is that it is through markets and institutions that the EU has consistently framed the issue, and it seems that the Commission is more than moderately successful in pushing in that direction.

The main vehicle for pushing for a more liberal energy market in the EU is the so-called Third Energy Package. The aim of the Package was to complete the internal energy market by 2014, but the Commission's implementation report from the same year made it clear that although significant progress had been made, the process was far from complete and that the problems resided mainly on the member state level (European Commission 2014b). As part of the process, the EU has started to enforce competition rules in a stricter manner with a view to facilitating market entry and increased competition. What is more, the EU seems to be making claims that companies operating in the EU market should abide by the EU rules also in their own domestic markets (Konoplyanik 2012: 51). In the field of gas, this has entailed growing demands for unbundling and indeed re-examining the long-term contracts and pricing formula behind Russia's role as one of the main energy suppliers for Europe.

In conjunction with this, in 2012 the Commission launched an antitrust investigation into the business activities of Gazprom and its subsidiaries and partners in the EU. In essence, the Commission suspected that Gazprom was in breach of internal energy market rules in three respects: market partitioning (resale prohibition or destination clauses in contracts), denial or limits of third-party access to its networks, and allegations of unfair pricing (oil indexation) (Riley 2012; Sartori 2013). In April 2015, the Commission made the first results of its investigation public by sending a Statement of Objections to Gazprom, alleging that some of its business practices indeed constituted an abuse of its dominant market position in breach of EU antitrust rules (European Commission 2015c). If found culpable, Gazprom may be forced to alter its business practices as well as ordered to pay retroactive fines possibly amounting to tens of billions of euros. This is a serious threat to both Gazprom as well as the Russian state, especially when one bears in mind that the Commission has had an almost impeccable record of pursuing antitrust cases in the European Court of Justice (Sartori 2013).

Most importantly, the Commission's possible anti-trust case – should it prove successful – is a direct challenge to the Russian business model and the preferred vision of energy order that Moscow has been advocating. It comes as no surprise, therefore, that Russia greeted the Commission's actions with growing indignation, arguing that by and large it has proven to be a reliable supplier that is working hard to meet European energy needs and one that hopes to have the right to operate in the whole spectrum of European energy markets (Perovic 2009: 9). Russia also emphasized that Gazprom was a foreign entity on the European market and that the EU should respect this position. For example, in its immediate reaction to the Commission, Gazprom stressed how the company is, in fact, 'registered outside the jurisdiction of the EU, is a business entity empowered, according to the legislation of the Russian Federation, with special social functions and a status of a strategic organization, administered by the government' (Gazprom 2012). Russia has also taken a stance on the topic at the highest possible level. For example, at the EU–Russia Summit in December 2012, when the president of the Commission, José Manuel Barroso, painstakingly explained how the Third Energy Package was not discriminatory against Russia, or indeed any other party, Putin reacted strongly, and even though the press conference had already been declared over, he grabbed the microphone and said, 'My friend from many years, Mr Barroso, has for so long and so emotionally spoken, because he knew that he is not right, he is guilty' (EurActiv 2012b). Russia has also made some accommodating gestures, suggesting its readiness to discuss price discounts to the tune of 5 billion dollars in 2013 (*Moscow Times* 2013). However, it seems unlikely that the Commission would be fazed by either Russian carrots or sticks. On the contrary, for the Commission, antitrust investigations are purely legal and technical measures that do not involve any political judgement in the process (Almunia 2012), although their eventual *timing* can have political undertones, one way or another. This technocratic approach, rooted in the rule of law, is, however, alien to Putin's and indeed wider Russian thinking about how 'administrative resources' are usually used (Hill and Gaddy 2015).

In addition to consolidating its domestic sphere, the EU has also continued to develop a broader European energy order that would eventually include Russia as well. The EU, and especially the Commission, has used the increased internal momentum in the field of energy as a springboard to re-energize the process of developing and consolidating the pan-European energy order as well, seeking to cajole, potentially even coerce, external partners into adopting the EU's norms, standards and practices in the field of energy. A case in point is the Energy Community, an international body that was created in 2005 to facilitate the stabilization and the eventual integration of the Western Balkans into the EU. For the EU, the Energy Community is about encouraging and assisting the partners to apply the EU internal energy market rules (European Commission 2012c: 5). It is also about gradually expanding this zone beyond its existing members with a view to creating a network of countries around the EU that would operate on the basis of the EU's norms and principles in the field of energy (Prange-Gstöhl 2009; Renner 2009). Indeed, since its inception, the Energy Community has accepted new members with Ukraine and Moldova as contracting parties since 2009, and Armenia, Georgia, Norway and Turkey as observers.

All in all, it seems that the EU has two main motivations for seeking to create a pan-European energy order. First is the security of supply, as the EU, and especially the Commission, seems convinced that only market mechanisms can guarantee reliable and affordable access to energy for the whole Union (European Commission 2012c). The second is more ideological, as the EU believes that its own liberal principles and integration are conducive to a wider economic and political space that is prosperous, stable and secure. In a sense, the EU's attempts at creating a pan-European energy order are a variant of democratic and economic peace theories. The EU's own history bears testimony to the transformative power of these ideas. Politically, it seems that the EU is engaged in a pincer movement, thereby internally beefing up its own Single Market with a view to using that as leverage to make Russia heed the EU's liberal agenda. At the same time, the EU seeks to lock the majority of non-EU European states into an EU-centric energy order through the Energy Community, thus constraining Russia's ability to engage in non-market business deals also in the so-called 'common neighbourhood' between the EU and Russia.

Trade as a political weapon: the impact of embargoes, other restrictive measures and sanctions

The discussion of energy relations above has already brought the contrasting visions and clashing interests between the EU and Russia to the fore. But economic ties have also been wielded by both sides to influence, even sanction, each other's behaviour. The use of economic incentives in modifying other countries' preferences is a well-established practice in international politics (Baldwin 1985). For example, the EU has made the use of conditional access to its Single Market one of the main and most successful modes of operation in its own foreign policy (K. E. Smith 2003). That said, it is Russian energy, a truly strategic commodity, that is usually seen as the most potent dual-use product (Sullivan 2014).

The question of the potential use of Soviet/Russian energy as a tool of influence, even blackmail, has long been a divisive issue. During the Cold War, the United States especially viewed the growing reliance on Soviet gas by some key Western European allies, particularly West Germany, with increasing concern, a trend that has persisted to this day and has undoubtedly once again been accentuated by the conflict in Ukraine (Rutland 2009). Yet, apart from one supply disruption in January 1981 (see Staar 1987: 140–1), the Soviets proved to be reliable partners who consistently shied away from using energy for political ends. By contrast, during the post–Cold War era, Russia has used energy as a foreign policy tool much more openly.

This is not to contend that Russia is somehow 'evil' and that it wants to use energy first and foremost to coerce others. In an interesting article, Orttung and Overland (2011) have argued that Russia's strategic use of energy is, in fact, an indication of its otherwise fairly 'limited toolbox' in foreign policy – in other words it reveals the chronic lack of other reliable levers of influence. In a similar manner, one can argue that Russia's hasty decision to first annex Crimea and then continue to destabilize Ukraine through hybrid means in 2014 was a reflection of policy failure and lack of other instruments to influence Ukraine, rather than a premeditated display of impressive strength. But be that as it may, the practice of Russian foreign policy has revealed a pattern where, particularly in the former Soviet space, Moscow has frequently wielded its energy influence. The background to this is the Soviet energy policy, which deliberately drew the Republics into a dense web of oil and gas dependency (Newnham 2011: 135). Russia has used this dependence both as a carrot and as a stick, as exemplified by the variance in gas prices between different customers in Europe that cannot be explained on commercial grounds alone (Smith Stegen 2011: 6509; for an overview, see Newnham 2011: 140–2). For a while, it seemed that the 2009 gas crisis with Ukraine had made Russia publicly downplay the role of energy as an instrument of its foreign policy. More recently, however, there seems to be more than anecdotal evidence that this is no longer the case. For example, in September 2012, in the space of a few days, both Moldova and Ukraine were faced with a situation whereby Russia linked the future prices of natural gas to the countries' willingness to consider joining the Eurasian Customs Union and giving up their pretentions of pursuing closer integration with the EU (*Moscow Times* 2012; Wierzbowska-Miazga 2012). In a similar vein, Putin has characterized Belarus's relatively affordable natural gas prices as 'integration discounts', making no secret of the fact that the price of commodities and the political choices of CIS countries are indeed inextricably linked in the eyes of Russia (Adomeit 2012: 4).

Having established this, we should take note that to view energy simply as a 'weapon' that Moscow can wield freely at will is too simplistic and misses some important nuances in Russia's international role. First is how singlehandedly unsuccessful Russia has been in using the 'energy weapon' for political gain (Drezner 1999; Smith Stegen 2011). On the contrary, the relationship is clearly not unidirectional as, interestingly, Russia has also suffered at the hands of the transit states (Stulberg 2012). Second is the wider fact that, for Russia, energy is also an important objective of its foreign economic policy: Russia needs stable demand, high prices and, in the final analysis, reliable customers. To that end, Russia has come to realize that it needs to use energy for political purposes with great caution and selectively: Moscow may be in a position to use energy for buying domestic peace and leverage in its immediate neighbourhood, but it needs to tread more carefully farther away. Indeed, especially in its relations with Western European states, and perhaps with the development of a more joined-up energy policy in the whole EU over time, there is a certain logic of mutually assured disruption at work: although Russia could conceivably use energy for coercion against the EU, it would simultaneously also destroy the basis for its own economic well-being and undo its prospects of being an energy power. This has spurred Casier (2011) to describe Russia's energy leverage over the EU as 'overrated'. That said, one should also note than in the last instance Russia and the EU operate in different time frames: A supply disruption would cripple the EU member states practically instantaneously, whereas the loss of revenue would affect Russia more slowly (Shaffer 2009: 39). Therefore, the use of the Russian 'energy weapon' against the EU cannot be entirely excluded, should a more serious crisis between the two develop.

But energy has not been the only bone of contention in trade relations. The Putin period in particular witnessed various kinds of disputes related to trade and other rules governing commercial activities. The EU repeatedly accused Russia of unfair economic practices and has used a series of anti-dumping measures against the country and its key industries, a practice that is usually equated with protectionism by the majority of economists (Davis 2009) and, as already noted, has increasingly aroused the ire of Russian officials (see above).

One of the longest-standing irritants deals with the dispute over the so-called Siberian overflight fees for European aircraft flying between Europe and Asia via Russian territory (Forsberg and Seppo 2009). It is also an instructive case in the sense that the issue has been 'resolved' on numerous occasions between the parties without actually being successfully solved, and deserves, therefore, to be examined at some length. The issue became topical in 2005 when the annually collected fees had reached a record level of €330 million, rising significantly from €250 million in 2004. From the EU perspective, such fees for air trafficking were not consistent with international law. Russia was, in fact, the only country in the world to collect such fees, which were not linked to any conventional payments levied on the basis of air traffic control, but were collected simply in order to support the national flag carrier Aeroflot. Thus, in the eyes of the EU, Aeroflot enjoyed an unfair competitive advantage, as it could provide cargo transfer services crossing Russian airspace on the Europe–Asia route which, in the final analysis, were essentially subsidized by its European competitors.

The European Commission linked the question of abolishing the overflight fees to Russia's WTO accession. This strategy seemed to be working and during the bilateral EU–Russia negotiations on Russian WTO membership in May 2004, the Russian government promised to abolish the fees. According to the agreement, the fees should have been replaced in 2013 with an open system and non-discriminatory, cost-based calculation. The Russian Ministry of Transport declared, however, that it opposed the demands for removing the air traffic fees as a matter of principle. In their view, Russia should not make any concessions to the EU without receiving something in return. The Ministry of Transport did not agree that the fees constituted a form of royalty payments, but, if anything, a system of business relations that took into consideration the interests of all 'economic subjects'. In the Russian view, the fees were also much lower than what the EU claimed. For Russia, the future of Aeroflot was essentially at stake as the company would not survive without the revenues generated by the fees. Moreover, the payments were also otherwise beneficial for Russia as they could be invested in necessary infrastructure, such as new railroads, air navigation and control systems in the country (Karaganov et al. 2005).

In 2006, the Council of the European Union (2006) declared that a viable solution to the issue was a precondition to Russia's WTO membership and authorized the Commission to negotiate a solution to the overflight fees. The Commission and Russia conducted negotiations, and a new solution was tabled at the EU–Russia summit in Helsinki in November 2006. The parties agreed that all payments after 2014 should be cost-based, transparent and non-discriminatory between foreign carriers and in line with the Chicago Convention. Yet, when the agreement was supposed to be signed at the subsequent EU–Russia Summit in Samara, the Russian Ambassador to the EU, Vladimir Chizhov, noted on the eve of the summit that the Russian government had not yet approved the agreement. The Russian ministries required further clearance with regard to the technical and economic provisions of the agreement. He further argued that 'the issue can be seen as a compromise, which is not approved by everyone' (Mason and Taylor 2007). This was clearly an unpleasant surprise for the EU, which had considered the issue a 'done deal' since the agreement was reached in November 2006.

After the failure of Samara, the EU believed that the agreement could be signed at the Aviation Summit scheduled for November 2007. These hopes were reinforced by a statement issued by President

Putin, who declared that the Russian authorities were almost ready to move forward with the agreement. However, just before the planned Aviation Summit, an unexpected dispute emerged between the Russian aviation authorities and the German Lufthansa Cargo over whether Lufthansa should move its hub from Kazakhstan to Siberia. The Summit was postponed due to the Russian reluctance to ratify the negotiated aviation agreement, which the EU set as a condition for its own participation.

The politicization of the issue by the EU seemed to be one reason why Russia did not want to yield in the dispute over the overflight fees. The Russian media reflected upon the postponement of the Summit by accusing Brussels of turning the issue into a serious irritant in EU–Russia relations. Sergei Sokolov, advisor to the chairman of the Council on Foreign and Defence Policy, argued that by 'deciding to boycott the summit, the EU lost a unique opportunity to discuss an important issue with the senior Russian government officials and aircraft industry managers'. In a similar fashion, the deputy director of research at the Council on Foreign and Defence Policy, Dmitry Suslov, argued that the decision to cancel the summit chimed with Russian interests because Moscow was facing 'exorbitant EU demands'. The EU could have tried to promote 'its own strategy of bilateral aviation relations, to impose its own environmental protection, including safety standards and regulations, and to persuade Moscow to establish a unilateral open-skies regime at the summit' (*Nezavisimaya Gazeta* 2007).

The issue remained pending until December 2011, when the parties, once again as part of Russia's bid to enter the WTO, made an agreement that from 1 January 2014 onwards Russia would gradually decrease the overflight fees until they were to be fully cancelled. But true to form, the deal once again faltered as in September 2013 Russia announced that the fees would, in fact, remain in place after 2014 but that they would be made 'more appropriate and transparent' and that the main beneficiary would be changed from Aeroflot to the Russian state corporation overseeing aviation (Panin 2013). Moreover, in November of the same year, some news reports indicated that Russia intended to use the fees as leverage to entice individual EU member states to enter into bilateral deals where, in exchange for dropping the fees altogether, Russia would be granted increased operational access in the airspace and airports of the state in question. For example, the Czech Republic was mooted as a potential partner in such an endeavour (Prikhodina 2013).

At the time of writing, Siberian overflights are still an open wound in EU–Russia relations. If anything, the issue has gained a sense of new urgency in the context of the Ukraine conflict, as Russia on several occasions hinted that it was considering banning Europeans from using Russian airspace altogether as part of its own counter-sanctions (G. Smith 2014).

Turning to embargoes and other restrictive measures, Russia is not the only party that has felt wronged in the field of trade relations. For its part, Russia has repeatedly used embargoes against products from some EU countries, such as Polish meat and Lithuanian dairy products, officially citing quality and health reasons, but for some reason these complaints seem to be associated with political problems between Russia and the member state in question (Forsberg and Seppo 2009). The EU has not been entirely exempted from energy embargoes either. Three cases in particular are worth highlighting. First, in 2006 Russia shut down the oil pipeline servicing the Lithuanian Mazeikiai refinery, citing a 'leak' in the pipeline after Lithuanians had refused to sell the refinery to the Russians. In 2007, during the so-called Bronze Soldier crisis between Estonia and Russia, Russia halted shipments of oil via rail to Estonia due to 'maintenance work'. And in July 2008, Transneft cut oil deliveries for 'commercial and technical reasons' to the Czech Republic in the aftermath of Prague's decision to base elements of US missile defence on its territory (Newnham 2011: 142; Orttung and Overland 2011: 84). The wrangling over hiked export duties that Russia set on raw timber between 2007 and 2009 is also instructive as it can be seen as an attempt at compelling Western countries to invest in pulp and paper mills in Russia.

As already noted, the conflict in Ukraine brought the question of sanctions in EU–Russia relations to the fore (see Chapters 2 and 8 for more). Yet 2014 was by no means the first time that the EU adopted sanctions against Russia. On the contrary, back in 1994–6 and again in 1999–2000 the EU applied economic pressure on Russia over the two wars in Chechnya, and the 2008 war in Georgia also resulted in a brief freeze of political relations in particular. That said, the gradually toughened EU and wider Western sanctions, or restrictive measures, have been an order of magnitude greater and have caused significant hardship for the Russian economy and especially many Russian companies, which have been shut off from Western financial markets and forced to rely on the Russian state for financing (Dobrokhotov 2015). For its part, Russia responded in kind, imposing its own food embargo against EU member states in August 2014 (Wegren 2014). Taken together, the conflict in Ukraine brought the EU and Russia to the brink of an open trade war.

Although EU sanctions definitely played their part in Russia's economic woes, they were not the primary culprits. As President Putin (2015b) also noted, sanctions 'are definitely contributing to our current problems' but they are 'not our biggest problem'. As already discussed, the structural problems and the consequent slowdown of the Russian economy were visible even in 2013, well *before* the conflict in Ukraine and the imposing of sanctions (see Tables 4.1 and 4.2 above). Indeed, in the opinion of Philip Hanson (2014: 2), Russia's economic problems are long-lasting, making it no longer an emerging, but a submerging economy. What is more, the dramatic devaluation of the rouble in December 2014 was not caused by the sanctions, but by the equally dramatic plummeting of oil prices. Yet Kudrin estimated in June 2015 that the international economic sanctions were reducing Russia's GDP by between 1 and 1.5 per cent per year (RFE/RL 2015).

Over the longer term, the impact of sanctions on the Russian economy will be far from insignificant (Aalto and Forsberg 2016). The fact that key Western technologies for deep offshore and fracking operations have been included on the list alone will entail severe difficulties for the future development of the Russian oil and gas industries. This can have serious consequences for Russia's future ability to sustain production, which, even before the conflict, had a question mark hanging over it because of the chronic underinvestment in greenfield production on the one hand and overinvestment in export infrastructure on the other during the post-Soviet era (Rutland 2014: 5; Gustafson 2012). In addition, although one should never underestimate the greed of investment bankers, the political risk factor has also been accentuated, and Russia's very reputation as a business partner has been damaged. These will have a longlasting effect on Russia's ability to attract FDI, which will be key to the country's future economic growth.

Russia has remained far from idle in the face of this economic onslaught. On the contrary, it has actively sought to blunt the edge of EU and wider Western sanctions. To begin with, Russia has embraced trade substitution, even flirting with some Soviet ideals concerning autarchy, namely complete self-sufficiency in certain key sectors of the economy. The policy of trade substitution has brought some economic benefits. In the words of Popescu (2015: 2), the crisis has acted 'like steroids for a sportsman – boosting performance in the short term at the expense of long-term health'. Indeed, by spurring domestic production import, substitution has brought some results particularly in the agricultural sector, but it has also exposed the clear limits of the Russian economy to rid itself of external dependence (Traub-Merz 2015; P. Hanson 2015: 19). Moreover, the process has also managed to accentuate one of the main ailments of the Russia economy by increasing state intervention therein (Connolly 2015b). At the same time, Russia has sought to offset these losses by launching its own 'pivot to Asia' and seeking to deepen both its economic and its political relations with China. On the face of it, Beijing seems to have been happy to reciprocate, but, ambitious political declarations notwithstanding, fairly little has been achieved in practice. In fact, it is hard to avoid the conclusion that China has been happy to welcome Russia into the fold, seeking to entangle Moscow in a web of economic ties with a view to turning it into a trustworthy junior partner in the process. It may very well be that Moscow will find Beijing a more wily and ruthless partner than Brussels ever was.

Yet the fact remains that for the foreseeable future Russia will remain dependent on economic ties with the EU and the wider West. An acknowledgement of this has been the third tactic adopted by Russia, namely a series of moves to evade the sanctions by overt changes in the ownership structures of certain key companies, using covert offshore safe havens often residing under Western jurisdiction to circumvent the sanctions, or by directly challenging some of the restrictive measures in EU courts (see Johnston 2015; Nesvetailova 2015: 16). Although Russia has had some success with these actions, the country is nevertheless facing tough times economically. One should, however, be cautioned against expecting, let alone hoping for, a rapid economic crisis and collapse of 'Putin's Russia', as the political crisis and turmoil it could unleash are far from comfortable prospects for anyone. An imminent collapse of Russia is not necessarily on the cards, as a great deal of Russian private debt is in fact 'intra-group debt', that is, owed to other Russian entities, enabling its restructuring with relative ease. In addition, Russian reserves remain robust enough to sustain the Russian state and economy, barring another severe crisis in the global/Russian economy or a renewed and prolonged slump in oil prices (Connolly 2015c). Finally, one should take note that increasing economic hardships do not necessarily turn the key elites against Putin. Ownership and economic positions in Putin's Russia have been built in such a way that rising against the man at the top is neither easy nor even feasible: One is in immediate danger of losing one's assets, reputation or worse in the process (Hill and Gaddy 2015: 215–6). It seems that at least from an economic and perhaps also from a political vantage point, the EU has to prepare itself for dealing with 'Putin's Russia' for the foreseeable future.

Environment and climate change

The last topic discussed in this chapter is cooperation in environmental matters and combating climate change. The PCA had already spelled out a wide-ranging agenda for environmental protection (PCA 1997: Art. 69). The issue was further developed in the context of the Common Economic Space, where Section 6 called for environmental issues to be 'mainstreamed' into all sectors of economic cooperation. To facilitate this process, in 2006 the EU and Russia launched a high-level Environmental Dialogue between DG Environment and the Russian Ministry of Natural Resources and Ecology (MNRE). This PPC on environment includes one working group and seven sub-groups dedicated to more specific topics: environmental policies, climate change, water and sea issues, biodiversity and nature protection, forest protection, clean production and pollution prevention. The Dialogue has taken place approximately every two years, and in 2013 a working group as well as sub-groups on biodiversity and climate change convened in Brussels. The 2014 meetings were, however, postponed on the EU's initiative due to the conflict in Ukraine.

Actual cooperation in environmental protection has taken place under the auspices of the ENP, where the European Neighbourhood and Partnership Instrument (ENPI) Eastern Region instrument has been used to develop a host of projects that have also included Russia. The key issues include air and water quality, waste management, nature conservation, energy use, land use and dealing with pollution in the Baltic, Barents, Caspian and Black Seas. These projects have typically been genuinely transboundary, including the EU and the Eastern Partners as well as Russia (ENPI 2013).

The EU–Russia P4M also included an environmental aspect. But despite this catalogue of high-level initiatives, for the most part the concrete day-to-day cooperation in environmental issues has, in the spirit of subsidiarity, been relegated to the regional level and has taken place in formats such as the Helsinki Commission (HELCOM) in the Baltic Sea and the Northern Dimension Environmental Partnership (NDEP) for the wider Northern areas. The NDEP is particularly noteworthy as it has been regarded as one of the success stories of EU–Russia relations (see Haukkala 2010, Ch. 9). Initiated in March 2001, the NDEP was created to combine funding from the EU, Russia and several international financial institutions (IFIs) to develop and finance environmental projects, including nuclear safety, in north-western parts of Russia and in Belarus (for an updated list of projects, see http://ndep.org/projects/). The flagship project has been the building of a €200-million wastewater treatment facility in St Petersburg, which has been instrumental in lessening the discharge of harmful phosphorus emissions into the delicate Baltic Sea. Notably, the NDEP continued its operation even during the Ukraine conflict, indicating that both parties envisaged low-politics environmental cooperation between the EU and Russia and an area that should be exempted from the otherwise near total freezing of relations.

Another success story in the environmental field, at least initially, was combating climate change. The issue, and in particular the adoption of the so-called Kyoto Protocol, was one of the EU's flagship international initiatives, where it sought to take the lead in fostering an international consensus concerning the topic, and also to lead by example by adopting ambitious climate goals itself (Groenleer and Van Schaik 2007). At the same time, the EU faced serious problems in gaining sufficient international traction for the Protocol, which required 55 industrialized nations, representing 55 per cent of the world's greenhouse gas emissions, to sign it before it came into effect. Once the United States and Australia refused to sign, it was up to Russia to ratify the treaty to save it from collapse. Initially, Russia was far from enthusiastic about the prospect of joining the Protocol. Putin prevaricated over the bill, saying that Russia would only sign it if it was in its own national interest, and suggested that it would need modifying. His key economic advisor at the time, Andrei Illarionov, cautioned against moving ahead with the issue, describing it in a less than politically correct way as an 'economic Auschwitz' that would cripple Russian economic development (Paton Walsh 2004).

At the end of the day, an initial agreement that Russia would join the Kyoto process was reached at the Moscow EU–Russia Summit in

May 2004. This was achieved by creating a linkage between Russia joining the Kyoto Protocol and the EU's readiness to conclude bilateral market access negotiations with Moscow that would facilitate Russia's accession into the WTO. After the Summit, Putin registered his satisfaction by noting how '[t]he fact that the European Union has met us halfway at the negotiations on membership in the WTO cannot but influence Moscow's positive attitude towards ratification of the Kyoto Protocol' (Paton Walsh 2004). The Russian Parliament took heed of this advice and ratified the Kyoto Protocol in October 2004, enabling it to come into effect in February 2005.

But even though environmental cooperation has been relatively successful, it has not been entirely without problems. To begin with, like all the other fields of cooperation discussed in this book, the environmental dialogue has also been plagued by problems of reaching a fully shared understanding concerning the issues at stake. In the words of Hønneland (2003), despite common projects, a tension between 'eco-centric' and 'techno-centric' approaches between the EU on the one hand and Russia on the other have been evident. In the final analysis this has entailed a crucial difference in emphasis, with the EU stressing environmental protection and conservation, and with Russia putting the accent first and foremost on regional development. A symbol of these differences was Russia's decision in 2000 to turn the previously independent Environmental Protection Committee into a department of the Natural Resources Ministry, the primary function of which is to promote the exploitation of natural resources. According to Nina Tynkkynen (2008: 73), the decision was the starting pistol for the gradual abolition of environmental policy in Russia.

The same asymmetry of interests has applied in combating climate change. Although Russia has benefited from selling 'hot air', in other words the extra emissions credits it acquired because of the rapid de-industrialization of the country after the dissolution of the Soviet Union, the issue has been more complex than that. Russia is also a major fossil-fuel exporter, and it has faced a trade-off between maximizing its permit revenue and its revenue from fossil energy exports (Bernard et al. 2003; for a discussion, see Korppoo, Karas and Grubb 2006; V.-P. Tynkkynen 2014). It has also been far from certain whether Russians genuinely subscribe to the notion of 'anthropogenic (human-induced) climate change' to begin with. A case in point has been the rhetoric of President Putin, who has repeatedly questioned the whole phenomenon. For example, in 2003 he declared in front of an international climate conference audience in Moscow that global warming entailed that Russians would 'spend less on fur coats' while 'agricultural specialists say our grain production will increase, and thank God for that' (Kuzmin 2015). Although since then Russia has not denied climate change as a phenomenon (in 2010 Putin indeed noted that 'it was happening'), it has nevertheless taken a sceptical stance on whether it is in fact induced by human activities at all. In the Russian reading, climate change is cyclical and has nothing to do with humans. This reading stands in stark contrast to the EU consensus that takes the issue as an undeniable fact (see European Commission 2014a: 1). The concrete manifestation of the increased dissonance in climate policy came at the Cancún climate conference in 2010, where Russia announced that it would not be participating in the second round of Kyoto commitments spearheaded by the EU (Tynkkynen 2014: 11). One may, however, argue that in this respect Russia was in fact in good company, as the climate change negotiations have increasingly been taken hostage by the narrow economic interests of the participating states across the board (Giddens 2011).

Conclusions

This chapter opened by arguing that economic relations – and in the final analysis trade in energy – are the glue that essentially binds the EU and Russia together. The discussion of economic relations that ensued confirms this proposition. The vast amount of trade and other economic links is a significant achievement. The interdependence is real and enduring. At the same time, the analysis that followed also suggests another conclusion, namely that instead of bringing the two closer together, economic ties have become an object of increasing political and economic contestation, which has, in fact, lessened the prospects of a wholly successful 'strategic partnership' between the EU and Russia. This field reveals what seems to be a recurring pattern of relations between the EU and Russia: Despite good intentions, natural synergies and the consequent massive size of the stakes involved have succumbed to mutual recrimination and have remained suboptimal. Instead of maximizing mutual utility and synergies, EU–Russia economic relations have succumbed to a vicious circle of what Bozhilova and Hashimoto (2010: 641) call *reactions on reactions*. What is more, one can also argue that the vast windfall generated by natural resources has resulted, or at least facilitated, Russia's drifting away from some key liberal norms concerning democracy and market economy, in effect alienating Russia from the EU and eroding the normative foundation of EU–Russia relations further.

In the light of this, it is hardly surprising that the question of energy in particular has become such a bitter bone of contention between the EU and Russia. At loggerheads are two different economic models and substantial disagreement over the content and nature of the energy order, or any order for that matter, in the post–Cold War Europe, and the role of liberal principles in the process. This chapter has tried to show that despite a brief moment of agreement at the beginning of the 1990s, the EU and Russia have come to adopt and push for diametrically opposed principles concerning the trade of energy in Europe. The EU, and particularly the European Commission, has been pushing for a very liberal market-based approach that has been gaining traction in the 2000s. By contrast, Russia, especially under Putin, has been galvanizing a state-capitalist model enhancing the economic and also potentially the political power of the Russian state. In between these two polar opposites, we found a host of EU member states and energy companies with differing views on, and stakes in, the relationship.

The end result is the current state of affairs, whereby instead of creating positive interdependence and synergies, the question of energy has become one of the toughest bones of contention between the EU and Russia. What is more, the bureaucratic and market-based approach promoted by the EU is in danger of becoming increasingly at loggerheads with Russia's more personified and politicized approach. This is well reflected in the Commission's investigation concerning Gazprom and the possibility that it will result in a public legal battle of wills similar to the one the Commission launched against Microsoft – in which the former of course prevailed. It also seems unlikely that Russia will simply fold under EU pressure and finally find its place in the energy order promoted by the Union. On the contrary, we should prepare for a period of further and most likely very intense politicization of energy, and a potential crisis between the two that can be expected to have significant and manifold impacts on EU–Russia energy relations, and indeed on the overall relations between the two 'strategic partners'.

The possible erosion of energy link may be a further concern for the future of EU–Russia relations, already heavily strained over the crisis in and over Ukraine. The continued securitization of energy is a case in point that has the potential, first, to undo the positive gains and interdependence achieved during recent decades while, second, potentially heralding a more conflictual relationship between the EU and Russia in the future (Ciuta 2010). The relationship is in danger of losing a significant part of one of its most important stabilizing factors: the interdependence and the mutual economic benefits that the trade in energy has brought to the parties. On the contrary, it is because of the EU's increasingly consolidated internal market in the sphere of energy that Russia's is sliding into the orbit of the EU's conditional market power (cf. Damro 2012), which it has done its best thus far to shy away from and avoid. To a degree, it seems that the EU has only bad choices on the table. It can go through with the process and potentially alienate Russia further from Europe. Alternatively, it may succumb under pressure from Russia, sending the final signal to Moscow that 'Brussels' perennially lacks teeth. Alternatively, Russia may try and perhaps even win some support from certain key member states against the Commission, increasing the tensions and cleavages inside the EU.

This raises the question concerning the future of economic relations and interdependence. With prospects for the Russian economy remaining weak and the EU's attempts at diversifying its energy away from Russia on the increase, we are headed towards gradually declining interdependence. This process will most probably not be rapid, but the trend seems clear. Although there is no unequivocal evidence of energy supply relationships preventing or alleviating conflicts (see Shaffer 2009: 67), it does not mean that the factor is entirely insignificant. Indeed, even if to date interdependence has failed to prevent relations between the EU and Russia from entering a downward spiral, one should refrain from thinking that severing economic ties would automatically help. This is admittedly a double-edged sword as the Russian propensity to use economic ties as sources of asymmetrical influence, even subversion, has shown. Nevertheless, one should be cautioned against lessening the interdependence between the EU and Russia too far: increased peace and harmony are not necessarily in store at the end of that road.

Chapter 5

Justice and Home Affairs

One of the key goals of the EU has been to promote good governance, human rights and democracy in the world (Manners 2002; European Council 2003; Keukeleire and Delreux 2014). This goal has also been regarded as central to the EU's relations with Russia, but its relative importance in comparison to other goals has been much disputed. There are those who consider that democracy promotion has been a utopian goal and that trying to push the agenda has been counterproductive, leading to grave problems in the relationship, while others have suggested that the EU has only tried to foster this agenda half-heartedly, and hence it has not only undermined its own values and principles but also contributed to the problems in EU–Russia relations. Still a third group sees the EU as not being genuinely interested in promoting noble goals, but just advancing its own self-interest hypocritically under the pretext of universal values. All the groups, however, agree in their own way that the EU has not been particularly successful in this area (see Saari 2010a).

Although traditionally it has been the EU that has taken the initiative to foster and influence a set of democratic values in Russia, more recently we can also discern increasing Russian attempts to shape the understandings and developments concerning human rights and democracy in Europe. However, to argue that this is an area where the partners compete with their systems of values and related interests is simplistic and neglects the perspective that these issues have also been very much a part of the common agenda. Indeed, and despite President Putin's repeated professions of how 'the West' took advantage of Russia's temporary weakness during the 1990s to impose a set of alien norms and values upon it, it is worth remembering that originally in the PCA, Russia did, in fact, both subscribe to and eventually also ratify this agenda (see Chapter 2). It also actively sought membership in the Council of Europe (CoE), committing itself to a wide-ranging set of obligations in this field, and has remained a member despite its voting rights in the parliamentary assembly being suspended due to the violations of international law in relation to the Ukrainian crisis (Saari 2010a).

The agenda of promoting democracy and human rights became problematic, however, on the agenda of EU–Russia relations due to Russia's resistance. Instead, the parties started to develop cooperation in justice and home affairs that is known as the Common Space of Freedom, Security and Justice. The idea of common values was not dropped entirely, but cooperation focused on solving problems related to management of the borders and societies to enhance freedoms but prevent crime and other detrimental activities. This area of cooperation has been seen as producing results and progressing substantially relative to the other spaces (Potemkina 2010), but also in these issues, the Ukraine crisis left its traces.

This chapter looks at the role of both 'human rights' as well as 'justice and home affairs' – two interconnected but partly separate issues – on the agenda of EU–Russia relations. We start by reviewing the way democracy, human rights and the rule of law have been debated and how dialogue and cooperation in these matters have evolved. We take a closer look at one particular problem, namely the Chechen wars, and discuss how the EU addressed human rights questions in that context, as they twice prompted a political conflict in the relations with Russia. We then move on to the items in the second common space, judicial cooperation between the law enforcement and border officials, and focus again on one topic in particular, namely the visa regime issue between the EU and Russia. The chapter concludes by contending how the parties started from the idea of shared values, how this idea upon which the relations would be based eroded and how Russia not only started to question the European interpretation of these values and the 'double standards' in their application but also offered its own set of values instead.

Human rights and democracy

The EU's relationship with Russia was, from the outset, based on the optimistic premise that Russia was transforming into a democratic 'European' country. The principles of democracy and human rights were also included as a normative basis of the Partnership and Cooperation Agreement and were a key part of the EU Common

Strategy on Russia adopted in 1999. Yet, as a shared background, it was narrowed down and neglected during the Putin era, and as a goal of EU policy towards Russia, the normative goal was gradually shifted increasingly to the future; with the Ukrainian crisis, it is uncertain whether this goal is still taken seriously or has it been abandoned entirely.

The EU started to give 'technical assistance' to Russia in 1992 under the heading of the TACIS (Technical Assistance to the Commonwealth of Independent States) programme, aimed at promoting democracy along with a market economy (Prozorov 2006). It was in this early period that hopes for a relatively smooth and swift transition into democracy prevailed. The EU programme consisted of various projects that were funded for strengthening democratic practices and civil society. On the Russian side, this assistance was welcome in the beginning, but over time the perception amounted that the representatives of the West were arrogantly lecturing about democracy in a context with which they were not familiar and that they were relying on double standards when pointing to the problems in Russia.

As already discussed in Chapter 2, the PCA had a strong commitment to democracy and human rights as a shared normative basis of relations. Article 2 of the agreement defined respect for democracy and human rights as 'an essential element of the partnership'. This shared goal was seen as a legitimate basis to which the EU could refer when criticizing Russian leaders about breaches in these questions. The EU Common Strategy on Russia set as a 'clear strategic goal' 'a stable, open and pluralistic democracy in Russia, governed by the rule of law and underpinning a prosperous market economy benefiting alike all the people of Russia and the European Union' (European Council 1999a). For political reasons, the EU did not raise too many questions during the Yeltsin era, because it was believed that Yeltsin would be the better guarantor of Russia's eventual progress in these matters than his key political competitors. Indeed, the Russian leadership also confronted EU criticism of their human rights by claiming that the criticism only strengthened undemocratic forces in Russia and was therefore 'irresponsible' (Saari 2010b: 19).

Initially, the key mechanism of the EU policy of promoting democracy in Russia was to establish missions to observe elections in the country (Allen 1997: 230–1). These missions, three in total, were originally launched on the invitation of Russia: the first free general elections were held in December 1993; the parliamentary elections, in 1995; and the presidential elections, in July 1996. The EU thereafter left the field of observing elections to the organizations that have this task as one of their key functions: the Office for Democratic Institutions and Human Rights (ODIHR) of the OSCE and the Council of Europe, which Russia joined in 1996. When these organizations faced difficulties in fulfilling that function, the EU leaders sought to persuade the Russian authorities to invite international observers, for example to the Duma elections and presidential elections in March 2008. Although the Kremlin's attitude towards the missions turned negative, the general perception of the role of the election observers among the Russian electorate was nevertheless mainly positive, albeit voters would not always subscribe to the criticism presented by the observers (Hutcheson 2011).

The EU continued to support democratic development and human rights through the Commission's European Instrument for Democracy and Human Rights (EIDHR). Since the instrument's launch in Russia in 1997, the EU has supported 350 projects; in 2014, the budget was €3 million, and 12 new projects were carried out. The EIDHR has tried to enhance respect for human rights and, fundamentally, to strengthen the role of civil society in promoting human rights and democratic reform, and to build confidence in democratic electoral processes through the further development of electoral observation and assistance (Delegation of the EU to Russia 2014).

During the 1990s, the EU started to focus more on good governance than elections. As Commission President Romano Prodi (2000) declared before meeting Putin for the first time as President of Russia, 'The first priority is to ensure strong and effective institutions to underpin the rule of law.' A key issue was corruption and money laundering, which the EU as well as the Kremlin regarded as a problem. After 2002, EU assistance was explicitly linked to the reform projects of the Russian government while democracy promotion was downscaled. The 'Common Space on Freedom, Security and Justice' still referred to respect for human rights and fundamental freedoms, democracy and rule of law as the overarching principles for cooperation within this Space, but in the road maps democracy was already pushed to the margins and freedom was discussed in terms of mobility. Indeed, the negotiations for the Space revealed an increasing divergence between the parties when it came to these issues (Haukkala 2010, Ch. 8).

During Putin's second term as president, the EU became increasingly concerned about the limitations of democratic and civil freedoms in Russia. Since 2005, Freedom House, for example, has no longer characterized Russia as 'partly free', but as 'not free' (Freedom House 2015; but for criticism, see Tsygankov and Parker 2015). The human rights questions became most visible in the context of the 2007 EU–Russia Summit in the Volga city of Samara, when the Russian authorities prevented an opposition demonstration and did not allow Garry Kasparov or members of his Other Russia movement to travel anywhere near the summit venue. At the same time, Russia started to accuse the EU of breaches of democracy of its own, referring particularly to the situation in the Baltic states and the Bronze Soldier case in Estonia. This old Soviet practice of so-called 'whataboutism', responding to concerns by pointing to problems elsewhere, has been gaining in prominence in the Russian attempts at deflecting Western criticism ever since (The Economist 2008).

The representatives of the EU also paid attention to well-known cases of arrest and murder that were seen as gross violations of the rule of law. One of the first and arguably the most spectacular of these cases was the arrest and imprisonment of the powerful oligarch and head of the Yukos oil company, Mikhail Khodorkovsky, in October 2003. The Khodorkovsky case was discussed at the EU–Russia Summit in Rome in November 2003. External Relations Commissioner Chris Patten stated that Russia had to apply the rule of law in the case of Yukos if it wanted close trade links with the EU (*Moscow Times* 2003b), and Javier Solana said that it was crucial to keep the entire legal proceedings transparent and in unison with the norms of a constitutional state. In stark contrast to this, the Prime Minister of Italy, Silvio Berlusconi, who was holding the EU presidency and hosting the meeting at the time, explained that all suspicions against Russia were unfounded and that he regarded the Khodorkovsky arrest as an internal affair (Deutsche Welle 2003). Overall, the EU remained relatively silent on the issue, despite some attempts to mobilize European public opinion through Khodorkovsky's associates. In 2010, when Khodorkovsky's sentence was prolonged, Catherine Ashton and Angela Merkel issued statements expressing their disappointment with the trial being a political process and Russia stumbling on its road to the rule of law.

The EU and its member states were somewhat more vocal with regard to the murder of Anna Politkovskaya in October 2006, the award-winning journalist who reported critically on Russia's behaviour in Chechnya, and Alexander Litvinenko, the former Russian spy who resided in the UK and who was poisoned by radioactive polonium a month later. Finland, which was holding the rotating EU presidency at the time, issued a statement expressing deep regret over the killing of Politkovskaya and called for 'a thorough investigation of this heinous crime and the bringing of its perpetrators to justice' (Foreign Ministry of Finland 2006), but overall, the European reaction was rather muted (Tisdall 2006). When visiting Germany three days after the murder, President Vladimir Putin promised a 'thorough investigation' of the crime, but the German hosts remained fairly subdued on the issue. The Litvinenko case was flammable because the murder had taken place on the soil of a EU member state. Putin called Litvinenko's death 'a tragedy' when attending the EU–Russia Summit in Helsinki just one day after the event, but he did not believe that it was a 'violent death' (Dombey 2006). The Kremlin dismissed allegations that the Russian government poisoned Mr Litvinenko because of his criticisms and revelations as 'sheer nonsense'. When the UK authorities then concluded on the basis of their investigations that the primary suspect in the case was a former Russian secret service officer, Andrei Lugovoi, a heated diplomatic row erupted between the UK and Russia over Moscow's refusal to extradite him to Britain. The Portuguese EU presidency duly expressed its 'disappointment at Russia's failure to cooperate constructively with UK authorities'. The British were satisfied with the European solidarity they received, but the issue was perceived as more bilateral than one which should have burdened EU–Russia relations (see Roth 2009: 19–21).

The arrest, torture and death in police custody of Russian lawyer and auditor Sergei Magnitsky, in November 2009 after one year of imprisonment, led to a major diplomatic conflict and sanctions in the relations between the United States and Russia. The adoption of the so-called 'Magnitsky Act' by the US Congress in 2012 entailed targeted travel bans and asset freezes against some Russian officials implicated in the affair. The EU and its member states also demanded the Kremlin to clarify the issue but, unlike the United States, it did not impose targeted sanctions over the case. The European Parliament nevertheless accepted several resolutions calling upon EU member states to consider imposing entry bans and freezing the assets of the Russian officials who played a direct role in the Magnitsky case, following the US example. EU President Herman Van Rompuy also weighed in on the issue. In a letter sent to President Medvedev, he called the case 'emblematic' of Russia and one that had 'come to symbolise the state of the rule of law and judiciary in the Russian Federation for Russia's friends and observers abroad' (Van Rompuy 2012).

As these cases demonstrate, Russia's commitment to democratic values and human rights was ambivalent at best. Russia had defended itself against the alleged violations and was rhetorically committed to upholding them, but actual conduct was increasingly deviating from them. When meeting with George W. Bush in February 2005, Putin stressed that 'Russia has made its choice in favour of democracy', and that the choice was irreversible but did not come about due to outside pressure, instead having been made by the people of Russia (Osborn 2005). In April 2005, Putin (2005) declared in his annual address to the nation that 'the ideals of freedom, human rights, justice and democracy have for many centuries been our society's determining values'. At the same time, however, the Kremlin started to cherish its concept of 'sovereign democracy', indicating that Russia is democratic in its own way, and the content of democracy cannot be defined from outside (Herd 2009; Mäkinen 2011). Before the EU–Russia Summit in November 2006, Putin (2006) wrote in an op-ed piece in the *Financial Times* that '[i]t would be useless and wrong to try to force artificial "standards" [of common values] on each other'. The bottom line was that Russians perceive human rights and democracy differently compared to people in Western Europe (Deriglazova 2013). For Russians, 'democracy was utopian, discredited and incomprehensible' (Hutcheson 2006: 170). The European way of talking about human rights is legalistic and based on logic, whereas Russian language is much more emotional and based on feelings and moral ideas (Zakharova 2013). As a result, rights are framed in terms of citizens' interests, and 'fairness' is more important than 'the rule of law'.

The Kremlin's growing antipathy towards Western views on democracy and human rights in Russia coincided with a series of policies and legislation that aimed to curtail civil freedoms. Particularly after the Orange Revolution in Ukraine, the Kremlin started to tighten its control over civil society organizations in Russia. It claimed that the revolution in Ukraine had been staged and funded by Western actors. It feared that the European Union when paying attention to the concerns of various nationalities in Russia were plotting against it. As a result, Russian non-governmental organizations (NGOs) that received funding from abroad were particularly suspect. Democracy promotion and minority protection by the West was seen as merely a cover for attempts at weakening the Russian state (Finkel and Brudny 2012).

Over time, Russia gradually started to take additional steps to resist the European and American interpretations of democratic values more openly, and accused the West of their own violations of democratic principles and the application of double standards in the process (Ambrosio 2009; Headley 2015a). In the mid-2000s, Russia launched a counter-campaign against the EU and its member states, criticizing them for human rights violations. Its key concern about such violations in Europe in the 1990s had focused on the alleged discrimination against the Russophone population in the Baltic countries, and many Russians expected that this would negatively affect the Baltic states' chances of joining the European Union. Russia was rather disappointed when the European human rights bodies contended that Russian speakers were not systematically discriminated against in Estonia or Latvia. Moscow's allegations about such discrimination nonetheless continued in the 2000s (Fawn 2009). Moreover, Russia extended its allegations of human rights violations to other EU member states. For example, it claimed that the rights of Russians were being violated in child custody cases in Finland and Sweden. Russia also founded a new think tank, the Institute of Democracy and Cooperation in Paris, which promoted Russia's democracy and human rights agenda. Russian representatives also dodged questions concerning democracy in Russia by criticizing the lack of democracy in international politics dominated by the US.

When Russia started to distance itself from the shared normative basis, the EU tried to find new ways to promote democracy and human rights in the country. To this end, in March 2005 the EU and Russia launched regular human rights consultations. These consultations were meant to provide a setting where the EU and Russia could raise concerns related to human rights, but on a more equal footing, so that it could be seen as a dialogue rather than a European monologue on Russia (Russia preferred the term *consultations* because the EU was having a 'dialogue' with China and Iran). As Gunnar Wiegand, the EU diplomat responsible for the relations with Russia, explained, 'When we talk about democracy, freedom, human rights and common values, what is important in the new way of interacting with Russia is that we do not discuss these things, . . . with us being the lecturers. What is important in this process is that we accept also when Russia raises critical points with us' (House of Lords 2008b: 76). The consultations were extended to NGOs, but they failed to result in substantive progress, and according to leading Russian human rights activists, they had reached a 'dead end'

(Rettmann 2010). Perhaps the most damning conclusion came from Klitsounova (2008: 19), according to whom:

> EU human rights promotion strategies seem ill-adapted to the current context of the EU–Russia relationship. These strategies are largely designed as an experimental, weaker derivative of the policy developed in the course of EU enlargement and are based on the belief that the EU acts as a magnet, leading neighbouring countries to revolutionary policy changes.

As a consequence:

> Russia puts EU policy to the test, as demonstrated by the lack of real progress in the ongoing dialogue between the two parties. This situation demands a profound rethink of the EU approach to human rights promotion: either existing EU policy will be reconstructed to meet new challenges or Russia will continue to limit EU–Russia human rights cooperation.

A report commissioned by the European Commission's Directorate-General for External Relations (DG RELEX) in 2011 concurred and concluded that 'the effectiveness of the EU–Russia consultations is widely regarded as very low or nil' (European Commission 2011a). Eleanor Bindman (2013) has argued that the EU's decision to concentrate almost solely on individual civil and human rights in its dealings with Russia is to be blamed for the lack of progress. According to her, economic and social rights are much more pertinent for the Russians, and concentrating on them instead could point towards a more fruitful agenda.

Joint goals of developing the rule of law in Russia were also included in the Partnerships for Modernisation that were concluded between the EU and its member states and Russia. Here too, it was evident how the EU and Russia put emphasis on different things. For Russia, modernization was largely an economic issue related to technology transfer and improved productivity, whereas the EU wanted to put emphasis on the rule of law and democratization (see Chapter 4). As President Medvedev had acknowledged that corruption is a key problem in Russian society, it became one of the most visible areas of cooperation in the framework of the P4M. Yet even in the issue of corruption, it seemed that the Russian and the EU readings of the issue had little in common (Pavlova 2014).

The neglect of democratic principles and restrictions on human rights increased when Putin returned to the presidency in 2012. Many human rights issues were raised by the representatives of the EU and its member states and were contested with Russia. Particularly antagonistic was the question concerning the rights of sexual minorities in Russia. The EU called on Russia to refrain from adopting federal legislation on 'homosexual propaganda', but for Russia such criticism was nothing but proof of the decadence of the EU (Rohrich 2015). Another thorny issue was the case of the punk band/activist group Pussy Riot, whose members were arrested in February 2012 following a provocative anti-Putin performance at the altar of the Cathedral of Christ the Saviour in Moscow. They were later given two-year prison sentences for 'hooliganism motivated by religious hatred'. EU foreign affairs representative Ashton (2013) announced her 'deep disappointment' with the verdict in the case and regarded the sentence as disproportionate. Moreover, laws related to freedom of expression and association and other measures that suppressed civil society were regarded as alarming by the EU. The so-called 'protest law' and the 'law on foreign agents' that required NGOs to register as foreign agents came in for particularly heavy criticism.

The Kremlin found such criticism and European attempts to interfere in the legislation and court cases biased and politically motivated. The Russian foreign ministry, for example, accused the European Parliament's resolution on human rights issues in Russia of being 'just another politicized and very unfriendly opus having nothing to do with the real situation surrounding democracy and human rights in Russia and strikingly contradicting the positive dynamism of relations between Russia and the European Union' (Interfax 2013). By contrast, the Russian Foreign Ministry started to publish its own reviews of the human rights situation in the world, accusing the West, the EU and the Baltic states in particular of serious neglect and wrongdoing (Ministry of Foreign Affairs of the Russian Federation 2011). Moreover, it launched its own agenda of human rights based on conservative social values, and rallied international opposition to lesbian, gay, bisexual, transgender (LGBT) rights in particular. From the Russian point of view, a political union with Europe was not possible because Europeans were abandoning Christianity and traditional norms (Karaganov 2014).

Putin's (2013a) speech at the prestigious Valdai meeting was famous for its defence of traditional values and concern about the erosion of Christian values and an exaggerated focus on the rights of sexual minorities in the West. Despite Putin's diatribe against Western liberalism, his conservatism was essentially defensive and geared towards protecting Russia's domestic sphere from the corrosive effects that any further Western encroachments would entail and the dangers that they would pose to the Russian body politic. Indeed, Putin alluded to this when referring to the words of Nikolai Berdyaev, an early twentieth-century Russian philosopher, according to which '[t]he point of conservatism is not that it prevents movement forward and upward, but that it prevents movement backward and downward, into chaotic darkness and a return to a primitive state' (Putin 2013b; see also Rodkiewics and Rogoża 2015).

In these circumstances, the EU and its member states variously wanted to revise their human rights policy towards Russia. Some member states wanted to put more emphasis on the human rights issues despite the Kremlin's negative attitude towards criticism from abroad. Others were of the opinion that human rights issues should not be pushed too hard without the consent of the Russian leadership. There was a broad consensus in the EU and its member states that it was nevertheless important to create and develop links with various NGOs and representatives of civil society in Russia. Yet this was seen as provocative by the Kremlin, and as an attempt at creating conditions conducive to a 'colour revolution' in Russia. As a consequence, Russia took steps to nip these developments in the bud, and the EU's ability to exert a direct influence on the nature of Russian civil society waned with the strengthening of Russian policies of nation-building, internal consolidation and control (Finkel and Brudny 2012). Of particular significance in this respect was the adoption of the so-called NGO law in 2013, which required the registration of all Russian entities operating with foreign financing as 'foreign agents' (Crotty, Hall and Ljubownikow 2014). That said, the European connection nevertheless remained as an indirect background force: subtle forms of the 'Europeanization' of civil society agendas, primarily as a result of pragmatic cooperation with EU partners in defining social agendas, could still be discerned (Belokurova 2010).

Overall, the issues related to democracy and human rights have been a very sensitive area in the cooperation between the EU and Russia. Although Russia wanted to have these issues promoted in the 1990s, it gradually rejected the common values base and then started to promote its own values. Sinikukka Saari (2010b: 22) argued that

> [t]he EU has made many drastic mistakes in its human rights policy towards Russia. First, the EU should have reacted faster and in a more consistent and coherent manner to early human rights violations in Russia. Instead, the EU has sent mixed messages to Russia and Russia has been able to play EU states and institutions off against each other on human rights questions.

The value distance between the EU and Russia seemed only to grow after the Ukraine crises. The EU regarded the human rights situation in Crimea as a new concern in Russia. Russia, in turn, accused the EU and its member states of massive human rights violations when they were struggling to find a solution to the refugee crisis. Russia was also less forthcoming as far as joint frameworks were concerned. A clear indication of this negative trend was the Kremlin's decision in December 2015 that enabled Russia's Constitutional Court to overrule decisions of the European Court of Human Rights (BBC 2015).

Chechnya

The Chechen conflict inside the Russian Federation in North Caucasus was primarily framed as a human rights issue by the EU. It constitutes an important case for EU–Russia relations because on two occasions the issue led to a significant, albeit temporary, worsening in the relationship. The Chechen conflict thus demonstrated the role and effect that human rights issues have had when it comes to EU–Russia relations (Forsberg and Herd 2005; H. Smith 2005). The exact importance of Chechnya for Russia's relationship with the EU has remained contested, however. Some analysts regarded Russian human rights abuses in Chechnya as one of the major obstacles to Russia's rapprochement with Europe, whereas others have seen it as of secondary importance for the overall relationship.

The Chechen war started in December 1994 when Russian armed forces advanced into Chechnya after the separatist region, led by President Dzhokar Dudayev, had declared independence three years earlier. The EU was not willing to recognize Chechnya as a sovereign state, but it argued that Russia had committed itself to uphold international norms, and a violation of these norms by Russian military and security forces in Chechnya undermined international stability. The argument was soon made that the EU's credibility in its relations with Russia depended on its ability to speak up unambiguously when treaties and norms were violated.

The EU decided that it would not consider the war in Chechnya a Russian internal affair in so far as human rights abuses had occurred there. Hence, the EU insisted that both Russia and Chechnya adhere to an OSCE presence in Chechnya, access to humanitarian aid, a cease-fire and the search for a political solution respecting the territorial integrity of Russia. The EU gradually sharpened the language, but there was very little support on the part of the member states for imposing sanctions on Russia. The EU's strongest demonstration of its determination to enforce its normative agenda was the decision to postpone the ratification of the PCA and the signing of the Interim Treaty on trade provisions in January 1995. The decision was still mainly symbolic because bilateral programmes remained in force, and the TACIS funds were not frozen.

Although the EU representatives continued to criticize human rights violations on both sides of the conflict, they were not seen as important enough to block the PCA with Russia. The Commission concluded as early as May 1995 that it was ready to sign the Interim Agreement and recommended the ratification of the PCA because it had detected enough progress related to Russia's Chechen policy. The signing of the Interim Agreement in July 1995 was then followed by Russia's admission to the Council of Europe, as well as the ratification of the PCA. The EU's human rights criticisms subsequently focused on the Chechen side, pointing to the public execution and kidnapping of humanitarian aid staff in the area controlled by President Aslan Maskhadov.

The second Chechen War, starting in August 1999, posed a renewed challenge to the rapprochement between the EU and Russia and represented an analogous story (on the war, see e.g. Russell 2007). The war was triggered by the expansion of the conflict outside of Chechnya's borders and a series of bomb blasts targeting civilians that occurred in major Russian cities, including Moscow. At first, the EU remained silent on the issue, but criticism emerged in September 1999, when Germany, France and Italy, sidelining the EU institutions, issued a joint statement in which they expressed their deepest concern about Russia's bombing campaign in Chechnya and urged Russia to find a political solution (see also *Die Zeit* 1999). This prompted the Finnish EU presidency to deliver another statement with similar content. The issue dominated the EU–Russia Summit in October 1999, although initially it was not the key issue. Moreover, as a protest, the key European foreign ministers decided not to take part in the meeting on Northern Dimension in November. The EU representatives stressed that they had no wish to isolate Russia, but they criticized the use of disproportionate military force and urged the country to seek a political settlement.

The second war in Chechnya reached its most severe phase in December 1999, when Russian forces delivered an ultimatum to the people of Grozny, threatening it with annihilation. As the siege of Grozny coincided with the European Council meeting held in Helsinki, it was clear that it had to react (Lintonen 2004). The European Council (1999b), indeed, issued a Declaration on Chechnya, which called upon the Russian authorities not to carry out the ultimatum, to respect international norms and to initiate political dialogue with the Chechen leaders. The Declaration threatened a review of the implementation of the EU's Common Strategy on Russia, the suspension of some of the provisions of the PCA and the freezing of some TACIS programme funds. By EU standards, the Declaration on Chechnya represented a relatively tough formulation of the EU position, but following a series of compromises, it was still a vaguely worded, ambivalent political document. In fact, it was unclear what the sanctions were exactly and when they should be invoked.

On the basis of the Declaration on Chechnya, the EU General and External Affairs Council subsequently accepted limited sanctions in January 2000: two-thirds of the TACIS funding was transferred to democracy, civil society and humanitarian assistance, and the finalizing of an agreement on cooperation in science and technology was suspended. EU unity on the issue was, however, rather fragile. While France and Germany had been in the vanguard, advocating the sanctions and also believing in their effectiveness, Britain adopted a sceptical stance. Its Prime Minister Tony Blair argued that the best way to get results was by engaging with Russia and not isolating the country. The newly appointed high representative of the EU foreign and security policy, Javier Solana (2000), also opined that the EU must address the Chechen issue without endangering future EU–Russia relations, and noted that it was important 'to discuss and respond to a problem like this constructively and in a manner of mutual respect'. In contrast, Foreign Minister of France Hubert Védrine justified the sanctions by arguing that 'we cannot pretend that everything is fine', and threatened that 'we might have to go further, regrettably'. In his view, 'The way in which the Russians are dealing with the Chechen tragedy is in total contradiction with the idea they have of closer relations between Russia and Europe' (quoted in Forsberg and Herd 2005: 464).

The limited EU sanctions and the continued verbal criticism did not have much impact on Russia. As soon as the fiercest phase of the war was over, the EU was willing to restore relations with Russia, as unacceptable as the situation was from the Brussels perspective. At the summit in Feira in June 2000, the Union decided to lift the sanctions in order to create a positive start with the administration of newly elected President Vladimir Putin (European Council 2000). This justification was perplexing, not least inasmuch as Putin had been de facto president since the launch of the second campaign. France, which had been the most vociferous EU member state in criticizing Russia's actions in Chechnya, regarded its EU presidency in the autumn of 2000 as a good opportunity to repair its relations with Russia. In the summit declaration, Russia agreed to pursue a political solution to the conflict, but that phrase meant little in practice. Védrine argued that 'we do not withdraw any of what we have said about Chechnya but Russia is a great country with which we want to maintain . . . good relations'. Germany's Foreign Minister, Joschka Fischer, in turn, defended the policy change by contending that 'we cannot force Russia to change its policy although we would use all available means' (quoted in Forsberg and Herd 2005: 466).

When the pressure lessened, Russia showed some gestures of its willingness to address the human rights issues related to the conflict in Chechnya. For example, Russia allowed an EU delegation to visit Chechnya on a fact-finding mission, and Putin signalled that the EU could be involved in helping to bring peace to Chechnya. Russian presidential aide Sergey Yastrzhembskiy reassured the EU that Russia was making efforts to investigate the criminal offences that had been committed in Chechnya, but impunity still prevailed; in fact, he denied that any gross violation of human rights had occurred there and demanded apologies from the French dailies for their distorted coverage of the conflict (Forsberg and Herd 2005: 466).

Another factor that led the EU to reduce and soften its criticisms of Russian actions in Chechnya was the terrorist acts of 11 September 2001. The EU nevertheless resisted the temptation to subscribe to the Russian view that the war in Chechnya was an integral part of the global war on terrorism. Yet, during Putin's visit to Berlin, Chancellor Gerhard Schröder declared that the Chechen conflict must be reassessed in the light of 11 September, and Blair too argued that 'the whole perception of Russia, in Europe and in the West, has been transformed', declaring that Russia had a legitimate right of self-defence against extremism and fundamentalism. French Prime Minister Lionel Jospin, however, contended that the fight against terrorism did not give Russia carte blanche to rely solely on the indiscriminate use of military power (Forsberg and Herd 2005: 468).

Although the issue of human rights violations in Chechnya was no longer central to the agenda of the EU–Russia Summits, it hovered in the background. The EU institutions and key politicians continued to remind Russia of its human rights commitments, and the EU also sponsored a declaration condemning Russia at the UN Commission on Human Rights. A more visible clash over Chechnya re-emerged when the exiled Chechens held their world congress in Copenhagen in 2002. Russia accused Denmark, which was holding the EU presidency at the time, of supporting terrorism by not prohibiting the meeting, and requested that Maskhadov's representative, Akhmed Zakayev, be extradited from Denmark. After Denmark refused, Putin announced that he would not travel to Copenhagen for the EU–Russia Summit scheduled for November 2002. As the EU wished to prevent an escalation of the dispute, the summit was relocated to Brussels, where the issue of Chechnya was publicly avoided until the final press conference, where Putin lost his temper when questioned about the Chechens (Forsberg and Herd 2005: 468).

The EU then shifted from criticism to supporting stability in Chechnya on the conditions imposed by Russia. The EU welcomed the constitutional referendum of 2003 in Chechnya, although it was clear that it was hardly conducted in a free and fair manner. At the EU–Russia Summit in May 2003, Prime Minister Costas Simitis of Greece, who was holding the EU's rotating presidency, stated that the EU would 'continue to support the efforts of Russian leaders to carry out a policy aiming to bring peace back to Chechnya' and characterized the constitutional referendum as 'an important step forward'. European leaders avoided the Chechen issue with Putin and focused on the economy instead. Even more strikingly, Italian Prime Minister Silvio Berlusconi defended Putin's Chechen policy and the rule of law in Russia at the EU–Russia Rome summit later in 2003 and accused the international media of 'spreading legends' (Forsberg and Herd 2005: 471). All in all, the EU had to tread a fine line between not provoking the Russians while not ignoring human rights and values entirely. When Romano Prodi (2004) visited Moscow, he delivered a speech in which he assured listeners that 'we have a common cause in the need to fight against terrorism', but then reminded the audience that 'terrorism cannot be defeated by force alone' but 'makes our continued attachment to our shared democratic values even more imperative'. Moreover, he regretted that 'our Russian partners' have not fully appreciated our humanitarian assistance to Chechnya, 'which has played a significant part in alleviating the suffering of many refugees and victims of the conflict'.

The EU's adoption of a more accommodating line helped to normalize the relations with Russia, but the EU had already earned a reputation for being a difficult partner as far as Chechnya was concerned, and it was clearly regarded as more hawkish than the United States in this respect. As one analyst (Khudoley 2003: 18) noted: 'While the US leaders appear to understand that the Chechen situation is rather complex and multi-dimensional and that Russia indeed has been compelled to deal with confirmed terrorists, West European politicians and analysts have often seen the Chechen problem as a violation of human rights on the part of the federal forces, with the terrorist activities of the Chechen separatists being completely overlooked.' When the Chechen terrorists attacked a school in Beslan in September 2004 and took hundreds of children hostage, the leaders of the major EU countries were quick to sympathize with the Kremlin and condemn Chechen terrorism. An incident occurred only when Bernard Bot, the foreign minister of the Netherlands, which was holding the EU's rotating presidency, asked the Russian government 'how this tragedy could have happened'. Russian Foreign Minister Sergey Lavrov labelled the question 'inappropriate and blasphemous', but European Commission officials were quick to assure Moscow that Bot's comments on the tragedy had been misunderstood by Moscow (Forsberg and Herd 2005: 472).

The Chechen issue faded into the background as news about atrocities decreased. Overall, the EU failed to elaborate a comprehensive policy on the Chechen issue, and its attempts to influence Russia with regard to the human rights questions in Chechnya were ineffective. Chris Patten (2005: 207), the external relations commissioner, explained in his candid memoirs of the 'depressing' Chechnya story how 'Russian officials – President Putin, prime ministers, foreign ministers obfuscated and lied. They ignored our letters. They denied that we had raised concerns about specific issues with them. Naturally they got away with it.' The EU council never discussed the issue thoroughly but switched its position in a rather arbitrary manner unrelated to the situation on the ground. The EU was not able to have much impact on Russia's behaviour in Chechnya, but neither was Russia able to convince the EU about its view of the conflict. For example, Russia was unable to get the Chechen representative, Akhmed Zakaev, extradited from Denmark or the UK, which Russia regarded as a clear example of double standards.

Police, border and judicial cooperation

The agenda dealing with justice and the police between the EU and Russia was already part of the PCA, including a special title devoted to counteracting unlawful activities. It mentions 'the prevention of illegal activities' (Title VIII), defined, among other things, in terms of illegal migration, money laundering, corruption and drug trafficking (Art. 84). The EU Common Strategy on Russia envisions that '[t]he Union wishes to support Russia in the consolidation of its public institutions, particularly its executive, legislative and judicial bodies and its police, in accordance with democratic principles'. The Road Map for the Common Space on Freedom, Security and Justice of 2005 stated that the objective was to contribute to the efficiency of the judicial system in EU member states and Russia, and to the independence of the judiciary (European Commission 2005). The aim was also to improve cooperation in tackling terrorism and all forms of organized crime as well as other illegal activities. Collaboration between Eurojust and the Russian General Prosecutor's Office was also a target for development but was complicated because of data protection regulations.

It should be pointed out that in this field it is not necessarily always the EU and its institutions that are the most relevant framework for cooperation. On the contrary, bilateral links between member states and Russia as well as other international fora such as the Council of Europe and Europol are equally and even more important than the EU (Hernández i Sagrera and Potemkina 2013: 11). Europol and Russia signed a cooperation agreement in November 2003 in Rome, making it possible to request assistance in combating serious forms of transnational criminal activities. The parties have tried to update this agreement by including provisions that would allow for the sharing of data, but the negotiations that started in 2010 have not been concluded, mainly because of EU concerns over the protection of information in Russia (Hernández i Sagrera and Potemkina 2013: 14). In general, police cooperation between the EU and Russia remains predominantly bilateral in nature. In terms of multilateral cooperation, Interpol is more important than Europol. Furthermore, the EU policy instruments have been of little relevance for police cooperation with Russia (Block 2007). Exchanging information in combating crime was deemed crucial, but cooperation was not always smooth on this level; according to one Europol representative, '[T]he Russians always want to have information but are never willing to give any' (Weltschinski 2014: 5).

Judicial cooperation between the EU and Russia consisted of various projects enhancing border control and combating organized crime, including human trafficking and drugs. On the face of it, these issues reveal a host of common interests. The EU Border Agency FRONTEX concluded a working arrangement with its Russian counterpart in 2006. The practical cooperation in this area comprised risk analyses, training, and research and development related to border management, as well as possible joint operations. The EU was pressing Russia particularly on human trafficking. The most important achievement was, however, the readmission agreement between the EU and Russia in 2007 (Korneev 2012). The EU and Russia have also launched a dialogue on migration since 2011 (Bisson 2014). This has included attempts to codify legislation concerning migration, starting with the very definition of *migrant*.

When it comes to drugs, both the EU and Russia are key destinations from South America and Afghanistan. Yet instead of achieving close cooperation based on these common interests, the two have remained mired in disagreements over the specific modalities of cooperation. For the EU, the priority has been tackling the Balkans as a traffic route for drugs and other criminal activities, whereas for Russia the onus has been put on Central Asia. Moreover, whereas the EU has been seeking to immerse Russia in the existing European bodies and networks of cooperation, such as the CoE and Europol, Russia has been vying for arrangements that would be more 'equal' in the sense that they would build cooperative arrangements between the 'Western' players and the gamut of organizations created in the Eastern part of the continent, such as the Collective

Security Treaty Organization (CSTO) and Shanghai Cooperation Organization (SCO) (Hernández i Sagrera and Potemkina 2013). The EU and Russia were, however, able to make progress in this area by concluding a cooperation agreement on the control of drug precursors in June 2013 at the EU–Russia summit in Yekaterinburg (European Commission 2013b).

The EU and Russia also started to develop a joint anti-terrorist agenda, particularly after the terrorist attacks in the United States in September 2001, but shaped also by the terrorist siege at the Dubrovka Theatre in Moscow in October 2002. The fight against terrorism was discussed in all the subsequent summits, in Brussels in October 2001 as well as in Moscow in May 2002, leading to a Joint Statement on Combating Terrorism issued at the EU–Russia Summit in November 2002 in Brussels. The statement condemned all acts of terrorism and declared joint commitment to strengthen bilateral as well as wider international cooperation in various ways. As new dramatic terrorist deeds followed in Madrid, Beslan and London, the issue remained on the agenda and was prominently discussed at the EU–Russia Summit in May 2006 and the EU–Russia Summit in December 2012, which included an assessment of the counterterrorism political dialogue. Though both sides understood the need for cooperation, finding ways to combat terrorism jointly was a long-term process burdened by organizational mismatch, bureaucratic thresholds and political disagreements on the roots of terrorism (Hernández i Sagrera and Potemkina 2013; Potemkina 2015). The parties were nevertheless working hard, holding regular meetings between the Russian MFA and the European External Action Service. This resulted in a new Joint EU–Russia Statement on Combatting Terrorism at the January 2014 summit (Council of the European Union 2014). The statement outlined concrete political actions in fighting terrorism and signalled readiness to negotiate substantial agreements on extradition, mutual legal assistance, passenger name record (PNR) and financing of terrorism (Potemkina 2015: 2–3). Yet, the Ukrainian crisis affected the cooperation on combating terrorism too, as the EU's sanctions targeted some of the key counterparts on the Russian side. Lavrov announced angrily that the EU was taking 'a complete turn away from joint work with Russia on international and regional security, including the fight against the spread of weapons of mass destruction, terrorism (and) organized crime' (Potemkina 2015: 2–3; Ministry of Foreign Affairs of the Russian Federation 2014).

The visa issue

The question of the visa regime and eventual visa freedom between the EU and Russia has had the paradoxical quality of being one of the rare negotiation processes seen as moving constantly forward while also eventually becoming a touchstone of trust and eventual progress between the parties. For Russia in particular, the visa question has been important both practically as well as symbolically and is one of the few issues in EU–Russia relations where Russia has been the *demandeur* and has driven the agenda (Mäkinen, Smith and Forsberg 2016).

Initially, the question of visas was not really prioritized on the agenda. For example, the only mention of the issue in the PCA is to be found in a Joint Declaration annexed to the agreement that makes reference to the need to 'facilitate the prompt entry, stay and movement of businessmen' with visas. The issue became more prominent in the context of the EU's Eastern enlargement in the early 2000s. The impending accession of Poland and Lithuania meant that the Russian Kaliningrad region was about to become an enclave within the enlarged EU. This in turn meant that the previous visa-free travel between Kaliningrad and mainland Russia would be disrupted when the new EU members adopted the Schengen *acquis*. The growing Russian realization of the hardships, both actual and symbolic, generated by this state of affairs resulted in one of the most heated exchanges between the EU and Russia.

To begin with, Russia framed the issue in terms of economic losses incurred and the rights of Russian citizens violated in the process, and put forward ideas for road and rail links or other 'corridors' where all Russians could continue to travel visa-free (Oldberg 2004: 49–50). Initially, the EU found these suggestions unacceptable, claiming that the Schengen system did not allow for such derogations and that the existing system could be adjusted to address Russian concerns (Potemkina 2003: 235). Commissioner Chris Patten (2001) reassured that these sensitive issues can in his opinion be resolved with no doubt to everyone's satisfaction, although the solutions will 'require us to make imaginative use of the flexibility permitted by EU rules'. Yet Russian concerns were not dispelled that easily, and the issue came to a head at the EU–Russia Summit in Moscow in May 2002, where Putin launched a vitriolic attack against the EU, claiming that its policies were essentially an affront to Russia's sovereignty when it was 'making proposals to us which essentially mean only one thing: [that] the right of Russians to free communication with relatives inside Russia will depend on the decisions of other states' (Traynor 2002).

The heated exchanges continued throughout the summer and early autumn, leading to a diplomatic incidence when a Danish newspaper labelled Kaliningrad a 'desperate and poor robbers den' and suggested that it should become a EU district (Etzold and Haukkala 2011: 256). Yet, in November 2002, at the EU summit that was relocated from Copenhagen to Brussels, the parties were eventually able to settle the issue through a compromise, albeit some Russian journalists, believing that a deal would have been a precondition for EU enlargement and therefore Russia should have had leverage, called it 'a defeat' for Putin (Shiskounova and Zhegulev 2002). The solution nevertheless came in the form of facilitated transit documents (FTDs) for road and rail passengers that Lithuania would grant to Russians travelling to and from Kaliningrad. In exchange, Russia signed and ratified a bilateral readmission agreement with Lithuania that would commit Russia to take back any illegal immigrants travelling from Russia to Lithuania.

Despite their name, in essence the FTDs amounted to facilitated visas in anything but name. Indeed, Russia used the positive momentum generated by the compromise to press ahead with further visa liberalization. Putin had already proposed visa-free travel between Russia and the EU in August 2002, and the issue was raised on the common agenda at the St Petersburg EU–Russia Summit in May 2003 as 'a long-term perspective' (EU–Russia Summit 2003). The Russians were optimistic that the long-term perspective was within reach, and they often circulated a Romano Prodi quote from July 2003, according to which '[v]isa-free travel for Russians could be a fact already in five years' time' (*Moscow Times* 2003a). When visiting Moscow a year later, Prodi, however, refrained from giving a timetable (Prodi 2004).

From the outset, the EU and Russia have assumed different perspectives concerning visa freedom. For Russia, the Schengen agreement was seen as being in direct conflict with one of the most basic freedoms – the freedom of Russians to travel. The Russians also regarded the EU's visa application processes as discriminatory and humiliating, reducing them to 'belonging to a second class in Europe' (Baranovsky and Utkin 2012: 77). Russia's ambassador to the EU, Vladimir Chizhov (2003b), accused the EU of building a 'Schengen Wall' that was becoming 'higher and more insurmountable over time' and that would produce 'uncomfortable memories of the Berlin Wall'. When the candidate countries started to apply the Schengen rules, the Russians concretely realized that their situation was getting worse and not better because of the EU. For these reasons, the visa question became a symbolic issue for the Russians, effectively rubber-stamping their exclusion from Europe (Averre 2005: 185). As a consequence, Russia has approached the issue as a matter of the greatest urgency and has constantly expressed its willingness to press ahead with the process as swiftly as possible. For example, in 2008, Foreign Minister Lavrov declared that Russia would be ready for visa freedom with the EU 'by tomorrow', given that the EU was willing to follow suit (Salminen and Moshes 2009: 43).

The EU, for its part, has assumed a much cooler stance concerning the issue, stressing the long-term nature of the perspective and insisting that the process would require numerous reforms on the Russian side and that clear benchmarks and strict timetables would have to be adhered to in order to qualify for eventual visa freedom. In a word, the EU was able to impose strict conditionality on the issue because it was Russia that clearly assumed the role of a *demandeur*. That said, the EU largely resisted the temptation to make inappropriate issue linkages to a host of other problematic issues on the EU–Russian agenda. Nevertheless, when the cooperation in most other areas where the EU was the *demandeur* stalled, awareness grew in Brussels and in some of the member states that the EU should not give its trump card away for free. At the same time, the EU has pursued a rather expansive notion of visa liberalization, entailing significant improvements in terms of Russia's human rights, rule of law and anti-corruption records. This has gone against the grain of Russian readings of the process, which have emphasized the limited and more technical nature of visa liberalization.

In the meantime, the parties embarked on a process of taking reciprocal steps to facilitate and expedite the issuance and practices related to visas and travelling. An EU–Russia Visa Facilitation Agreement, the first of its kind that the EU negotiated with any country, was signed in Sochi in 2006 and entered into force in June 2007. The agreement introduced 'privileged categories' of citizens who can obtain visas with fewer supporting documents than previously; lowered and fixed the overall visa fee; made obtaining multiple-entry visas easier; and waived visas entirely for diplomats (Van Elsuwege 2013: 16). Linking visa facilitation with readmission agreements was a conscious choice on the part of the EU to make its partners move forward with the latter, and it became the staple of EU policy in the field of visa facilitation (Trauner and Kruse 2008: 418). The readmission agreement with Lithuania over the Kaliningrad transit issue had already sparked some criticism in the Russian debates. Olga Potemkina (2003: 246) has argued that Russia made a bad deal when signing the agreement:

> As a rule, a country signs a readmission agreement in exchange for a visa-free regime, at least that was the case of the candidate countries. Russia is going to sign the agreement with Lithuania, having obtained just a feasibility study on visa-free transit to Kaliningrad, an FTD scheme and a non-stop train in future. . . . The inequality and asymmetry of relations between the European Union and Russia has thus been re-established.

Be that as it may, the parties kept making steady progress in the field, launching in spring 2007 a Visa Dialogue, which the Russians tellingly called a Visa-free Dialogue, to further facilitate travel across the borders. In the context of the dialogue, the parties agreed in 2011 on a so-called Common Steps document to facilitate the process towards eventual visa-free, short-term travel (Common Steps 2011). The document spelled out four thematic blocks – document security, including biometrics; illegal migration, including readmission; public order, security and judicial cooperation; and external relations, including a comprehensive set of steps to be implemented in order to reach eventual visa freedom. Despite its concrete and operational nature, the document also contains a catch, particularly in the EU reading, as although the path towards visa liberalization is dependent on the full implementation of the Common Steps, there is nevertheless no automaticity in the process: on the contrary, in its final provisions, the Common Steps document notes that once the implementation of the Common Steps is completed, 'the Parties will decide, in accordance with their respective internal procedures, on starting negotiations on an EU–Russia visa waiver agreement' (Common Steps 2011). In essence, this means that while committing itself to a road map and Common Steps towards visa freedom with Russia, the EU simultaneously retained the right to have a separate and final say in the matter. This has not escaped Russian criticism. For example, Russia's EU Ambassador Vladimir Chizhov argued that negotiations for abolishing visas should have begun right after the implementation of the Common Steps as '[a]ny other scenario would contradict the very logic of the agreed document approved by Russian and EU leadership' (Chizhov 2012).

This basic tension notwithstanding, the visa dialogue has generated a great deal of concrete results and actual implementation, making it one of the rare cases where the EU and Russia have been able to make significant progress towards a shared objective. Of particular significance is the fact that in this field Russia has made strides in implementing the Common Steps: significant legislative changes have been made; document security has been improved, including the adoption of biometric passports; a network of readmission agreements have been negotiated between Russia and its various neighbours; and so on. Russia has clearly shown a unity of purpose and willingness to implement decisions in a way that has not been met practically in any other issue-area discussed in this book.

Russia's actions have not gone entirely unreciprocated by the EU. An important development was the adoption of a so-called local border traffic (LBT) regime between Kaliningrad and the adjacent region in Poland in December 2011. LBTs are a tool afforded by the Schengen *acquis*, which allows visa-free travel for residents of border areas who frequently need to cross the external border of the EU. The LBT regime became a success story, facilitating movement and economic activities between Kaliningrad and Poland and acting as a 'confidence building measure' between Russia and Poland, and indeed between the EU and Russia (Van Elsuwege 2013: 18). The Russian side in particular has appreciated the LBT regime as a rare case of flexibility on the part of the EU, in their view (Hernández i Sagrera and Potemkina 2013: 8).

Progress was also notable in other areas related to visas, but the visa dialogue failed to make a decisive breakthrough. This was largely due to different understandings concerning the very nature of the process. From the Russian perspective, the question of visa freedom was largely a question of political will, namely of the willingness to move ahead swiftly in order to reach the desired objective. On the EU side, however, the issue was viewed more in technocratic terms. Indeed, the visa question revealed a clear divergence when it came to interpreting the term *political will*: for Russia, it meant papering over the remaining differences, whereas for the EU it entailed a diligent implementation and monitoring of agreed deliverables.

Having established this, one should also note that the EU did accentuate the technocratic nature of the visa dialogue in order to deliberately camouflage the internal tensions concerning the issue in several member states. Whereas Italy and Spain were in favour of a faster timetable, the Baltic countries and Poland were more willing to put the brakes on the process. For these countries bordering Russia, fears concerning the increased migratory pressures and organized crime from Russia were paramount, overriding any considerations for improved ties with the country (Van Elsuwege 2013: 12). Overall, the EU had serious concerns regarding Russia's ability to guarantee border security and the integrity of documents free of corruption or other problems dealing with the lack of the rule of law. As a consequence, the key ingredient for the successful adoption of visa freedom – reciprocal trust – has been missing (for a detailed discussion of EU reservations, see Salminen and Moshes 2009, Ch. 4).

The EU's alleged foot-dragging aroused the Russians' repeated ire over the years, and they regarded the technocratic demands as simply a pretext for the lack of political will. For example, right at the beginning of the visa dialogue Vladimir Pankov (2007) argued, 'The usual allegations by leading European politicians and high-ranking officials from Brussels and Strasbourg, which say that Russia is denied visa-free travel due to its so-called instability, are absolutely unconvincing considering Russia's real situation.' Pankov opined that the EU offered visa-free entry to citizens of many countries that are less stable than Russia (e.g. Argentina). Deputy Foreign Minister Aleksandr Grushko (2010) argued that there were no insurmountable technical obstacles to a visa-free regime – it just needed a political decision.

Unfazed, it seemed, Russia kept pushing for a positive solution to the issue. At the EU–Russia Summit in Rostov-on-Don in June 2010, President Medvedev handed his EU counterparts a draft agreement for the abolition of visas, repeating Russia's essential willingness to move forward with the issue 'tomorrow'. By contrast, EU President Herman von Rompuy only referred to the issue in the usual EU refrain as 'a long-term goal' and one where the EU remained 'committed to making concrete progress as soon as possible on the ground' (News Conference following EU–Russia Summit 2010).

Russia's final push for visa freedom, at least for the time being, coincided with the preparations for the Sochi Winter Olympics in

February 2014. Moscow clearly hoped that the occasion would have served as a natural date of conclusion for the process (Chizhov 2012). The EU was, however, never enthusiastic about this prospect, and it avoided any commitment to strict deadlines. For example, in March 2013, Commission President José Manuel Barroso stated that it would be better not to speak about any deadlines for the abolition of visas (Pavlova 2014: 113). The EU's lack of eagerness concerning the process was clearly a disappointment for the Russians. In an emotional broadside against the EU, Foreign Minister Lavrov (2013) noted how

> [w]e are disappointed with insufficient progress towards visa-free travel for short-term visits between Russia and the EU. The visa regime has long been an anachronism in our relations. From the technical point of view, Russia and EU Member States have been ready to waive visas for each other. This issue is symbolic; it exemplifies all the differences between Russia and the EU. It is ironic that our Western partners, who were so adamant about freedom of movement when negotiating the Helsinki Final Act, are now reluctant to create conditions for free human communication on the European continent.

Indeed, the Russian wishes for a Sochi deadline were not met. The EU ambassador to Russia, Vygaudas Usackas, said that the EU had been prepared to conclude an agreement on the relaxation of visa formalities in 2012, but Russia suddenly made a new demand that the so-called official passport-holders be granted visa-free travel (Kyiv Post 2013). Although the first Common Steps Progress Report noted that Russia had made good progress with many steps already fulfilled, further work was seen as necessary before all the elements contained in the Common Steps would be fully implemented (European Commission 2013c: 52). As a consequence, visa-free travel could not be implemented before the Sochi Olympics. On the contrary, in a meeting in Moscow in January 2014, in an atmosphere already soured by the pending Ukraine conflict, the two sides exchanged barbs concerning the topic. EU Commissioner Cecilia Malmström argued that although the EU was still committed to visa freedom with Russia, it still had several concerns regarding Russia's commitment to 'values shared by EU countries'. According to her, 'We [the EU] want a visa-free regime to be established in a safe and secure environment, which means there is no corruption, and human rights and the rule of law are observed.' The Russian Minister for Justice, Alexander Konovalov, retorted, 'We have a feeling that our colleagues in the EU are not committed and do not feel a need to eliminate the barriers between Russia and the EU', and that '[w]e are trying not to turn our relations completely sour and maintain a certain level of dialogue' (Kravtsova 2014).

Yet even this was not to transpire. Instead, the conflict in Ukraine suspended the visa process as well because the EU, as part of its first set of sanctions in March 2014, froze the visa dialogue with Russia. The Russian consternation was captured by Putin (2014), who, in his 'victory speech' after the annexation of Crimea, concluded:

> We are constantly proposing cooperation on all key issues; we want to strengthen our level of trust and for our relations to be equal, open and fair. But we saw no reciprocal steps. On the contrary, they have lied to us many times, made decisions behind our backs, place us before an accomplished fact. . . . It happened with the endless foot-dragging in the talks on visa issues, promises of fair competition and free access to global markets.

In essence, all the good intentions and mutual give and take notwithstanding, the visa dialogue too had become both a victim and the symbol of the wider problems and malaise in EU–Russia relations. The Russians were still hoping that the dialogue on the abolition of visas with the EU could be resumed as soon as possible, but, as Ambassador Anwar Azimov noted, 'The ball is in the EU's court' (Lenin 2015). In December 2015, as a move that was seen as mocking Russia, the EU commission announced that it would grant visa freedom to Ukraine and Georgia.

Conclusions

This chapter has dealt with democracy and human rights as well as cooperation in police and border matters. This has been a difficult field and one that is often seen as a major source of problems because of its relation to values. During the past ten years in particular, the values gap between the EU and Russia has grown steadily and has clearly affected the level of cooperation. The EU did not have a very consistent and coherent policy towards human rights violations in Russia. At the same time, Russia increasingly denied that the EU had any legitimate say in human rights issues in Russia, and it was able to cherry-pick its European partners among those who did not insist on human rights violations. For the most part, the EU member states were happy to leave the human rights agenda to the EU and its institutions, but its mandate and consequent leverage remained rather limited.

However, cooperation in the framework of the Common Space of Freedom, Security and Justice, focusing on police, border and antiterrorism matters, has taken place and has brought some positive results. Despite of its pragmatic nature of this cooperation, it has not been possible to erase the value questions entirely. Equality was also at stake because it was important for Russia to avoid the impression that it was the origin of the various cross-border problems. At the same time, Russia suspected that the EU benefits more from the joint achievements (Potemkina 2010: 564). Moreover, the area has been difficult for cooperation because of complex and inflexible bureaucratic structures.

The most important item on the agenda related to these issues, and perhaps one of the most important issues overall for Russia, was the goal of visa-free travel with the EU. As the discussion above testified, the visa dialogue can indeed be seen as an area of intensive cooperation, showcasing that interest-driven cooperation with Russia can lead to significant achievements, providing that a strong Russian self-interest is present. At the same time, the difficulties in bringing the process to fruition show that in this field too, a certain asymmetry of interests existed, with the EU being less than enthusiastic about taking the process forward and Russia becoming frustrated with the slow pace of progress. Russia regarded the issue as a symbol of the EU's true commitment to partnership, but the problems along the way also revealed the different readings between the EU and Russia when it comes to understanding the conception of 'political will' and what it entails – willingness to compromise or arduous implementation. As a consequence – and despite its vast promise and results – the visa question also became part of the negative background noise precipitating the dramatic rupture in relations over Ukraine, as a result of which cooperation in this field also became an immediate casualty.

Two broader issues underline these trends. The first concerns the increasingly divergent readings of the so-called 'shared values' in the domestic development of Russia and in the wider framing of EU–Russia relations. Here we can see a trend whereby Russia has increasingly moved away from and even actively challenged the applicability of norms and values to which it committed itself in the 1990s as legitimate starting points and benchmarks, in both respects. In addition, we have seen Russia turning the tables on the EU. Not only has it accused the member states of applying double standards and undue pressure against Russia, as well as towards other countries in the so-called common neighbourhood, but it has also advocated the view that Russia rather than the EU represents the true European values, reflecting the conservative Christian heritage. As a consequence, the EU has often been pushed onto the defensive when it comes to these issues, while it has effectively been hampered in achieving its own aims.

The second trend follows from the first but also stems from the actual practice of cooperation between the EU and Russia. Interaction and cooperation in the field of internal security especially requires a great deal of trust. Instead of building this trust, relations in this field have in fact suffered from and contributed to the lack of it (Hernández i Sagrera and Potemkina 2013). Here, the EU and Russia seem to be confronted with a chicken-and-egg dilemma, where the effective cooperation that would be of importance in generating mutual trust effectively requires more than a modicum of initial trust in order to take off successfully. Yet instead of generating that trust, cooperation in this field seems mired in mutual suspicion and mistrust, as exemplified by the mutual recriminations over the conflict in Ukraine.

Chapter 6

Security and Defence

The EU and Russia have been developing cooperation in the field of foreign and security policy, including defence, since the early 2000s. It is worth pointing out that security issues fell outside the remit of the PCA, and cooperation between the erstwhile Western European Union (WEU) and Russia in the 1990s was mainly informal and irregular (Assembly of the Western European Union 1998). In EU–Russia relations, this field started to be relevant only when the EU had first formed its Common Foreign and Security Policy (CFSP) and complemented it with the European Security and Defence Policy (ESDP, later the Common Security and Defence Policy, CSDP). In the Four Common Spaces initiative of 2003, cooperation in this area was defined as the space for external security.

Despite some clear common interests and natural synergies, cooperation in foreign, security and defence policy between the EU and Russia has not developed much. There were some high expectations in the early 2000s that the two could move rapidly towards positive developments in the field of security, but for several reasons very little of a concrete nature was achieved, prompting one of us to wonder back in 2004 'why the opportunity was missed' (Forsberg 2004). Russia warmly welcomed the creation of the CSDP, only to be subsequently frustrated by how it evolved (Merlingen 2012: 226). One problem was related to institutional questions as the EU could not offer Russia the status it craved in this area: Moscow wanted acknowledged decision-making, or at least shaping rights, whereas the EU was mainly interested in preserving its own autonomy as a fledgling security actor (Webber 2001). Despite common interests in principle in preserving the overall stability and security order in the wider European space, the cooperation was limited and strained when it came to actual problems. The parties were not able to establish joint approaches to the militarized crises in the region, such as the Yugoslav wars and the frozen conflicts in the former Soviet Union, as they held different views on these issues. At the same time, it was understood in the EU that the frozen conflicts in the former Soviet area could only be resolved if Russia was involved, and the EU did not want to set against it directly. Cooperation in security issues dealt with Iran and the Middle East too, mainly in coordination with the United States, and to a lesser extent with regional conflicts in Africa.

This chapter looks first at the institutional questions before moving on to the conflicts in the former Yugoslavia, Moldova and Georgia and the security issues in the Middle East and Iran. After that, the chapter discusses Medvedev's proposal concerning the European security treaty, before finally turning to the Ukrainian crisis. The chapter concludes that, once again, despite some progress being achieved in many issues during Putin's first term as well as during Medvedev's term, the actual fruits of cooperation remained scant and half-hearted. Yet, in light of the common interests that both parties have acknowledged and the mounting problems in the wider regional security environment, it is an area where it would be paramount to restore cooperation.

Institutional beginnings

The European Union started to develop its security and defence policy in the summer of 1999 (see e.g. Jones 2007; Mérand 2008; and Merlingen 2012). This policy was not launched with the Russian threat or its assets in mind: the attitudes towards enhancing European foreign and security policy did not seem to correlate with views of Russia (Russo 2016). The background of boosting European Union as an international security actor was related to regional conflicts and the need to have capabilities of its own for crisis management and a political profile distinct from that of the United States. The Kosovo war in particular exposed European shortcomings in terms of capabilities and inter-operability with the US forces, with some 85 per cent of the munitions delivered by NATO coming from America (Grant 1999: 3). Aspirations for a more independent and robust European defence identity did precede the Kosovo war, however, and sprang largely from the self-declared desire to manage the Bosnian crisis and the frustration that it caused when it did not turn out to be 'the hour of Europe'. The 1997 Treaty of Amsterdam had already incorporated crisis management into the Common Foreign and Security Policy, but the real kick-off for the process of developing defence policy in the framework of the EU was the Franco–British Saint-Malô Declaration of December 1998. This declaration set the bar rather high for the EU by declaring that it 'must have the capacity for autonomous action, backed up by credible military forces, the means to decide to use them, and readiness to do so, in order to respond to international crises' (Rutten 2001: 8). This ambition was duly confirmed by the Union at the EU summit in Cologne in June 1999.

At the time, Russia was generally seen as a valuable and in some regards even indispensable partner in security cooperation. The EU Common Strategy on Russia regarded maintaining European stability, promoting global security and responding to the common challenges of the continent through intensified cooperation with Russia as a clear strategic goal (European Council 1999). The European Security Strategy that was adopted in December 2003 emphasized joint efforts in finding solutions to various security questions and contended that '[w]e should continue to work for closer relations with Russia, a major factor in our security and prosperity' (European Council 2003: 14). Still, most key issues to be sorted out for the EU in developing its security and defence policy were internal, and the partners with which it most urgently needed to resolve the security relationship were the US and NATO as well as Turkey (Missiroli 2002; Bailes 2003).

Russia also saw many advantages in creating ties with the EU in security issues. Moscow had not paid much attention to the security and defence aspects of European integration in the 1990s and did not quite believe that the attempt to launch a common security and defence policy would change the nature of the European Union much, but when it seemed to develop, its potential role in undermining NATO was seen in a positive light. Russia's medium-term strategy on EU relations made this explicit by arguing that increased ESDP cooperation would help diminish 'NATO-centrism in Europe' (Russian Federation 1999). The partnership between the EU and Russia in security questions was not seen as a bad idea as such, and Russians were soon putting forward ideas for an action plan (Danilov 2005b). Analysts envisaged a host of joint interests in the area of security. Sergei Karaganov (2003: 23) argued that the EU's security and foreign policy was developing with great difficulty and was failing to meet the pressing needs of the fast-paced international environment, but '[i]t would be advantageous for Russia to work side by side with a European Union that acts as a more powerful and efficient partner in foreign and security policy areas' as 'most of our views and interests are similar'. Russia's interest in achieving rapprochement with the EU was, in Karaganov's view, also 'predicated on an increase in the efficiency of the EU's foreign policy, which could counterbalance that of the US'. Vitaly Zhurkin (2003) similarly contended that 'the general state of relations between the EU and Russia constantly demonstrates an identity and conformity of views and positions on a majority of present international issues'. Alexei Arbatov (2003) argued that '[t]he Iraqi crisis may facilitate a practical dismantlement of NATO on both sides of the Atlantic and construction of a truly European defence system in its place'. As a consequence, the security sphere did appear to be one of the most promising areas of cooperation on which to found a meaningful long-term partnership (Mahnke 2001; Rontoyanni 2002; Splidsboel-Hansen 2002a).

During the early years of the 2000s, cooperation in security issues started to take shape but did not yet have much substance. For example, negotiations over the possibility of the EU leasing longhaul aircrafts from Russia, as it did from Ukraine, did not bring results. Joint approaches to disaster management were also discussed, but ambitious plans remained on the table. The EU–Russia Summit in Paris in October 2000 was considered an institutional 'breakthrough' in EU–Russia security cooperation because Russia became the first non-member state with which the EU's Political and Security Committee (COPS) started monthly consultations. In the following year, in the aftermath of the 9/11 terrorist attacks in the United States, the emphasis was placed on terrorism. Half a year later at the Seville European Council in June 2002, the EU defined the arrangements for third-party participation in EU crisis management operations. The arrangements did not quite satisfy Russia, however, because the EU did not grant the country any decision-making rights on an equal footing (Council of the European Union 2002).

Security cooperation between the EU and Russia was given a further boost in the framework of the Common Space for Cooperation in the Field of External Security, which was agreed at the St Petersburg summit in May 2003 (EU–Russia Summit 2003). The parties declared that they 'have agreed to reinforce their co-operation in the area of external security as they both have a particular responsibility for security and stability on the European continent and beyond'. The road map accepted at the Moscow Summit in May 2005 defined five priority areas for enhancing EU–Russia cooperation: strengthening dialogue and cooperation on the international scene, combating terrorism, non-proliferation of weapons of mass destruction and their means of delivery, strengthening export control regimes and disarmament, cooperation in crisis management and, finally, cooperation in the field of civil protection (European Commission 2005). Michael Emerson (2005: 2–3) regarded the document as disappointing, particularly when it came to crisis management. The parties had held long negotiations on the content of the document because it was difficult to agree even on terminology, as Russia rejected the concept of 'common neighbourhood' (hence, the document refers only to adjacent areas), and the frozen conflicts could not be explicitly named. Indeed, the document revealed a clear asymmetry in readings concerning security between the partners: the EU was interested in crisis management in the wider European area, whereas Russia, for its part, wanted to put more emphasis on the fight against terrorism and preventing proliferation of weapons of mass destruction.

It is worth pointing out that, for Russia, cooperating with the EU in security and defence policy security and defence policy was always seen in the context of its overall perception of security and position in the international system. Initially, security cooperation with the EU was perceived in Russia as a means of counterbalancing the US by strengthening the UN and the OSCE and reducing the importance of NATO. The run-up to the Big Bang Eastern EU enlargement and the launch of the ENP in 2004 coincided with the high-water mark of European–Russian rapprochement in the field of security. In its opposition to the Iraq war in 2003, Russia relied on European partners and issued joint statements with France and Germany to that effect, including cooperation in blocking the UN Security Council mandate for the commencement of the war. This short-term success seemed to vindicate Russia's hopes of prising at least some of the most influential EU member states away from the US, while auguring a more multipolar world in the process. As the anti-war alliance of the continental great powers proved to be short-lived and did not in fact change the alliance loyalties in Europe in any meaningful way, the hopes of a European counterweight to the United States waned. Rather, Russia concluded that European states will ultimately side with the US on most security-related issues. As one Russian research report noted even before the Iraq war (Zhurkin 2001: 295):

> Attempts to view cooperation between Russia and the European Union as an alternative or a counterbalance to the policy of

NATO and the United States may be described as wishful thinking. Such attempts would have an opposite effect, that is, increase the Atlantic accent of the European policy and diminish the interest of the European Union in the development of a partnership with Russia.

On the other hand, it was not always clear that the EU was Russia's favourite partner in security policy and that NATO was to be counterbalanced. First of all, Russia's improved relationship with the US after 9/11 somewhat decreased its interest in European security cooperation as a mere balance-of-power strategy. Moreover, many Russians were disappointed with the pace of the developments and the bureaucratic complexity of the Brussels machinery that vindicated their initial scepticism. With the EU enlargement, they started to detect politically motivated attitudes in the EU against cooperation with Russia and a potential danger (Baranovsky 2002). As one Russian newspaper article (Sycheva 2002) stated: 'It is far simpler to deal with NATO and Washington' than 'with individual European nations and politicians, some of whom are openly anti-Russian', and, '[i]t is becoming convenient for Russia and NATO to be friends against the uncooperative European Union.' The Russia–NATO cooperation did not, however, develop any faster, and with the Iraq war, the Kremlin returned to anti-American stances (Forsberg and Herd 2015).

It was thus no surprise that the assessment provided by analysts on the security cooperation between the EU and Russia in the mid-2000s was rather disappointing: 'Plans exist but very little of real substance has taken place. Cooperation has been problematic and low profile – and frankly on a very small scale' (Monaghan 2005: 9). The Council Report on the implementation of the European Security Strategy in December 2008 noted that '[n]ew concerns have arisen over the so-called "frozen conflicts" in our eastern neighbourhood' and contended that 'relations with Russia have deteriorated over the conflict with Georgia' (European Council 2008). Yet the Georgian war did not change the EU's strategic outlook much, and the Russians still regarded the EU strategic concept as being close to their own but wondered why there was no place for cooperation with Russia in it. Indeed, and as Steve Marsh (2008: 195) noted, in a broad range of issues, the EU and Russia enjoyed a greater degree of at least potential convergence than either of them did with the United States.

The Yugoslav wars

The breakup of Yugoslavia in the 1990s constituted the most severe security issue and a test case for the European post–Cold War security architecture at the time. Russia had religious ties and traditional links with Serbia as its ally, and the dissolution of Yugoslavia was often compared with that of the Soviet Union, but the main issue at stake was Russia's status as a European great power without whose contribution and eventual consent such issues should not be resolved (Headley 2008). Yet there was no inherent reason why the Yugoslav issue would have created a conflict between Russia and the EU. The special relationship between Russia and Serbia was largely a myth, and the direct strategic stakes in the area were relatively modest. Nevertheless, the Yugoslav conflict had a major impact on the relationship between Russia and the West, although the major culprit from the Russian point of view was NATO rather than the EU. Nevertheless, cooperation between Russia and the EU in the area has since suffered from the same root problems instigated by the events during the Yugoslav wars (Andersen 2000).

At the beginning of the 1990s, Russia largely accepted the Western lead in managing the conflict in the former Yugoslavia and supported the key resolutions related to the conflict in the UN Security Council. Russia was also part of the great power Contact Group that dealt with the issue. Russia started to become more critical when NATO resorted to the use of military force, first in Bosnia in 1995 and then directly against Serbia in the 1999 Kosovo war. Russia condemned NATO's military involvement but was eventually willing to participate in the NATO-led post-conflict crisis management operations in Bosnia and Kosovo.

The Balkans constituted the key area where the EU regarded its role as that of a security actor, and it was willing to cooperate there with Russia. The first EU crisis management operation was a police mission in Bosnia and Herzegovina (European Union Police Mission [EUPM]) that was launched in 2003. Russia had been present in the UN's International Police Task Force and decided to continue its role in the EU operation when the task was shifted from the UN to the EU, with the goal of supporting the reform of the Bosnian police force. A Russian police contingent of 100 men operated under the EU command without special arrangements, but there was nevertheless a technical problem when the EU and Russia negotiated over the Russian participation in the mission, as Russia refused to sign the agreement in English and demanded a Russian version of the document. In the field of military crisis management things were more complicated, however, as Russia was not willing to participate in the EU's military crisis operation Althea in Bosnia at all, although it had been in the preceding NATO Stabilization Force (SFOR) operation before it was handed over to the EU in 2004. It nevertheless supported the mandate in the UN Security Council when the transfer of the operation was decided. In this regard, things changed only a decade later when, in November 2014, Russia abstained from voting in the UN Security Council to extend the EU crisis management operation in Bosnia. From the European perspective, Russia was not acting constructively, but rather was flexing its muscles and importing a tit-for-tat game from the Ukraine conflict to an unrelated issue (Jukic 2014).

Kosovo was also an issue over which the EU and Russia clashed, although it most directly affected Russia's relations with NATO. Initially, however, the key EU members wanted the EU to play a bigger role in managing the crisis, and that is why the peace talks were held in Rambouillet near Paris (the Bosnian peace negotiations were held in Dayton, Ohio, in the US). The EU's role became secondary, however, when the negotiations ended without a result and NATO decided launch a military intervention in March 1999. NATO's bombing of Yugoslavia without the consent of Russia and the UN mandate seriously damaged the relations between Russia and the West in general (Averre 2009b). Although the EU was not actively bombing, it supported NATO's air strikes politically, and of course, most of the EU member states were also NATO members, which cast a shadow over the EU too, at least from Russia's perspective. Under the German presidency, the EU nevertheless actively sought a diplomatic solution to the conflict that was achieved in the negotiations with Slobodan Milosevic carried over by Russia's envoy Viktor Chernomyrdin and Finland's President Martti Ahtisaari representing the EU.

After the mediated peace in Yugoslavia, a period of cooperation ensued. Russia participated in the NATO-led stabilization operation Kosovo Force (KFOR) in Kosovo, but it withdrew its contingent in July 2003. Russia remained, however, part of the Contact Group, which also consisted of Britain, France, Germany, Italy and the United States. Although the EU was not nominally part of the Contact Group, it backed it diplomatically, and EU representatives participated regularly in the meetings. The EU committed to the reconstruction of Kosovo by assuming responsibility for the macroeconomic reforms there under the authority of the United

Nations Interim Administration Mission in Kosovo (UNMIK). In 2008, the EU also launched a civilian crisis management operation, European Union Rule of Law (EULEX), consisting of police and judicial experts.

The biggest problem was, however, the question of Kosovo's independence (see Weller 2008 and Perritt 2010). In October 2005, the UN Security Council authorized the Contact Group to conduct formal negotiations over the status issue between Belgrade and Prishtina. At the same time, the UN Secretary General appointed former Finnish President Ahtisaari as a special envoy to coordinate the process. The Western policy community as well as a number of independent analysts had concluded that the status question had to be resolved because postponing the decision would only destabilize the situation. The EU members in the Contact Group differed slightly as Britain and France were – together with the United States – more outspoken in their support for the independence of Kosovo, while Germany and Italy were more reserved or cautious in voicing their positions and put more emphasis on Russia's concerns, which reflected Belgrade's position. Nevertheless, at the start of this process the group agreed on principles upon which the negotiations would be based, including the fact that the outcome had to be acceptable to the people of Kosovo, and that there would be no return to the pre-1999 situation (Contact Group 2005). It was implicitly understood that this meant the independence of Kosovo.

On the basis of the negotiations, Ahtisaari drafted his plan, which would have created supervised independence first and full independence after a transition period and referendum. The western members of the Contact Group believed that they had agreed with Russia that there was no sensible alternative to the independence of Kosovo, and the key question for Russia was therefore how to formulate the precedent in a satisfactory manner. Although Lavrov had agreed to the initial principles as a member of the Contact Group, Russia decided to actively resist the plan. Most likely, there was no disconnect between Putin and Lavrov in this issue, but Russia's position had either been badly misunderstood by the other members of the Contact Group or else Russia did not feel committed to the group as a whole. From the perspective of the other members of the Contact Group, Russia's behaviour was motivated simply by its goal to derail the solution (Perritt 2010: 257–8). In Ahtisaari's view, the problem was that Lavrov's stance was made public by the US diplomats, and this irritated Russia (Merikallio and Ruokanen 2015: 349–50).

Although Russia was defending a matter of principle in refusing to recognize separatist entities, calling Kosovo a precedent, it did not seem to be the core issue at the early stage of the negotiations, and it was not honoured when Russia recognized South Ossetia and Abkhasia as independent states in the aftermath of the Russo-Georgian war. Russia seemed to feel that in the Kosovo case the United States in particular was forcing it to accept an exception to international principles without proper deliberation or meaningful incentives (Ker-Lindsay 2011). During the process, Russian diplomats consistently emphasized Russia's willingness to continue the dialogue with the West, even though the gap between the positions started to widen. It was quite clear from his famous Munich speech in February 2007 that Putin (2007) was referring not only to Iraq but also to Kosovo when he stated, 'We are seeing a greater and greater disdain for the basic principles of international law' and a 'desire to resolve a given question according to so-called issues of political expediency'. When directly asked what he thought of Kosovo, he replied: 'If one of the participants in this difficult process feels offended or humiliated, then the problem will last for centuries. We will only create a dead end.'

Hence, when the resolution of the Kosovo status question based on the Ahtisaari Plan was brought before the UN Security Council in March 2007, Russia did not abstain, but voted against it. As the plan was not accepted, Kosovo unilaterally declared its independence in February 2008. The EU did not have a unified view of the issue: the majority of member states recognized Kosovo as an independent state, whereas five states (Cyprus, Greece, Romania, Slovakia and Spain) did not. Putin (2008) called support for Kosovo's independence immoral and illegal, regarded it as a deception, a policy based on 'double standards', and refused to recognize Kosovo. For him, Kosovo was a 'terrible precedent that will come back to hit the West "in the face"'. Sergei Yastrzhembsky (2008), Russian envoy to the EU, went further by stating: 'Only a blind person would not see the destructive consequences for Europe from the game being played out over Kosovo. We have warned the EU.' Lavrov (2008a) did not see any sense in punishing the EU, but he stressed that the Kosovo precedent could lead to a new conflict in the Balkans and would have serious consequences for international stability. Although the EU was often portrayed as acting under heavy pressure from the US, it was also seen as an aggressive actor in its own right and responsible for undermining the international order (EU–Russia Centre 2008).

Russia continued to criticize the EU in the process leading up to the independence of Kosovo, despite the fact that Serbia and Kosovo were able to normalize their relations on the basis of an agreement mediated by EU High Representative Catherine Ashton and concluded in Brussels in April 2013. Indeed, in the Russian reading of the situation, the Kosovo case as a whole represented a failure of multilateralism (Hughes 2013) and justified not only the independence of South Ossetia and Abkhazia in 2008 but also Crimea's unification with Russia in 2014.

The Transnistrian question

The Transnistrian question in Moldova constituted one of the frozen conflicts in the post-Soviet space, which the EU could not avoid tackling when it assumed more responsibility for its neighbourhood and was enlarging to the East. Transnistria – or the Pridnestrovian Moldavian Republic (PMR) as the entity calls itself – is a strip of land north of the River Dniestr in Moldova, bordering Ukraine, with a population of half a million. It had already declared independence in 1990 and achieved it *de facto* with the help of Russian military support in 1992 after a short armed confrontation. A peace agreement between Moldova, Transnistria and Russia was concluded, whereby the parties agreed to define Transnistria's final legal status at a later date. The conflict remained unresolved, and no UN member state recognized the independence of the breakaway area.

Initially, the Transnistrian issue was not particularly important for the Russian Federation, but the conflict that started in March 1992 and the involvement of the 14,000 men strong 14th Army massively increased its political symbolism. Russia's influence in the region became one of the key elements in its policy of its near abroad, with which the opposition forces challenged the liberal foreign policy of Yeltsin and Kozyrev. Although the conflict was more political than ethnic, the presence of Russia's army was seen as safeguarding the rights of Russian speakers as well as Russia's influence in the wider Balkan region. The commander of the Army, General Aleksandr Lebed, became a national hero in Russia and his slogan 'If the 14th Army retreats from Transnistria, then Russia has retreated' was widely quoted among the population (Socor 1993).

Until the early 2000s, the EU had not paid much attention to the Transnistrian question, regarding it as a matter falling more within the remit of the OSCE (Tolstrup 2014: 91, 131; Popescu 2011: 42).

The EU wanted to see Russia pull its troops out of Moldova in accordance with the commitments made in the OSCE framework, but otherwise it was rather passive and relieved that the conflict had not escalated. Yet, when the EU launched its security and defence policy in 1999 and the eastern enlargement was approaching (although Moldova's neighbour, Romania, did not join the EU before 2007), and the European Neighbourhood Policy (see Chapter 8) was about to be launched, this frozen conflict started to be discussed more often in various EU fora. In February 2003, the EU – together with the US – imposed a travel ban on the Transnistrian leadership, referring to 'the continuation of illegal activities and clandestine flows originating in Transnistria' and 'the continued obstructionism of the leadership of the Transnistrian region of the Moldovan Republic'. The EU urged both parties to engage actively in the peace negotiations but declared that the unwillingness of the Transnistrian leadership to change the status was unacceptable (Council of the European Union 2003). The possibility of sending EU peacekeepers to the region emerged as a topic at the Council deliberations. EU Institute for Security Studies researcher Dov Lynch (2003) also raised awareness of the issue and suggested the adoption of a joint approach with Russia to settle the conflict in Moldova. Such a joint approach was, however, rejected by Russia, and the EU abandoned the idea.

Perhaps the most dramatic episode in the Transnistrian conflict happened in November 2003 when Russia prepared a solution known as the 'Kozak Memorandum', and the EU, together with the US, torpedoed it. This initiative, carried out by the deputy head of the Russian presidential administration, Dmitry Kozak, was an attempt to resolve the conflict on the basis of creating a federation that would have given the Transnistrian federal subject a de facto veto power in all important matters of the federation, and would have legitimized the continued Russian military presence in the region. The initiative was clearly a Russian response to the increased EU activism over the issue, but it was also a unilateral attempt at sidelining the joint OSCE-based framework. William Hill (2012: 183), the American head of the OSCE mission, held that 'the Russian approach throughout the year was heavy-handed and clumsy, and thus almost bound to fail. More than seven years later I still do not understand how otherwise intelligent Russian colleagues could expect to get away with introducing the last-minute fait accompli of a long-term troop presence without provoking serious Western objections'. Indeed, the Russian plan did not succeed since, at the last minute, EU High Representative Javier Solana intervened and declared that the EU did not support it, which induced the Moldovan government to reject it. The case clearly highlighted the importance of the EU. Although it could not provide any solution to the protracted conflict – with its sanctions policy remaining rather ineffective for example – the episode showed that no solution to the Transnistrian problem was likely to emerge without EU support (Popescu 2011: 46).

The EU became more committed to stabilizing the situation in Moldova after the Kozak Memorandum incident. A key aspect of this policy was strengthening the Moldovan state structurally and economically, as well as channelling funds for civil society projects to the Transnistrian side too. Nonetheless, the EU realized that the conflict could not be solved without Russia's input, and therefore the tools that the EU chose were of low profile in order not to irritate Russia too much and avoid the internal tug of war in the issue between the member states (Popescu 2011: 48). In June 2004, when the situation was in danger of escalating again, Solana wrote to Lavrov asking him to 'persuade the Transnistrian leadership in Tiraspol to halt their campaign against the Moldovan schools, and to return to the settlement negotiations in the "five-sided format talks" without delay' (European Council 2004). In 2004, the Commission adopted a country strategy on Moldova, where it declared, 'The EU is actively supporting the process of settlement of the conflict with the separatist region of Transnistria, in full coordination with the OSCE' (European Commission 2004a). It stressed that Russia was tied to the commitments it had made in the context of the OSCE to withdraw its troops and ammunition from Transnistria. The country strategy was followed by an Action Plan that entailed '[e]ffective co-operation between the EU and Moldova towards a settlement of the Transnistria conflict', reflecting the Moldovan aspirations (European Commission 2004b). To underscore its commitment to solving the conflict, the EU also designated an EU Special Representative for Moldova, Dutch diplomat Adriaan Jacobovits de Szeged, in March 2005. In this context, based on Moldova's desire, the EU also became an external observer along with the US in the OSCE-led peace talks in the 5+2 format in which, in addition to the OSCE, Transnistria, Moldova, Ukraine and Russia participated. Moreover, in November 2005, the EU deployed a border assistance mission to Moldova and Ukraine (European

Union Border Assistance Mission [EUBAM]), based on a request submitted jointly to the European Commission by the presidents of the Republic of Moldova and Ukraine. The mission's task was to advise the authorities of the two states on best practices to prevent cross-border crime and improve the border and customs services, but in essence the purpose was to control smuggling and shut down 'illegal' Transnistrian trade (Dura 2009). Yet, in order to soften its nature and not to provoke the Russians, the mission was presented as technical support without executive functions and not as a crisis management operation, and indeed it was led by the EU commission rather than by the council (Kurowska and Tallis 2009).

Russia, in turn, was clearly frustrated and felt humiliated because the Kozak plan was rejected by the Moldovan leadership with the backing of the EU. The Kremlin duly started a campaign against Moldova, which included economic sanctions such as imposing embargos on Moldovan wine and food products, raising the price of gas and even turning off the delivery of gas for a short while in 2005. It protested that EUBAM excluded Russian and Transnistrian participation but tolerated the mission. In this situation, in September 2006, the Transnistrian leadership organized a referendum where 97 per cent of those who cast a vote supported 'the course towards the independence of Transnistria and the subsequent free association with the Russian Federation' (Electoral Geography 2006). Although Russia did not recognize the result of the referendum, it was less forthcoming in international efforts to resolve the conflict (Tudoroiu 2012). In his Munich speech, Putin (2007) assured listeners that 'we constantly discuss this issue with Mr Solana and he knows our position'. Putin stated that Russia was ready to work towards withdrawing its troops, but accused the US and NATO of simultaneously building new bases close to Russia's borders.

The negotiations over the resolution of the Transnistrian conflict in the 5+2 format that got underway in October 2005 but then halted for a while were initiated again in 2006 but did not yield any results in this fraught political climate and were continued on an informal basis only. Russia was not willing to change its policy, and the EU remained reluctant to assume a bigger role, for example by pressing Russia to accept EU participation in the peace-keeping mission, as it did not want to jeopardize its relations with Russia by challenging it directly (Popescu 2011: 60; Gordon 2012: 120). However, in the aftermath of the Georgian war, the EU and its key member states became more active and tried to push Russia to take a more 'constructive' attitude towards resolving the conflict. As is discussed later, this was regarded as the litmus test to determine whether Russia was willing to build a joint European security architecture with the EU.

During the Medvedev era, the conflict resolution in Moldova indeed progressed step by step in the joint framework, and Russia clearly worked towards a negotiated solution by putting pressure on the Tiraspol leadership as well (Devyatkov 2012). In February 2011, the 5+2 talks were duly resumed. The idea was to focus more on the practical issues instead of territorial status, with the aim of facilitating cooperation and forging trust between the parties to the conflict and their societies. Joint working groups discussed issues such as economic and social affairs, transport and telecommunications, and health and education. Lavrov signalled his willingness to compromise, calling for a 'new format for the peace mission' (New Europe 2011). He urged both parties to make concessions, stating, 'Transnistria's government must accept that the international community will never allow the region the formal status of an independent nation, while Chisinau for its part must accept that Transnistria must be semi-autonomous once it returns to Moldovan sovereignty.' In April 2012, the 5+2 talks led to agreement on the principles and the agenda for further negotiations. Acknowledging the progress, in September 2012 the EU lifted the travel ban that it had imposed on the Transnistrian leadership a decade earlier.

The Ukraine crisis, however, put a stop to this joint process, whereby both Russia and the EU had committed themselves towards a negotiated solution. The Association Agreement between the EU and Moldova had already complicated the situation, leading Russia to impose a ban on Moldovan wine during the negotiation process. The round of 5+2 talks that was scheduled to take place in April 2014 was postponed. Even more worrisome was the fact that tensions between the conflicting parties seemed to be increasing, and fears that the Ukrainian conflict could spill over to Moldova were palpable.

Georgia

The EU security policy towards Russia faced a severe test after the Russian military invasion of Georgia and its subsequent recognition of South Ossetia and Abkhazia as independent states in August

2008. Throughout the 1990s, the EU had followed a 'Russia-first approach' toward the Caucasus region and had little interest in involving in the region's conflicts, as the UN and the OSCE were already present and some of the member states also had diplomatic ambition to play a mediating role (Popescu 2011: 69). Gradually, and at least partly as a result of the 2004 Rose revolution in Georgia, the EU started to pay more attention to the area, was concerned about its stability and supported Georgian integrity against Russian pressure and interference. The EU repeatedly urged a de-escalation of tensions between Moscow and Tbilisi, which had intensified after Mikhail Saakashvili became president in the Rose revolution in January 2004, and demanded both parties re-establish a dialogue. But it was reluctant to take a greater role in the region: it refrained from taking over the OSCE border monitoring mission when it was terminated in 2004 and tended to overlook many minor incidents and provocations, such as the August 2007 missile incident, where an unidentified aircraft dropped a large air-to-surface missile that failed to detonate near a newly upgraded Georgian military radar station in the vicinity of the South Ossetian conflict zone (Bosse 2011: 136–7; Popescu 2011: 73–5; Cornell, Smith and Starr 2007). A lack of coherence with regard to the policy towards the region was clearly evident (Tocci 2007), but there were also instances that showed a certain level of commitment on the part of the EU. For example, when visiting Georgia in May 2008, Solana (2008) complained, 'The last Russian measures don't contribute to a lower temperature' and asserted that the EU was supporting Georgia: 'I came here in the name of the EU, to again show the friendship, the deep ties, which Georgia has with the EU.' At the same time, the EU leaders were also worried that Saakashvili might act too quickly and that his expectations towards the West were unrealistic.

The outbreak of the Russo–Georgian war in August 2008 came as a major shock to the EU and its member states (see Antonenko 2008; Asmus 2010). Many facts related to the conflict are still contested, but it started when the Georgian army launched a military operation over the border of the breakaway territory of South Ossetia on the eve of the opening ceremony of the Olympic Games in Beijing on 7 August, killing a number of Russian peacekeepers and, as Russia claimed, hundreds of civilians (Felgenhauer 2009; Fawn and Nalbandov 2012). Russia responded with military force the very next day by launching its offensive through the Roki Tunnel from North Ossetia and dispelling the Georgian troops from South

Ossetia. Within a couple of days, Russian troops advanced over the South Ossetian border towards the Georgian capital of Tbilisi and opened a second front in the west of the country.

The first European reactions to the Georgian war reflected some degree of disunity within the EU. Britain and many of the new Eastern members condemned Russia and called for international sanctions against the country, whereas Germany and some others tended to understand Russia's behaviour. France, which was holding the rotating presidency, was more cautious in passing judgement. In a matter of days, however, the EU swiftly reacted to the crisis and managed to broker a ceasefire between the conflicting parties.

It was indeed France rather than the EU institutions and the high representative who acted and organized the response. Foreign Minister Bernard Kouchner flew to Tbilisi on 10 August. Together with the OSCE chairman, Finland's Foreign Minister Alexander Stubb, he drafted a peace plan, received President Saakashvili's acceptance of it and then flew to Moscow in order to negotiate with the Russians.

Moreover, French President Nicolas Sarkozy also decided to play a role in the conflict mediation, and having also travelled to Moscow, he presented a six-point plan to Dmitri Medvedev, based on the Kouchner proposal on 12 August. The six principles were first, the non-use of force; second, cessation of hostilities; third, free access to humanitarian aid; fourth, withdrawal of Georgian forces to their normal bases; and fifth, withdrawal of the Russian military to the lines prior to the start of hostilities. The fifth clause included the much-disputed Russian claim for 'additional security measures' pending international mechanisms. The final clause called for international discussions on achieving lasting security in Abkhazia and South Ossetia. The reference to respecting the territorial integrity of Georgia that was part of Kouchner's draft was, however, omitted from the final French proposal. Medvedev accepted the plan on the same day with obvious backing from Prime Minister Vladimir Putin, who participated in the negotiations.

The modified plan was then accepted by Saakashvili, who nonetheless requested the removal of the sixth clause referring to talks on the future status of South Ossetia and Abkhazia, to which President Medvedev concurred. A key session of the UN Security Council was held on 19 August, where the Russian ambassador rejected the draft resolution presented by France because it insisted on respecting Georgia's territorial integrity and its internationally acknowledged borders. The Russian ambassador claimed that the French draft 'separated individual elements of the six-point "Moscow Peace Plan" and reinterpreted them for propaganda purposes' (UN Security Council 2008). Russia then circulated its own UN Security Council Resolution, reiterating, among other things, the view that the peace plan allowed it to implement 'additional security measures' before leaving Georgia.

Russia's recognition of the independence of Abkhazia and South Ossetia on 26 August was strictly condemned by the French presidency and other EU institutions (European External Action Service 2008). Moreover, the EU criticized Russia because it had neither respected the agreed six-point agreement nor begun to withdraw its troops in a timely manner. Some member states called for immediate countermeasures. Amid the turmoil, an EU emergency summit of foreign ministers was called in Avignon on 1 September. At the meeting, the EU member states decided to freeze the negotiations on a new cooperation agreement with Russia, but there was no agreement on imposing additional sanctions on Russia. The EU was also not willing to send armed EU peacekeepers to Georgia. Instead, the possibility of establishing an autonomous civilian monitoring mission in Georgia was discussed (Spiegel 2008). The EU summit decisions were regarded as favourable by Russia, with Putin commenting on the EU's summit by saying, 'Thank God, common sense prevailed. We do not see any extreme conclusions or proposals, and this is very good. We have a foundation to continue dialogue with our European partners' (RIA Novosti 2008).

Talks between the EU and Russian representatives conducted after the summit led to the agreement on Russia's military withdrawal from the Georgian territory surrounding South-Ossetia and Abkhazia and the deployment of an international monitoring mission. The EU Council decided on 15 September to establish an autonomous civilian monitoring mission (EUMM) of 200 European monitors in Georgia, which was swiftly deployed on 1 October (Freire and Simão 2013; Lewington 2013). Despite Georgian wishes, the mission did not include any US observers. The EU Council also nominated a Special Representative for the Crisis in Georgia, Pierre Morel, in addition to the Special Representative to South Caucasus, Peter Semneby, who was already operating in the area. Russia pulled out its forces in piecemeal fashion, and in October the European Union Monitoring Mission in Georgia attested that 'Russia seems to have completed most of the withdrawal' (EUMM 2008).

The EU Monitoring Mission (EUMM) monitored and reported on the ceasefire conditions on the border between Georgia proper and South Ossetia. It was unable to prevent minor incidents, but it contributed at least psychologically to the overall stabilization and normalization of the situation. The EUMM was, however, unable to fully utilize its mandate, as Russia was unwilling to grant the EU monitors access to South Ossetia and Abkhazia because the EU mandate – according to the Russian interpretation – covered only Georgia's territory. As a consequence, the EUMM has not been conducive to resolving the conflict and has acted more as a refreezing exercise (Popescu 2011: 90; Sinkkonen 2011; Haukkala 2013). In effect, it actually helped Russia to fortify its claim concerning the independence of South Ossetia. In this light, it is understandable that the part played by the EU was welcomed by the Russians. As Russian foreign minister Sergei Lavrov (2008a) commented, '[we are] glad that the settlement of the Caucasus crisis has provided a serious subject for our cooperation with the European Union in regional affairs', expressing his satisfaction that 'a European solution to the problem' had been found.

During the crisis and the subsequent negotiations, the EU introduced an array of actions that reflected more the model of an impartial mediator than a party to the conflict (Forsberg and Seppo 2011). It refrained from apportioning blame to either party for the outbreak of the war. A good example of such action was the EU-sponsored fact-finding mission to investigate the roots and causes of the conflict. The mission was led by Swiss diplomat and former UN special envoy to Georgia, Heidi Tagliavini, and the group consisted of legal and military experts from EU countries. The key message of the report, published in October 2009, was that the Georgian side initiated the conflict but that Russia was not an innocent victim (Independent International Fact-Finding Mission 2009).

The EU's capability to assume a more active role was limited. It clearly could not influence Russia much through freezing the negotiations on the post-PCA settlement because everybody knew that it was only a symbolic act and not a real effort to produce results. The EU did not consider wielding any heavier sticks in order to force Russia to withdraw its troops more quickly or to backtrack its recognition of the independence of Abkhazia and South Ossetia. Nor did the EU use its economic leverage to influence Georgia or the breakaway republics. It granted an aid package amounting to €500 million or thereabouts, but this aid was unconditional with no political strings attached. Essentially, the EU aimed at 'rebuilding confidence in the Georgian economy, boosting investment in critical infrastructure including energy and providing shelter, food, and other basic services to the internally displaced' (Ferrero-Waldner 2008b).

Relations between the EU and Russia were normalized at the EU–Russia Summit held in Nice in November 2008. The EU saw no further reason to freeze the start of the negotiations for the new strategic partnership agreement, because Russia had 'fulfilled a very large part of its commitments' with regard to Georgia. Russia had, however, not withdrawn its recognition of the breakaway republics and still maintained a small troop presence in Georgia in addition to Abkhazia and South Ossetia, prompting Lithuania to criticize the decision to normalize relations. That said, the atmosphere of the negotiations was deemed positive, and the main focus of the meeting dealt not with Georgia, but with the global financial crisis and its effects on both the EU and Russia (Schlamp 2008).

The role of the EU in the Russo-Georgian war was nevertheless highly valued by the EU representatives. Solana (2008), whose own role was minimal, nonetheless argued that 'the EU rose to the occasion. We have acted in unity, with determination and we have achieved clear results.' Jean-Pierre Jouyet (Jouyet and Coignard 2009: 88), the French minister for European Affairs, held that the Georgian crisis was as important for European diplomacy as the euro was for European economic politics. The EU Council report on the implementation of the European Security Strategy also highlighted the Georgian experience by declaring, 'Our Georgia mission has demonstrated what can be achieved when we act collectively with the necessary political will' (Council of the European Union 2009). In their report, the House of Lords (2008a) concluded, 'The EU was the obvious and perhaps only credible body to act as intermediary in the conflict, and acted with unaccustomed confidence and authority.' But the EU – or its 'strong Presidency with whom the Russians were prepared to negotiate' (House of Lords 2008a) – was able to play an effective role in the conflict largely because Russia allowed it to play that role, and neither the US nor the OSCE was competing with the EU in the mediation efforts. The success was often attributed more to France than to the EU (McNicoll 2008).

The Georgian war in 2008 thus constituted a mixed package of success and failure in EU–Russia relations. The ability of the EU to mediate the ceasefire between the conflicting parties when contrasted with the failure to deal with the Balkan crisis during the 1990s was celebrated (Whitman and Wolff 2010). Yet it should also be taken into account that the EU was not able to prevent the war in the first place, and the EU-mediated conditions of the ceasefire remained vague and not thoroughly implemented. Moreover, the EU was unable to restore Georgia's territorial integrity or bring the parties towards a more lasting peace. In Nicu Popescu's view (2011: 93), EU impact remained very low because too many member states regarded the conflict resolution through the prism of EU relations with Russia. The open question related to the conflict is, in hindsight, whether the willingness of the EU to restore relations with Russia so quickly, despite the key commitments not being fulfilled, sent the wrong signal to Moscow with regard to the EU's resolve.

The Middle East, Iran and Africa

The EU has worked together with Russia and the United States in trying to find a solution to three key international issues: the Middle East Peace Process, the civil war in Syria and the Iranian nuclear issue. Russia is a participant in the so-called Middle East Quartet, and with regard to the Israeli-Palestinian question the EU's positions have been closer to those of Russia than those of the United States. The US, in fact, has eyed the EU's role in the process with some suspicion, allotting it a role as 'chief financier' in managing the conflict (Siniver 2012: 88). This has contributed to the EU and Russia effectively 'finding each other' over the issue. To this end, they have issued joint statements on the Middle East, urging the parties to conduct political dialogue and supporting the two-state solution. Indeed, Russia's contribution has mostly been seen as positive by the EU.

This positive attitude towards EU–Russia cooperation did not extend to the handling of the bloody civil war in Syria that has been raging since spring 2011. The destructive conflict in the country gave rise to different strategic and normative perspectives on how to bring the crisis to the fore internationally and how to manage it. It was one of the key issues at the first EU–Russia Summit in June 2012, but when Lavrov was asked whether he expected the summit to narrow the gap on Syria, he told reporters, 'I don't think so' (EurActiv 2012a). An especially tough bone of contention was the question concerning UN legitimation for an intervention in Syria. The EU, and France in particular, were willing to explore all avenues for containing the conflict, including harsh condemnation of the Syrian government, imposing sanctions aimed at curtailing its ability to wage war on its people and entertaining the possibility of a military intervention to remove President Bashar Al-Assad from power (Giumelli and Ivan 2013). Russia, however, adopted a much more conservative stance, stressing the essential legitimacy of Assad and his government and resisting and blocking calls for a forced regime change in the country in the UN Security Council, effectively aligning itself with Damascus to the growing consternation of the key Western actors, the EU included. In the first instance, Russia's stance seemed to be principled, seeking to uphold the norm of non-intervention in the internal affairs of states (R. Allison 2013; Averre and Davies 2015). In October 2015, Russia changed its policy and launched a military operation in support of the Assad regime. EU foreign ministers criticized Russia for attacking not only the Islamic State of Iraq and Syria (ISIS), which was regarded as a common enemy, but also the more moderate opposition groups, and demanded an immediate cessation of Russia's use of military force against them. High Representative Federica Mogherini refused to characterize Russia's role as either 'positive' or 'negative', but called it a 'game changer' instead (Gotev 2015). Somewhat later, in a speech that she delivered in Strasbourg, she urged Russia to seek a political solution, arguing that 'Russia risks being trapped in another quagmire like Afghanistan unless it helps orchestrate a political transition in Syria' (Borger 2015).

The Iranian nuclear issue, negotiated in the E3+3 framework since 2003, included three EU states as well as the United States, Russia and China. Once again, Russia's input was deemed valuable, although there were differences of opinion between the EU countries and Russia. The Europeans would have wanted Russia to play a more active role as a broker in the issue. Yet Russia did not share the view that Iran was attempting to build nuclear weapons, and it opposed the EU sanctions against the country. Russia was no spoiler in the process, however, which ultimately and crucially depended on the bilateral US–Iran dynamics, despite the multilateral framework. In November 2013, an interim agreement between the negotiating parties was reached in Geneva. There were fears that the Ukraine conflict would spill over to this negotiation process, but few signs of a clash seemed to exist, and these primarily concerned the continuation of the arms embargo and restrictions on technology that could be used for missiles. Hence, the historic deal on Iran's nuclear programme was finally struck in July 2015.

Turning to other past, actual or potential areas of security cooperation between the EU and Russia, it is noteworthy that there have been very few joint activities with regard to conflicts and emergencies in Africa. Overall, Russia's policy towards this region has not been systematically developed (Schumacher and Nitoiu 2015). Russia abstained when the UN voted on the Libyan no-fly zone in March 2011, but so did Germany – the EU was not united in the issue. Russia did, however, provide four helicopters with 140 personnel to assist the EUFOR mission in Chad in 2008, right after the Georgian war. The negotiations over the support as well as cooperation on the ground were carried out professionally, and the experience was generally positive (Jozwiak 2008). Yet the Russians were not entirely happy, but complained that their participation was made unduly complicated (Ginsberg and Penksa 2012: 181). The EU and Russia have also coordinated their activities in fighting piracy in the Western Indian Ocean near Somalia.

Although conflicts in Africa and the Middle East were seen as being a potential area of cooperation already at the early stage of the ESDP, because they would not challenge Russia's view of its vital sphere of interests, they did not give the necessary boost for a security partnership (Herd 2003: 142). Sergei Lavrov (2011), for his part, expressed Russia's willingness to develop practical cooperation 'related to our ability to react properly and rightly to the unpredictable situations like the ones we're witnessing in the Middle East and North Africa'. Despite Russia's commitment to Responsibility to Protect (R2P) as a principle (Piiparinen 2014; Averre and Davies 2015), the normative basis for crisis management operations remained largely contested, as the case of Syria demonstrated, and Russia had only limited security interest in supporting the EU's crisis management operations in these more distant geographical areas.

Medvedev treaty proposal

Russia's dissatisfaction with the existing security arrangements in Europe, as well as globally, became evident when Vladimir Putin delivered his speech at the Munich Security Conference in February 2007. 'I am convinced', he declared, 'that we have reached that decisive moment when we must seriously think about the architecture of global security' (Putin 2007a). A treaty proposal for a new European security architecture soon became the dominant theme of President Medvedev's diplomatic agenda in Europe (Layton 2014). For Bobo

Lo (2009: 1–2), the timing of the proposal was no coincidence, but reflected 'a confidence that Russia was finally able to assume a more active role in international affairs, and that others – great powers and small states alike – must respect its interests'.

For the first time, Medvedev presented the idea of a new treaty in Berlin in June 2008. The proposal was rather loose and mainly repeated the idea that a new binding treaty was needed to reflect the notion of 'indivisibility of security', but the concrete principles upon which it would rest were not clearly spelled out. It was hard to escape the conclusion that the aim of the initiative was to resist the growing role of the US and NATO in European security (Diesen and Wood 2012). Although many rounds of discussions were conducted, diplomatic meetings organized in various settings and diverse issues ranging from nuclear weapons to human rights probed, there was not much progress, and the European reception remained rather lukewarm. Medvedev (2009b) nevertheless presented a draft treaty in November 2009 that affirmed the core security principles of 'indivisible, equal and undiminished security'. The main content comprised phrases that were already part of the OSCE agreements, and upon closer inspection the only exception was the idea that the treaty would prevent any further enlargement of NATO. The key article of the treaty, stipulating that countries are prohibited from enhancing their security in a way that actually harms that of another, was deemed too contentious and subjective by the Western counterparts (Weitz 2012). In her speech at the Munich Security Conference, Catherine Ashton (2010) argued that the OSCE should be 'the primary place for discussions on the Russian initiative for a European Security Treaty'. She indicated, 'We are open to discussing any idea that could enhance European security', but the discussion should be anchored to certain agreed principles: that states are free to join the security alliance they wish and human rights are part of the security agenda.

Despite their widespread scepticism, many European capitals did not want to ignore Medvedev's initiative entirely. One reflection of this was the so-called Corfu Process initiated under the aegis of the OSCE to discuss the issues – but not the initiative – raised by Russia, although it soon transpired that it was a dialogue of the deaf leading nowhere (Zagorski 2009; Herd and Dunay 2011; Cliff 2011).

Of its own volition, Germany decided to develop an alternative way to bind Russia more closely to the European security architecture without scrapping the existing principles. The bilateral meeting in Meseberg Castle near Berlin, between Merkel and Medvedev in June 2010, put forward ideas concerning Russia's tighter integration into the European structures. Merkel and Medvedev signed a brief memorandum on a joint EU–Russia Committee on Security and Foreign Policy (ERPSC) that would be chaired jointly by the EU High Representative for Foreign and Security Policy, and Russia's Foreign Minister. The purpose of the forum would be to exchange views on issues of international security and foreign policy and to establish ground rules for joint crisis management operations. The test case for cooperation, explicitly named in the document, was Transnistria. This initiative also dissolved, however, partly because the test case turned out to be too difficult and partly because Medvedev was soon replaced by Vladimir Putin. It is also important to point out that the German initiative was not greeted with enthusiasm by all the member states. Although Berlin had consulted Chisinau in the run-up to the summit, there was a feeling in many member states that their voices and interests had been sidelined in the process (Socor 2010).

Putin's return to the presidency in 2012 did not immediately affect the security relations between Russia and the EU. Russia was still signalling its willingness to deepen security cooperation with the EU. Sergei Lavrov (2013), for example, in an article that he wrote for the *Journal of Common Market Studies*, suggested that Russia and the EU could boost their military cooperation as a confidence-building measure. In his view, military-to-military working groups should become an organic part of the EU–Russia dialogue. Crisis management could be developed on the basis of equality, meaning that the EU would have no obligation to participate in crisis management operations conducted by Russia, and Russia would similarly have no obligation to participate in operations conducted by the EU. Yet these and other positive perspectives in the field of security seemed increasingly ephemeral in the light of the conflict in Ukraine that commenced in 2014.

The Ukraine conflict as a security issue

In the first instance, the main impact of Russia's actions in the Ukraine conflict on EU–Russia security relations has been to nullify those relations by freezing the dialogue between the EU and Russia concerning these issues. The dialogue, if any, has become dominated by the Ukrainian issue in the regional context, resulting in growing acrimony between the EU and Russia (see Chapter 2). At the same time, an interesting side development has been both sides' attempts to 'compartmentalize' the conflict in the sense that other issues of international security (Iran, Syria, North Korea, etc.) were cordoned off from the wider conflict dynamic. This is an approach that the United States has also been pursuing in its relations with Russia, and with some success, as exemplified by the Iranian nuclear deal already discussed.

At the same time, the lack of almost any meaningful EU role in the Ukraine conflict has been striking. After some initial EU steps, the handling of the crisis has been taken over almost entirely by key member states, Germany and France in particular, that have come to dominate the Western response to the crisis through their role in the so-called Minsk process and the Normandy group, also consisting of Ukraine and Russia (Juncos and Whitman 2015). Moreover, the tense situation has underlined the role of other actors and institutions in European security. The OSCE has once again been elevated to the main talking shop about European security, although its actual ability to settle the conflict has remained severely constrained by its strict unanimity principle. The rapid increase in Russian military activity in Northern Europe – but also elsewhere in the North Atlantic region (see Frear, Kulesa and Kearns 2014; Kearns, Kulesa and Frear 2015) – has prompted NATO and the US to reassume a much more visible role in European security by 'deterring' and 'containing' the Russian military actions in Europe. The re-militarization of European security has spelled trouble for the EU as it directs attention and processes in directions where the EU does not enjoy any significant comparative advantage, or even credible actorness for that matter.

None of this should be taken to imply that the EU has remained entirely on the sidelines in these developments. On the contrary, the debates about the role of the EU as a security actor in its own right have been gaining momentum. Perhaps the most spectacular opening in this respect has come from Commission President Jean-Claude Juncker, who, in March 2015, proposed that 'in the very long run' the EU should eventually form its own army to ensure the territorial defence of its members. According to him, a 'common European army would convey a clear message to Russia that we are serious about defending our European values' (EurActiv 2015). Juncker's statement remained, however, a rather separate output, as the majority of member states were less than enthusiastic about the proposal, preferring to revitalize NATO and the US security guarantees instead.

At the same time, the 'hybrid' or 'the full spectrum' (Jonsson and Seely 2015) nature of the Russian security challenge has meant that the EU has been seen as having some relevance of its own in responding to the potential Russian threat. In particular, the increased attention directed at societal resilience in withstanding externally directed destabilization has accentuated the EU's role in the debates. The EU's own 'comprehensive approach' (European Commission and the HR 2013) has made it in certain respects an interesting candidate to assume a larger role and a burden in countering the Russian tactics. At the same time, the actual results to date have remained fairly slim. One key deliverable in this respect has been the EU's decision to set up a small 'rapid response' team at the EEAS to counter Russian disinformation campaigns. Established in September 2015, the team of some ten Russian-speaking officials will pay special attention to the Russian destabilizing media influence in Eastern Europe and the Baltic region (Tigner 2015).

The EU's decision to enhance its ability to drive and counter information campaigns, particularly in the Russian language, aroused Russia's immediate ire. Even the EU's announcement of plans to create such a team was greeted by the MID as a reprehensible attempt 'to ostracize Russia from the international media stage'. In addition, Moscow resorted to the old Soviet trick – which itself is part of Russia's information assault against the West (see Snegovaya 2015) – of turning the guns on the EU by claiming that with these decisions the EU was, in fact, infringing on the 'fundamental and universally recognized right to the freedom of expression and its commitments to media plurality and the freedom of information' (Ministry of Foreign Affairs of the Russian Federation 2015).

Conclusions

Global and regional security questions can be regarded as a potentially very prominent area of cooperation between the EU and Russia. In the beginning, when the EU started to develop its security and defence policy in the late 1990s, there were promising signs that Russia could be tightly integrated into this cooperation, highlighting the idea of a 'strategic partnership': not only the EU but also Russia showed initial interest in such cooperation. At the time, the two did not consider each other threatening, and they identified joint security concerns such as international terrorism and regional conflicts in the neighbourhood, as well as supporting the stability of the international system in a general sense. The threat assessments in their strategy concepts were largely overlapping, focusing on international terrorism, the spread of nuclear weapons and regional conflicts.

Nevertheless, there were fundamental problems that soon became plain to both parties. The EU prioritized cooperation with the United States, and the institutional status of Russia in the framework of the Union's security policy decision-making was difficult to resolve in a satisfactory manner. The root causes of regional conflicts were interpreted differently, and particularly the emphasis based on democracy and human rights was not shared. The EU was not welcome to carry out crisis management in the area of the former Soviet Union, which Russia considered its sphere of interest, and Russia in turn was not willing to contribute much to crisis mangement in Africa, where the EU was active. The cooperation ran into problems at the practical level too, although the problems were not that often related to the military-to-military cooperation. The EU rules for cooperating with third parties were rigid and did not allow for the flexibility that Russia demanded. The underlying problem was often related to status. Russia wanted to be equal to the European Union in deciding and conducting crisis management operations, whereas the EU regarded Russia as a 'third party' on a par with other key partners (Forsberg 2004; see also Webber 2001). This proved hard for Russia to accept, although it would not allow outsiders to affect its own policymaking either.

All in all, the discussion in this chapter reveals the theme of this book. Despite common interests, the EU and Russia have repeatedly found themselves in a position of mutual frustration. The logics informing their respective policies have simply not been compatible. The EU has not been willing to irritate Russia in assuming a bigger role in the crisis management in the former Soviet area, but it was not able to persuade Russia to accept the EU approach either. One key aspect of the problematique has been the differing accents put on security. For the EU, security has entailed soft security issues and promotion of good governance and democracy. For Russia, the onus has been put on hard security issues and the inviolability of state sovereignty and spheres of interest – where the very principle of state sovereignty is often violated. These divergent interests and readings of security, evident well before the tragic events in Ukraine, have diminished the prospects of sustained EU–Russia security cooperation (Marsh 2008: 192). This basic incompatibility has resulted in a situation of growing suspicion and even mistrust concerning the very underlying motives and objectives of both parties, leading to a view of security as a zero-sum game and eroding the prospects of mutually satisfactory cooperation in the field of security even further.

Although the crisis in Ukraine has accentuated the role of the EU as a security actor somewhat, the conclusion must nevertheless be that it is NATO that will remain dominant in the field of security for the majority of member states. When the mutual defence clause of the Lisbon Treaty was invoked in November 2015, it was not because of Russia, but because of Jihadist terrorism. In all likelihood, this will entail that it will be the US and NATO and not necessarily the EU that will be the main interlocutors and objects of contestation for Russia when it comes to security issues on the European continent. It goes without saying that eventually a new *modus vivendi* will have to be negotiated between the West and Russia. Undoubtedly, this will give the EU and Russian security dialogue a new role to play as well. We return to these questions at the end of the book.

Chapter 7

Science, Education and Culture

Cooperation between the EU and Russia in the field of science, education and culture is an interesting field to look at because it represents 'low politics' – issues that are traditionally seen as less important from the perspective of political decision-makers – but also 'soft power' – tools that can wield general influence in politics. These issues are therefore not entirely devoid of political purpose and content. On the one hand, the field can be seen as an area where cooperation between the parties could be continued and extended despite political conflicts, as well as a potential vehicle for overcoming some of the barriers to 'higher' political cooperation. If the key problem in EU–Russia relations derives from stereotypical views of each other and a relative lack of practical experience of working with each other, then scientific, educational and cultural cooperation would be a functional way of enhancing the depth of the partnership. On the other hand, cooperation in this field can also be perceived as a one-sided and biased strategy to influence the views and images each has of the other.

EU–Russia cooperation in the scientific, educational and cultural field, known as the fourth of the common spaces, has been marked by achievements but marred by a lack of progress. It enjoyed its golden era in the early 2000s, when Russia joined the Bologna Process, but more recently all kinds of obstacles to cooperation have become visible. Initially, the models and principles advocated by the EU were seen as shared objectives, the ties expanded and clear results were achieved. Although more disagreements related to the shared norms and objectives in this field started to emerge in the 2010s, and cooperation was affected by the increasing tensions in the relationship in general, it did not come to a complete standstill due to the Ukraine crisis.

In this chapter, we first look at the institutional development of the cooperation largely related to the creation of the common space. Next, we focus the discussion on EU–Russia cooperation in research, education and culture in turn. Finally, we expand our analysis by examining the role that history and various interpretations of it have played in EU–Russia relations, as this has been one of the sensitive issues in this field of cooperation.

Institutional frames

Science, education and culture are areas of cooperation where many national and subnational actors interact, and their activity seldom depends on wider institutional schemes and framework agreements to any great extent. Hence, various programmes between the EU member states and Russia, partly dating back to Soviet times, already existed in this area before the parties decided to foster them in a more systematic manner.

This area of cooperation was already covered by the PCA, but the EU–Russia Summit in St Petersburg in May 2003 represented a landmark by creating a 'Common Space of Research and Education, including Cultural Aspects'. Indeed, the whole summit revolved around Russia's European cultural heritage, as it commemorated the 300th anniversary of St Petersburg as a European city. The aim of the Space was to 'reinforce people-to-people contacts, promote common values and contribute to increase the competitiveness of the EU and Russian economies'. The road map that was designed two years later reiterated these objectives and listed a number of largely technical instruments based on existing mechanisms for potentially developing and intensifying links between the EU and Russia in this field (EU–Russia Summit 2005).

EU representatives recognized the promise in this field and saw the expansion of ties as both natural and important. In his speech delivered in the Tretyakov Gallery, then-President of the European Commission Romano Prodi (2004) reminded the audience that 'the partnership has to embrace the whole of our societies' and that 'by widening and deepening contacts [the Common Space] will foster mutual understanding among our peoples'. Michael Emerson (2005: 3) opined that it would take a generation or two before the (Western) European and Russian mindsets could truly converge, and hoped that resources could be directed more towards educational rather than technical assistance projects.

Russian views on scientific, educational and cultural cooperation with the EU were rather positive throughout the 2000s. Mark Entin (2006: 33–8) described the cooperation on the Common Space of

Science, Education and Culture as being different from the political and economic common spaces as 'cooperation in this area is less vulnerable to political and ideological disagreements, with both sides seeming to recognize that it is a win–win situation'. Gennady Konstantinov and Sergei Filonovich (2008: 142–3) argued that the fourth common space was 'becoming not only an example of the rapprochement of Russia and the EU but also an example of effective measures to form all four common spaces'. Writing on the eve of the Ukraine conflict, Irina Busygina (2013: 64) still contended how the fourth Common Space 'may be viewed as the most promising . . . the least contentious, the most successful and most useful to both parties'. From the Russian point of view, the objective was not only to learn from Europe but also to enhance knowledge about Russia within Europe, because a major problem, according to Tatiana Zonova (2013), was that young Europeans knew little about Russian culture, history or politics.

However, in the years leading up to the Ukraine conflict, problems started to crop up in this field as well, with increasingly critical views being expressed on both sides. This clearly affected the lower levels of practical cooperation too, where interest in fostering joint projects waned. Nevertheless, neither side has entirely abandoned the idea that this area could serve the purpose of creating common understanding and preserving links, despite the difficult political situation.

Research

Research cooperation has been one of the most long-standing elements in the relations between the EU and Russia. Within the framework of the PCA, the parties already decided that 'a joint scientific and technological committee will be established, with the aim of increasing discussion and ensuring the smooth functioning of cooperation between the two' (CORDIS 1996). Since its establishment, the EU–Russia Joint Science and Technology (S&T) Cooperation Committee has met annually. Russian scientists also started to participate in EU-funded research projects, especially within INCO-COPERNICUS, a specific programme for international cooperation in the field of technological research and development.

The EU and Russia concluded a Science & Technology Agreement in 2000, which was renewed in 2003 after the common space was created. Cooperation expanded quickly as science and technology were top priorities for Putin's programme at the beginning of the 2000s. At the time, the EU and Russia were particularly active in matters relating to the European Space Agency (ESA) and the Russian space industry (European Commission 2000). In October 2001, the EU Commission signed deals with Russia on energy and space research cooperation during a visit to Brussels by President Putin. The agreements were seen as major achievements, fostering long-term cooperation in nuclear energy and safety, as well as space technology, between Europe and Russia (CORDIS 2001). Another step was taken in March 2003 when Russia was invited to the steering committee of the Global Monitoring for the Environment and Security (GMES) satellite programme, and the Russian Space Agency offered to make available the data from the Russian Earth observation satellites. The cooperation was lauded as a win-win situation for both sides as it would boost the industrial competitiveness of both (*Times Higher Education* 2003).

Scientific cooperation between the EU and Russia was subsequently furthered by creating a joint vision for research cooperation. The Joint Committee established working groups in diverse areas such as energy, food, life sciences, nanotechnologies and environmental research. One of these was the Working Group in Civil Aeronautics Research, established in 2007, which was seen as breaking new ground as it was supposed to have a common decision-shaping process aimed at creating closer mutually beneficial links between research agendas and researchers (European Commission 2012b). At the same time, Russia increasingly participated in the EU's Framework Programmes, ranking highest among all third-country partners in terms of both funding received and number of participating researchers (Sokolov, Haegeman, Spiesberger and Boden 2014). Scientific research and innovation were also one of the priority areas of the EU–Russia Partnership for Modernisation, established in June 2010 (The EU–Russia Partnership for Modernisation 2012).

Assessments of the progress in research cooperation remained fairly positive at the beginning of the 2010s, although the degree of optimism that prevailed in the early 2000s had waned. A review of the S&T Cooperation Agreement between the European Union and Russia, prepared in spring 2013, regarded the cooperation in science and technology as 'one of the most successful and promising areas in EU–Russia relations which provides strong positive signals to the general EU–Russia relationship' (European Commission

2013a). Although cooperation under the aegis of the fourth Common Space was considered successful, the review nevertheless paid attention to 'a number of administrative obstacles and fundamental barriers, which are hampering still more deepening, more efficient cooperation'. One of these was the fact that Russians were not able to access the European Strategy Forum on Research Infrastructures (ESFRI) and its road map, despite the competence on offer. Moreover, 'technical and administrative barriers such as customs and visa issues, and differences in administrative procedures of funding organizations' complicate the S&T cooperation in practice (for a similar Russian assessment, see Busygina 2013: 64).

In this conjunction, the Skolkovo technology village should also be mentioned. Established in 2010, Skolkovo was one of the flagship projects of President Medvedev's attempts at modernizing the Russian economy. According to him, the new venture was to serve as a motor for Russia's modernization, nothing short of creating a Russian 'Silicon Valley' that would radiate technological innovation throughout Russia (Kremlin 2010). Indeed, the initiative highlights a wider Russian propensity to focus almost exclusively on the technological R&D aspects of its partnership with the EU (Yurgens 2013: 69). Although Skolkovo has never been an official EU–Russia initiative, it has had repercussions at this level as well. One of Skolkovo's aims has been to attract Western, including European, high tech, know-how and investments to Russia. To a degree, this succeeded as a host of Western companies accepted the invitation. At the same time, the process was plagued by problems already familiar in the overall economic relations between the EU and Russia, one of them being the lack of continuity (Chapter 4 and Graham 2013).

At the same time, Russia set ambitious goals for its reform of higher education in its entirety. When it was reported that Russian universities perform poorly in the international university rankings, President Putin declared in December 2013 that five Russian universities should be among the 100 top universities by 2020 (Povalko 2015). Russians were also thinking how they could create an alternative ranking system of their own to measure the performance of universities more 'objectively'. Nonetheless, since internationalization was one key indicator of the international quality of universities, more effort was put particularly to international research collaboration and publishing. The government programme was not, however, particularly directed to boost cooperation with European countries but one key part of it was to attract Russian scientists abroad and reverse the brain drain.

One sign of the continuing mutual willingness to develop research cooperation was the fact that 2014 was declared the 'EU–Russia Year of Science' in conjunction of the EU–Russia Summit in December 2012. The Year of Science was formally opened in Moscow in November 2013 'as a platform highlighting the intense EU–Russia relations in the area of scientific collaboration' (Year of Science 2014 2013). It was not cancelled because of the Ukrainian crisis and the restrictive measures by the EU, but the events suffered from the lack of any high-level political attention. At the closing event in November 2014, the EU representative highlighted the strategic character of cooperation and the necessity for maintaining strong scientific ties with Russia. The Russian representative, in turn, explained that Russia had developed links with the Eurasian Union and BRICS countries (Brazil, Russia, India, China and South Africa) in scientific cooperation, but European cooperation attracted the most successful research teams. The Ukraine crisis did not play any role in the presentations at the closing event (Year of Science 2014 [2013]).

Despite the Ukraine conflict, scientific cooperation has also been carried out in other frameworks. An interesting link was forged between the ESA and the Russian Federal Space Agency, Roscosmos, in October 2015, when the two sides announced a joint project to send a probe to the moon to prepare for a possible permanent base on its surface (Ghosh 2015). For Russia, the project is a return to the Soviet Moon projects discontinued in the 1970s, but with an important twist that underlines the close links and interdependence between Russia and the Western and European scientific community. In the words of Professor Igor Mitrofanov from the Space Research Institute in Moscow and one of the lead scientists on the project:

> We have to go to the Moon. The 21st Century will be the century when it will be the permanent outpost of human civilisation, and our country has to participate in this process. But unlike efforts in the 1960s and 70s, when the Soviet Union was working in competition with the US and other nations, we have to work together with our international colleagues (quoted in Ghosh 2015).

Indeed, science cooperation remained the area that was least affected by the restrictive measures and the negative overall political climate. In June 2015, EU Research Commissioner Moedas asserted, 'We are working to maintain this important bridge to Russia, preserving a precious link through the common language and ideals of science' (Kelly 2015).

Education

The key areas of cooperation in education have focused on higher education: creating shared standards and recognition of diplomas, and fostering student mobility and multidisciplinary European studies programmes. Cooperation between the EU and Russia in education started as part of the TACIS programme and continued under the aegis of the PCA. In the 1990s, the Western-sponsored programmes and schemes were generally welcomed and indeed regarded as highly important amid the financial difficulties that emerged during the post-Soviet transition period of Russia.

The milestone in educational cooperation was Russia's decision to sign the Bologna Declaration in 2003. The aim of integrating Russia into the European Higher Education and Research Area through the Bologna Process met with resistance from academia, both from the national conservative circles, who feared that Russia would lose its identity, and from those who argued that common standards concerning academic degrees and curricula would lower existing Russian requirements. Yet there was rather broad political support for Russia to accept the wider European framework (Entin 2006; Konstantinov and Filonovich 2008). It was, indeed, framed not as an EU-centric project but as a truly pan-European process, where harmonisation was combined with an effort to maintain diversity and respect for the cultural traditions of the participating states. Entin (2006: 33–8) regarded the goals of the Bologna Process as paramount for non-English-speaking Europeans and Russian university students because having broad mutual recognition of university degrees across Europe and in Russia would open up new opportunities for young academics. Moreover, joining the Bologna Process was seen as 'a means to upgrade [Russia's] global attractiveness and competitiveness, and to capitalize on its most precious national resource, the human potential' (Pursiainen and Medvedev 2005: 21).

As a result of the Bologna Process, multiple joint study programmes, cooperative higher education institutions and exchange programmes for students and academic staff between Russia and the EU have been created and sustained. Russian higher education institutions, students and academic staff were integrated into the Union's Erasmus+ programme, which subsumed the previous TEMPUS and Erasmus Mundus programmes. The parties aimed at adopting comparable higher education degrees with similar credit systems (European Credit Transfer System [ECTS]), cooperating in the provision of learning quality and increasing the attractiveness of the higher education systems in Russia and in the EU (European External Action Service 2015b). Student exchanges evolved progressively, although only a small number of students could participate in the programmes. Nevertheless, the number of Russian students visiting the EU rose from 10,000 in the late 1990s to 30,000 in the early 2010s, the largest proportion visiting Germany. The Russian numbers were roughly on a par with the number of Chinese students in Europe (GHK Consulting and Renmin University 2011), two and half times higher than the number of Russian students in Chinese universities (13,000) and six times higher than in the US (5000). At the same time, the number of EU students who were studying in Russia remained on a very low level (under 2000), despite the official attitude being in favour of mobility.

The Bologna Process had an effect on the Russian system of higher education, impacting curricula, university diplomas and educational standards and quality. Yet these effects should not be exaggerated or generalized (Telegina and Schwengel 2012: 45; Esytina, Fearon and Leatherbarrow 2013; Gänzle, Meister and King 2009). Many indicators assessing the implementation of the agreement show that the results have remained rather modest. International educational cooperation is still burdened by bureaucratic factors as well as a lack of language skills. The ECTS system, although formally introduced, has been vague in practice in most Russian universities, while curricula reforms have been sporadic and the overall academic mobility limited. The mutual recognition of diplomas, programmes and courses has functioned best in the framework of bilateral agreements. Some of these issues were secondary for Europeans as, for example, the recognition of diplomas abroad was largely a problem for Russian citizens who had studied abroad, rather than a problem for Europeans seeking a job in Russia.

Although the tensions in EU–Russian relations started to increase in the mid-2000s, the field of education was not directly affected, and some very tangible forms of cooperation were established. One of the practical achievements was the opening of the European Studies Institute (ESI) in Moscow in 2006. The ESI was built on the basis of the Moscow Institute of International Relations (University) of the Russian Ministry of Foreign Affairs (MGIMO), together with the European Commission and the College of Europe. The ESI focuses on EU–Russia dialogue, teaching European studies with higher education standards adopted from EU universities, including postgraduate training and retraining of government officials and businesspeople (see MGIMO 2015).

Another notable EU initiative that succeeded was the setting up of a host of 'Europe Centres' in Russian universities. The Centres were the continuation of the Commission's previous programme to establish 'European Union Centres' in North America to encourage the further development of European studies. In Russia, the EU has established six such centres altogether, seeking a wide geographical distribution ranging from the Barents region in Petrozavodsk to Siberia in Tomsk and in between. The centres engage in several activities, including teaching European studies and conducting research on the topic, as well as acting as information centres and hubs for visitors and networking with other Russian and European universities (EU Centres World Meeting 2012: 19–24).

Despite these positive dynamics, cooperation in education has been turning into a field of competition as well. In this field, too, Russia is looking increasingly towards the east and trying to gain a better foothold in the Chinese educational market (RIAC 2014). Moreover, Russia is viewing higher education as an important tool for socializing its own younger generation, as well as the surrounding Eurasian space, into its own system of education and values (Mäkinen 2016). As a consequence, the use of English language in teaching has increasingly been discouraged and exchange programmes with the EU discounted, while the Russian language has once again taken pride of place as the lingua franca of the post-Soviet space, and attempts to attract students from the Commonwealth of Independent States (CIS) partners have been strengthened (Jokisipilä 2014).

Culture

Institutional cooperation between the EU and Russia in the field of culture began as early as the 1990s, but was intensified in the second half of the 2000s. The EU–Russia Permanent Partnership Council (PPC) on Culture held its first meeting in Lisbon in October 2007, where the benefits of cultural cooperation between the EU and the Russian Federation in the framework of the EU–Russia strategic partnership were highlighted. The parties agreed that cooperation in cultural matters would foster the creativity and mobility of artists, public access to culture, the dissemination of art and culture, intercultural dialogue and knowledge of the history and cultural heritage of other peoples of Europe. The cultural exchange was seen as an important channel for activating civil society and people-to-people contacts between Russian and EU citizens. The parties also underscored culture's role in creating common memory between the EU and Russia. (The Preparatory Action 'Culture in EU External Relations' 2015b: 31; Permanent Mission of the Russian Federation to the European Union 2015).

One of the key instruments in this field was the EU's Institution Building Partnership Programme's (IBPP) Cultural Cooperation Initiative, which, together with Russian counterparts, funded around 20 different grass-roots projects in 2007–9. The projects sustained NGOs, local and regional authorities, artistic universities, museums and other cultural institutions in the EU and Russia. Another round of the IBPP-Culture Programme was launched in 2010–12 in the framework of which the EU participated in a new set of diverse cultural projects (see The Preparatory Action 'Culture in EU External, such as Investing in People as part of the Development Cooperation Instrument - Human and Social Development (DCI-HUM) and Cooperation In Urban Development and Dialogue (CIUDAD), and the Non-state Actors and Local Authorities Programme for the Baltic Sea Region (see The Preparatory Action 'Culture in EU External Relations' 2015b: 44–5).

Cultural cooperation between the EU and Russia has also taken place at the regional level. The so-called Northern Dimension Partnership on Culture (NDPC) was launched in 2010 as the fourth partnership in the Northern Dimension policy (for more about the ND, see Chapter 8). According to a Memorandum of Understanding signed in St Petersburg in May 2010, the aim of the NDPC is to serve as a 'focal point for networks, projects and other cultural activities' in the ND area. To that end, the NDPC facilitates dialogue, promotes cooperation and provides information concerning cultural activities in the region, among other things, through its dedicated web portal (NDPC 2010).

For Russia, its key direction in promoting its culture and language abroad had always been the post-Soviet area, and lately these activities have been effectively incorporated as part of its foreign policy (Putin 2013b). Russia intended to increase the budget of *Rossotrudnichestvo*, a federal agency that maintains Russia's influence in the Commonwealth of Independent States (Armenia, Azerbaijan, Belarus, Kazakhstan, Kyrgyzstan, Moldova, Russia, Tajikistan and Uzbekistan), from about 45 to 220 million euros by 2020. The agency is also working together with the Ministry of Education and Science to promote Russian language and culture around the world. With its cultural heritage, Russia tries to influence 'brother nations', seeking to create a 'we-feeling' among ethnic Russians and beyond that it can use to mobilize support and even put pressure on some of the countries in its immediate vicinity (Saari 2014). The Kremlin's attempts at using cultural cooperation to engage the Russian diaspora have not been entirely confined to the post-Soviet space, but have also employed the same methods to mobilize its compatriots in EU countries, such as Britain (Byford 2012). The results have, however, been anything but unequivocal, casting doubt on whether ethnic Russians living abroad can be considered a homogenous group to begin with.

From the Russian perspective, cultural cooperation was not thwarted by the growing value gap and political clashes between Russia and the EU. Russia regarded itself as a cultural leader in Europe, and the cooperation on cultural matters as a means of paving the way for further economic and political cooperation. Improving the mutual knowledge and understanding of each other's culture would be crucial for strengthening the shared European identity. Yet, in its state cultural policy, Russia adopted a very restricted view of what passes for Russian culture, cautioning against forms of culture and art that diverge from 'traditional values' and promoting the slogan that 'Russia is not Europe' (Golubock 2014).

For the EU, indeed, the cooperation on culture with Russia started to look more challenging, and a downward turn after 2012 was noted in the official documents. The fact that Russia had not ratified the 2005 UNESCO Convention on the Protection and Promotion of the Diversity of Cultural Expressions was particularly problematic from the point of view of the EU, since it regarded the Convention as the key framework for its external action dealing with cultural matters (The Preparatory Action 'Culture in EU External Relations' 2015b: 18).

The EU's most recent funding programme, Creative Europe, does not include any projects in Russia. This is a remarkable change compared to the earlier cultural policy in the Commission's funding. The EU-funded initiative, Preparatory Action 'Culture in EU External

Relations', published a report about culture as a part of the EU's foreign policy. The report (The Preparatory Action 'Culture in EU External Relations' 2015a), while still naming Russia as a Strategic Partner of the EU, found that Russia's way to take culture into account in its foreign policy had changed during the last few years. According to the report, Putin's government has built a cultural strategy for Russian foreign policy that aims at transforming Russia into a 'great and famous culture' in a way that can be construed as propaganda, or bordering on it (for a detailed account of Russian methods, see Sherr 2013: 87–91 and 109–12). The report claimed that Russia's instrument in this cultural policy is the government-sponsored international RT television channel that the Kremlin is actively using (The Preparatory Action 'Culture in EU External Relations' 2015b: 3–4). Perhaps the most problematic finding of the report was this:

> The Russian government has a top-down approach to culture and rarely enters into a dialogue with its citizens on the formulation of cultural policy. In general, the Ministry of Culture and the Ministry of Foreign Affairs are not very popular and are strongly criticised by civil society. Cooperation with foreign NGOs and Russian NGOs receiving foreign funds does not operate smoothly either, as their freedom to operate in Russia has been tightened. All these NGOs need to be registered as 'foreign agents' and cannot apply for government funding. (The Preparatory Action 'Culture in EU External Relations' 2015b: 3–4)

Hence, cultural cooperation has also suffered from the general trend of mutual suspicion and sense of incompetence in the field. The more politicized the field of culture became in the relations, the less it reflected the attitude that low politics could facilitate cooperation in other areas.

Politics of history and collective memory

History, although in most orations seen as a unifying Russia and the EU, has also been a thorny subject between them. This is because collective memories between Russia and many of the new eastern member states, in particular, have clashed. Russia's relations have been largely unaffected by historical problems, or they have been practically resolved with most of the Western European countries, including countries such as Germany and Finland, which fought against the Soviet Union in WWII; but they have been more strained, even contested, with former Soviet camp members such as Poland and the Baltic states. The participation of heads of state in the commemorations in Moscow to mark the anniversaries of the Soviet victory over Nazi Germany and the end of WWII in Europe are indicative of the degree to which the historical problems related to the war still exist between Russia and European countries.

The standard account of how Russia has been dealing with its past is that Mikhail Gorbachev made the first moves towards addressing the historical problems, but resolving them was not at the top of his perestroika agenda. By contrast, Boris Yeltsin distanced Russia more radically from the wrongdoings of the Soviet Union and condemned them without reservation. During Yeltsin's second term as president, Russia started to move into a more conservative and nationally self-conscious direction that integrated the Soviet past more closely with Russian national pride. This also meant a decreased willingness to admit the historical culpability of the Soviet Union, in particular in relation to WWII, as the Great Patriotic War served a key role in building the new Russian identity. This trend continued when Vladimir Putin became president in 2000. There was a clear movement towards more conservative interpretations of history – effectively sanitizing it and glorifying the Soviet Union, according to critics (Sherlock 2011; Koposov 2011). This trend was most visible in the teaching of history, but the need to defend the Soviet account of the past also influenced public debate and research. An overwhelming majority, 90 per cent of Russians, rejected the idea that Russia should acknowledge that the Soviet Union was a criminal state that committed genocide against its own people and was responsible for starting the Second World War (Krizhanskaya 2011). Some civil society and human rights organizations, such as Memorial, have tried to raise the difficult history issues of the Stalin era on the political agenda, but only during the Medvedev presidency was the idea of reconstituting and modernizing the Russian identity through re-evaluating the Soviet past articulated more prominently and afforded wider attention.

The Western European countries that had fought along with the Soviet Union against Nazi Germany tended to ignore the Soviet role in the war rather than objecting to Russian interpretations of it. History disputes with Russia came on the EU agenda only after the eastern enlargement, and were politicized mainly by the European Parliament. In April 2009, it adopted a resolution on

'European Conscience and Totalitarianism', which called for the proclamation of 23 August, the date of the Molotov–Ribbentrop Treaty between the Soviet Union and Nazi Germany, concluded in 1939, as a Europe-wide Day of Remembrance for the victims of all totalitarian and authoritarian regimes; and called on the European public to commemorate these victims with dignity and impartiality. The Parliament then visibly commemorated the 70th Anniversary of the Pact in 2009. The national-conservative Union for Europe of the Nations (UEN) group of the European Parliament sponsored a controversial documentary, *The Soviet Story*, directed by Edvīns Šnore in 2008, which advanced the argument that the Soviet Union and Nazi Germany and their corresponding ideologies, communism and Nazism, shared many similarities and had close political connections before WWII (Jutila 2016).

In response, Russia started to vigorously defend the Soviet Union in the face of historical accusations from abroad in particular, accusing others of misinterpreting history (Benn 2011). For example, although otherwise seen as liberal in his worldview, President Medvedev decided to establish an Orwellian-sounding Commission to Prevent the Falsification of History to the Detriment of Russia's Interests. Yet Putin and Medvedev were also willing to selectively re-address historical problems that burdened Russia's relations to the neighbouring countries, albeit without overly compromising the prevailing political ethos in Russia that underlined pride in the achievements of the country and its people, especially in WWII. Medvedev, in particular, was sometimes willing to open the gates to a reinterpretation of the Soviet past. He declared in his speech on the day of political repression in 2009 that remembering the dark pages of Russia's history was as important as remembering its moments of glory. As Medvedev contended: 'Accepting our past the way it is – this is mature citizenship. It is just as important to study our past, overcoming indifference and desire to forget its tragic aspects' (RT 2009). The Russian-Polish Group on Difficult Issues that was reactivated in 2009 and delivered its report in 2010 is perhaps the most prominent example of the attempts to write shared history jointly (Rotfeld and Torkunov 2015). Such attempted changes in Russia's policy of history towards its neighbours can be seen as resulting from the idea of reworking history for domestic purposes, but it also went hand in hand with the need to improve relations with the neighbouring EU member states. As Dmitri Trenin (2011a: 232) argued, 'Russia can do much more to promote reconciliation with its neighbours: it can start by acknowledging crimes committed by Stalin against all the people of the Soviet Empire starting with the Russian people'. 'It can win many hearts through genuine signs of compassion'. Yet the trend was, in fact, the reverse: the historical justification for the annexation of Crimea reflected the attitude that interpretations of history are both nationally sensitive and politically loaded.

Conclusions

Scientific, educational and cultural cooperation between the EU and Russia expanded quickly after the dissolution of the Soviet Union. The key achievement in this field was Russia's entry to the pan-European Bologna Process, despite problems in its implementation. Scientific cooperation, educational exchange as well as the number of joint cultural projects grew steadily after the early 1990s, but to a certain extent they too fell victim to the growing tensions in EU–Russia relations. The Russian growing self-consciousness that manifested in the aim of developing joint schemes on a more equal footing was not a problem as such, as the Russians also willingly paid their share of the cooperation. However, the EU wanted to put emphasis on the low politics cooperation that would help to create a more 'European' civil society in Russia, whereas Russia started to view any cooperation that it could not directly control with increasing suspicion. Russia duly created its own cultural policy, distanced itself from Europe and increasingly viewed research, higher education and culture as a competitive field. One particularly sensitive question has dealt with interpretations of history and collective memories that have been politicized on both sides.

The crisis in Ukraine and the sanctions imposed by the EU against Russia did not bring this cooperation in science, education and culture to a complete standstill, but it has become more difficult and limited in its scope. The problem can be partly attributed to the political climate, which discourages joint projects, but also to bureaucratic uncertainties as well as some very concrete restrictions concerning travel, which have served to slow down cooperation. Nevertheless, the belief that links in this field are important is still preserved and serves as a legitimation for fostering various people-to-people contacts. There is perhaps not enough genuine grass-roots pressure that the successful examples of cooperation would currently radiate to other areas, but even small achievements are interpreted as positive signs on both sides.

Chapter 8

The 'Common Neighbourhood' and Regional Cooperation

The question of a 'common neighbourhood' – that is, the countries residing between the EU and Russia – and the interaction of the policies the EU and Russia have adopted for their respective neighbourhoods, is one of the most difficult and pressing issues in EU–Russia relations (Averre 2009a; Carnap and Trotskyi 2014; Bechev 2015; Smith 2015). It was, indeed, where the clash in 2014 between the EU and Russia took place, and that is why it is essential to ask whether the divergent and incompatible views concerning the region were, in fact, the root cause or just a symptom of the deepened conflict between the two.

The question of a 'common neighbourhood' is closely intertwined with the question of EU enlargement. As already noted in Chapter 2, the issue of EU enlargement has been historically contentious, but not always equally so. During the Cold War, the Soviet Union viewed enlargement with suspicion and even outright hostility. During the 1990s, the Russian Federation approached the topic in a much more relaxed manner, even flirting at times with its own eventual membership in the Union, but it helped that the former states of the Soviet Union, apart from the Baltic states, were not intent upon becoming EU members. Since the early 2000s, however, the debate has taken an increasingly fractious turn, as the EU approached what Russia regarded as its vital zone of interests. The shared neighbourhood was thus part and parcel of the wider deterioration of relations between the EU and Russia while increasingly becoming an independent factor contributing to the continued downward spiral of relations in its own right.

The successive rounds of enlargements are indeed key to understanding a good deal of the essential dynamic, both positive and negative, between the EU and Russia. In the first instance, the process of the EU's rapid post–Cold War enlargement has resulted in the current situation whereby previously physically far-removed partners have, in fact, become close neighbours: Since the accession of Finland in 1995, the two have shared a common physical land border, a feature that was significantly expanded in the 2004 Big Bang Eastern enlargement. But the impact of enlargement on the EU's external relations obviously extends far beyond geography. In general terms, enlargements have always affected the EU's international role and relations with partners (Allen 1998; Preston 1997: Ch. 8). Therefore, it is only natural that the repeated accession of new members had an impact on EU–Russia relations in several respects. As already discussed in Chapter 4, it has increased the economic stakes between the two. It has also affected the image the two have of each other. In the case of the EU, the accession of former Soviet satellites resulted in a more critical edge emerging in the internal debates and even in certain EU-level policies – although a certain element of moderation and convergence of positions has also been notable in recent years (see Chapter 3). As a consequence, there has been a process of 'customization' (Ojanen 1999) of the EU's Eastern policies, whereby some member states with specific interests have sought to shape the Union's external agenda in the East. None of these developments have gone unnoticed in Russia which, as becomes clear below, has taken an increasingly critical stance on both the EU's Russia policy and its increasing role and ambitions in Eastern Europe under the aegis of the European Neighbourhood Policy (ENP) and the Eastern Partnership (EaP) (see also Haukkala 2013).

This chapter does not, however, dwell on the question of EU enlargement any further. Instead, it analyses the policies the EU and Russia have adopted for their respective neighbourhoods, as well as examines their interaction in what has been dubbed by the EU as 'the common neighbourhood' in Eastern Europe, which includes the countries residing in between Russia and the enlarged EU – Belarus, Moldova and Ukraine – as well as the countries of the Southern Caucasus, Armenia, Azerbaijan and Georgia. But the common neighbourhood is not the only regional facet of EU–Russia relations. Hence this chapter also discusses other forms of regional cooperation, such as cross-border cooperation, the Northern Dimension (ND) as well as the role of the Arctic, Baltic and the Black Sea cooperation in EU–Russia relations. Here we see, perhaps somewhat surprisingly, that although the common neighbourhood has become a flashpoint between the EU and Russia, some other forms of regional cooperation have fared much better. The ND in particular deserves to be analysed at some length as it reflects some key characteristics and themes in wider EU–Russia relations while also representing one area where cooperation has been ongoing despite other serious problems, and even crises, in relations.

The discussion in this chapter proceeds via four stages. First, the development of the EU approach towards its Eastern neighbourhood is discussed, followed by a similar treatment concerning Russia. After that, the role of the neighbours themselves is briefly added to the mix. We then move on to the other facets of regional cooperation before the chapter ends with some conclusions concerning the impact that the interaction over the common neighbourhood has had, and can be expected to have, on the evolution of wider relations between the EU and Russia.

The EU approach towards its Eastern neighbourhood

The question of a 'common neighbourhood' between the EU and Russia emerged in the early 2000s in the advent of the Big Bang Eastern enlargement that took place in 2004. By and large, the EU approach towards its neighbourhood has been in gestation since then, reflecting both the political tug of war within the enlarged Union as well as the pre-existing mindsets and policy templates developed by the EU during the post–Cold War era. Indeed, with the accession of Poland and other Central and Eastern Europeans, the EU acquired, first, a set of new neighbours that presented it with a host of fresh challenges and, second, a group of new member states with interests and new ideas for the development of EU relations with that area. As a consequence, for the first time, the EU acquired a direct stake in the volatile dynamics of Eastern Europe, including the Southern Caucasus, as well as an internal imperative to develop appropriate policy responses towards the countries. In addition, the EU was also faced with the pressing question of how to deal with calls for accession that started to emerge from the forthcoming 'new neighbours'. For example, both post-Rose revolutionary Georgia and Orange Ukraine were pressing hard for full accession perspectives. For the EU, however, enlargement had to all intents and purposes become a veritable perpetual motion engine, a fact not all the member states and wider public were equally comfortable with (Dangerfield 2011).

It is against this backdrop that the emergence of the European Neighbourhood Policy in 2003 should be examined. It is hardly a coincidence that the essential blueprint for the new ENP was launched prior to the emergence of both new members and neighbours. It was an attempt, and a successful one at that, by the 'old' members to set the agenda and ensure that the new policy would not overstretch matters in terms of promises made concerning future enlargements in particular. More generally, the adoption of the ENP can be seen as having had a fourfold function for the Union: First, it was an attempt both to placate as well as anticipate and defuse the demands of the new Central and Eastern European member states for a new and robust neighbourhood policy towards the East. In this respect, one need not be a conspiracy theorist to understand that the fact that the adoption of the ENP preceded the Big Bang enlargement was hardly a coincidence: it was a deliberate move on the part of some key member states to take the initiative in the development of ties with the Eastern neighbours in order to control and contain the process that was in any case forthcoming.

Second, the ENP was meant to balance the interests between the Eastern and Southern neighbourhoods by bringing them under the common rubric of a single policy template (the Southern neighbourhood is not discussed further on this occasion; see Schumacher and Bouris 2016 for more). Third, the ENP was an attempt to devise an alternative to further enlargements of the Union. Instead of full integration and institutional immersion, the 'neighbours' were offered wide-ranging cooperation and association. Fourthly, it was an attempt at (re-)injecting the Union's normative agenda and the application of conditionality more strongly into the relations with non-candidate countries as well. As such, and taken together, the ENP was a conscious attempt at squaring the circle of relinquishing enlargement and retaining the Union's normative power in Eastern Europe while controlling and perhaps even curtailing the internal dynamics concerning the issues within the post-enlargement EU itself. Indeed, one noteworthy aspect of the ENP is that a good many Eurocrats tasked with developing the new policy template were, in fact, people made largely redundant by the successful completion of the Eastern enlargement. Keeping this in mind, it is hardly surprising that in several key respects the ENP has come to resemble the accession process – with one key difference: the golden carrot of full EU accession (Missiroli 2004) was not at any point seriously on the table.

All in all, the EU's policies towards its new Eastern neighbours were largely predicated on the same integrationist and essentially post-sovereign approach already discussed in Chapter 2. At the heart of the ENP has been the EU's offer of enhanced relations and closer integration based on shared values between the Union and its neighbours. The mechanism was simple: in return for effective implementation of reforms (including aligning significant parts of national legislation with the EU *acquis*), the EU would grant closer economic integration and association with its partners. The approach has been twofold, as the EU wanted first to tap the full potential of the already existing PCAs, namely the gradual harmonization of legal norms with the EU *acquis* and the creation of free trade, and only then move towards a set of new 'neighbourhood agreements' that would include a deep and comprehensive free trade area (DCFTA) as well as the prospect of closer political association with the Union.

The ENP envisaged a process based on clear differentiation between countries and regular monitoring of progress. It is, however, here that the Union's attempt at normative hegemony also in its neighbourhood becomes clearly visible, as the process is built on a set of bilateral relationships between the individual neighbours and the EU. Scholars seem to be in agreement that this has been a deliberate choice on the part of the Union to maximize its leverage over the neighbours (Dannreuther 2006; Haukkala 2008; J. Kelley 2006; Sasse 2008). Therefore, to all intents and purposes the Union, especially in the early stages of the ENP, did not give much meaningful say to the neighbours in setting the normative agenda: the objectives and the means were non-negotiable, and the only time that the partners were consulted was when individual action plans with benchmarks and timetables were being agreed. As such, the Union was offering (or withholding) economic benefits depending on the neighbours' ability and willingness to implement the Union's normative agenda, and the EU was willing to give its neighbours influence basically only over *when* they wanted to implement the Union's demands and not *how* that was to be done (Bicchi 2006).

The ENP has also included an aid component. The main instrument is the European Neighbourhood and Partnership Instrument (ENPI, currently the European Neighbourhood Instrument ENI) that was introduced in 2007 and replaced the TACIS funding in Eastern Europe. The budget for the Financial Framework 2007–13 was €12 billion, and for the period 2014–20, €15 billion, showing a steady, although by no means dramatic, increase in resources. This is a substantial amount of financial resources, although it pales in comparison with the scale of challenges and expectations in the region. It is also a far cry from the resources the EU has devoted to the countries with clear accession perspectives, be it the Central and Eastern European countries (CEECs) in the 1990s or the countries of the former Yugoslavia in the 2000s.

Although the EU itself has been convinced about the credentials of its initiative, the neighbours themselves have been less impressed (Bengtsson 2010; Bechev and Nicolaïdis 2010). Ukraine has been a case in point, repeatedly voicing its frustration over the lack of credible accession prospects as well as the negligible level of market access and economic aid coming from the Union (Haukkala 2008; Sasse 2008). At the same time, the lack of any serious progress in reforms in many of the neighbours has made it fairly easy for the Union to defer from making any further concessions. Nevertheless, to allay some of the criticisms, the EU launched the EaP in 2009. At the same time, it is worth bearing in mind that much of the motivation for the Polish–Swedish initiative was, in fact, EU internal, as the EaP was mooted as a counterweight to the Union for the Mediterranean, an initiative that was launched unilaterally by French President Nicolas Sarkozy during the French EU presidency in 2008.

Compared to the ENP, the main innovation in the EaP was the new multilateral platform that encouraged the convergence of the partner countries' legislation, norms and practices with those of the Union. The practical implementation of the multilateral track has taken place through four thematic platforms: (i) democracy, good governance and stability; (ii) economic integration and convergence with EU policies; (iii) energy security; and (iv) people-to-people contacts. The multilateral track has also provided for civil society participation through a separate Forum whose results will feed into the thematic platforms. Visibility and concrete substance for the EaP have been brought about through a number of regional flagship projects ranging from border management to energy efficiency and environmental concerns. Once again, political association and deeper economic integration were on offer for those partner countries that advanced in the agreed reforms. A related plan was to encourage free trade within the region itself. Of concrete and most immediate interest to the citizens of the partner countries is the facilitation of mobility. The EaP expands on the already-set goal of country-by-country advancement to visa facilitation and readmission agreements with prospects for a visa dialogue and the possibility of eventual visa freedom. Integral to the success of this path is the partner countries' ability to deal with the challenges posed by illegal immigration and other border security–related issues. Despite an impressive catalogue of new instruments and initiatives, the actual results from this flurry of activism have remained fairly meagre. To a degree, this is due to Russia's suspicions, discussed in detail in the next section, but also to the nature of the EU's own policy template. As Christou (2010) has argued, both the ENP and the EaP have been based on the simultaneous and uneasy co-existence of two binary logics, whereby cooperation and containment and the essential securitization of the Eastern neighbourhood have effectively limited and prevented the EU from facilitating meaningful change through its policies. Instead of being able to offer its neighbours the full benefits of freedom and interaction, the EU ends up shielding and protecting itself behind various policies that undercut the transformative potential of the EU in the East.

The EU's response to these criticisms was presented in May 2011 when – largely in response to the events in the Southern neighbourhood in the form of the Arab Spring – it presented a new policy template for the ENP (European Commission 2011b). The revised ENP sought to re-insert differentiation and conditionality into the process by adopting 'a more for more' approach whereby the neighbours were more clearly rewarded for their positive efforts as well as potentially penalized for the lack of them (for a discussion of the revised ENP, see Beauguitte, Yann and France 2015; Schumacher and Bouris 2016). It also introduced the notion of 'deep democracy', which was ostensibly intended to make a distinction between democracy based on genuine civic liberties and mere electoral democracy that is content with simply holding elections. It has also sought to operationalize the ENP Action Plans by opening up the prospect of signing Association Agreements – a feat that was achieved with some partner countries at the Vilnius Eastern Partnership Summit in November 2013 (more on this below).

All in all, the EU has sought a more joined-up approach to its neighbourhood. Internally, this has entailed attempts at bringing the different strands of EU policies together and ensuring their coherence, an opening that has been made possible by the Treaty of Lisbon (Gebhard 2011). Externally, the EU has sought to engage its neighbourhood more strategically, consistently and in a more flexible manner (European Commission 2012a), all objectives that have been highlighted in the most recent review of the ENP, launched by the EU in the aftermath of the Ukraine conflict in 2015 (European Commission and the HR 2015). That said, it is still too early to make a final assessment concerning the long-term efficacy of the constant stream of reviews and reforms in the EU policy. To date, there is in fact fairly little evidence that a change for the better has been achieved by the EU in and through its policies towards the East. On the contrary, the fact that the EU, first, did manage to 'lose' Ukraine during the run-up to the Vilnius Summit, to be discussed at length below, and then succumbed to a crisis with Russia suggests an entirely different conclusion. Although the EU has been manifestly disinterested in pursuing spheres of influence and has, in fact, declined to frame its role in the East in this manner, the underlying reality has nevertheless been Russia's insistence on framing the EU's role in largely negative and competitive terms. As a consequence, the EU has been locked into an integration competition with Russia over Eastern Europe, although it has been both unwilling and ill-equipped to play that game. On top of this, the two also adopted conflicting regime preferences concerning the countries in between, Ukraine in particular, with Russia pursuing increasingly coercive zero-sum strategies to win the key countries over (Smith 2015). In the following, both the Russian policies for the region as well as the reactions of the countries in between are discussed in turn.

Russian policies for its 'near abroad'

Although the EU did its best to convince the Russians that it was not interested in exclusive spheres of influence, but was seeking consensual win–win outcomes instead, Moscow decided to treat its presence in the region largely in a classical zero-sum manner. This was mainly because the Russian elites frame international relations in general in terms of fierce competition and consequent spheres of interest and influence (Trenin 2009). This was reflected in the fact that Russia decided to opt out of the value-laden ENP but insisted on, and was granted, a more interest-driven strategic partnership with the EU instead.

To better understand the Russian reactions, a closer look at Moscow's evolving responses to the CIS area is in order. The question of the 'near abroad' and Russia's inability to protect its own interests – be they strategic or economic benefits, the human rights of ethnic compatriots, or historical glory – in this area was seen by a majority of the Russian foreign policy elite as being the key issue in its foreign policy in the 1990s. Russia required a 'belt of good neighbourliness' that would prevent an anti-Russian bloc from penetrating its borders. In the early 1990s, only a relatively small group of liberal Westernizers were willing to prioritize relations with the West over preserving Russia's hegemonic role in the CIS. In fact, it was largely the alleged neglect of Russia's interests in this area, not the overly friendly relations with the West as such, that was the key reason why the era of 'romanticism' in Russian foreign policy came to an end. As Alexei Arbatov (1993: 42), a self-defined 'moderate liberal', argued in an *International Security* article at the time, 'Only one issue may create a serious problem [between Russia and the West], and that is the issue of Russia's relations with the other former republics of the Soviet Union.. He suggested that a modus vivendi with Russia and the West could be formed on the basis of Russia having 'a free hand' in establishing, by whatever means it considered appropriate, 'security and stability' across the space of the former Soviet Union (the Baltic states perhaps excepted). In exchange, Russia would follow the Western lead in other international questions of consequence.

Such an arrangement never transpired, but the issue was never formally discussed or resolved. On the contrary, the key Western institutions, both NATO and the EU alike, continued their drift towards the East. Initially, however, it seemed evident that Russia did not take the EU's neighbourhood policy seriously, focusing rather on the enlargement of NATO (see Asmus 2002; Stent 2014) and relegating the role of the whole topic in EU–Russia relations to the status of a non-issue. The wake-up call for Russia was Ukraine's Orange Revolution in 2004, which showed that Russia could not take its own standing in the CIS area for granted. For one, it revealed the limited appeal of the Russian model of integration and seemed to augur an era where the neighbours' delicate balancing act between Moscow and Brussels would be resolved in favour of the latter (Gretskiy, Treshchenkov and Golubev 2014: 378). Moreover, the EU's active role in brokering the conflict over the presidential elections and in securing the victory of Western-oriented Victor Yuschenko also showed that Moscow was no longer the only power centre that counted and that Russia's previously hegemonic role in the Western CIS was potentially in full retreat (Sherr 2013: 57–8).

Indeed, it was the evolution of the ENP, and especially the emergence of a more ambitious and institutionally more robust Eastern Partnership in 2009, that finally changed Russia's tack. The EU's strategy of developing hard law contractual frameworks with a view to eventual EU association for the Eastern partners has raised the stakes and changed the nature of the game for Russia. On the one hand, the process has raised the spectre of loosening Russia's grip in several key post-Soviet states – Ukraine, in particular. On the other hand, the potential success of systemic transformation along the EU model in Eastern Europe could result in a situation where Russia's own system could be exposed to unfavourable comparisons with its Western neighbours, with potentially negative political consequences for the standing and legitimacy of Russia's current elites. In light of this, it hardly seems surprising that Russia has repeatedly deplored the EU's attempts at 'carving its own sphere of influence in the East' (Pop 2009), and has made no secret of its growing displeasure. On the contrary, Russia has actively started to take steps to blunt the edge of the EU's policies in the region.

In his book *Post-Imperium*, the respected Russian analyst Dmitri Trenin (2011a) argued that one of the biggest stories concerning post–Soviet Russia dealt with the explicit and knowingly effected renunciation of any pretence towards having or re-achieving an empire in the post-Soviet sphere. On the contrary, Trenin argued, especially during the 2000s, Russia was busy building relationships along more equal and mutually equitable lines. Although probably accurate in the formal sense – Russia indeed did not want to physically reintegrate the CIS countries into its own body politic – it is, however, only part of the story. Indeed, and as Trenin himself admits, Russia still takes an acute interest in who 'controls' the CIS area (Trenin 2011b: 33). In fact, Bertil Nygren (2008: 18–19) has gone as far as to argue that especially during the 2000s Russia actively sought political domination of the post-Soviet space. For Russia, this entailed two things: first, it sought to ensure that no alien – that is, Western – power or bloc could penetrate the area. In the first instance, this meant resisting further NATO enlargements in the East. Second, and although Russia shied away from seeking formal control of the CIS as such, it preferred and indeed actively sought and promoted softer forms of domination – or coercion (Sherr 2013) – in the region (Tolstrup 2013).

To better understand Russia's policies towards its post-Soviet neighbours, a brief excursion into the foundations of Russian thinking about international relations in general is perhaps called for. The starting point could be that the emphasis Russia puts on equality and sovereignty as a cornerstone of international relations is based on an underlying understanding of world politics as an arena of an uncompromising battle of interests and a struggle for domination. The notion of ruthless global competition – economic, military and normative – seems to resonate strongly with the current Russian elites (see, for example, Haukkala 2010). Perhaps the most famous occasion when such sentiments were voiced in public was in the aftermath of the tragic school siege in Beslan in September 2004, when President Putin argued how Russia had shown itself to be weak and that the weak get beaten (Putin 2004). Putin voiced similar interpretations and concerns about international relations during his election campaign to return to the presidency in 2012, a theme he has revisited during his presidency as well (Putin 2012; Putin 2013a).

In the current situation, this thinking is reflected in Russian views that the world is about to enter, or has already entered, an era of competitive multipolarity (or polycentrism), where a group of leading great powers manage the international system and agree on the major rules of the game in concert while feverishly competing with each other at the same time (Trenin 2011a: 208–10; Lo 2015: passim.). In policy terms, this has entailed clamouring after a sphere of influence that would act both as the resource base and as a political springboard for Russia's claim to great power status.

But the post–Soviet Russia has not always been bent on dominating its neighbourhood. On the contrary, at the beginning of the 1990s, Russia went through a period of disorientation and disinterest towards its neighbourhood, which resulted in a policy of benign neglect towards the region. As Trenin (2011a: 85–6) has argued, Russia was busy severing its ties and relieving itself of the burden of propping up regimes in the former Soviet Union. Instead, Moscow's focus was on developing ties with key Western players, the United States in particular. At the same time, there was an underlying expectation that the post-Soviet countries would eventually naturally gravitate towards Russia. Yet this was patently not the case: by the end of the 1990s, Russia had largely lost its standing in the CIS, and the whole post-Soviet space was drifting towards growing impotence and even irrelevance.

The arrival of Vladimir Putin on the scene in 1999 changed the Russian tack towards the region. True to style, Putin assumed a no-nonsense approach towards the CIS that sought to safeguard Russia's own interests in the region while beginning to cultivate a set of bilateral relations that would bring the CIS countries closer to Russia's orbit. To be sure, the growing presence of key Western institutions in Eastern Europe also helped to focus Russia's mind. This has obviously been the case with repeated rounds of NATO enlargement, which have been cast in negative terms in and by Moscow, but to a degree the same has applied to the EU's growing involvement in the East as well. For example, the adoption of the EaP was greeted by Foreign Minister Sergei Lavrov with disdain, and he characterized the process as a crude attempt on the part of the EU at carving up a sphere of influence in the East (Pop 2009). In a similar fashion, President Medvedev, at the press conference of the EU–Russia Summit in May 2009, noted that 'any partnership is better than a conflict, but it is confusing for us that some states attempt to use the structure as a partnership against Russia (quoted in Tumanov, Gasparishvili and Romanova 2011: 135; for a fuller discussion, see Haukkala 2009a).

As a consequence, Russia has come to actively resist not only NATO's but also, and perhaps increasingly, the EU's perceived encroachments on its backyard (for a discussion, see Greene 2012). This resistance has taken many forms, all of which have effectively sought to curtail the impact of the EU's policies in the East:

1. Russia has had no qualms about actively supporting authoritarian regimes in the CIS area (Kramer 2008). This has been done at least partly in direct opposition to the EU's voiced ambitions of encouraging liberal democracy in the region. By contrast, Russia has clearly preferred the status quo to the prospects of normative change advocated by the EU. By providing political and economic support for authoritarian regimes in the region, Russia has to a large degree managed to curtail the transformative potential of the EU presence in the region.

2. Russia has used energy resources and linkages with post-Soviet countries to lock them into economic and political dependence on Moscow (Nygren 2008). Even in the 1990s, Russia was accustomed to trying to buy political benefits by providing its neighbours with subsidized gas and oil, but with very limited success. By contrast, during the 2000s, Russia has become more adept at playing the game, using both carrots and sticks to cajole and coerce its neighbours in the required direction.

3. Russia uses so-called frozen conflicts to control the European aspirations of its neighbours. Moscow is a player (in one form or another) in all the still simmering conflicts in the region. For example, the independence-minded 'kleptocracy' of Igor Smirnov in Transnistria relies on Moscow's political and economic support. Russia also holds considerable sway in the deadlocked settlement of Nagorno-Karabakh between Armenia and Azerbaijan. In most cases, it seems as if Russia is playing the role of spoiler, frustrating the Union's and other international actors' attempts to resolve the conflicts; essentially preferring the status quo and the perceived spheres of influence to the risk of the EU and its normative and economic reach achieving stronger sway in the region, perhaps even supplanting Russia's role in the process (Akçakoca, Vanhauwaert, Whitman and Wolff 2009: 23–25; Meister 2011: 17). If need be, Russia has not shied away from using military or other more hybrid forms of force projection to secure its foothold in the region.

4. Russia has started to put forward its own ideas for economic and political integration in the East. Although the CIS proper has remained fairly moribund, in its shadow Russia has promoted arrangements based on more selective engagement, which seem to show more promise. For example, the Eurasian Economic Union (EEU), an idea advanced by Vladimir Putin in 2011, is slated to become 'the European Union of the East' in stark competition with the ideas of European integration promoted by the EU. Further, in the field of security, the Collective Security Treaty Organization (CSTO) has some potential to organize the security dynamics in the CIS region around Russia's leadership.

All in all, and well before the conflict in Ukraine, Russia increasingly positioned itself as a counterforce to the EU's approaches to their 'common neighbourhood'. Indeed, Russia was investing increasing political and economic energies in developing alternative models of economic modernization and societal development to those promoted by the EU. Of these initiatives, it is the EEU that deserves closer examination. The EEU can be seen as a significant break in the main post–Cold War narrative outlined in Chapter 2 in at least three overlapping respects. First, philosophically, it rejected the notion of an EU-centric order in which the transference of norms and values is entirely one-sided. Second, politically, it sought to build an alternative pole that has the potential to augur a more bipolar setting in the wider Europe, at least for the time being. To an extent, this can be seen as an attempt by Russia to delineate its privileged sphere of influence – or interests – in a clearer and more institutionalized manner. Third, and largely as a consequence of the previous two points, it has repercussions both for EU–Russia relations as well as for the policies the EU has been promoting in its Eastern neighbourhood (Haukkala 2013).

At least initially, the EEU seemed to have a forward-oriented and aspirational side in the form of joint institutions based at least ostensibly on supranationality and an emphasis on economic growth and prosperity (Dragneva and Wolczuk 2013; Roberts and Moshes 2015). Yet the underlying realities seemed to suggest a much more mixed picture. Despite the accent put on the expected positive outcomes of closer Eurasian integration, Russia's invitations for other CIS countries to join the initiative always seemed to be laced with subtle, and at times less than subtle, threats of economic hardships imposed by Russia if the invitation was not duly heeded. In addition, the EU has voiced its concern over whether accession to the EEU is indeed voluntary, as exemplified by Russia's use of energy as a carrot and a stick to induce the CIS countries to join the organization (see Chapter 4).

These differences were brought into the sharpest of reliefs in autumn 2013 in the run-up to the Vilnius Eastern Partnership Summit, already discussed in Chapter 2. There is hardly any need to repeat that discussion here, but one aspect that has been particularly contested deserves addressing. During the Ukraine conflict, Russia repeatedly accused the EU of ignoring Moscow in the preparation of the Association Agreements, and regarded the EU approach as unilateral and imperialistic, essentially forcing a false choice between the East and the West on the partners. Moreover, Russia claimed that the repeated concerns it raised with regard to the effects of the AAs did not receive any resonance in Brussels. The EU officials, in contrast, claimed that Russia was kept in the loop and that the economic effects that the agreements would have on Russia were going to be marginal and largely beneficial. Moreover, and as already discussed in Chapter 2, the EU repeatedly reminded Russia that the Association Agreements were bilateral between the EU and its Eastern partners and that under international law third parties have no right to interfere in the conclusion of such treaties. In December 2014, Commission President Barroso argued to this effect:

For five years the Russian government was informed about the details of the Association Agreement with Ukraine. Also Putin was fully informed. When he says today that he was surprised by it, it is not true. (Eder and Schiltz 2014)

For Russia, the problem was not, however, the content of the agreement or knowledge about the details, but the fact that the EU policy as a whole contradicted Russia's own project of establishing a 'Eurasian Union'. This was not entirely lost on the EU. Speaking admittedly after the fact, Barroso declared:

> 'We were perfectly aware of all of the risks,' he said, his voice rising with pique. 'I spoke with Putin several times, and he told us how important for him was the customs union, the Eurasian Union, and the specific role he saw for Ukraine. But should we have given up? Should we say, "OK, Vladimir, Ukraine is yours, do whatever you want?" That is the logical consequence of what they are saying. That's perfectly unacceptable.' (Spiegel 2014)

This basic incompatibility of visions and consequent institutional designs explains the growing Russian resistance, even belligerence, towards the EU policies in the region. To a degree, Russia was successful in its efforts to stymie the EU's approach. Its heavy-handed tactics persuaded President Yanukovych to retreat from signing the AA in Vilnius, and even before the conflict, the EU had been rendered quite timid in its approaches towards the region. It factored Russian sentiments and objections into its policies and shied away from developing responses that could be seen as being threatening from Moscow's vantage point. As a consequence, the EU approach entailed tacit approval and unintentionally lent support to Russia's claims to its special 'sphere of influence' in the East. As Carl Bildt explained in an interview in March 2015:

> I think we should have reacted more strongly towards Russia when they started to misbehave in the summer of 2013. Clearly, when they started the sanctions against Ukraine, we didn't see clearly the implications of that, and I remember that [former Polish Foreign Minister] Radek [Sikorski] and myself were trying to alert Brussels and Brussels was more or less asleep. (RFE/RL 2015)

That said, it would be an exaggeration to argue that Russia's policies towards the CIS had been an unalloyed success either. On the contrary, and despite increased purposefulness and activism, Russia was put on the defensive: its economic standing among the CIS countries had been declining with the EU challenging Russia in the West and China in the East (Trenin 2011a: 149). The proliferation of regional integration schemes left a lot to be desired in terms of the marching order and strategic purposefulness of these endeavours (for a useful discussion, see Zagorski 2012). Some have even gone as far as to characterize the Russian policies as a total failure with potentially catastrophic consequences for the whole of Eurasia (see Tsygankov 2012b). To date, however, it seems that Russia's effectiveness has been hindered by two factors: first, Moscow's failure to come up with an idea or theme to provide its policies with sound programmatic underpinnings that would have wider international resonance; second, Russia's own lack of credibility as an economic hub, given its weak standing and integration into the world economy. As a consequence, and compared with the magnetic pull of the EU, Russia's 'soft power' has been lacking (Tsygankov 2006a: 1079).

In addition, the bilateral relations that Russia enjoys with its CIS brethren are hardly trouble-free. Georgia is by no means the only post-Soviet country that has had serious problems in its relations with Russia. On the contrary, even a cursory glance at the EU's immediate Eastern neighbourhood reveals a host of problematic relationships. As Arkady Moshes (2013) has argued, even before the conflict the 'marriage of unequals' between Ukraine and Russia was fraught with tensions and problems (see also Bogomolov and Lytvynenko 2012). One is indeed hard pressed to envisage a return to any normality in the Ukrainian–Russian relations in the present circumstances. To a degree, the same applies to the relationship between Belarus and Russia, which has assumed a negative dynamic of oscillating between cooperation and conflict (Nice 2013). Similarly, Moldova is trying to carve out a niche for itself that would allow it to inch closer to the European Union, while in Central Asia Kazahkstan has engaged in a delicate balancing act between Russia, the regional hegemon in the making, and China (Boonstra 2015). All these tendencies and tensions have been exacerbated by the conflict in Ukraine: in practically all quarters of the CIS, Russia's actions have heightened wariness and concern about its motivations and have lessened the positive power of attraction for its neighbours, making them think hard about how to sustain the freedom of manoeuvre in the drastically worsened situation (Kuchins 2015: 152; for a country-by-country analysis, see Gröne and Hett 2015). Indeed, it is to the role of those countries in between that we turn next.

The role of the neighbours

Usually, the countries in between are treated either as bones of contention between the EU and Russia or simply as mere passive objects of their respective policies. Yet a story worth pondering deals with the increasingly independent role these countries have been able to assume in European affairs. In this respect, the starting point must be that the element of competition between the EU and Russia has not gone unnoticed by these countries. In fact, the present constellation has invited and enabled a recurring political pattern whereby the states in the 'common neighbourhood' have alternated their allegiances between the EU and Russia, always looking for a better political and economic deal. Therefore, instead of fully Europeanizing or falling loyally into Russia's orbit, the countries use the two protagonists as bargaining chips and sources of political leverage to buttress their own sovereignty and freedom of manoeuvre (Popescu and Wilson 2009). As a result, there exists the potential for an unhappy outcome where neither the EU nor Russia manages to achieve their aims, but both end up being played by the countries in between. What is more, this process feeds into the feeling of more than latent competition in the region, eroding trust and hindering the development of further cooperation while creating the potential for conflicts in the future, including the often frail domestic dynamics in the countries in question. All are trends that came to negative fruition in Ukraine in 2013–14.

Russia's relations with the countries in question have already been touched upon. For the EU, the nature of the Eastern neighbours, and indeed the very neighbourhood, has also been a source of complications, but for different reasons. Countries in the region are usually weak states with limited administrative capacity. Corruption is entrenched, and they are often divided states, either physically, as is the case with Georgia or Moldova, or mentally and politically when it comes to their place in Europe, as is the case with, for example, Ukraine. As a consequence, the countries have faced severe limitations in their ability and even basic willingness to engage in the kinds of reforms propagated by the Union (see Gnedina and Sleptsova 2012).

A case in point is Ukraine. Despite repeatedly professing its European calling and credentials, Ukraine has failed to fully embrace the kind of societal change and reforms that would take it genuinely closer to the European Union, as exemplified by the dramatic U-turn on the eve of the Vilnius Summit in 2013, already discussed above. The brief 'romance' with the EU that followed the Orange Revolution of 2004 was increasingly replaced with fatigue and disillusionment on both sides. Members of the Ukrainian elite have often acknowledged this conundrum and called for domestic reforms and closer integration with the EU. Yet the fate of the Orange Revolution shows how even the best intentions for reform can crumble under the pressure of the clannish and oligarchic political and economic structures present in Ukraine (for useful discussions, see Kuzio 2011; Hale 2015: Ch. 9). In the process, EU-led initiatives for reform can be distorted to serve the needs of local elites in prolonging and even enhancing their grip on power (Börzel 2010). As a consequence, the EU has been in danger of ending up propping up regimes with authoritarian tendencies instead of reforming them.

The difficulties the EU faces in trying to strike the right balance have been exemplified in the EU's policy towards Ukraine during the conflict with Russia. On the one hand, there has been an imperative to show 'strong political support' for Ukraine. This was reflected in the hasty signing of the political provisions of the AA in March 2014 and the continued rhetorical support for Kiev ever since. On the other hand, the EU has become increasingly frustrated with the Ukrainians dithering both in terms of implementing the Minsk Accords as well as engaging in significant domestic reforms. None of this is to say that Ukraine would find itself in an enviable position where achieving these things would be easy. On the contrary, the continued Russian destabilization, combined with the chronic economic and political weaknesses of Ukraine itself, has conspired to make them very difficult indeed. At the same time, the EU is in danger of being locked into a situation where it must assume significant political and fiscal responsibilities over Ukraine that it is clearly unwilling to accept. This is probably part of Russia's game plan in the conflict: by overstretching its capacity to engage Ukraine, the EU might in the future be more easily persuaded to strike a 'Grand Bargain' concerning the future of the country over the heads of the Ukrainians after all (see also Lo 2015:111).

The Northern Dimension

Since the early 1990s, the EU and Russia have been developing regional and cross-border cooperation. Of particular significance in this respect is the Northern Dimension. The origins of the Northern Dimension have their roots in the early 1990s when, with the accession of Finland and Sweden, the EU acquired an entirely new 'northern dimension', as what had previously been a predominantly western and southern European project was introduced to a host of new geographical realities. Early on, there was an expectation that the enlargement would also spell changes to the Union's external relations. This was reflected in the fact that it had brought the Union for the very first time into direct contact with the Russian Federation in the form of a 1300-kilometre Finnish–Russian border. Since then, this exposure has grown with the accession of Poland and the three Baltic states in 2004.

Finland was eager to prove its mettle as a new member state and launched the initiative with a new policy proposal in September 1997 (for a discussion on the background of the Finnish initiative, see Heininen 1999: 150–78; for a more detailed account of the subsequent development of the initiative than the one given here, see Joenniemi and Sergounin 2003: Ch. 2). In a speech delivered at the Barents Conference in Rovaniemi, Prime Minister Paavo Lipponen argued that the Union and its member states shared vital common interests in northern Europe and that those interests warranted a new EU policy (Lipponen 1997). Geographically, Lipponen's original vision was rather Russia-centric, but it also included a wider interpretation of the reach of the initiative, including the three Baltic states and Poland as well as the United States and Canada. The main emphasis was, however, put on a host of different threats emanating mainly from the north-western parts of Russia, such as the poor state of the environment, including the burning question of nuclear safety. Another set of challenges derived from the existence of what was perhaps one of the widest welfare gaps in the world on the Finnish–Russian border: the fear of uncontrolled immigration together with the danger of transmittable diseases, such as HIV and drug-resistant forms of tuberculosis. These threats were indeed a legitimate source of concern: the north-western parts of Russia, and the Kola Peninsula and the Kaliningrad region in particular, represented, as they still do, one of the most toxic environmental hotspots on the planet (these challenges have been analysed in detail in Moroff 2002).

But Lipponen's speech was not only a list of hardships and obstacles. The positive side of the initiative was based on the idea that, in the future, the EU would become increasingly dependent on imported energy and that the north-western parts of Russia contained vast reserves of these resources. However, and in order to exploit these reserves, the region would require an immense amount of investment in basic infrastructure, including rail and road connections, harbours, airports, border-crossing facilities as well as improved telecommunications systems. These were all things which, according to Lipponen, the Northern Dimension could help to provide.

In addition to its strategic ambitions, the Finnish initiative also echoed the EU's post-sovereign emphasis on its relations with Russia. Therefore, for Lipponen (1997), one of the key aims of the Northern Dimension was to 'facilitate Russia's integration into European structures' on the basis of the Partnership and Cooperation Agreement of 1994. It was understood 'as an arena where both the EU and its member states are attempting to export specific policy objectives, principles, values and norms to neighbouring areas' (Haglund 2005: 93–4; see also Romanova 2005). That said, in one interesting respect the Finnish initiative did differ from the Union's existing approach to Russia in calling for a partner-oriented approach where the views of 'all interested parties' would be taken into consideration with a view to developing 'a real partnership' between the EU and Russia. In the Russian debate, this promise of equality was initially greeted with some enthusiasm. For example, according to Igor Leshukov (2001: 135–6), the Northern Dimension was 'the only [EU–Russia] framework where Russia is not treated as an outsider.... This is exactly what Russia is struggling for – to be equally treated and to have a say (to be truly heard and not just politely listened to).'

From early on, the European Commission was entrusted with the further development and eventual implementation of the Finnish initiative. Making the Commission responsible for the policy had the effect of emphasizing the post-sovereign qualities of the initiative. This was reflected in the two Northern Dimension action plans (2000–3 and 2004–6), which included numerous points and paragraphs about the steps to be taken by other actors under the umbrella of the policy. There is hardly any need to dwell on their content at length as such an assessment appears elsewhere (see e.g. Haukkala 2010: Ch. 9). In essence, the action plans merely re-affirmed the EU's post-sovereign approach to its relationship with Russia in the form of unilateral demands, without engaging, for example, the acute Russian concerns regarding the negative effects of regionalization around the turn of the millennium in any meaningful way (see Ivanov 2001b; Ivanov 2002: 150).

By the adoption of the second action plan in 2003, it was clear that the ND predominantly reflected EU principles and interests over those of Russia (Haglund 2005: 105; Haukkala 2005: 39; Romanova 2005). The Russian disillusionment was accentuated by the fact that, initially, Russia was interested in the possible funds that could flow from the initiative, but once its non-existent budget became clear, Russia started to lose all interest. Even where considerable external funds were finally made available – a case in point being the so-called Northern Dimension Environmental Partnership (NDEP) (see Chapter 4) – the main political attention and financial resources were nevertheless directed at issues of first-order importance for the Union, sidelining Russian concerns about receiving aid and investments to develop its north-western regions with the help of the EU. Therefore, unsurprisingly, Russia became frustrated with its inability to influence the content of the policy. In the words of Romanova (2005), the Russians 'took the Northern Dimension as a regime that can be either taken or ignored (but not modified and supplemented)'. As a consequence, Russia, to all intents and purposes, withdrew itself from the implementation of the policy (Van Elsuwege 2007: 39; Romanova 2005).

The Russian resistance resulted in certain modifications to the EU approach towards the ND. The change took place incrementally, at first taking the form of rhetorical and, later, actual policy concessions as the Union sought to accommodate the Russian concerns. The increasingly apparent policy paralysis spurred the Finnish government, together with the European Commission, to take action to save the policy. Beginning in 2005, this was done through a series of consultations held with the European Commission and three partner countries, Iceland, Norway and Russia. The conclusion of the consultations was that in order to reinvigorate the initiative, a rather radical overhaul in the way the policy was organized was required. In essence, this meant turning the EU policy into a genuinely joint programme between the Union and its partners (Tuomioja 2007; see also European Commission 2007b: 5–6).

The first steps towards that end were taken at the fourth ministerial meeting in Brussels in November 2005, where the guidelines for the development of a new political declaration and a policy framework document were adopted by the EU and the partner countries, Russia included. The guidelines noted that after the expiration of the second action plan at the end of 2006, the ND should be put on a more permanent footing by adopting jointly drafted documents between the EU, Iceland, Norway and Russia (Council of the European Union 2005b; see also European Commission 2005). At the meeting, the Russian Foreign Minister, Sergei Lavrov, welcomed the new approach with satisfaction, noting that many of the key Russian concerns and priorities were – for the very first time – being taken into consideration by the Union (Lavrov 2005). Of particular significance for Russia was the fact that, in future, the ND would be transformed from an EU policy into a common one for both Russia and the Union.

The negotiations on the political declaration and the policy framework document took place during 2006, culminating in the Northern Dimension Summit, organized peripherally to the regular EU–Russia Summit in Helsinki in November 2006. In the post-summit news conference, Russian President Vladimir Putin noted, in a clear change of Russian rhetoric, how it had been a 'genuinely significant event' that would allow the parties to 'fundamentally update and modernize' the Northern Dimension (European External Action Service [EEAS] 2006). Putin had good grounds for feeling content at the Helsinki City Hall. The political declaration was merely a brief statement of the collective intentions of the EU and Russia as well as the other partner countries, Iceland and Norway. As such, the guiding principles for the future policy were good neighbourliness, equal partnership, common responsibility and transparency (EEAS 2006). Crucially, the new principles guiding the policy lacked any references to the Union's post-sovereign agenda. The Northern Dimension was no longer linked with the goal of integrating Russia into European structures, nor was it seen as facilitating the country's transition towards European norms and values. Instead, the policy should provide 'concrete and pragmatic activities with the objective to achieve tangible results' – a very traditional agenda of cooperation indeed (see Haglund-Morrissey 2008).

The new Northern Dimension policy was greeted with delight in Russia. Archer and Etzold (2008) argued that it enabled 'Moscow increasingly to act as a policymaker, or co-policymaker, rather than the obviously disliked role of policy-taker'. This was reflected in the official communications as well. For example, in a seminar in Helsinki in January 2007, the Deputy Minister for Foreign Affairs, Aleksandr Grushko, heaped praise on the policy. In a speech full of strong positive adjectives, Grushko (2007) noted how the new policy was 'a promising tool' with the potential to 'give a considerable impetus' to cooperation in 'the vast region' of Northern Europe. In a similar vein, in an article written for *Mezhdunarodnoye Zhizn* – the journal of the Russian foreign ministry – Deputy Chairman of the Federation Council of the Federal Assembly Mikhail Nikolaev (2007: 84) applauded the new equality between the EU and Russia as 'an absolutely new format, a format of the 21st century'. For Nikolaev, the proper marching order in the future should be that the ND would be turned into a tool for implementing national development strategies. In the case of Russia, this would entail 'that if Russia implements its national projects, the projects drawn up as a part of the Northern Dimension policy should correspond to these national projects'. In essence, this would seem to imply a reversal of the EU's and its Commission's earlier attempts at delegating tasks to regional actors and replacing them, with Russia's insistence that the policy should start to serve its own developmental needs.

Since then, the ND has continued its operation in a concrete and low-key manner. By 2014, the ND had generated a portfolio of projects worth €1.3 billion (EEAS 2014). In the process, the web of sectoral partnerships has expanded to four and now includes partnerships on environment (NDEP), public health and social wellbeing (NDPHS), transport and logistics (Northern Dimension Partnership on Transport and Logistics [NDPTL]) and culture (NDPC) (see Haglund-Morrissey 2008). It is also interesting to note that the parties have decided to exempt the ND from their otherwise increasingly frozen relations. This was already the case after the Georgian War, when the French EU presidency decided to proceed with the ND Summit in St Petersburg in October 2008, even though the EU had officially frozen its other relations with Moscow following the war. Speaking in front of the media after the event, Foreign Minister Lavrov noted with satisfaction, and in clear reference to the still contentious Georgian issue, how the parties had 'agreed on all of the issues discussed. It is currently not often that in international discussions consensus can be observed on all issues' (Lavrov 2008c). In his earlier opening remarks, Lavrov had also emphasized Russian satisfaction with the renewed Northern Dimension, claiming that the new 'format can lay its small brick in the construction of … [a] comfortable common home for all Europeans' (Lavrov 2008b). The EU side has concurred and decided to exempt the ND from the set of restrictive measures adopted over the conflict in Ukraine in 2014.

Arctic, Baltic and Black Sea cooperation

The final set of issues deals with other forms of regional cooperation. In this context, the Arctic in particular has been gaining in relevance in recent years. This is largely due to the climate change that is resulting in the opening up of possibilities for the growing economic utilization of the resources in the area. The melting of polar ice is opening prospects for exploiting the natural resources and opening logistical routes between Europe and North America and Asia.

Russia has found itself at the centre of attention in the Arctic. In the Russian debates, the thawing of the Arctic Sea has been seen to entail significant economic prospects but also increased military liabilities (Emmerson 2013; Zysk 2011). Russia has tried to proceed on both tracks simultaneously, seeking to develop the economic potential of the High North while enhancing its military capabilities in the region (Antrim 2011). To a large degree, the accent in the Russian rhetoric has been put on seeking cooperative solutions with other states in the region and developing joint ventures with key Western companies: the remote, difficult and – by extension – expensive conditions in the Arctic have also witnessed Russia embracing a largely cooperative stance (Hough 2012: 78). As a consequence, the Arctic has, to a large extent, remained insulated from the ebb and flow of wider EU/Western–Russian relations (Wilson Rowe and Blakkisrud 2014: 82).

The Ukraine conflict has, however, had a negative effect on these developments as well. To begin with, the sanctions imposed by the EU and the United States (see Chapter 4) are hampering the economic development of the Arctic by Russia. The increased geopolitical tensions between Russia and the West are also raising concerns about the securitization, even growing militarization, of previously relatively well-functioning Arctic cooperation. For example Conley and Rohloff (2015) have speculated whether a new 'Ice Curtain' is in fact in the process of being erected in the High North.

The EU, for its part, has for the last decade been developing its own Arctic policies. The Union is, in a sense, also an Arctic actor, as three of its member states – Denmark, Finland and Sweden – have Arctic territories and are founding members of the Arctic Council, but it has also taken steps to acquire a more formal role in Arctic governance. To this end, the Commission announced in 2008 that it would be seeking a permanent observer status in the Arctic Council (European Commission 2008: 11). Although the Council did receive the EU's application 'affirmatively' (Arctic Council 2015), the actual decision to grant the role has not been taken due to Canada's, and to a lesser extent Russia's, resistance. In the meantime, the EU has been granted an interim right to observe the Council's meetings on an ad hoc basis.

The difficulties in securing a foothold in Arctic governance structures have not discouraged the EU from developing its common policies for the region. An indication of this was the joint report by the EU high representative and the European Commission in June 2012 (European Commission and the HR 2012). In May 2014, the Foreign Affairs Council highlighted the Arctic in its conclusions and called it 'a region of growing strategic importance', urging the EU to 'further enhance its contribution to Arctic cooperation' (FAC 2014). Commission President Jean-Claude Juncker has raised the issue on the agenda, commissioning a study concerning the EU Arctic policy from the Father of the Northern Dimension initiative, former Finnish Prime Minister Paavo Lipponen. All these activities point towards the EU's aim to increase its engagement and stake in Arctic issues and governance with a view to resolving environmental challenges and fostering sustainable development of natural resources in the High North. Whether this ambition will be realized in the current tense atmosphere remains to be seen.

Other areas where tensions have arisen are over the Baltic and Black Sea cooperation. In both regions, the EU and Russia have undertaken significant attempts at developing cross-border cooperation during the post–Cold War era. The first arena was the Baltic Sea, where the attempts began immediately at the turn of the 1990s and resulted in a wide-ranging agenda of economic and environmental cooperation (Tassinari 2004). The EU's Eastern enlargement in 2004 resulted in the Baltic Sea almost becoming an EU internal sea. This was reflected in the launching of the EU Baltic Sea Strategy to develop its internal policies and regional cohesion, but also resulted in the EU trying to enhance its regional cooperation with Russia as well.

The Black Sea cooperation is a more recent addition brought about by the EU accession of Bulgaria and Romania in 2007. The European Commission's communication on the topic in 2007 noted how 'more than ever before, the prosperity, stability and security of our neighbours around the Black Sea are of immediate concern to the EU' (European Commission 2007a). The EU established the Black Sea Synergy initiative as a regional cooperation scheme of the EU, and it was formally launched at a joint meeting of EU and Black

Sea region foreign ministers in Kiev in February 2008. To a degree, the Black Sea Synergy has been modelled on the ND example, and the development of cooperation has taken place under sectoral partnerships, such as environment, transport and energy. Other cooperation has taken place in a number of focus areas, for instance in the cross-cutting integrated maritime policy. Since 2009, the EU has invested nearly re-militarization €140 million in the development of the region (EEAS 2015a).

All in all, both the Baltic and Black Seas have showcased the potential for mutually beneficial, low political and sector-specific cooperation between the EU and Russia. In both cases, however, the mainly economic and soft security agendas have more recently been jeopardized by the increased political tensions and even re-militarization of the regions. The Baltic Sea has become the primary arena where Russia and NATO now meet (see Chapter 5). Military tensions have been rising in the Black Sea as well. The disheartening conclusion for these two regions for the time being must be that the conflict in Ukraine has also increased their role as potential flashpoints between Russia and the EU, and indeed the wider West. Unfortunately, the positive outcomes of the past two decades are not entirely secure in the regional setting either.

Conclusions

This chapter has examined the difficulties that the EU and Russia have faced in managing their shared or 'common' neighbourhood, including regional cooperation. It has highlighted the different starting points the two have had concerning the region, as well as discussed the contrasting and even competing policies the two have adopted to deal with their respective neighbours. The bottom line of the analysis is that both adopted largely incompatible and even irreconcilable approaches towards the countries in between. The two might have overlapping neighbourhoods, but the notion of a genuinely 'common' neighbourhood that the EU has been promoting remained far from a reality.

As the crisis in Ukraine showed, neither the EU nor Russia was, in effect, very successful in reaching their voiced ambitions, nor were they able to manage the region and its many challenges in any meaningful way on their own. The process around the Vilnius Eastern Partnership Summit in November–December 2013 undermined mutual trust and, as a consequence, both parties felt betrayed. The consequent drastic deterioration of relations in this key sector of cooperation between the EU and Russia had the full potential to 'spill over' to other fields, a process that has been duly achieved. Clearly, the 'common neighbourhood' has proved to be a significant catalyst in the process towards the serious rupture of relations between the EU and Russia.

Although this chapter unveils a largely negative overall dynamic between the EU and Russia in the common neighbourhood, the starting point nevertheless must be that, at least initially, the two were not engaged in a traditional geopolitical battle over spheres of influence in the East, not to speak of a clash of two civilizations whose fault line has run through Ukraine for centuries (Huntington 1996). That said, this does not mean that there was no competition between the EU and Russia. On the contrary, the contest was real, as demonstrated by the dramatic disruption of EU–Russia relations and wider European security over Ukraine. At the same time, the situation is also more subtle than traditional geopolitical rivalries alone might entail. In essence, the two have become locked into what can be called an integration competition of who gets to integrate the countries in between and under what terms (Smith N. R. 2015). This is geopolitics with a postmodern twist befitting the twenty-first century.

Yet to argue that the EU and Russia would be locked in a Battle Royal over Eastern Europe is only partially true. The 'problem' is that, thus far, there has been only one really interested contender, namely Russia, with the EU clearly unable and unwilling to vie for the mastery of Eastern Europe. Russia has exercised considerable influence in these countries ever since the dissolution of the Soviet Union, whereas the EU has become more and more active after the 2004 Eastern enlargement (Tolstrup 2014). What is more, neither contender has really been up to the task of dominating and consequently effectively ordering the 'common neighbourhood': as a result, both the EU and Russia have ended up being played by the countries in between and have failed to achieve almost any of their most important objectives. In future, the key issue will be how to overcome this detrimental dynamic between the two that is not doing the main contenders or the countries in between any favours.

To a degree, regional cooperation has acted as a safety valve in relations, allowing concrete and low political interaction even during periods fraught with disagreement. At the same time, the evolution of formats and forms of cooperation regionally has pointed to some crucial changes in the way the two have jointly framed their relationship (Haukkala 2010: Ch. 9). Therefore, it would be wrong to say – as the majority of scholars working on the topic seem to have done – that regional cooperation has largely been a failure as well (for a representative sample, see Averre and Reut 2005; Ojanen 2000; Volk 2004; Voronov 2003). The NDEP alone is clear proof of the impact the policy has had, and is having, on the ground in Russia. Yet it is also true that most of the original, and largely post-sovereign, objectives of the policy have remained unrealized, mainly due to the growing passive resistance on the part of Russia. By deciding on a policy of non-engagement with the ND, Russia in actual fact constrained the impact of the policy and forced the Union to draw conclusions from the ineffectiveness of its approach. This process reached its culmination during the Finnish EU presidency in 2006, which witnessed the 'reinvigoration' of the policy that resulted in the substantive erosion of the post-sovereign principles in the logic of interaction between the EU and Russia; this perhaps created an expectation on the Russian side that this would increasingly be the norm in other areas of cooperation as well. The fact that this did not transpire could be a contributing factor pointing towards an explanation for the current rupture in relations, a task we turn to in the next chapter.

Chapter 9

Explaining EU–Russia Relations

During the more than 20 years that EU–Russia relations have existed in the institutional sense, the scholarly literature on the topic has expanded. To a large extent, the literature has been descriptive and/or prescriptive, and policy-oriented in nature. Various think tanks and research institutes have been more visible in the field than universities. The research has posited some general explanations (Prozorov 2006; Pursiainen 2008; Haukkala 2010; Sergunin 2016) along with some issue-specific attempts at explication (Medvedev and Neumann 2012; Kuzemko 2014), but there is no concentrated academic debate on the competing explanations concerning the nature of EU–Russia relations. Explanations are often embedded in the analysis, but they are not systematically developed, tested or contrasted with alternative explanations. They are also often singular, ad hoc and related to events and political leaders rather than general patterns or complex mechanisms. As a consequence, EU–Russia relations do not figure to any significant degree in general IR discussions dealing with the accuracy and utility of various theoretical approaches and explanatory models (Schmidt-Felzmann 2015: 605).

With the Ukrainian conflict marking the end of an era in the relations between the EU and Russia, it is high time we revisited various theoretical approaches to the topic. Such an exercise is needed not only for the purposes of academic rigour but also to gain a better understanding of how the ruptured relations could possibly be repaired. A knowledge of explanatory mechanisms is also required in order to make better predictions. We can only improve relations if we know what the key problems are and where they originate (Chernoff 2007).

After these bold words, it is, however, important not to be overly ambitious or too naïve about the possibility of 'explaining EU–Russia relations'. First of all, if we are to trace the evolution of the relationship after the Cold War, it is clear that this pattern of cooperation and conflict can be attributed to a number of factors. This point of departure calls for caution when it comes to believing that there is one key perspective through which we can understand

EU–Russia relations. We can have a debate over the relative importance of causal factors, but even such factors that have relatively little impact on the whole should not be neglected as they can bring added value and help to unravel some crucial aspects. In this sense, we can never attain a complete explanation of something like EU–Russia relations. Second, definitive evidence that would conclusively prove one explanation correct and another erroneous is often impossible to find. As a rule, we do not have direct access to the decision-making process either in Brussels or in Moscow, and even if all the possible archives and witness statements were available, ample room often remains for diverging interpretations.

This chapter endeavours to outline the possible explanations for EU–Russia relations, based on previous chapters that have examined the various issue areas. It revisits the existing literature on the topic and examines how the 'explanatory discourses' that emerge are related to the more general theoretical 'IR discourse'. We first construct alternative narratives of the relationship, but then try to back up the explanatory endeavour and structure the debate by framing the question of what is to be explained more explicitly. EU–Russia relations per se do not yet constitute an explanatory puzzle. Instead, we suggest that explanatory puzzles need to be formed in a contrastive way. Why is the EU policy towards Russia x, rather than y? Why is Russia behaving towards the EU in an x manner, rather than a y manner? Why have the EU–Russia relations evolved according to x, rather than y? Sometimes, the ability to spell out meaningful contrastive puzzles is more important than the ability to offer correct explanations. They also point to potentially interesting political choices that were made, and hint at roads that were not traversed. As a consequence, they also give us some grounds to contemplate the choices that lie ahead for both the EU and Russia, which is a topic we return to in the concluding chapter of the book.

The discussion in this chapter proceeds in three successive steps. We first look at EU foreign policy, then at Russian foreign policy and finally at the dyad of relations between the two. We conclude by refining our statement about the importance of being clear about the explanatory contrasts and offer our view of what the possible fruitful and accurate explanations of EU and Russian foreign policy and the dynamics of their relationship might be. In the final analysis, the question we need to answer is why we are dealing with 'a partnership that failed'. Indeed, one key contention of this chapter is that the failure of the partnership was not pre-ordained: Neither side wanted nor actively sought it, but due to a myriad of reasons, including some key events to be discussed below, they just arrived at it. We start, however, with a brief section concerning the nature of explanations, discussing both narrative and contrastive versions.

Narratives and contrastive explanations

If we are to explain the evolution of the EU–Russia relationship after the Cold War, it is clear that there are many factors that have constituted this pattern of cooperation and conflict. This observation is trivial to the extent that all social phenomena are multicausal. We should be wary of believing that there is one key perspective through which we can understand these relations, such as power or identity. And it hardly makes sense to try to subsume EU–Russia relations in some covering law dealing with great powers in general, without taking a closer look at the kind of explanations that make sense on the basis of the evidence to hand.

One way of advancing such explanations, favoured by historians and other interpretivists, is to see them in terms of narratives. The issue is explained through an integrative story that describes how it evolved over time: there is a beginning; some events take place; and there is an outcome. Historians typically believe that narrative accounts can provide causal explanations for an outcome without assuming that there are any general laws that dictated the chain of events that resulted in the outcome. Hidemi Suganami (1997), who has defended and developed the narrative explanation in the study of IR, has argued that a narrative explanation combines four kinds of information concerning the background, chance coincidences, mechanistic forces and human acts. In Suganami's view, what distinguishes explanations of the social and natural phenomena is not the presence or absence of narratives, but the ingredients of the narrative explanation.

Narrative explanations have sometimes been criticized on the grounds that providing information about the development of the events and other factors leading up to the outcome does not prove that they have been causally effective. A causal narrative typically provides a lot of information about factors and conditions that are not relevant to an explanation, but which, at the same time, can be misleading as a form of genuine explanation. Nevertheless, rich narratives consisting of details can be important in better imagining and comprehending the explanations as well as ruling out possible alternative explanations.

Explanations, which are more precise than general narratives, spell out some causal mechanisms that have been essential in contributing to the outcome. Such explanations do not need to be complete as such an objective is often too idealistic in an open system. The main idea of the contrastive view of explanations is precisely that explanations focus on an aspect that is either explicitly or implicitly contrastive: we do not ask 'why *p*?' but 'why *p* [fact] rather than *q* [foil]?' Framing the question in contrastive terms forces us to sharpen our explanatory focus. For example, when asking why World War I broke out, we can pose the question in different ways: 'Why did World War I break out in July 1914 rather than sooner or later?'; 'Why, when the war broke out in July 1914, was it a "World War" and not a regional conflict?'; or 'Why, when the war broke out in July 1914, was it so devastating and protracted?' Which question we are answering depends on our explanatory interests and existing knowledge. In the words of Eric Grynaviski (2013: 832), 'Contrastive why-questions, like a microscope, zoom in on theoretically important questions, whereas simple why-questions risk losing important trees in the forest.'

The contrastive nature of explanations is not a new discovery, but it has only relatively recently been seen as a distinctive approach to thinking about the nature of explanation (Ylikoski 2007). In the IR literature, Kenneth Waltz (1979/2010: 7) is famous for his position that 'theory explains some part of reality', because 'a full description would be of least explanatory power'. Many representatives of other theoretical approaches, such as Alexander Wendt (1999: 88), who notes that 'what counts as explanation is relative to an interrogatory context', share the view that we have multiple perspectives on explanations, depending on what it is exactly that we want to explain. In this sense, various explanations do not necessarily compete with, but rather complement, each other by explaining different aspects of the same phenomena. We agree with this perspective to a certain extent and see a great deal of individual merit in the competing narratives outlined below.

Four narratives

As already noted, explanations often take the form of narratives. But the narratives usually revolve around the question of whose fault it is that things have gone awry between the EU and Russia, rather than competing theoretical approaches. The Ukrainian conflict and the concomitant crisis in EU–Russia relations can therefore be seen in terms of four narratives. The first puts the blame on Russia, the second on the EU, the third on the United States and the fourth on no particular actor, but on a gamut of misunderstandings, misperceptions and other happenstance factors.

According to the first narrative, EU–Russia relations failed due to Russia's conflict-seeking behaviour, manifested in its unwillingness to accommodate itself to European norms and values and its decision to undermine stability in its neighbourhood and eventually illegally annex Crimea. There are two versions of the narrative that focuses on Russia's role: one puts the emphasis on Russia's offensive behaviour, whereas the other regards it as more defensive, acting out of despair rather than hegemony, but nonetheless fully acknowledging the risk of conflict with the EU. Some Western leaders have expressed views that support this narrative. For example Donald Tusk, the president of the European Council, has noted that Putin's policy is 'simply to have enemies, to be stronger than them, to destroy them and to be in conflict' (Traynor 2015). In this reading, the key origins of Russia's conduct were either inherent in the Russian state and deriving from its imperial legacy, or domestic and related to the rise to power of Putin and the *Siloviki* group, who first started to usurp all the domestic power for the Kremlin and then project that power onto the neighbourhood. There is the cynical view that these people were simply obsessed with power and, according to some (Dawisha 2014), were even kleptocratic. The alleged difference in values was only used to mask the fact that they could not play by the general rules and survive. At the same time, cooperation with the EU was possible to the extent that it served the function of bringing direct benefits and buying time.

The domestic political explanation has become a commonly held Western view of the root causes of the crisis between Russia and the EU. Michael McFaul (2014), for example, argues that Putin reacted to the home-grown protest movement, feared the possibility of a colour revolution in Russia and created an external crisis in order to consolidate the Kremlin's domestic power. Similarly, in Roger Kanet's (2015: 519) view, 'Confrontation with the West is a useful stimulant for the nationalism necessary to generate domestic support.' Some prominent Russians, such as Sergey Karaganov (2003), have also subscribed to this narrative category when explaining problems within EU–Russia relations:

> Whatever the failings of Europe, a considerable part of the problem in the EU-Russian relationship should be placed at

Russia's doorstep. The most obvious failing is Russia's economic backwardness. The country's level of corruption and criminality, the frequently illegal intervention by the state in economic activity and the sorry state of its court system cannot but baffle and infuriate the Europeans.

The second narrative turns the tables and blames the EU and its actions for the crisis. In this view, the EU has conducted imperial policies in the shared neighbourhood, squeezing Russia into a corner in the process. Moreover, according to this line of thought, the EU has constantly tried to force its values upon Russia and has employed double standards, criticizing Moscow while trying to cover up its own wrongdoings and egoistic interests. The EU's worst mistake was the exclusionary Eastern Partnership and the attempt to foster a regime change in Ukraine and consequently in Russia. Richard Sakwa (2014: 41) has argued that the aim of the Eastern Partnership was to give the division of Europe an institutional form and to 'engineer Ukraine's separation from Russia'. Therefore, it 'rendered the EU as much of a threat in Russian perceptions as NATO'. In this reading, the West, including the EU, ignored the legitimate interests of Russia and was a source of constant humiliation for the country. In a word, the EU has been out 'to get' Russia.

This is the narrative recounted by the Russian leaders. As Putin (2015a) has asserted:

> I firmly believe that Russia was not responsible for the deterioration in relations between our country and the EU states. This was not our choice; it was dictated to us by our partners. It was not we who introduced restrictions on trade and economic activities. Rather, we were the target and we had to respond with retaliatory, protective measures.

Similarly, Lavrov (2014a) has argued that '[i]f it was not for Crimea and South-Eastern Ukraine, the West would have invented something else.' According to Lavrov, the goal was set 'to unbalance Russia at any price' a long time ago. But many Western scholars and pundits have also entertained similar readings of the situation. Perhaps most famously, John Mearsheimer (2014) has explained Russia's actions in Ukraine as a legitimate and rational reaction to NATO enlargement, European Union enlargement eastwards and the provocation of colour revolutions in the immediate sphere of

Russia's interests. Even if the EU had not harboured any malign intent towards Russia, it was nonetheless insufficiently sensitive and respectful towards its prerogatives.

The third narrative is a derivation of the previous one, but it accentuates the role of the United States as the main culprit. According to this view, Washington prevented the EU–Russia partnership from developing on its own merits because it would have challenged its position as the leading global power. In this reading, the US did have an active and largely negative role to play in EU–Russian relations. To begin with, Washington did not allow for a genuinely independent EU foreign policy to emerge. Instead, with the help of its Trojan horses in Europe, it undermined the possibility of a common European home and a partnership between Russia and the European Union. Sakwa (2015) has advanced this thesis too and claims that US-led 'New Atlanticism' has been instrumental in undermining mutual trust and cooperation between the EU and Russia. In other words, the key problem has been the hapless immersion of the EU into the objectives and policies of the United States, to the detriment of both the EU and Russia. Putin himself has argued that 'the Americans do not want Russia's rapprochement with Europe. I am not asserting this, it is just a hypothesis' (Corriere della Sera 2015).

Finally, the fourth narrative envisages the eventual confrontation between the EU and Russia as a tragedy that nobody really intended but that came about due to a series of misunderstandings, misperceptions and even misfortune. If a parallel is sought with the First World War (Clark 2012), the key players were 'sleepwalking' into a conflict (House of Lords 2015: 63). On the EU side, nobody took real responsibility for designing and carrying out the ENP and the wider Russia policy, and the repeated warning signs from Moscow went ignored. In the Kremlin, by contrast, the EU was seen as acting more purposefully than it actually was, and Moscow launched countermeasures without understanding, again, how seriously the EU would respond to them. Reporters from the German *Spiegel* magazine concluded that the run-up to the Ukraine crisis in the relations between the EU and Russia was 'filled with errors in judgement, misunderstandings, failures and blind spots' (Spiegel Staff 2014):

> Russia and Europe talked past each other and misunderstood one another. It was a clash of two different foreign policy cultures: a Western approach that focused on treaties and the precise

wording of the paragraphs therein, and the Eastern approach in which status and symbols are more important.

As a result, 'it was the interaction between the two sides, rather than the actions of only one side, that created the spiral in tensions' (Legvold 2014: 84). In the background, we find the widening gap between individual and mutual expectations and the actual deliverables of the relationship, with both sides increasingly blaming the other, rather than the circumstances, for the failures. As a consequence, the mutual disillusionment – even exasperation – with relations acted as an important backdrop to the conflict, in effect 'priming' both the EU and Russia to assume the worst about each other.

All of the basic narratives are crucially important in the sense that they reveal different aspects of the relationship, inform judgements made in the present and frame choices related to its future. Both Russia and the EU can be blamed for the failure to build a cooperative partnership. At the same time, they have not conducted their relations in a vacuum, but rather in a global environment that has been largely conditioned by US hegemony and the market forces of the international economy. Moreover, the decisions that the parties made were path-dependent and produced outcomes that were not fully intended. In that sense, the narratives are not mutually exclusive, but rather entail various causal claims and theoretical schemes, to which we turn next.

EU foreign policy

EU foreign policy towards Russia constitutes a key case for examining the classic questions of who drives it, what motivates it and how much impact it has (Telo 2013), but with regard to relations with Russia these questions have not been addressed as systematically as they could have been. Russia certainly constitutes both a different and a difficult case, but it should be better integrated with the existing conceptual and theoretical literature in the Euroepean studies.

The first question, who runs the foreign policy, is framed in terms of intergovernmental and supranational perspectives, the former putting more emphasis on the member states, particularly the large ones and their decisions, and the latter on common institutions, 'Brusselization' and the impact of Europeanization on national foreign policies in general. With regard to EU–Russia relations, this question has been politically loaded with accusations that Russia is playing divide-and-rule tactics and is not respecting the role of the European institutions. Overall, it can be stated that there has been a bureaucratic Brussels-centric track manifested in developing the broad agendas and carrying out negotiations in those areas where the EU institutions have had competence, such as trade or visa issues. However, the EU has had an undeveloped general strategy towards Russia and the ability of the high representative or other leaders of the EU institutions to lead this overall policy has been notoriously weak. At the same time, various member states have been able to 'customize' EU policies – such as Finland in the Northern Dimension, Poland and Sweden in the Eastern Partnership, or Germany in creating modernization partnerships – or they have been able to put a brake on the relations at times, or foster them at least symbolically, particularly when they held the EU presidency. Moreover, it is often claimed that there was a shift in the EU policy towards Russia as a consequence of the eastern enlargement due to the growing influence of the member states that were critical towards Russia. The Ukraine crisis has tipped the balance in favour of the member states compared to Brussels and has underlined Gemany's role in particular (Forsberg 2016). This has served to increase EU unity, at least nominally. Yet it is difficult to conclude that the situation will prevail in the future as it was clearly an outcome of the crisis.

The second question about the nature of the EU as a kind of foreign policy actor that has or does not have a distinct quality has revolved around three alternatives. First, there is the view that the EU is, or at least is developing into, a traditional self-interested great power with military resources. This view has not been mainstream, because the realists usually downplay the EU as an actor, whereas those who highlight the EU's role in world politics regard it as a new kind of power, as a civilian power or 'postmodern superpower' (McCormick 2007: 33). The second view is that the EU is a trade power, whose primary interest and driving force in international affairs is its economic might. Third, there is the idea of the EU as a normative power, whose power resides in persuasion, ability to invoke norms, shape discourses and show example (Manners 2002; see also Forsberg 2011). The primary interest of the EU as a normative power is to promote universal norms, such as human rights norms, and to wield power through them.

The Russian view, but also the understanding of many Western scholars, is that in the Ukraine conflict, and even prior to it, the EU had been acting as a traditional kind of geopolitical power or as 'an empire' trying to expand its territorial area and enhance its relative power position through such manoeuvres (see Zielonka 2006). Yet the EU has been very reluctant to use the traditional methods of great power, particularly military force, in issues and areas that are of concern to Russia. The alternative view, that the EU is primarily a trading power, can be seen in the emphasis that the EU has placed on trade relations in its relations with Russia. The emphasis on trade can be seen as having undermined the view that the EU is a 'normative power', if 'normative' is defined here as an attempt to foster democracy and human rights in international politics. Nevertheless, the EU's overall preference for tying EU–Russia relations to a shared normative framework, and conducting negotiations on various issues on this basis rather than on attaining short-term benefits, can be seen as reflecting the ideal conceptualization of normative power. The same goes for the defence of values and international law in the context of the Ukrainian crisis, as manifested in targeted sanctions rather than in prioritizing trade interests with Russia. The Ukrainian crisis does not unequivocally settle the issue of whether normative goals matter for EU foreign policy or whether it is merely acting out of material self-interest, however. Moreover, it is important to note that these concepts of geopolitical power, trade power and normative power often serve to summarize the behaviour rather than explain it.

The concepts of normative power or civilian power explain the EU's behaviour to the extent that they are shared identities on the basis of which EU foreign policy is made. These concepts are indeed widely accepted and adopted by European leaders as descriptions of self-image. To a certain extent, these identities exist in contrast to the traditional powers. The key traditional power to which European identity is contrasted, however, is the United States, not Russia. Moreover, the identity of the EU is often contrasted with Europe's past rather than with an external 'Other' (Wæver 1996: 128).

The effectiveness of the EU's foreign policy has become a much-debated issue precisely in its relations with Russia. The EU's lack of impact has been blatant, despite the idea of a strategic partnership (Piccardo 2010; Haukkala 2010). According to Chris Patten (2009), the former Commissioner for External Affairs, 'Dealing with Russia has probably been the biggest failure in the attempt to make European foreign policy.' A Power Audit on EU–Russia Relations, conducted by the prestigious European Council on Foreign Affairs in

2007, found that the EU has hardly been able to influence Russia at all, although it is a far bigger power than Russia in conventional terms (Leonard and Popescu 2007). In the view of Hiski Hauk-kala (2009b), 'The Union has failed to reach practically any of the original objectives with Russia.' Other authors have been somewhat more optimistic, however. Charlotte Bretherton and John Vogler (2006: 153), for example, conclude that 'The record of EU–Russia relations is thus mixed, with evidence of EU influence in relation to economic matters.'

The EU's ability to influence developments in Russia and aspects of Russian foreign policy has been disappointing to many, particularly to those who share the EU's ambition to play a significant role in world politics. The EU's inability is puzzling insofar as it has been seen as possessing more traditional power resources than Russia. So the contrastive question is, in effect, why has the European Union only had a limited (or at least more limited than could be expected) instead of a wide impact on Russia; rather than why has the EU had less influence on Russia than on some other third parties, or why has the EU had less influence than some other actors?

There are at least four possible explanations for the EU's poor performance in EU–Russia relations (see Forsberg 2013). The first of these is related to the type of power resources. Traditional realists argue that the EU is weak because it lacks military power resources. This assumption is already somewhat problematic as the member states collectively outstrip Russia in terms of military power. More-over, a closer examination of many instances of EU–Russia relations reveals that it is seldom the lack of military resources that makes the EU weak. This is in line with the general perception that 'the absence of military capability was not identified as an issue by any of the third party representatives' (Bretherton and Vogler 2006: 9). As military power was virtually irrelevant on the EU–Russia agenda, at least up to recent years, we need to come up with other reasons to explain why the EU has been unable to influence Russia effectively.

A second explanation is related to power perceptions. It may be true that the EU possesses objective resources of power, but Russia does not perceive itself as being dependent on the EU. Russia sees itself as a great power that is gaining in significance in world politics and believes, furthermore, that the EU is in decline and dependent on its energy resources. The EU acknowledges the dependency but considers that the relationship is based on interdependency and stresses Russia's own dependency on the EU as a market area. As a shared hierarchy of power does not exist, the parties are unable to influence each other in any meaningful way.

A third explanation for the EU's relative weakness in EU–Russia relations has to do with immaterial power components, such as coherence, strategic skill and the will to exercise its power. These deficiencies are often apparent in the EU's policy towards Russia, but as a standard explanation for the failures, there is a danger that they may take on mythical proportions. Indeed, the lack of success often explains the lack of unity, rather than the other way around. In most cases, the EU would not have been able to have any significant impact on Russia even if it had been united. Indeed, even when the EU has been united and has had a relatively coherent strategy, it has still been unable to have any effect on Russia. It seems that the increased cohesion of the EU does not always raise the likelihood of an agreement, because it is in the interests of Russia to resist a more united EU from emerging, and therefore it has all the more reason not to 'budge'. Although the EU has been rather unified in its policy towards Russia since the Ukrainian crisis, the impact has been mixed at best.

Against this background, it is advisable to bear the fourth explanation in mind, namely that the expectations that the EU should be able to influence Russia in a vast number of issues are often false to begin with. Most cases predicated on the impression that the EU is not able to influence Russia are those where the EU has 'offensive' objectives and Russia has 'defensive' objectives. In other words, the EU wants to change Russia's policy in matters that Russia can control by virtue of its sovereignty. In such cases, it is difficult to imagine that any actor, regardless of the power resources, unity, determination and strategies at its disposal, would be able to get its own way. A fuller picture emerges when we see that in most cases to which Russia has attached primary importance, Moscow has not been able to influence the EU, or individual member states for that matter. Framed in a broader historical perspective, this can be seen as an achievement too.

To sum up, it is not easy to pinpoint one clear-cut factor that explains the successes and failures of the EU's attempts to exert its influence over Russia. Lack of unity and lack of coherence and political will certainly play a role, but equally it is implausible to think that greater unity and increased political determination would have helped to achieve radically different outcomes. There is no unified theory of power, and it may be futile to even look for one.

Indeed, in most episodes of power, small things and co-incidents may determine the outcome.

Russian foreign policy

For researchers interested in Russian foreign policy, the main question is often whether this policy is driven by power or ideology, as classically stated by George Kennan (1947) with regard to the Soviet Union or whether Russia's national interest is defined by geopolitics, security, economic interest, status or identity. It can be argued that all of the above are enduring goals of Russia's foreign policy (Donaldson and Nogee 2014: 4), but there are also more nuanced discussions on the basis of which both temporal and geographical variation is explained. Nonetheless, Russia's policy towards Europe has typically been seen as indicative of its overall essence.

The old debate concerning Russian foreign policy was mostly framed between what – in IR parlance – are known as offensive and defensive realists, namely those who see territorial expansion as the ultimate goal of Russia's foreign policy, and those who see Russia's interests more in terms of its defensive security needs. Alongside these two accounts, a growing number of scholars and pundits see Russia's foreign policy more in terms of economic gain. Some associate the economic gain with the nation as a whole; some, with the interests of the leading sector – gas and energy; while still others think that the economic interest is defined by an even smaller group of people who hold power and want to profit from it. In the words of Dmitri Trenin (2007), Russia's business is business. Sometimes the debate over the nature of Russian foreign policy can be simplified between two positions, namely between those who emphasize Russian national interest understood rationally (Schleifer and Treisman 2011) and those who think that various cultural, sociological and psychological factors play a significant role in Russian foreign policy, making it not irrational as such but changing the content of rationality (Forsberg and Pursiainen 2016). Moreover, it can also be asked whether various interests and psychological factors, such as power, economic profit or belief systems, are most relevant at the level of the national level, in the collective level of the foreign policy elites and decision-makers or even at the individual level of the leaders.

Domestic political explanations indeed surface quite often when Russian foreign policy is analysed (Kaczmarski 2014). There are two basic variants. On the one hand, domestic political explanations may refer to the changes in the domestic constellations of power and the policy shifts deriving from these changes. In the case of Russia, there have been no conspicuous changes of the governing elite, but alleged changes within the elite. The interests of the business elite were geared towards cooperation with Europe (Russia Beyond 2000 2000; Stowe 2011). Hence, the relative decline of the liberal elite and the rise of the *siloviki* in the early 2000s potentially explains the shift in Russia's foreign policy away from the Western and European orientation (Bukkvoll 2003; Kryshtanovskaya 2008). Another variant of domestic political explanation would be the diversionary theory of conflict, whereby conflict is an outcome of power holders who have domestic difficulties and who want to increase or restore their popularity by creating an external conflict. This chimes quite well with Russia's behaviour to a degree, as Yeltsin started to adopt a critical stance towards the EU as his popularity waned. The recent phase of the conflict between the EU and Russia can be related to fears that Putin's regime might be challenged at home, but the more conflictual period started well before Putin had any problems with the support of the masses in Russia. Margot Light and David Cadier (2015: 9) have concluded that regime consolidation has been the main objective of Russia's contemporary foreign policy behaviour.

The sociological and psychological perspectives often start from the premise that Russian foreign policy is driven by identity concerns, because interests are defined on the basis of a certain identity (Hopf 2002). Identity-based explanations are most often linked to the view that Europe has been Russia's most significant 'Other' and that Russia is a status seeker trying to restore and strengthen its position as a great power and acquire recognition for its equality in relation to European great powers (Clunan 2009; Leichtova 2014), but they also entail Russia's desire to be regarded as a European country endowed with attributes like democracy and a market economy (Splidsboel-Hansen 2002b). Status is not always seen as a separate foreign policy motivation, but it is quite intriguing to take this perspective seriously with regard to Russia, given Russia's often expressed desire to be a great power respected as such by others (Larson and Shevchenko 2010; Tsygankov 2012a). These identity theories may explain why Russia has been interested in creating and developing a partnership with the EU, because Russian leaders have seen Russia as a European power, and cooperation with other European great powers has been a traditional reference group and symbolic arena of its diplomatic presence. At the same time, identity theories can account for Russia's constant problems in its relations with the EU, as the EU has both questioned the Russian commitment to the European values and relegated its position of a great power to that of a junior partner. Although Russia had the privileged status of a strategic partner, it was still a third party rather than equal to the EU when rules and norms were negotiated, and not even on a par with great powers inside the EU when decisions in Brussels were taken. Russia's identity thus changed, and it distanced itself from Europe as defined by the EU (Tsygankov and Fominykh 2010; Schiffers 2015). Stephen White and Valentina Feklyunina (2015) have identified three basic identity discourses in Russia, arguing that the first discourse regarded Russia as a part of Europe, as defined by the West – a view that was predominant in the early 1990s. But subsequently, the mainstream view was based on the understanding that Russia was an equal and constituent part of a 'Greater Europe', while the third discourse, emphasizing Russia's normative superiority vis-à-vis the EU-centric 'Europe', has been in the ascendancy recently.

There is again no hard evidence to hand that would validate one account and disprove the others. They all offer valid perspectives on Russia–EU relations. One means of combining them has been through neoclassical realism; as Elena Kropatcheva (2012b: 38) has argued, in order to understand Russian foreign policy towards the West 'Both the domestic context of action – material power capabilities, subjective self-perception and perception of international realities – as well as objective changes in the international context, that is the actions of the West, have to be taken into account.' Typically, however, we would expect that Russia would seek cooperation with Europe if defensive security, long-term economic gain or just European identity were the primary driving forces behind Russia's foreign policy. On the other hand, if Russia's foreign policy is driven by the goal of territorial expansion or the short-term economic interest of a particular ruling elite, we would expect conflict. We would also expect conflict if Russian foreign policy is driven by identity, if identity duly means that there is a growing need to underline that Russia is special in some way and different from Europe (Neumann 1996). Status – or honour – would, according to Andrei Tsygankov (2012a), lead to cooperative behaviour if granted to Russia, but to conflict if status were denied, particularly when Russia itself is confident of its own status.

Although Russian foreign policy in general would be driven by all of the aforementioned goals, there are certain emphases in Russia's relations with the EU. As the EU is not a fully-fledged military actor, it is rather understandable that security concerns have not been primary in Russia's policy towards the EU. Most prominently, security concerns have emerged when Russia has assumed that EU enlargement would also lead to NATO enlargement. Yet security cooperation has been rather limited, even when the threat perception has been mutual. Economic interests have often predominated, but economic motives cannot provide an explanation for every political objective or trade dispute with the EU. Russia's identity position towards the EU has been contested in the Russian domestic debate. Russian leaders have emphasized both Russia's Europeanness and its distinctive features. Status often seems to be at stake. For example, foreign minister Sergey Lavrov (2013) very clearly indicated that the biggest problem in the EU's attitude towards Russia is that it does not treat it as an equal partner. Russia's willingness to establish a Eurasian Union comparable to the European Union can also be seen as a sign of status politics.

Overall, Russian policy towards the EU has mainly pursued its economic interests. Russia has favoured partnership and cooperation, refraining from using energy as a weapon against the EU, but it has also safeguarded its own economic benefits in various disputes. Security questions entered into the relations when the eastern enlargement started to encroach on critical areas, Ukraine in particular, with Russia vehemently protecting its sovereignty in all fields. Status concerns explain why Russia has been willing to cooperate with the EU but has been disappointed and has protested when its status as an 'equal partner' or as a great power with its own sphere of influence has not been respected. Identity concerns and the need for 'Europe' as an 'Other' became more visible only after the Russian attempt to become accepted as legitimately and fully 'European' failed towards the end of Putin's first term as president. Yet there is a lot of uncertainty when it comes to validating explanations for the true motivations behind Russian foreign policy because access to the decision-making process has been so restricted: the competition between two perspectives – domestic political motivation or the elite interests driving Russian foreign policy on the one hand, and national interests defined in terms of humiliating experiences, fears and strategic objectives on the other – are not easy to resolve.

There has been some discussion over Russia's influence on the EU and the policies of the member states. Although Russia has had a degree of success in fostering its objectives with regard to the individual member states, its access and lobbying capacity at the EU level have been rather limited. Since the mid-2000s, but particularly against the backdrop of the 2014 crisis and conflict in Ukraine, the debate over Russia's influence has concerned its 'soft power' in particular. Divergent views exist in this regard. On the one hand, some argue that Russia's soft power poses a danger to its neighbours and EU member states, undermining policies and creating undemocratic practices, for example through supporting right-wing groups. Peter Pomerantsev and Michael Weiss (2014) see that '[t]he Kremlin exploits systemic weak spots in the Western system, providing a sort of X-ray of the underbelly of liberal democracy'. On the other hand, others hold that Russia's attempts to use soft power do not wield much influence (Cwiek-Karpovic 2012). Joseph Nye (2013) is equally sceptical about Russia's soft power: 'Although Putin has urged his diplomats to wield soft power, Russia does not have much.' The debate has become sensitive as not all those who subscribe to Russia and its behaviour, particularly in the Ukraine crisis, can be seen as evidence of Russian influence. What we know is that influence attempts exist; some politicians as well as segments of the public support Russian views, but the majority of the EU populace has not been persuaded by the Russian positions and information campaigns. Russia's image has certainly not been enhanced, and very few believe in Russia's narrative of the Ukraine conflict, while the concrete decisions at the EU level have not been to Russia's liking.

EU–Russia interaction

The dyadic relationship between the EU and Russia has thus oscillated between conflict and cooperation (Webber 2000; Averre 2005; Piccardo 2010; Nitoiu 2014). The period of cooperation in the early 1990s after the end of the Cold War and the dissolution of the Soviet Union gave way to further conflicts in the latter half of the 1990s, renewed cooperation in the early 2000s and gradually more conflict in the latter part of the 2000s, with some hopeful signs during the Medvedev era, despite the war on Georgia ultimately culminating in the ongoing crisis and conflict in Ukraine. This leads us to seek an explanation for the dynamism in EU–Russia relations, as the pendulum swings back and forth between cooperation and conflict, or periods of optimism and pessimism in mutual relations.

The fact that cooperation between the EU and Russia improved and deteriorated at a roughly similar time across various issue-areas suggests that the central problem in cooperation was not so much related to the nature of the issues on the agenda, but to the formation of the relationship in general. It is intriguing to note that if the key to the puzzle concerns the relative frequency of conflicts and the lack of progress in the relationship, then our background theory suggests that the relationship between the EU and Russia should have been cooperative from the outset. By contrast, if we are to explain cooperation in the relationship, then our general theoretical expectations would suggest that the relationship between the EU and Russia should be conflictual by nature. If liberals expect cooperation, they should be puzzled by conflicts, and conversely, if realists expect conflict, they should be puzzled by the amount of cooperation in the relationship.

A typical way of explaining this pattern of variation in EU–Russia relations, and especially the negative trend leading to the Ukrainian conflict, is to look at the changes in the power relations between the parties. As Russia became stronger, and the EU gradually weaker, particularly during the financial and economic crisis that started in 2008, it was only natural that Russia would challenge the EU, and conflict would prevail over cooperation. These kinds of power political explanations are, however, problematic in many ways, but most significantly, the changes in power relations do not quite correlate with the cooperative and conflictual periods in EU–Russia relations. The period when Russia was most vulnerable coincided with the period when the country was also very critical towards the EU and the West, namely the late 1990s. Even fairly recently, before the Ukrainian crisis, Europeans were not considering how to adjust their policies towards a strong Russia, but how to cope with a weakening one (see e.g. Moshes 2012). As Fraser Cameron (2007: 117) has argued, it was Russia's weakness that increased its defensive attitude and made it difficult for the country to be flexible in its relations with the EU.

Theories of economic interdependence would explain EU–Russia relations from the perspective of economic dynamics. As already noted, interdependence is normally regarded as a source of cooperation rather than conflict, and thus a factor that pushed the EU and Russia closer together rather than pulled them further apart.

Nevertheless, both parties have also tried to decrease their mutual dependence, particularly in the field of energy, in order to gain more political as well as economic freedom of action. As Krickovic (2015) has argued, interdependence has not worked in EU–Russia relations because both sides have been concerned that, in the future, any interdependence would become asymmetrical, allowing the other side to take advantage. Moreover, the simple contact hypothesis postulating that increased interaction between the EU and Russia and their citizens would linearly improve the relations has turned out to be deficient.

Along with these material explanations, there are also ideational explanations of EU–Russia relations, such as those based on cognitive theories focusing on the belief systems, values and other elements related to the way they see and process information about the world. There is a long pedigree of these kinds of explanations, referring to the 'conflict between two distinct attitudes towards life and society: the Russian and the Western European' (Crankshaw 1946: 502). Hiski Haukkala (2010) and Christian Thorun (2009) have argued that different worldviews best explain the difficulties in the relationship. The EU cherished postmodern values, whereas Russia was committed to more traditional ones. Andrey Makarychev (2014) also offers a constructivist explanation, arguing that Russia and the EU have different views of normativity, and therefore their ideas of freedom, human rights or sovereignty clashed and affected cooperation; also in more technical issues. These explanations, which have become quite popular, have also been criticized, however (Klinke 2012). For example, Tom Casier (2013) has suggested that the value gap explanation is overrated and oversimplified. The difference in values does not matter as such, but it is essential that the parties construct the values in such a way that they are meaningful: a value gap has not created a similar antagonistic process in the relations between the EU and China. Samuel Huntington (1996: 242) famously regarded the West and Russia as representing different civilizations, but in his view, the relationship was not particularly conflictual and could be mitigated on the basis of an agreement on their basic equality and respective spheres of influence: the sensitive fault line in this clash ran across Ukraine.

Identity theories offer another often-used approach to EU–Russia relations. As identity and status theories of Russian foreign policy have suggested, historically, the recognition of identity was important for Russia in its relations with Europe (Neumann 1996), while the interpretation of Russia as a European 'Other' has been used in creating a distinctive identity for the European Union in general and some of its member states in particular (Neumann 1999). Against this background, Sergei Prozorov (2006) sees the EU–Russian conflict as arising out of the incompatibility of the subject positions of the two parties, which is established in the course of the interface of their policy discourses. But the identity theories, in addition to the problem of often circular inference, are quite static too, and they have a hard time explaining why the identities mattered at some point, but not at another.

The dynamism needed in the identity theories could therefore be seen as a result of the interaction between the parties (DeBardeleben 2012). From the perspective of structuration theory, the formation of identities is not a single act, but was rather an ongoing process whereby the EU and Russia were mutually reinforcing the negative image of each other. These negative images on both sides then legitimized practices that again reproduced the negative image of the other. In the period after 2004, as Sanjoy Banerjee (2015) has argued, the practices that the West and Russia generated were reproduced, and this created a negative spiral. Both sides repeatedly rejected each other's offers and, in the process, simultaneously vindicated the critical categorizations each formed of the other. The political dynamic started to reinforce what psychologists have called the fundamental attribution error (FAE), where actors perceive the hostile or otherwise problematic actions of others as emanating from their inherent dispositions or characteristics, instead of merely reflecting the situation they find themselves in (e.g. Kahneman and Renshon 2009). In other words, both the EU and Russia perceived the actions of the other as stemming from malign intent, instead of simply reflecting the happenstance of any given moment.

The EU and Russia were also prone to talking at cross purposes and understood basically all the key concepts defining their mutual relationship differently. Therefore, the two have put forward different interpretations concerning, for example, what democracy (Makarkin 2011: 1471), modernization (Mäkinen 2011) and reciprocity (Romanova 2010: 80) entail in the context of their relationship. Even relatively technical issues, such as corruption, have been based on radically different understandings of key terms (Pavlova 2014). But the biggest elephant in the room was arguably the notion of equality: for Russia, equality meant equal to the EU, while for the EU, it meant equal to the other non-members aspiring to have a relationship with the Union. These two views were never compatible. The EU thought it was doing Russia a great favour by conferring a special status upon it, but that was not enough as it did not include the EU's recognition of a sphere of influence. The Russian plan to create a Eurasian Union could be seen in this light as an attempt to form an entity equal to the EU and through which Russia could negotiate shared rules and principles.

The fact that the EU and the West in general did not recognize Russia's identity in the way that Russians wanted thus caused a setback in relations (Splidsboel-Hansen 2002b; Tsygankov 2012a). Russia's quest for equal status led rather to 'quixotic' practices that were dismissed by the West (Neumann and Pouliot 2011). Yet this way of explaining the conflict often ignores the fact that the EU and the Western leaders in general attempted, on several occasions, to offer Russia special treatment and to grant the country symbolic recognition: the practice of biannual summitry and the talk of 'strategic partnership' were primary indications of this (Forsberg 2014). With regard to the deterioration of the relations with the West, Andrew Wilson (2014: 183) considers that, in the final analysis, Russia's policy is driven by a victim syndrome, and the country has not been able to give credit to the chances that it has had, but has instead created a story where it has been mistreated and surrounded by enemies. Moreover, Russia equally often wanted to deny the EU vision of itself, and the Kremlin signalled disrespect, for example, by not returning calls or letting the EU representatives to wait for meetings. In addition, the negative spiral was not a linear process, with both Russia and the West willing to give their partnership another chance during the Medvedev era. The bottom line, however, remains that the Eastern Partnership, particularly in the run-up to the Ukraine crisis, generated a negative reading of the EU's intentions and the West in general in Russia.

Conclusions

This chapter has reviewed existing theories and explanatory accounts related to EU–Russia relations. We have looked at theories that explain the EU's foreign policy towards Russia and its alleged lack of influence, the driving forces behind Russian foreign policy as well as explanatory accounts of why EU–Russia relations have evolved in the way they have between conflict and cooperation. In summary, there are many plausible explanations of the development and eventual failure of relations. These range from power relations to economic interdependence and from domestic developments to psychological interaction dynamics. Their relevance largely depends on what we want to explain. Power relations explain why the relationship matters to both parties in the first place and why neither of them has been able to gain the upper hand. Of course, the perception of power relations is that Russia was weaker relative to the EU in the 1990s compared to the 2000s, and this explains under what terms cooperation was possible, but it does not explain the pattern of cooperation and conflict as such. At the same time, economic interests and interdependence have not protected the parties from conflict, and even if they have formed incentives for cooperation, they have also created problems in their own right. Identity constructions have also been sources of both cooperation and conflict.

EU–Russia relations are important enough that this relationship should also be seen as a possible test of the theories typically applied in the field of international relations as well as European and Russian studies. The limits of standard IR theories become rather clear when we see that the variation between more cooperative and conflictual periods did not follow in any logical way the changes in the power relations between the parties. Nor do liberal domestic politics or interdependence explanations offer any quick solutions to fully understanding the big picture. Social constructivist theories of identity are no longer helpful, because – if identity and cooperation are not defined in a mutually constitutive way – then cooperative and conflictual periods existed both when there was more of a shared idea of common identity as well as when there was less. Yet it is undeniable that power, interests, domestic politics, economic interdependence as well as identities and values do shape the relations. Perhaps one way of grasping the big picture of the ups and downs in the relationship between the EU and Russia is to think that realist and liberal factors of common interests push the parties towards cooperation, but problems with finding a partnership that would satisfy both parties' self-understanding of their status and normative visions tended to create recurring setbacks.

The development of EU–Russia relations has to be seen in a framework where it was structured by the international system shaped by the US hegemony and international economy. At the same time, from the early 1990s onwards, both the EU and Russia were in the process of developing their international identities and foreign policies, and in this process domestic priorities were often more important than investing in their mutual relations in the long term (see also Maass 2016). The paradox is that at the very start of these individual and mutual processes, they decided to create a highly institutionalized relationship that locked the two into detailed legal commitments that consequently constrained what was politically possible. Although both parties appreciated the importance of relations and have sought cooperation in good faith *as they have understood it*, they were not able to diplomatically solve the key issue related to the status of, or re-negotiate the foundation of, their relations in a mutually satisfactory manner. Ultimately, the relations were shaped by events and developments they were not able to control, but were forced to react to.

The significance of the Ukraine crisis can be seen in this light: it was more important symbolically than materially, and the parties lacked the means to manage the clash based on different conceptions of their rights and visions of themselves. Although Russia, from the very beginning, had two caveats that the EU and the West in general should respect, namely Russia's sovereignty and its privileged (although not necessarily exclusive) sphere of interests in the CIS, the EU could neither agree to, nor necessarily even correctly decipher and understand, these terms. It believed that Russia had committed to certain values that not only limited its own sovereignty but also that of the European great powers. In the same way, the geographical spheres of interest were recognized, but not fully respected, because the EU regarded the sovereignty and the subjective will of the countries in between as more important than Russia's view of its privileged rights in the area. Differences in understanding key terms and communicating intentions were pervasive. At the same time, we must take note of the fact that, to a degree, Russia was disingenuous in the sense that it framed, and effectively camouflaged, its criticism and increasing belligerence towards EU policies in technical terms. For example, in 2013–14, the key question in Ukraine was ostensibly the negative trade effects of the DCFTA, not the potential slipping away of the country from Russia's orbit. This made it easy for the EU to keep 'misunderstanding' (willingly or otherwise) the Russian complaints and insisting on the continuation of its policies without the perceived need to address the Russian concerns until it was too late. This is not to say that the EU should have simply caved in and accepted Russia's claim for a sphere of influence. Yet the failure to successfully address any of these issues resulted in mutually diminishing expectations and eventual attribution error and fatigue, as well as a chain of events that neither party could fully control. In a word, the Ukrainian conflict of 2013–14 was the perfect storm whereby all of these issues came together: the end result was the rupture of relations, leading to further diminishing trust and fading horizons for the relationship in general, all issues we turn to in the final concluding chapter of the book.

Chapter 10

Conclusions: The Past and the Future of EU–Russia Relations

We have never viewed Europe as a mistress. I am quite serious now. We have always proposed a serious relationship. (Putin 2015b).

I think Russia stays a strategic player in the regional and global challenges, [regardless if] we like it or not, but I don't think it's a strategic partner anymore. I wish it could go back in the future, I wish Russia would choose to go back to be a strategic partner in the future, but I don't think this is what is happening now. (Mogherini quoted in EurActiv 2014)

In this book, we have provided a comprehensive overview and analysis of the evolution, or perhaps degradation, of EU–Russia relations. The purpose of this concluding chapter is not to summarize the findings of the previous chapters. To that end, we have offered comprehensive sectoral conclusions along the way. Instead, this chapter revisits the question of why the partnership failed by looking at what the way forward could look like.

On the preceding pages, we have painted a vivid picture of a drawn-out political process between two 'strategic partners', which has included several ups and downs but which has also always been imbued with deep promise, meaning and importance by both parties. Yet the sum total of a quarter of a century of deepening interaction and institutionalization is grim indeed: Currently, the relations between the EU and Russia are steeped in a deep crisis, if not a dead end. Despite a flurry of activities over the years, undeniable successes have remained few and far between. On the contrary, mutual disillusionment has set in, with the conflict in Ukraine resulting in an open rupture in relations. A longer period of malaise and tensions between the EU and Russia seems to be in the offing.

Yet this is not what the two set out to achieve in the early 1990s, nor what they have aspired to along the way. In this book, we have offered our interpretations concerning how the EU and Russia have ended up in this state of affairs, while fleshing out some potential explanations for it. In short, the crisis was not predetermined, and it did not reflect a fully rational choice on the basis of their strategic or economic interests. Rather, the crisis is a strikingly suboptimal outcome that the parties could and should have avoided. Although a deepening partnership was no longer likely in the mid-2000s as it would have required a shift in domestic political priorities and values in Russia, neither was the scenario of confrontation: the slow stagnation of relations was regarded as the most probable development (Medvedev 2006). But due to various reasons, the parties were not able to avoid, or perhaps even chose not to avoid, the increasingly confrontational path, on the basis of assumptions and beliefs that they had formed of themselves and of each other. The attribution of malign intentions and the consequent perception of the actions of the other in this light led to the situation in spring 2014 where no agreement seemed plausible anymore.

That said, we must take issue with some of the received wisdom concerning the root causes of the crisis. As we have sought to demonstrate, relations between the EU and Russia have never been based on a one-sided imposition of objectives, norms and values. On the contrary, the institutionalized logic in EU–Russia relations was the product of mutual and hard bargaining, and the deal was one that Russia wilfully signed and ratified in the PCA. In a similar fashion, the subsequent events have shown how Russia has been anything but a hapless object of the EU's policies and hectoring. In fact, the reverse seems to be the case as on many occasions it has been Russia that has shaped the nature of the relations.

Neither was a geopolitical competition for power a key determinant of the downward turn in the relationship. Although the EU had geopolitical interests too, in terms of enlargement and having a 'ring of friends', and these clashed with what Russia regarded as its zone of vital interest, the EU was always reluctant to expand its influence in the former Soviet Union (apart from the Baltic states), and it did not want to directly challenge Russia. It was unwilling, however, to give up the right to conclude relations of its own with the states in the area. Nevertheless, after the big eastern enlargement in the mid-2000s, and due to the financial crisis that had plagued the Union since 2009, there was little general willingness to start new rounds of enlargement and to make extensive commitments to the states in the east.

It is also too simplistic to think that the key reasons for the deterioration of EU–Russia relations can be fully traced back to Russia's domestic politics, the civilizational divide and diverging societal values. Although it can be argued that there were differences with regard to these matters and that the pro-Western policy that Russia followed in the early 1990s, when Yeltsin was president, was not sustainable, Russia tried to improve relations with the EU both under Putin as well as under Medvedev, although the difference in key values had become plain. The EU was also willing to soften its demands regarding Russia's domestic value questions. The gap in values, worldviews and identities does explain why the chances of deepening the relationship have been rather slim, but the conflictual course was not preordained by these background factors.

Indeed, in our view, the problems in EU–Russia relations have emerged during and due to the course of interaction. In this respect, we contend that one of the main reasons for the dramatic rupture between the two was the existence of two separate levels, or dimensions, of relations. On the discursive level, the objectives and rhetoric of the early 1990s remained intact. This enabled the EU to keep insisting on the implementation of the PCA and other deliverables while Russia continued to pay lip service to these ideals. On the other, practice side, the everyday reality of EU–Russia relations had simultaneously progressed in an entirely different direction, where the implementation of agreed deliverables was the exception and not the rule, and where Russia was effectively traversing away from the common objectives, norms and values – and getting away with it with minimal resistance on the part of the EU. It was the existence of these two levels that enabled the continued pretence of a 'strategic partnership' while acting as the backdrop to the crisis that was perhaps bound to eventually come to a head between the two.

Although there were mounting problems in practically all issue areas due to the growing distrust, frustration and conflicting interests, the key problem that led to the explosion was the shared neighbourhood, where the objectives and modes of operation that the parties had adopted turned out to be incompatible, even mutually exclusive. Russia wanted to have its sphere of influence, a claim the EU refused for various reasons to accept, perhaps even to hear or understand. Other problems that the parties had were difficult to solve, but not as inflammatory. At the same time, they did act as the background noise to the relations, a negative overall backdrop that did contribute to the steady erosion of mutual trust and expectations concerning the future of relations. Therefore, once the crisis over Ukraine had erupted, both parties were in fact ready to think the worst about the intentions and actions of the other. Indeed, and to continue using the lens of two levels of relations, one can argue that to a degree the discursive level has now collapsed to the level of practices. This is understandable in the light of the severity of the crisis, but it is also regrettable because, if continued, it has the potential to rob EU–Russia relations of future potential and ambition as well.

In essence, one can envisage four basic scenarios for the future of EU–Russia relations: (i) the continuation of the current stalemate and confrontation; (ii) a return to the cooperation and business as usual that existed on a pragmatic basis before the crisis; (iii) a Russia-dominated outcome, whereby the EU is fractured and remains weak, with Russia building up its own sphere of influence not only in Ukraine but also elsewhere in Eastern Europe; and (iv) the opposite scenario, where the EU dominates and Russia is forced to acquiesce in the face of European values and policies. Some are tempted, perhaps, to add a fifth scenario that would entail a major war in Europe with all the potential nuclear horrors that it might unleash. At the time of writing, any of these scenarios are possible, although luckily not equally likely. Barring irrational and/or catastrophic mistakes or acts of desperation from a collapsing Russia, the fifth scenario can fairly safely be excluded. At the same time, the very fact that such a scenario warrants mentioning to begin with speaks volumes about the damage incurred to European security and stability in recent years.

There have been some attempts to create alternative visions for the future. The German Friedrich Ebert Foundation outlined four scenarios in its 2014 report (Scenario Group EU + East 2030, 2014). The first scenario was the benign 'Shared Home' built on pragmatic reasons. After a lost decade, the EU and Russia find shared interests from 2020 onwards and conclude a new free trade agreement which also integrates the Eastern countries in between. The second scenario, called 'Common Home', is based on common European values. 'Broken Home', on the other hand, is a scenario where the current confrontation between the EU and Russia continues and deepens, and a zone of instability emerges in the East. The fourth scenario is 'Divided Home', where 'Europeans live next door, but apart from each other' – a continuation of the current status quo. The German Marshall Fund of the United States (Forbrig 2015) published another scenario paper that starts from the assumption that 'conceivable scenarios are all based on different degrees of regime cohesion in Russia, and of unity among European and transatlantic partners'. The alternatives for Russian-Western relations are (i) standoff, (ii) Western decline, (iii) Russian decline or (iv) chaos. Each scenario is, according to the report, possible in the mid-term. As the author notes, none of these scenarios is bright, but they all 'defy the many hopes and efforts invested by the West in the transformation of Europe, and Russia, over the last quarter-century'.

There have also been similar exercises on the Russian side. For example, the influential Russian International Affairs Council published a report on the eve of the Ukraine conflict that fleshed out three scenarios for the future of EU–Russia relations: (i) political convergence with the EU alongside economic inter-dependence – essentially the realization of the agenda of the 1990s; (ii) the creation of a declarative political distance from the EU – effectively Russia walking away from partnership with the EU; and (iii) inertia – where close economic interaction is combined with the steady erosion of prospects for a future EU–Russia partnership. According to Irina Busygina, the author of the scenarios, continued inertia was the most apt characterization of relations between the EU and Russia, and she warned almost prophetically that the continuation of the trend was 'fraught with inherent contradictions and conflicts . . . lead[ing not] to a resolution, but rather to the *further accumulation* of issues . . . [that] may result in a gradual "slide" towards the scenario of open distancing [that] will drive Russia into a kind of a trap' (Busygina 2013: 71 [emphasis in the original]). The Institute of World Economy and International Relation's (IMEMO) forecast, written after the Ukrainian crisis had soured the Russia–EU relationship, expected that 'Moscow's relations with the West will most likely stay in place in the medium term' (Dynkin et al. 2014: 134). According to the report, the interdependency of the global economic system and the need to resolve the security questions on the global agenda, particularly the threat of radical Islamist terrorism, put limits on the sharpening of the tensions in the relations and brings some hope for normalization, although the political climate does not make quick progressive steps possible.

In our view, these different scenarios suggest two conclusions. First, they all include recognition of the essential vastness of the economic and political stakes in EU–Russia relations and the consequent imperative to develop mutually acceptable and advantageous relations between the two 'strategic partners'. This is also a recurring theme manifest in the previous chapters as well as a factor which, to a large degree, explains the repeated drives for 'fresh beginnings' in EU–Russia relations over the past two decades. It seems that practically no one in their right mind can envisage a feasible alternative to the building of relations between the EU and Russia. This applies to political leaders as well – the two quotes that open this chapter attest to that effect. Nor are these isolated utterances as it is not hard to come across statements to this effect on both sides. For example, in October 2015, Commission President Juncker noted how the EU 'must make efforts towards a practical relationship with Russia . . . we can't go on like this' (BBC 2015). Similarly, Foreign Minister Lavrov has argued how:

> There is no doubt that the European Union is our largest collective partner. No one intends to 'shoot himself in the foot' by renouncing cooperation with Europe, although it is now clear that business as usual is no longer an option. This is what our European partners are telling us, but neither do we want to operate the old way. They believed that Russia owed them something, while we want to be on an equal footing. For this reason, things will never be the same again. That said, I'm confident that we will be able to overcome this period, lessons will be learned and a new foundation for our relations will emerge. (Lavrov 2014b)

Interestingly, the public – at least on the Russian side – shares the sentiment. A poll conducted by Levada in November 2015 revealed that 75 per cent of respondents said that Russia should mend fences with the West. At the same time, 65 per cent of respondents saw that Russia should seek to accomplish this without undue compromises in its policies vis-à-vis the West (Hartog 2015). Indeed, Lavrov's – and perhaps Russia's in general – more hard-nosed approach hints at one of the key bones of contention, namely on *whose* terms the possible restoration of ties should take place. Or as president Medvedev (2016) pleaded with his audience at the Munich Security Conference, 'The challenges we are facing today will not lead to conflict but rather will encourage us to come together in a fair and equal union . . .' Otherwise, 'we are rapidly rolling into a period of a new cold war'. We return to this topic shortly, but for the time being, suffice it to conclude that the foundation for the restoration of ties still exists, and the necessity to eventually achieve that feat is widely acknowledged by the parties.

The second conclusion is no less sobering. The scenarios and public statements reveal a tacit recognition of the conflict potential in relations while they also seem to recoil in the face of that possibility due to the negative, even destructive, consequences such a rupture would entail. There seems to be a shared understanding that an open conflict between the EU/West and Russia is not in anybody's interests. At critical junctures, this shared understanding has probably had a steadying effect on the actions of both parties. For example, Russia refrained from pushing too hard militarily in Ukraine (although they pushed far too hard in any case), and the EU and the wider West clearly refrained from seeking to bring Russia to its knees through their sanctions against the country. As Sergei Karaganov has asserted (2015: 53):

> We should and can look for a new détente because the sides have already got much of what they wanted to get. Russia wanted to teach her partners to respect its interests by force, since persuasion and appeasement had failed. . . . The West wanted to prove that it is not a "paper tiger" and that it can deliver heavy blows.

Although tempting, we will not be offering our own forecast for the future of relations between the EU and Russia. For many, it seems that the question has already been answered: unless no major structural change internally on either side or in the international system follows, the present contestation, even conflict, is likely to continue. In our view, this seems a woefully suboptimal outcome of 25 years of relations and institutionalized interaction and one that hardly serves anybody's long-term interests. It is also normatively undesirable and one could argue that all the parties – the EU and its member states, Russia and the countries in between – deserve better. Therefore, the remainder of this chapter is devoted to pondering how the calamitous spectre of a continued conflict between the EU and Russia could be avoided and how the two could perhaps be re-steered along the path of partnership. In this respect, we would rather reword the title of this book 'partnership deferred', however indefinitely, rather than failed once and for all.

What might a sensible way forward look like? Traditionally, and to cut a very long story short, it seems that there have been two major strands of policy advice concerning the future of EU–Russia relations. On the one hand, we have had a school that has promoted the development of relations based on a strict adherence to 'European values' and a stringent application of political conditionality in the process. On the other hand, we have had another school that has argued that the root cause of the problems has precisely been the accent put on values and that the sensible way forward is to concentrate on common (economic) interests and to seek to develop ties in a piecemeal, almost neo-functionalist fashion (for a discussion of both strands, see Schuette 2004).

The current understanding concerning the two is that both value-based and interest-driven approaches have been tried, and both have been found wanting. We are not entirely convinced that this is really the case, as the discussion in this book has given ample examples of instances where the value dimension has, in fact, been sacrificed or at least short-changed by other political or economic considerations. In fact, it is little wonder that Russia has ceased to take the EU seriously as an international, let alone a normative international, actor in the process, and has come to view the EU as a 'cynical power Europe' that uses norms and values as double standards and shields under which the real business of economic and financial interests is nevertheless conducted.

To a degree, the current crisis has created an opening for the EU to reassert itself as a credible normative actor in world politics. But a unidimensional insistence on values and principles is not enough. The EU will also need a level-headed understanding of interests and an ability to pursue them when it is sensible, without unduly sacrificing its key values in the process. Therefore, it is not either/ or values and interests that are required, but both in order to have a sensible policy. Indeed, we argue that the distinction between values and interests is a false one, as the two are intimately linked, even fully immersed in each other. It seems to us that the EU's decision – taken unanimously by all the member states – not to accept Russia's actions in Ukraine highlights how widely this understanding is shared by the EU as well.

The essential question is whether a desirable, or perhaps more to the point, realistic scenario might be one where the EU and Russia can develop a common agenda of deepening and broadening their mutual relations towards some kind of 'Greater Europe' based on far-reaching economic integration and a set of shared values. There have always been some who do not deem such a goal feasible because of 'civilizational' or at the very least political differences that are seen as being fundamental obstacles to such a process. Today, there also exists a growing number of people who do not necessarily think that the goal as such should be rejected, but that for the time being all attempts in that direction are likely to be counterproductive. A less ambitious goal is therefore some kind of modus vivendi that would make mutual cooperation feasible again and perhaps over time create some progressive agendas. The minimalist goal is to think of EU–Russia relations in terms of damage limitation and to think that a realistic goal is one that avoids the relations going from bad to worse, and particularly to do everything to avoid a potential escalation of tensions into a military confrontation between the parties. The problem with such a minimalistic goal is that the other party, if cold-blooded enough, can always exploit this desire by using brinkmanship tactics. As Henry Kissinger (1957: 1) famously argued, 'Whenever peace – conceived as the avoidance of war – has been the primary objective of a power or a group of powers, the international system has been at the mercy of the most ruthless member of the international community.'

Yet a way forward must nevertheless be sought. Basically, one can see two avenues for rapprochement between the EU and Russia. The first is the striking of some kind of 'Grand Bargain' between Brussels and Moscow. The idea is not new (see e.g. Arbatov 1993). For example, after the Georgian war Russian analyst Timofei Bordachev (2008) suggested that a 'big deal' – energy in exchange for full-scale Russian participation in common institutions – would make relations between Russia and Western Europe stable for a long time. During the conflict in Ukraine, many commentators, particularly but not only Russians, raised the possibility of a 'new Yalta', or 'Yalta II' – an agreement, implicit or explicit, on the spheres of influence between Russia and the West over the countries in between – as the only feasible solution to the conflict and other similar proposals for finding a new basis based on realism and complementary of interests between the EU and Russia have been put forward recently (Buckley and Hille 2015; see also Pravda 2015; Charap and Shapiro 2014; van Ham 2015; Bordachev 2015).

But such a bargain is far from a panacea, and it has been strongly resisted both on moral as well as practical grounds. To begin with, there is no 'natural' way of dividing such spheres of influence, and countries whose fate would be regulated against their will would not accept such a system. Yet objections run deeper than this. As the realists have always argued, politics is at its core about making adjustments to changing power relations, but the parties should be able to form a common view of what the power relations are, how they have changed or how they are likely to change in the future. The EU and Russia currently not only lack a shared view of the values, but they also do not have a shared view of the power relations. The EU assesses that Russia is relatively weak and will only get weaker over time as its economic hardships multiply. Even admitting its own problems, the EU sees Russia's options as narrowing down. It does not think that China or any other alternative power centre can support Russia on terms better than the EU would be able to offer. The Russian view is exactly the opposite: the Kremlin thinks that it is the EU that is in decline, not only because of economic problems but also because of its flawed values and political institutions. Russia believes that the EU will collapse under its own weight and that there will be new leaders who are ready to compromise with Russia. In other words, both the EU and Russia think that time is on their side. In these circumstances, without a very concrete and palpable change in the material power conditions, no bargain can be attained because the perceptions differ so fundamentally. Power, after all, is not a language that both parties automatically understand.

These mutual failings have paradoxical effects on the interaction between the two. The EU's continued weakness gives Russia cause for hope in seeing whether it can wait out the EU's resolve. Russia's manifold problems can make the country more unpredictable, even aggressive and harder for the EU to deal with. In the past, Russia's 'weakness power' has managed to sway EU decision-making in at least equal measure as its strength. Therefore, one must ask whether we might be facing a scenario where the EU is forced to accommodate Russia out of concern for its weakness. But here we have the final and perhaps the most vexing problem at hand. A weakening Russia might not be one with which a stable accommodation could be reached. Paradoxically, it might very well be easier to deal with a strong rather than a weakening Russia. Kissinger's (1957: 146) insight about how a power will never accept a settlement that does not respect its 'vision of itself' is difficult to reach – and even more difficult to sustain – in a situation where that power is facing a downward trajectory: the appetite and the means to digest what it found enticing simply may not meet.

The impracticality is not the sole reason why an EU–Russia 'Grand Bargain' is not an option. To begin with, for Russia the

EU is not the only, or necessarily even the most relevant, actor. To a large extent, Washington is. Discussing the complexities of US–Russian relations goes way beyond the remit of this book (for a recent overview, see Stent 2014), but at the time of writing, it seems that Washington has even less appetite to accommodate Russian wishes for a recognized sphere of influence than the EU does. More importantly, and turning back to the EU, such a bargain would be Faustian in a sense that it would discredit the EU and the European project that underpins it. Moreover, the EU does not want to have a deal based purely on the logic of power because it would represent old-fashioned diplomatic culture that has so many times led to later catastrophic consequences in Europe.

In other words, it is not likely that the EU and Russia can find a way out of the present crisis through a package deal based on common interests or norms. This is a rather pessimistic conclusion indeed, and that is why we do not want to offer some simple policy advice: follow these three simple rules and all the problems will, like magic, vanish! The problem with such policy recommendations is often that they are either truisms or unrealistic wishes, impossible to follow or unclear how to execute. For example it is easy to recommend that the EU should stay united, but it is more difficult to say how this unity can be achieved and preserved in any given situation. In the same vein, it is easy to recommend that the parties should be realistic, but if the realities of the two parties differ diametrically, whose 'realism' is correct? We argue that unless a common view, even if minimalistic, either on power relations, long-term interests or normative arguments is achieved, cooperation will yield to conflict.

Assuming that a grand vision that trickles down to the practical level is not feasible, the second option would be to seek restoration of ties through pragmatic grass-roots cooperation in areas where it is most promising, with the hope that it 'trickles up', affecting the mutual overall understanding of the relationship between the two. But bottom-up approaches have their difficulties as well. To begin with, for years Russia has sought to control and curtail these activities – a trend that has only been increased during the Ukraine conflict. Although many pockets of cooperation still exist, the current dynamics do not point towards prospects of positive spillover. On the contrary, the reverse seems to be the case with many forms of cooperation, interaction between civil societies included, increasingly under threat and the difficulties at the grass-roots level negatively affecting the overall relations.

The failure to pinpoint an easy way forward, we argue, is not only a failure of our imaginations but one that points to the undeniable truth that the way forward, and we firmly believe there will have to be one, for EU–Russia relations, will not be an easy one. It entails, first, navigating the conflict in Ukraine in a sensible manner. This is far from guaranteed. Second, it requires an eventual arrangement, an accommodation of sorts, that takes into consideration the key interests and visions on both sides. This is a tall order indeed, in a situation where the basic problem remains the inability to conduct an open and honest dialogue. But it is a challenge that the EU and Russia must meet in order to avoid getting stuck in conflict mode. Talk of a 'partnership restored' is premature and remains way off our radar screens, but it seems clear to us that the current partnership that failed will simply not serve the long-term interests of either the EU or Russia and will, therefore, not be sustainable over the long term.

If the EU and Russian leaders are serious about restoring their relations, it is fundamental to rebuild some trust. For that, the EU and Russia not only should look to future cooperation but also need to address the past. It is not possible to simply wipe the slate clean and merely let bygones be bygones. But here we are faced with a genuine dilemma: as already mentioned, the narratives concerning the past are diametrically opposite, with both parties squarely blaming the other. The same applies also to the future, where the visions concerning the future of relations, to the extent they have been put forward at all, remain largely incompatible. At the same time, overcoming the current conflictual dynamics does not *necessarily* require the ironing out of all the current differences, however desirable that may be. Nor do the two need to aspire to perfect commonality in their respective visions concerning their future and past relations (cf. Haukkala 2010) to get their interaction on a more positive footing. Sociologist Richard Sennett, in his book *Together* (2012: 274), has pointed towards one avenue for achieving this when arguing how 'we frequently don't understand what's passing in the hearts and minds of people with whom we have to work. . . . a lack of understanding shouldn't keep us from engaging with others; we want to get something done together.'

There is no reason to think that this mundane everyday observation cannot apply to EU–Russia relations as well. But in order to get there, the improvement of ties requires restraint and reciprocity from both sides. Both parties should avoid the attribution error and appreciate the fact that not all the negative actions are due to the adversary's malign character, but could be attributed rather to situational factors. Russia in particular should relax its view that the EU and the West are 'out to get it', trying to influence the developments in the shared neighbourhood to Moscow's permanent disadvantage. It should not exaggerate concrete problems and turn them into a zero-sum game whereby all actions that it does not necessarily perceive as the best option taken by the West are targeted against it. By extension, the EU, and indeed the West in general, will have to pay much better heed to Russia's essential interests and viewpoints. Russia has made it clear that developments that do not take its interests into consideration will not fare well in the shared neighbourhood. This is a message that will need to be heard. At the same time, Russia will have to realize (and we believe that it eventually will) that it too cannot impose solutions on its neighbours: Russia will have to find other ways to deal with these issues or face the negative consequences.

A big leap in the form of a package deal that would magically restore the relations and sweep the problems away is not realistically possible. Therefore, both parties need to seek moderation in the short term and aim at taking baby steps to rebuild trust. The parties need to adopt a long-term strategic perspective and be ready to develop their relations and take bigger and bolder steps in recreating trust when the first experiences have been sufficiently encouraging. Over time, both parties will come to realize that although it was easy to break relations, their rebuilding will take a lot of patience and time. Whether this can be achieved by the current leaders remains to be seen. It is to be hoped that this realization will eventually lead the EU and Russia back to a path of partnership.

Milestones of EU–Russia Relations

December 1991	The Soviet Union is dissolved; the Commonwealth of Independent States is founded.
February 1992	The Treaty of Maastricht is signed.
March 1992	Negotiations for a Partnership and Cooperation Agreement begin.
June 1993	Negotiations for Russia's accession to WTO begin.
September 1993	Yeltsin disbands the Russian parliament.
November 1993	The Treaty of Maastricht enters into force.
June 1994	Negotiations for the PCA are concluded; Russia joins North Atlantic Treaty Organization's (NATO) Partnership for Peace.
December 1994	The first Chechen war commences.
January 1995	Austria, Finland and Sweden join the EU.
June 1996	The first Chechen war ends.
May 1997	NATO–Russia Founding Act signed.
June 1997	Russia joins the G8.
December 1997	The PCA enters into force.
August 1998	Russia defaults on its debts and the rouble crashes.
January 1999	The common currency euro comes into existence.
March 1999	NATO starts bombing Serbia over the Kosovo war.
May 1999	Treaty of Amsterdam enters into force.
June 1999	The EU Common Strategy on Russia is adopted.
August 1999	Vladimir Putin becomes Prime Minister; the second Chechen war commences.
October 1999	Russia presents its Mid-Term EU Strategy to the EU.
March 2000	Vladimir Putin is elected the President of Russia.
October 2000	EU and Russia normalize relations; the Common Economic Space concept is introduced.

September 2001	9/11 occurs; Putin gives a speech in the German Bundestag.
February 2003	Treaty of Nice enters into force.
March 2003	The European Neighbourhood Policy is first introduced.
May 2002	NATO–Russia Council established.
May 2003	The Four Common Spaces concept is introduced.
May 2004	The Big Bang Eastern enlargement of the EU takes place.
May 2005	The Four Common Spaces Road Maps are adopted.
January 2007	Bulgaria and Romania join the EU.
February 2007	Putin gives a speech at the Munich Security Conference.
July 2008	Negotiations for a new basic agreement begin.
August 2008	Russo–Georgian war begins.
September 2008	The EU freezes negotiations for a new basic agreement with Russia over Georgia.
September 2008	Lehmann Brothers collapses; the global financial crisis begins.
November 2008	The EU resumes negotiations for a new basic agreement with Russia.
May 2009	The Eastern Partnership is launched.
September 2009	The EU's Third Energy Package enters into force.
December 2009	The Treaty of Lisbon enters into force, the euro crisis begins.
January 2010	Eurasian Customs Union (ECU) is established.
August 2012	Russia accedes into the WTO.
September 2012	The European Commission opens an antitrust investigation against Gazprom.
July 2013	Croatia joins the EU.
November 2013	The Vilnius Eastern Partnership Summit occurs.
February 2014	President Victor Yanukovych flees Ukraine; the conflict in Ukraine begins.
March 2014	Crimea is annexed; the Russian destabilisation of Eastern Ukraine begins; EU imposes targeted sanctions against Russia and freezes political relations; Russia is suspended from G8.
July 2014	MH-17 is downed over Ukraine.

August 2014	EU imposes sectoral sanctions against Russia; Russia retaliates with its own counter-sanctions.
September 2014	Minsk I is signed.
January 2015	ECU is turned into the Eurasian Economic Union (EEU).
February 2015	Minsk II is signed.

Bibliography

Aalto, P. (2002) 'A European Geopolitical Subject in the Making? EU, Russia and the Kaliningrad Question', *Geopolitics*, 7(3): 143–74.

Aalto, P. (2006) *European Union and the Making of a Wider Northern Europe* (London and New York: Routledge).

Aalto, P. (2011) 'The Emerging New Energy Agenda and Russia: Implications for Russia's Role as a Major Supplier to the EU', *Acta Slavica Iaponica*, 30: 1–20.

Aalto, P. (2012) 'Introduction', in P. Aalto (ed.) *Russia's Energy Policies: National, Interregional and Global Levels* (Cheltenham: Edward Elgar).

Aron, L. (2015) 'Putinology', *The American Interest*, 11–(1), July 30, http://www.the-american-interest.com/2015/07/30/putinology, accessed 16 February 2016.

Aalto, P. and T. Forsberg (2016) 'The Structuration of Russia's Geo-economy under Economic Sanctions', *Asia Europe Journal*, 14(2): 221–237.

Aalto, P. and D. Korkmaz Temel (2014) 'European Energy Security: Natural Gas and the Integration Process', *Journal of Common Market Studies*, 52(4): 758–74.

Abdelal, R. (2013) 'The Profits of Power: Commerce and Realpolitik in Eurasia', *Review of International Political Economy*, 20(3): 421–456.

Adomeit, H. (2012) 'Putin's "Eurasian Union": Russia's Integration Project and Policies on Post-Soviet Space', *Neighbourhood Policy Paper 04*, July (Istanbul: Centre for International and European Studies).

Akçakoca, A., T. Vanhauwaert, R. Whitman and S. Wolff (2009) 'After Georgia: Conflict Resolution in the EU's Eastern Neighbourhood', *EPC Issue Paper No. 57*, April (Brussels: European Policy Centre), http://www.epc.eu/documents/uploads/961937412_EPC Issue Paper 57 - After Georgia.pdf, accessed 10 July 2015.

Allen, D. (1997) 'EPC/CFSP, the Soviet Union, and the Former Soviet Republics: Do the Twelve Have a Coherent Policy?', in E. Regelsberger, P. de Schoutheete de Tervarent and W. Wessels (eds) *Foreign Policy of the European Union: From EPC to CFSP and Beyond* (Boulder, CO: Lynne Rienner).

Allen, D. (1998) 'Wider But Weaker or the More the Merrier? Enlargement and Foreign Policy Cooperation in the EC/EU', in J. Redmond and G. Rosenthal (eds) *The Expanding European Union: Past, Present, Future* (Boulder, CO: Lynne Rienner).

Allen, D. and M. Smith (1990) 'Western Europe's Presence in the Contemporary International Arena', *Review of International Studies*, 16(1): 19–37.

Allison, G. (1971) *Essence of Decision: Explaining the Cuban Missile Crisis* (Boston: Little, Brown).

Allison, R. (2006) '"Russia in Europe" or "Russia and Europe"?', in R. Allison, M. Light and S. White, *Putin's Russia and the Enlarged Europe* (London: Royal Institute of International Affairs & Oxford: Blackwell).

Allison, R. (2013) 'Russia and Syria: Explaining Alignment with a Regime in Crisis', *International Affairs* (London), 89(4): 795–823.

Almunia, J. (2012) 'Perspective from the European Commission: Competition as a Tool for Sustainable Recovery', speech at the 6th Annual Global Antitrust Enforcement Symposium, Washington, DC, 19 September, http://europa.eu/rapid/press-release_SPEECH-12-620_en.htm, accessed 26 April 2016.

Ambrosio, T. (2009) *Authoritarian Backlash: Russian Resistance to Democratization in the Former Soviet Union* (Abingdon: Ashgate).

Andersen, M. (2000) '*Russia and the Former Yugoslavia*', in M. Webber (ed.) *Russia and Europe: Conflict or Cooperation* (Basingstoke: Palgrave Macmillan).

Andrews-Speed, P. (1999) 'The Politics of Petroleum and the Energy Charter Treaty as an Effective Investment Regime', *Journal of Energy Finance and Development*, 4: 117–35.

Antonenko, O. (2008) 'A War with No Winners', *Survival*, 50(5): 24–36.

Antrim, C. L. (2011) 'The Russian Arctic in the Twenty-First Century', in J. Kraska (ed.) *Arctic Security in an Age of Climate Change* (Cambridge and New York: Cambridge University Press).

Arbatov, A. (1993) 'Russia's Foreign Policy Alternatives', *International Security*, 18(2): 5–43.

Arbatov, A. (1994) 'Russian Foreign Policy Priorities for the 1990s', in T. Pelton Johnson and S. E. Miller (eds) *Russian Security After the Cold War: Seven Views from Moscow*. CSIA Studies in International Security No. 3 (Washington and London: Brassey's).

Arbatov, A. (1997) 'Russian Foreign Policy Thinking in Transition', in V. Baranovsky (ed.) *Russia and Europe: The Emerging Security Agenda* (Stockholm & Oxford: SIPRI & Oxford University Press): 135–59.

Arbatov, A. (2003) 'Russia Needs Military Industrial Cooperation with the West', *Nezavisimia Gazeta* (WPS Monitoring Agency), 7 April.

Archer, C. and T. Etzold (2008) 'The EU's Northern Dimension: Blurring Frontiers between Russia and the EU North', *Zeitschrift für Politik, Wirtschaft und Kultur*, vol. 18.

Arctic Council (2015) *Observers*. 7 May 2015, last updated 27 October 2015, http://www.arctic-council.org/index.php/en/about-us/arctic-council/observers, accessed 17 November 2015.

Aron, L. (2015) 'Putinology', *The American Interest*, 11(1), July 30, http://www.the-american-interest.com/2015/07/30/putinology, accessed 16 February 2016.

Ashton, C. (2010) 'Remarks by HR Catherine Ashton, at the Munich Security Conference', *Munich A 12/10*, 6 February, http://www.consilium.europa.eu/uedocs/cms_Data/docs/pressdata/EN/foraff/112774.pdf, accessed 13 December 2015.

Ashton, C. (2012) 'Statement by EU High Representative Catherine Ashton on the sentencing of "Pussy Riot" punk band members in Russia', A 370/12, European Union, 17, August Brussels, http://www.consilium.europa.eu/uedocs/cms_data/docs/pressdata/EN/foraff/132192.pdf, accessed 16 February 2016.

Ashton, C. (2013) 'Statement by EU High Representative Catherine Ashton on Ukraine', *European Union External Action*, Brussels, 21 November.

Asmus, R. D. (2002) *Opening NATO's Door. How the Alliance Remade Itself for a New Era* (New York: Columbia University Press).

Asmus, R. D. (2010) *A Little War That Shook the World: Georgia, Russia and the Future of the West* (Basingstoke: Palgrave Macmillan).

Assembly of Western European Union (1998) 'WEU's Relations with Russia', report submitted on behalf of the Political Committee.

Averre, D. (2005) 'Russia and the European Union: Convergence or Divergence', *European Security*, 14(2): 175–202.

Averre, D. (2009a) 'Competing Rationalities: Russia, the EU and the Shared Neighbourhood'. *Europe-Asia Studies* 61(10): 1689–713.

Averre, D. (2009b) 'From Pristina to Tskhinvali: The Legacy of Operation Allied Force in Russia's Relations with the West', *International Affairs* (London), 85(3): 575–91.

Averre, D. and L. Davies (2015) Russia, Humanitarian Intervention and the Responsibility to Protect: The Case of Syria, *International Affairs*, 91(4): 813–34.

Averre, D. and O. Reut (2005) 'EU–Russia Security Relations and the Republic of Karelia', in Antonenko, A. and Pinnick, K. (eds) *Russia and the European Union: Prospects for a New Relationship* (London: Routledge and International Institute for Strategic Studies).

Axelrod, R. S. (1996) 'The European Energy Charter Treaty: Reality or Illusion?', *Energy Policy*, 24(6): 497–505.

Baev, P. (2003) 'Putin's Western Choice: Too Good to Be True'. *Eurasian Security*, 12(1): 1–16.

Bailes, A. (2003) 'Russia's Place in European Defence', in G. Gorodetsky (ed.) *Russia between East and West* (London: Frank Cass): 75–85.

Baldwin, D. A. (1985) *Economic Statecraft* (Princeton: Princeton University Press).

Balfour, R., C. Carta and K. Raik (eds) (2015) *The European External Action Service and National Foreign Ministries. Convergence or Divergence?* (Aldershot: Ashgate).

Banerjee, S. (2015) 'Rules, Agency, and International Structuration', *International Studies*, 17(2): 274–97.

Baranovsky, V. (2000) 'Russia: A Part of Europe or Apart from Europe?', *International Affairs* (London), 76(3): 443–48.

Baranovsky, V. (2002) *Russia's Attitude Towards the EU: Political Aspects.* Programme on the Northern Dimension of the CFSP No. 16 (Helsinki: Finnish Institute of International Affairs).

Baranovsky, V. and S. Utkin (2012) 'Europe as Seen from Russia', *New Perspectives*, 20(2): 63–81.

Barysch, K. (2006) 'Is the Common Economic Space Doomed?', *The EU–Russia Review*, Issue 2: 11–16, November (Brussels: EU–Russia Centre).

Barysch, K., C. Coker and L. Jesien (2011) *EU–Russia Relations: Time for a Realistic Turnaround* (Brussels: Centre for European Studies).

BASF (2015) 'BASF and Gazprom Agree to Complete Asset Swap', press release, 4 September, https://www.basf.com/en/company/news-and-media/news-releases/2015/09/p-15-330.html, accessed 12 November 2015.

Bastian, K. (2006) *Die Europäische Union und Russland: Multilaterale und Bilaterale Dimensionen in der Europäischen Außenpolitik* (Wiesbaden: VS Verlag).

Bátora, J. (2013) 'The "Mitrailleuse Effect": The EEAS as an Interstitial Organization and the Dynamics of Innovation in Diplomacy', *Journal of Common Market Studies*, 51(4): 598–613.

BBC (2014) 'Negative Views of Russia on the Rise: Global Poll', *BBC World Service*, 3 June, http://www.globescan.com/images/images/pressreleases/bbc2014_country_ratings/2014_country_rating_poll_bbc_globescan.pdf, accessed 13 December 2015.

BBC (2015a) 'EU Must Improve Russia Ties, Says Commission Chief Juncker', *BBC News*, 9 October, http://www.bbc.com/news/world-europe-34486157, accessed 4 December 2015.

BBC (2015b) 'Russia Passes Law to Overrule European Human Rights Court', *BBC News*, 4 December, http://www.bbc.com/news/world-europe-35007059, accessed 20 February 2016.

Beauguitte, L., R. Yann and G.-P. France (2015) 'The EU and Its Neighbourhoods: A Textual Analysis on Key Documents of the European Neighbourhood Policy', *Geopolitics*, 20(4): 853–79.

Bechev, D. (2015) 'Understanding the Contest between the EU and Russia in Their Shared Neighbourhood', *Problems of Post-Communism*, 62(6): 340–49.

Bechev, D. and C. Nicolaïdis (2010) 'From Policy to Polity: Can the EU's Special Relations with Its "Neighbourhood" Be Decentered?', *Journal of Common Market Studies*, 48(3): 475–500.

Belokurova, E. (2010) 'Civil Society Discourses in Russia: The Influence of the European Union and the Role of EU–Russia Cooperation', *Journal of European Integration*, 32(5): 457–74.

Bengtsson, R. (2010) *The EU and the European Security Order: Interfacing Security Actors* (London and New York: Routledge).

Benn, D. W. (2011) 'Russian Historians Defend the Molotov–Ribbentrop Pact,' *International Affairs* (London), 87(3): 709–15.

Bernard, A., S. Paltsev, J. M. Reilly, M. Vielle and L. Viguier (2003) *Russia's Role in the Kyoto Protocol*. MIT Global Science Policy Change Report No. 98, June 2003, http://dspace.mit.edu/bitstream/handle/1721.1/3584/MITJPSPGC_Rpt98.pdf?sequence=1, accessed 12 November 2015.

Bicchi, F. (2006) '"Our Size Fits All": Normative Power Europe and the Mediterranean', *Journal of European Public Policy*, 13(2): 286–303.

Bindman, E. (2013) 'The EU's Strategy on Economic and Social Rights in Russia: A Missed Opportunity?', *East European Politics*, 29(4): 461–78.

Binns, C.A.P. (1977) 'The Development of the Soviet Policy Response to the EEC', *Co-Existence*, 14(2): 240–65.

Bisson, L. (2014) 'Cooperation between Russia and the EU in the Sphere of Migration', *Russian Politics & Law*, 52(6): 76–93.

Black, J. L. (2015) *The Russian Presidency of Dmitry Medvedev 2008–12: The Next Step Forward or Merely a Time Out?* (Abingdon: Routledge).

Block, L. (2007) 'International Policing in Russia: Police Cooperation between the European Union Member States and the Russian Federation' *Policing and Society: An International Journal of Research and Policy*, 17(4): 367–87.

Bogomolov, A. and O. Lytvynenko (2012) 'A Ghost in the Mirror: Russian Soft Power in Ukraine', *Chatham House Briefing Paper*, January, http://www.chathamhouse.org/publications/papers/view/181667, accessed 10 December 2015.

Boonstra, J. (2015) 'Kazahkstan: The Emerging Power Project', in G. Grevi and D. Keohane (eds) *Challenges for European Foreign Policy in 2015: How Others Deal with Disorder* (Madrid: FRIDE).

Bordachev, T. (2003) 'Strategy and Strategies', in A. Moshes (ed.) *Rethinking the Respective Strategies of Russia and the European Union*, Special FIIA-Carnegie Moscow Center Report (Helsinki and Moscow: Finnish Institute of International Affairs and Carnegie Moscow Center).

Bordachev, T. and Moshes, A. (2004) 'Is the Europeanization of Russia Over?' *Russia in Global Affairs*, 2(2): 90–102.

Bordachev, T. (2006) 'Toward a Strategic Alliance', *Russia in Global Affairs*, 2(2): 112–123.

Bordachev, T. (2008) 'The Limits of Rational Choice', *Russia in Global Affairs*, No. 4: 90–105.

Bordachev, T. (2015) 'Russia and Europe: A New Round?', *Russia in Global Affairs*, 17 December, http://eng.globalaffairs.ru/book/Russia-and-Europe-A-New-Round-17897, accessed 16 February 2016.

Bordachev, T. and A. Moshes (2004) 'Is the Europeanization of Russia Over?', *Russia in Global Affairs*, 2(2): 89–102.

Bordachev, T. and T. Romanova (2003) 'Russia's Choice Should Provide for Liberty of Action', *Russia in Global Affairs*, 1(2): 56–70.

Borger, J. (2015) 'Russia Risks a Repeat of Doomed Afghan War in Syria, Says EU Foreign Policy Chief', *The Guardian*, 28 October.

Borko, Y. (2004) 'Rethinking Russia-EU Relations', *Russia in Global Affairs*, 2(3): 168–78.

Börzel, T. A. (2010) *The Transformative Power of Europe Reloaded. The Limits of External Europeanization*. KFG Working Paper, No. 11, February 2010, http://www.polsoz.fu-berlin.de/en/v/transformeurope/publications/working_paper/WP_11_February_Boerzel1.pdf, accessed 20 February 2016.

Bosse, G. (2011) 'The EU in Georgia: Towards a Coherent Crisis Management Strategy', in E. Gross and A. Juncos (eds) *EU Conflict Prevention and Crisis Management: Roles Institutions and Policies* (Abingdon: Routledge).

Boussena, S. and C. Locatelli (2013) 'Energy Institutional and Organisational Changes in EU and Russia: Revisiting Gas Relations', *Energy Policy*, 55: 180–9.

Bovt, G. (2010) 'Russia: Customs Union Instead of WTO?', *EurActiv*, 9 April.

Bozhilova, D. and T. Hashimoto (2010) 'EU–Russia Energy Relations: A Choice between Rational Self-interest and Collective Action', *European Security*, 19(4): 627–42.

Braghiroli, S. (2015) 'Voting on Russia in the European Parliament: The Role of National and Party Group Affiliations', *Journal of Contemporary European Studies*, 23(1): 58–81.

Bretherton, C. and J. Vogler (2006) *The European Union as a Global Actor*, 2nd edn (Oxford: Routledge).

Broadman, H. (2004) 'Global Economic Integration: Prospects for WTO Accession and Continued Russian Reforms', *Washington Quarterly*, 27(2): 79–98.

Browning, C. and P. Joenniemi (2004) 'Regionality Beyond Security? The Baltic Sea Region after Enlargement', *Cooperation and Conflict*, 39(3): 233–53.

Buckley, N. and K. Hille (2015) 'Russia: Powers in the Balance', *Financial Times*, July 5, http://www.ft.com/intl/cms/s/0/1b27cd0e-209e-11e5-ab0f-6bb9974f25d0.html, accessed 4 December 2015.

Buckley, N. and R. Olearchyk (2013) 'Ukraine Refuses to Sign up to Europe Deal', *Financial Times*, 29 November, http://www.ft.com/intl/cms/s/0/2a1380b2-58de-11e3-9798-00144feabdc0.html, accessed 13 December 2015.

Bukkvoll, T. (2003) 'Putin's Strategic Partnership with the West: The Domestic Politics of Russian Foreign Policy', *Comparative Strategy*, 22(3): 223–42.

Bull, H. (1982) 'A New Course for Britain and Western Europe', *SAIS Review*, 4: 41–51.

Busygina, I. (2007) 'Russia's Regions in Shaping National Foreign Policy.', in J. Gower and G. Timmins (eds), *Russia and Europe in the Twenty-First Century: An Uneasy Partnership* (London: Anthem Press).

Busygina, I. (2013) 'Russia–European Union Relations: Current Status and Development Prospects: Analytical Report', in I. S. Ivanov (ed.) *Russia–European Union: Potential for Partnership* (Moscow: Russian International Affairs Council).

Byford, A. (2012) 'The Russian Diaspora in International Relations: "Compatriots" in Britain', *Europe-Asia Studies*, 64(4): 715–35.

Camacho, J., Y. Melikhova and M. Rodrigues (2013) 'Russia's WTO Accession and Trade in Services: An Examination into Russia-EU Relationships', *Eurasian Geography and Economics*, 54(3): 322–41.

Cameron, F. (2007) *An Introduction to European Foreign Policy* (London and New York: Routledge).

Caporaso, J. (1996) 'The European Union and Forms of State: Westphalian, Regulatory or Post-Modern', *Journal of Common Market Studies*, 34(1): 29–51.

Carlsnaes, W. (2004) 'Where Is the Analysis of European Foreign Policy Going?', *European Politics*, 5(4): 495–508.

Casier, T. (2011) 'Russia's Energy Leverage over the EU: Myth or Reality?', *Perspectives on European Politics and Society*, 12(4): 493–508.

Casier, T. (2013) 'The EU–Russia Strategic Partnership: Challenging the Normative Argument', *Europe-Asia Studies*, 65(7): 1377–95.

Charap, S. and J. Shapiro (2014) 'How to Avoid a New Cold War', *Current History*, 113(765): 265–71.

Charap, S. and M. Troitskiy (2014) 'Russia, the West and the Integration Dilemma', *Survival*, 55(6): 49–62.

Charter of Paris (1990) *Charter of Paris 1990 for a New Europe*, CSCE 1990 Summit, Paris, 19–21 November.

Checkel, J. (1997) *Ideas and International Political Change: Soviet/Russian Behavior and the End of the Cold War* (New Haven: Yale University Press).

Chernoff, F. (2007) *Theory and Metatheory in International Relations* (Basingstoke: Palgrave Macmillan).

Chizhov, V. (2003a) 'From St Petersburg to Rome', *International Affairs* (Moscow), 49(5): 8–16.

Chizhov, V. (2003b) 'From Utopia to Reality', *Russia in Global Affairs*, No. 2, http://eng.globalaffairs.ru/number/n_1071, accessed 13 December 2015.

Chizhov, V. (2005) 'Russia–EU Cooperation: The Foreign Policy Dimension', *International Affairs* (Moscow), 50(6): 79–87.

Chizhov, V. (2006) Remarks at the 135th Bergedorf Round Table: 'Interests and Partners of German Foreign Policy', Berlin, 29 September–1 October, www.koerber-stiftung.de/bg/recherche/pdf_protokoll/bnd_135_en_text.pdf, accessed 27 June 2007.

Chizhov, V. (2012) 'Russia–EU Strategic Partnership: The Eurocrisis Is Not a Reason to Pause', *International Affairs* (Moscow), July 2012, http://www.russianmission.eu/en/interviews/russia-eu-strategic-partnership-eurocrisis-not-reason-pause-article-ambassador-chizhov-in, accessed 5 November 2015.

Chowdhury, A. (2003) 'WTO Accession: What's in It for Russia?', *William Davidson Institute Working Paper no 595*, July; http://www.wdi.umich.edu/files/Publications/WorkingPapers/wp595.pdf, accessed 26 June 2007.

Christou, G. (2010) 'European Union Security Logics to the East: The European Neighbourhood Policy and the Eastern Partnership', *European Security*, 19(3): 413–30.

Christou, G. (2011) 'Bilateral Relations with Russia and the Impact on EU Policy: The Cases of Cyprus and Greece', *Journal of Contemporary European Studies*, 19(2): 225–36.

Chryssochoou, D. N. (2001) *Theorizing European Integration* (London: Sage).

Ciuta, F. (2010) 'Conceptual Notes on Energy Security: Total or Banal Security?', *Security Dialogue*, 41(2): 123–44.

Clark, C. (2012) *The Sleepwalkers: How Europe Went to War in 1914* (London: Allen Lane).

Cliff, I. (2011) 'The Corfu Process – What Was It All About?', in *The OSCE Yearbook 2011* (Hamburg: CORE), http://ifsh.de/file-CORE/documents/yearbook/english/11/Cliff-en.pdf, accessed 1 July 2015.

Clunan, A. (2009) *The Social Construction of Russia's Resurgence: Aspirations, Identity and Security Interests* (Baltimore, MD: The Johns Hopkins University Press).

Common Steps (2011) *Common Steps Towards Visa Free Short-Term Travel of Russian and EU Citizens (Russia-EU Visa Dialogue)*. Final. December 2011, http://ec.europa.eu/dgs/home-affairs/what-we-do/policies/international-affairs/russia/docs/common_steps_towards_visa_free_short_term_travel_en.pdf, accessed 5 November 2015.

Conley, H. A. and C. Rohloff (2015) 'The New Ice Curtain. Russia's Strategic Reach to the Arctic', a report of the CSIS Europe Program, August, http://csis.org/files/publication/150826_Conley_NewIceCurtain_Web.pdf, accessed 16 November 2015.

Connolly, R. (2011) 'Financial Constraints on the Modernization of the Russian Economy', *Eurasian Geography and Economics*, 52(3): 428–59.

Connolly, R. (2015a) 'Economic Modernisation in Russia: The Role of the World Trade Organization', *European Politics and Society*, 16(1): 27–44.

Connolly, R. (2015b) 'Troubled Times: Stagnation, Sanctions and the Prospects for Economic Reform in Russia', *Chatham House Research Paper*, February (London: Chatham House).

Connolly, R. (2015c) 'Russia's Finances Are Not as Vulnerable as They Appear', *Chatham House Expert Comment*, 8 June, http://www.chathamhouse.org/expert/comment/17826?dm_i=1TYG,3G4MC,BLOMQG,CC9KI,1, accessed 12 June 2015.

Connolly, R. and P. Hanson (2012) 'Russia's Accession to the World Trade Organization', *Eurasian Geography and Economics*, 53(4): 479–501.

Contact Group (2005) 'Guiding Principles of the Contact Group for a Settlement of the Status of Kosovo', *UN Security Council S/2005/709 Annex*, http://www.securitycouncilreport.org/atf/cf/%7B65BFCF9B-6D27-4E9C-8CD3-CF6E4FF96FF9%7D/Kos S2005709.pdf, accessed 13 December 2015.

Cooper, J. (2006) 'Can Russia Compete in the Global Economy?', *Eurasian Geography and Economics*, 47(4): 407–25.

CORDIS (1996) 'EU and Russia to Reinforce Cooperation in Science and Technology', press release, 31 October, http://cordis.europa.eu/news/rcn/7207_en.html, accessed 23 June 2015.

CORDIS (2001) 'Busquin Signs EU–Russia Energy and Space Deals', press release, 4 October, http://cordis.europa.eu/news/rcn/17432_en.html, accessed 23 June 2015.

Cornell, S. E., D. J. Smith and S. F. Starr (2007) *The August 6 Bombing Incident in Georgia: Implications for the Euro-Atlantic Region*, Silk Road Paper, October (Washington, DC: Johns Hopkins).

Corriere della Sera (2015) Vladimir Putin, interview to the Italian newspaper *Corriere della Sera*, 6 July.

Council of the European Union (2002) Annex IV Arrangements for Consultation and Russia European Union Crisis Management.

Council of the European Union (2003) 'Common Position concerning restrictive measures against the leadership of the Transnistrian region of the Moldovan Republic', 139/CFSP, Brussels, 27 February.

Council of the European Union (2005) 'Joint Press Release on the IV Northern Dimension Ministerial Meeting', Brussels, 21 November, available at http://www.consilium.europa.eu/uedocs/cms_data/docs/pressdata/en/er/87071.pdf, accessed 26 April 2016.

Council of the European Union (2006) '2721st Council Meeting: Transport, Telecommunications and Energy', press release, 27 March, Brussels.

Council of the European Union (2009) 'European Security Strategy – A Secure Europe in a Better World', report on the implementation of the European Security Strategy, http://www.consilium.europa.eu/en/documents-publications/publications/2009/pdf/european-security-strategy-secure-europe-better-world/, accessed 26 April 2016.

Council of the European Union (2014) 'Joint EU–Russia Statement on Combatting Terrorism', 5816/14, 28 January, Brussels, http://www.consilium.europa.eu/uedocs/cms_Data/docs/pressdata/EN/foraff/140835.pdf, accessed 12 November 2015.

Crankshaw, E. (1946) 'Russia in Europe: The Conflict of Values', *International Affairs*, 22(4): 501–10.

Crotty, J., S. M. Hall and S. Ljubownikow (2014) 'Post-Soviet Civil Society Development in the Russian Federation: The Impact of the NGO Law', *Europe-Asia Studies*, 66(8): 1253–69.

Ćwiek-Karpowicz, J. (2012) 'Limits to Russian Soft Power in the Post-Soviet Area', *DGAPanalyse 8* (Berlin: German Council on Foreign Relations).

Damro, C. (2012) 'Market Power Europe', *Journal of European Public Policy*, 19(5): 682–99.

Dangerfield, M. (2011) 'Belarus, Moldova and Ukraine: In or Out of European Regional International Society?', *Journal of European Integration*, 33(2): 215–33.

Danilov, D. (2005a) 'European Choice of Russia', *International Affairs* (Moscow), 51(5): 144–58.

Danilov, D. (2005b) 'Russia and European Security', in D. Lynch (ed.) *What Russia Sees*, Chaillot Paper No 74: (Paris: European Union Institute for Security Studies).

Dannreuther, R. (2006) 'Developing the Alternative to Enlargement: The European Neighbourhood Policy', *European Foreign Affairs Review*, 11(2): 183–201.

Darczewska, J. (2014) *The Anatomy of Russian Information Warfare: The Crimean Operation, a Case Study* (Warsaw: Centre for Eastern Studies), http://www.osw.waw.pl/sites/default/files/the_anatomy_of_russian_information_warfare.pdf, accessed 10 November 2015.

David, M., J. Gower and H. Haukkala (eds) (2013) *National Perspectives on Russia: European Foreign Policy in the Making?* (London and New York: Routledge).

Davis, L. (2009) 'Ten Years of Anti-dumping in the EU: Economic and Political Targeting', *Global Trade and Customs Journal*, 4(7–8): 213–32.

Dawisha, K. (2014) *Putin's Kleptocracy. Who Owns Russia?* (New York: Simon & Schuster).

Debaere P. and T. Haesebrouck (2015) 'European Council', in K. E. Jørgensen, Å. Kalland, E. Drieskens, K. Laatikainen and B. Tonra (eds) *The Sage Handbook of European Foreign Policy* (London: Sage).

DeBardeleben, J. (2012) 'Applying Constructivism to Understanding EU–Russian Relations', *International Politics*, 49(4): 418–33.

Delegation of the EU to Russia (2014) 'Overview – The EU and Human Rights in Russia', *Moscow*, available at http://eeas.europa.eu/delegations/russia/eu_russia/civil_society_dialogue/overview/index_en.htm, accessed 11 December 2015.

Dempsey, J. (2004) 'EU Admits Flaws in Relationship with Russia', *Financial Times*, 23 February.

Deriglazova, L. (2013) 'Human Rights in EU–Russia Relations: A Human Rights Mechanism', *Vestnik IKBFU*, Issue 6: 58–69.

Dettke, D. (2011) 'Europe and Russia: from neighborhood without a shared vision to a modernization partnership', *European Security* 20–(1): 127–142.

Deutsche Welle (2003) 'Yukos Affair Overshadows EU–Russian Summit', *Deutsche Welle*, 6 November.

Devyatkov, A. (2012) 'Russian Policy Toward Transnistria', *Problems of Post-Communism*, 59(3): 53–62.

Diesen, G. and S. Wood (2012) 'Russia's Proposal for a New Security System: Confirming Diverse Perspectives', *Australian Journal of International Affairs*, 66(4): 450–67.

Dobrokhotov, R. (2015) 'Sanctions Against Russia: Economic and Political Consequences', in A. Pabriks and A. Kudors (eds) *The War in Ukraine: Lessons for Europe* (Riga: University of Latvia Press).

Dombey, D. (2006) 'Putin's Uncomfortable Day in Helsinki', *Financial Times*, 24 November, http://www.ft.com/intl/cms/s/0/678a75ec-7be4-11db-b1c6-0000779e2340.html#axzz40VUiCED6, accessed 16 February 2016.

Donaldson, R. and J. Nogee (2014) *The Foreign Policy of Russia: Changing Systems, Enduring Interests*, 5th edn (Abingdon: Routledge).

Dragneva, R. and K. Wolczuk (2013) 'Commitment, Asymmetry and Flexibility: Making Sense of Eurasian Economic Integration', in R. Dragneva and K. Wolczuk (eds) *Eurasian Economic Integration: Law, Policy and Politics* (Cheltenham: Edward Elgar).

Drezner, D. W. (1999) *The Sanctions Paradox: Economic Statecraft and International Relations* (Cambridge and New York: Cambridge University Press).

Duke, S. (2015) 'Presidencies: The Tale of Two and a Half Presidencies', in K. E. Jørgensen, Å. Kalland, E. Drieskens, K. Laatikainen and B. Tonra (eds) *The Sage Handbook of European Foreign Policy* (London: Sage).

Dura, G. (2009) 'EUBAM Moldova-Ukraine', in G. Grevi, D. Helly and D. Keohane (eds) *European Security and Defence Policy: The First 10 Years (1999–2009)* (Paris: The European Union Institute for Security Studies).

Dynkin, A., V. Baranovsky, I. Kobrinskaya, G. Machavariani, S. Afontsev, Y. Mirkin, A. Kuznetsov, et al. (2014) 'Russia and the World 2015 – IMEMO Forecast', *Perspectives*, 22(2): 113–36.

ECFR (2016) *European Foreign Policy Scorecard 2016* (London: European Council on Foreign Relations). The Economist (2008) 'Whataboutism', 31 January, http://www.economist.com/node/10598774, accessed 16 February 2016.

Eder, F. and C. B. Schiltz (2014) 'Russland Wird Schwächer: José Manuel Barroso Hält einen Zusammenbruch für Verkraftbar', *Welt am Sonntag*, 21 December.

Electoral Geography (2006) 'Transnistria (part of Moldova). Independence Referendum, 2006', *Electoral Geography*, http://www.electoralgeography.com/en/countries/t/transnistria/2006-independence-referendum-transnistria.html, accessed 4 December 2015.

Emerson, M. (2005) 'EU–Russia Four Common Spaces and the Proliferation of the Fuzzy', CEPS Policy Brief No. 71, May (Brussels: Centre for European Policy Studies).

Emmerson, C. (2013) 'The Artic: Promise or Peril?', in J. H. Kalicki and D. L. Goldwyn (eds) *Energy and Security. Strategies for a World in Transition*, 2nd edn (Washington, DC, and Baltimore: Woodrow Wilson Center Press and Johns Hopkins University Press).

English, R. D. (2000) *Russia and the Idea of the West: Gorbachev, Intellectuals, and the End of the Cold War* (New York: Columbia University Press).

Entin, M. (2006) 'EU–Russia: The Common Space of Science, Education and Culture', *The EU–Russia Review*, Issue 2, November (Brussels: EU–Russia Centre).

Esytina, M., C. Fearon and N. Leatherbarrow (2013) 'The Bologna Process in Higher Education: An Exploratory Study in a Russian Context', *Quality Assurance in Education*, 21(2): 145–61.

Etzold, T. and H. Haukkala (2011) 'Is There a Nordic Russia Policy? Swedish, Finnish and Danish Relations with Russia in the Context of the European Union', *Journal of Contemporary European Studies*, 19(2): 249–60.

EU Centres World Meeting (2012) *Networking Conference, Centre Profiles*, Brussels, 22–24 October, http://eeas.europa.eu/eu-centres/eu-centres_brochure_2012_en.pdf, accessed 6 November 2015.

EurActiv (2012a) 'Syria Crisis Tops EU–Russia Summit Agenda', *EurActiv.com*, 4 June, http://www.euractiv.com/global-europe/syria-crisis-tops-eu-russia-summ-news-513101, accessed 3 November 2015.

EurActiv (2012b) 'Putin Slams Barroso: "You Know You Are Wrong, You Are Guilty"', *EurActiv.com*, 21 December, available at http://www.euractiv.com/energy/putin-barroso-right-guilty-news-516827, accessed 13 November 2015.

EurActiv (2014) 'Mogherini: Russia Is No Longer the EU's Strategic Partner', *EurActiv.com*, 2 September, http://www.euractiv.com/sections/global-europe/mogherini-russia-no-longer-eus-strategic-partner-308152, accessed 10 July 2015.

EurActiv (2015) 'Juncker: NATO Is Not Enough, EU Needs an Army', *EurActiv.com*, 9 March, available at http://www.euractiv.com/sections/global-europe/juncker-nato-not-enough-eu-needs-army-312724, accessed 2 November 2015.

European Commission (2000) 'Commissioner Philippe Busquin Visits Russia', press release, 8 September, Brussels, http://europa.eu/rapid/press-release_IP-00-987_en.htm, accessed 23 June 2015.

European Council (1999b) 'Presidency Conclusions. Annex II: Declaration on Chechnya', Helsinki 10–11 December.

European Commission (2004a) *Country Strategy Paper 2004–2006, National Indicative Programme 2005–2006 – Moldova*, Brussels, http://eeas.europa.eu/moldova/csp/csp04_06_nip05_06_en.pdf, accessed 13 December 2015.

European Commission (2004b) *Proposal for Council Decision on the position to be adopted by the European Communities and their Member States within the Cooperation Council established by the Partnership and Cooperation Agreement establishing a partnership between the European Communities and their Member States, of the one part, and* the Republic of Moldova, of the other part, with regard to the adoption of a Recommendation on the implementation of the EU-Moldova Action Plan, COM(2004) 787 final, Brussels, 9.12.2004, http://eur-lex.europa.eu/legal-content/EN/TXT/PDF/?uri=CELEX:52004PC0787&from=FI, accessed 13 December 2015.

European Commission (2005) *Guidelines for the Development of a Political Declaration and a Policy Framework Document for the Northern Dimension Policy from 2007*, adopted 21 November, http://www.eeas.europa.eu/north_dim/docs/guidelines05_en.pdf, accessed 13 December 2015.

European Commission (2007a) *Black Sea Synergy – A New Regional Cooperation Initiative*, Communication from the Commission to the Council and the European Parliament, COM(2007) 160 final, 11 April, Brussels, http://eur-lex.europa.eu/legal-content/EN/TXT/PDF/?uri=CELEX:52007DC0160&from=EN, accessed 17 November 2015.

European Commission (2007b) *2006 Annual Progress Report on the Implementation of the Northern Dimension Action Plan*, Commission Staff Working Document, SEC(2007) 791, 4 June, http://register.consilium.europa.eu/doc/srv?l=EN&f=ST 10612 2007 INIT, accessed 13 December 2015.

European Commission (2008) 'The European Union and the Arctic Region', COM(2008) 763 final, Brussels 20 November.

European Commission (2011a) 'EU Human Rights Policy towards Russia', EXPO/B/DROI/2010/07 (Brussels: Directorate General for External Policies).

European Commission (2011b) *A New Response to a Changing Neighbourhood: A Review of European Neighbourhood Policy, Joint Communication by the High Representative of the Union for Foreign Affairs and Security Policy and the European Commission*, Brussels, 25 May, http://eeas.europa.eu/enp/pdf/pdf/com_11_303_en.pdf, accessed 13 December 2015.

European Commission (2012a) *Delivering on a New European Neighbourhood Policy*, JOIN(2012) 14 final, Brussels, 11 May, http://eur-lex.europa.eu/LexUriServ/LexUriServ.do?uri=JOIN:2012:0014:FIN:EN:PDF, accessed 9 December 2015.

European Commission (2012b) 'EU and Russia Agree to Work More Closely in Aeronautics Research', *News*, http://ec.europa.eu/research/transport/news/items/eu_and_russia_agree_to_work_more_closely_in_aeronautics_research_en.htm, accessed 23 June 2015.

European Commission (2012c) 'Making the Internal Energy Market Work', COM(2012) 663 final, Brussels, 15 November, http://eur-lex.europa.eu/legal-content/EN/TXT/PDF/?uri=CELEX:52012DC0663&from=EN.

European Commission (2013a) 'Review of the S&T Cooperation Agreement between the European Union and Russia', *Ref. Ares (2013)2859814*, 8 April, http://ec.europa.eu/research/iscp/pdf/policy/eu-russia-st-report-080413.pdf, accessed 22 June 2015.

European Commission (2013b) 'Fight Against Illicit Drugs: EU Signs New Agreement with Russia', Joint press release of the Council of the EU and the European Commission, 4 June, Brussels, http://europa.eu/rapid/press-release_IP-13-499_en.htm, accessed 26 April 2016.

European Commission (2013c) *First Progress Report on the Implementation by Russia of the Common Steps towards Visa Free Short-Term Travel of Russian and EU citizens under the EU–Russia Visa Dialogue*, COM(2013) 923 final, Brussels, 18 December.

European Commission (2014a) *Communication from the Commission to the European Parliament and the Council: European Energy Security Strategy*, COM(2014) 330 final, Brussels, 28 May.

European Commission (2014b) *Progress towards Completing the Internal Energy Market*, COM(2014) 634 final, 13 October, http://ec.europa.eu/energy/sites/ener/files/documents/2014_iem_communication.pdf, accessed 12 June 2015.

European Commission (2015a) *Intra-EU Trade in Goods – Recent Trends*, 2 February, http://ec.europa.eu/eurostat/statistics-explained/index.php/Intra-EU_trade_in_goods_-_recent_trends, accessed 4 June 2015.

European Commission (2015b) *European Union, Trade in Goods with Russia*, 10 April, http://trade.ec.europa.eu/doclib/docs/2006/september/tradoc_113440.pdf, accessed 28 May 2015.

European Commission (2015c) *Antitrust: Commission Sends Statement of Objections to Gazprom for Alleged Abuse of Dominance on Central and Eastern European Gas Supply Markets*, press release, 22 April, http://europa.eu/rapid/press-release_IP-15-4828_en.htm, accessed 11 June 2015.

European Commission and the HR (2012) *Developing a European Union Policy towards the Arctic Region: Progress since 2008 and Next Steps*, a joint communication to the European Parliament and the Council, JOIN(2012) 19 final, Brussels, 26 June.

European Commission and the HR (2013) *The EU's Comprehensive Approach to External Conflict and Crises*, a joint communication to the European Parliament and the Council, JOIN(2013) 30 final, Brussels, 11 December.

European Commission and the HR (2015) *Towards a New European Neighbourhood Policy*, a joint consultation paper, Brussels, 4.3.2015, JOIN(2015) 6 final.

European Council (1999a) *Common Strategy of the European Union on Russia*, 4 June, (1999/414/CFSP).

European Council (1999b) *Presidency Conclusions. Annex II: Declaration on Chechnya*, Helsinki, 10–11 December.

European Council (2000) *Conclusions of the Presidency*, Santa Maria Da Feira, 19–20 June.

European Council (2002) *Presidency Conclusions and Annexes*, Seville, 21–22 June.

European Council (2003) *A Secure Europe in a Better World – European Security Strategy*, Brussels, 12 December.

European Council (2004) 'Javier Solana, EU High Representative for the CFSP, Writes to Russian Foreign Minister Sergey Lavrov on Deteriorating Situation in Transnistria', Brussels, 30 July, http://eu-un.europa.eu/articles/en/article_3722_en.htm, accessed 16 February 2016.

European Council (2008) *Report on the Implementation of the European Security Strategy: Providing Security in a Changing World*, Brussels, 11 December.

European External Action Service (EEAS) (2006) *Political Declaration on the Northern Dimension Policy*, Helsinki, 24 November.

European External Action Service (EEAS) (2008) *Declaration by the Presidency of the Council of the European Union after the Russian Authorities' Recognition of the Independence of Abkhazia and South Ossetia*, Brussels, http://eeas.europa.eu/delegations/georgia/press_corner/all_news/news/2008/20080826_01_en.htm, accessed 13 December 2015.

European External Action Service (2014) *Northern Dimension – Practical, Practical, Result-Oriented Cooperation in the Baltic Sea and Barents Regions*, Europe Day Factsheet, 9 May, http://eeas.europa.eu/factsheets/docs/factsheets_europe_day_2014/factsheet_northern-dimension_en.pdf, accessed 16 November 2015.

European External Action Service (2015a) *Black Sea Synergy: Review of a Regional Cooperation Initiative*, Joint Staff Working Document SWD(2015) 6 final, 20 January, Brussels, http://eeas.europa.eu/blacksea/doc/swd_2015_6_f1_joint_staff_working_paper_en.pdf, accessed 28 August 2015.

European External Action Service (2015b) *EU Relations with Russia*, http://eeas.europa.eu/russia/about/index_en.htm, accessed 24 June 2015.

European Neighbourhood and Partnership Instrument (ENPI) (2013) *EU and the Eastern Partners: Cooperation to Face the Environmental Challenge*, Press Packs, 04-06-2013, http://www.enpi-info.eu/maineast.php?id_type=3&id=435, accessed 12 November 2015.

European Parliament (2014) Infographic: 'Energy Supply in the EU28', 24 June, http://www.europarl.europa.eu/EPRS/140816REV2-Energy-supply-in-the-EU28.pdf, accessed 4 June 2015.

European Union Monitoring Mission in Georgia (2008) *EUMM Witnesses the Withdrawal of Russian Troops*, press release, 8 October, http://www.eumm.eu/en/press_and_public_information/press_releases/96/?year=2008&month=10, accessed 13 December 2015.

Eurostat (2014) *Energy Production and Imports*, May, http://ec.europa.eu/eurostat/statistics-explained/index.php/Energy_production_and_imports, accessed 4 June 2015.

Eurostat (2015) 'Extra-EU28 Trade, by Main Partners, Total Product', http://ec.europa.eu/eurostat/en/data/database, accessed 26 April 2016.

EU–Russia Centre (2008) 'Kosovo Dominates Russian TV Screens on Eve of Elections', 28 February, http://www.eu-russiacentre.org/2008/02, accessed 13 December 2015.

EU–Russia Industrialists' Round Table (2015) *About Us*, the website of the IRT, http://www.eu-russia-industrialists.org/aboutirt.php, accessed 9 December 2015.

The EU–Russia Partnership for Modernisation (2012) 'Work Plan for Activities within the EU–Russia Partnership for Modernisation: Working Document', revision 1, 23 May, http://eeas.europa.eu/delegations/russia/eu_russia/tech_financial_cooperation/partnership_modernisation_facility/index_en.htm, accessed 26 April 2016.

EU–Russia Summit (2003) 'Joint Statement', *EU–Russia Summit*, St Petersburg, 31 May, 9937/03 (Presse 154).

EU–Russia Summit (2005) 'Conclusions – Four Common Spaces', *EU–Russia Summit*, Moscow, 10 May.

Fawn, R. (2009) 'Bashing about Rights? Russia and the 'New' EU States on Human Rights and Democracy Promotion', *Europe-Asia Studies*, 61(10): 1777–803.

Fawn, R. and R. Nalbandov (2012) 'The Difficulties of Knowing the Start of War in the Information Age: Russia, Georgia and the War over South Ossetia, August 2008', *European Security*, 21(1): 57–89.

Federal State Statistics of Russia (2015) 'External Trade of the Russian Federation with Other Countries', http://www.gks.ru/bgd/regl/b15_12/IssWWW.exe/stg/d02/27-06.htm, accessed 26 April 2016.

Felgenhauer, P. (2009) 'After August 7: The Escalation of the Russo-Georgia War', in S. Cornell and F. Starr (eds) *The Guns of August 2008: Russia's War in Georgia* (Armonk, NY: M.E. Sharpe).

Ferrero-Waldner, B. (2008a) 'The European Union and Russia – Future Prospects', speech at Salzburg Global Seminar 'Russia: The 2020 Perspective', Salzburg, 6 April, http://europa.eu/rapid/press-release_SPEECH-08-175_en.pdf, accessed 7 July 2015.

Ferrero-Waldner, B. (2008b) 'Donors Conference for Georgia: Time to Walk or Talk', Speech/08/549, Brussels, 22 October, http://europa.eu/rapid/press-release_SPEECH-08-549_en.htm?locale=en, accessed 13 December 2015.

Finkel, E. and Y. M. Brudny (2012) 'No More Colour! Authoritarian Regimes and Colour Revolutions in Eurasia', *Democratization*, 19(1): 1–14.

Finon, D. and C. Locatelli (2008) 'Russian and European Gas Interdependence: Could Contractual Trade Channel Geopolitics?', *Energy Policy*, 36(1): 423–42.

Fischer, S. (2013) 'EU–Russia Relations: A Partnership for Modernisation?', in Bertelsmann Stiftung (ed.) *From Cooperation to Partnership: Moving Beyond the Russia-EU Deadlock*, Europe in Dialogue 1/2013 (Berlin: Bertelsmann Stiftung).

Fish, M. S. (2005) *Democracy Derailed in Russia: The Failure of Open Politics* (Cambridge and New York: Cambridge University Press).

Fleming, J. (2013) 'Russia: Cyprus Bailout Shows EU's "Lack of Values"', *Euractiv.com*, 3 April.

Flenley, P. (2005) 'Russia and the EU: A Pragmatic and Contradictory Relationship', *Perspectives on European Politics and Society*, 6(3): 435–61.

Forbrig, J. (2015) 'What's Ahead for Russia and the West? Four Scenarios', *Europe Policy Paper 3/2015* (Washington, DC: The German Marshall Fund of the United States).

Foreign Affairs Council (FAC) (2014) 'Council Conclusions on Developing a European Union Policy towards the Arctic Region', Foreign Affairs Council meeting, Brussels, 12 May.

Foreign Ministry of Finland (2006) 'EU Presidency Statement on the Killing of Anna Politkovskaya', press release, 8 October, http://formin.finland.fi/public/Print.aspx?contentid=81692&nodeid=15154&culture=en-US&contentlan=2, accessed 13 December 2015.

Forsberg, T. (2004) 'The EU–Russia Security Partnership: Why the Opportunity Was Missed?', *European Foreign Affairs Review*, 9(2): 247–67.

Forsberg, T. (2011) 'The EU as a Normative Power, Once Again: A Conceptual Clarification of an Ideal Type', *Journal of Common Market Studies*, 49(6): 1183–204.

Forsberg, T. (2013) 'The Power of the EU: What Explains the EU's (Lack of) Influence on Russia?', *Politique Européenne*, 39(1): 10–30.

Forsberg, T. (2014) 'Status Conflicts between Russia and the West: Perceptions and Emotional Biases', *Communist and Post-Communist Studies*, 47(3–4): 323–31.

Forsberg, T. (2016) 'From Ostpolitik to 'Frostpolitik'? Merkel, Putin and German Foreign Policy towards Russia', *International Affairs* (London), 92(1): 21–42.

Forsberg, T. and G. Herd (2005) 'The EU, Human Rights, and the Russo-Chechen Conflict', *Political Science Quarterly*, 120(3): 455–78.

Forsberg, T. and G. Herd (2015) 'Russia and NATO: From Windows of Opportunities to Closed Doors', *Journal of Contemporary European Studies*, 23(1): 41–57.

Forsberg, T and C. Pursiainen (2016) 'The Psychological Dimension of Russian Foreign Policy'. 'Paper presented at the Annual Convention of the International Studies Association, Atlanta, 16–19 March.'

Forsberg, T. and A. Seppo (2009) 'Power without Influence? The EU and Trade Disputes with Russia', *Europe-Asia Studies*, 61(10): 1805–23.

Forsberg, T. and A. Seppo (2011) 'The Russo-Georgian War and the EU Mediation', in R. Kanet (ed.) *Russian Policy in the 21st Century* (Basingstoke: Palgrave Macmillan).

Forster, A. and W. Wallace (2000) 'Common Foreign and Security Policy: From Shadow to Substance?', in H. Wallace and W. Wallace (eds) *Policy-Making in the European Union*, 4th edn (Oxford: Oxford University Press).

Frear, T., L. Kulesa and I. Kearns (2014) 'Dangerous Brinkmanship: Close Military Encounters between Russia and the West in 2014', *European Leadership Network Policy Brief*, November (London: European Leadership Network).

Freedom House (2015) *Freedom in the World 2015* (Washington, DC: Freedom House), https://freedomhouse.org/report/freedom-world/freedom-world-2015 - .Vmt8Ik08LIU, accessed 13 December 2015.

Freire, R. and L. Simão (2013) 'The EU's Security Actorness: The Case of EUMM in Georgia', *European Security*, 22(4): 464–77.

Frellesen, T. and C. Rontoyanni (2008) 'EU–Russia Political Relations: Negotiating the Common Spaces', in J. Gower and G. Timmins (eds) *Russia and Europe in the Twenty-First Century: An Uneasy Partnership* (London: Anthem).

Gaddy, C. and B. Ickes (2013) *Bear Traps on Russia's Road to Modernization* (London: Routledge).

Galeotti, M. (2016) 'Free Sergei Lavrov!', *Foreign Policy.com*, 17 February 2016, http://foreignpolicy.com/2016/02/17/free-sergei-lavrov-putin-russia-syria/, accessed 20 February 2016.

Gänzle, S., S. Meister and C. King (2009) 'The Bologna Process and Its Impact on Higher Education at Russia's Margins: The Case of Kaliningrad', *Higher Education*, 57(4): 533–47.

Gazprom (2012) 'Gazprom Statement on Formal Stage of European Commission Antitrust Investigation', September 5, http://www.gazprom.com/press/news/2012/september/article143314/, accessed 12 November 2015.

Gazprom (2015) 'Gazprom, BASF, E.ON, ENGIE, OMV and ShellSign Shareholders' Agreement on the Nord Stream 2 Project', press release, 4 September, http://www.gazprom.com/press/news/2015/september/article245837/, accessed 12 November 2015.

Gebhard, C. (2011) 'Coherence', in C. Hill and M. Smith (eds) *International Relations and the European Union*, 2nd edn (Oxford and New York: Oxford University Press).

Gegout, C. (2010) *European Foreign and Security Policy* (Toronto: University Press of Toronto.)

Gel'man, V. (2015) *Authoritarian Russia: Analyzing Post-Soviet Regime Changes* (Pittsburgh: University of Pittsburgh Press).

Gessen, M. (2012) *The Man Without a Face: The Unlikely Rise of Vladimir Putin* (New York: Riverhead Books).

GHK Consulting and Renmin University (2011) 'EU–China Student and Academic Staff Mobility: Present Situation and Future Developments', a report submitted by GHK Consulting and Renmin University, 29 April, http://ec.europa.eu/education/international-cooperation/documents/china/mobility_en.pdf, accessed 6 November 2015.

Ghosh, P. (2015) 'Europe and Russia Mission to Assess Moon Settlement', *BBC News*, 16 October 2015, http://www.bbc.com/news/science-environment-34504067, accessed 6 November 2015.

Giddens, A. (2011) *The Politics of Climate Change*, 2nd edn (Cambridge: Polity Press).

Ginsberg, R. and S. Penksa (2012) *The European Union in Global Security* (Basingstoke: Palgrave Macmillan).

Giumelli, F. and P. Ivan (2013) 'The Effectiviness of EU Sanctions. An Analysis of Iran, Belarus, Syria and Myanmar (Burma)', EPC Issue Paper No. 76, November (Brussels: European Policy Centre), http://www. epc.eu/documents/uploads/pub_3928_epc_issue_paper_76_-_the_ effectiveness_of_eu_sanctions.pdf, accessed 1 July 2015.

Gnedina, E. and E. Sleptsova (2012) 'Eschewing Choice: Ukraine's Strategy on Russia and the EU', *CEPS Working Document No. 360*, January 2012, http://www.ceps.eu/book/eschewing-choice-ukraine's-strategy-russia-and-eu, accessed 10 December 2015.

Goldman, M. I. (2008) *Petrostate: Putin, Power, and the New Russia* (Oxford and New York: Oxford University Press).

Golubock, D. G. (2014) 'Culture Ministry Affirms 'Russia Is not Europe'', *Moscow Times*, 7 April, http://www.themoscowtimes.com/arts_n_ ideas/article/culture-ministry-affirms-russia-is-not-europe/497658. html, accessed 13 December 2015.

Gordon, C. (2012) 'The EU as a Reluctant Conflict Manager in Moldova', in R. Whitmann and S. Wolff (eds) *The European Union as a Global Conflict Manager* (Abingdon: Routledge).

Gorski, V. and Y. Chebotareva (1993) 'Maastricht and Russia', *International Affairs* (Moscow), 39(3): 45–52.

Gotev, G. (2012) 'Putin Promotes Eurasian Union at EU Summit', *EurActiv. com*, 5 June, http://www.euractiv.com/europes-east/putin-promotes-eurasian-union-eu-news-513123, accessed 13 December 2015.

Gotev, G. (2015) 'Mogherini Says Russian Intervention in Syria Neither Positive nor Negative', *EurActiv.com*, 12 October, http://www.euractiv. com/sections/global-europe/mogherini-says-russian-intervention-syria-neither-positive-nor-negative, accessed 13 December 2015.

Gower, J. (2007) 'The European Union's Policy on Russia: Rhetoric or Reality?' In J. Gower and G. Timmins (eds), *Russia and Europe in the Twenty-First Century: An Uneasy Partnership* (London: Anthem).

Gower, J., and G. Timmins (eds) (2008a) *Russia and Europe in the Twenty-First Century: An Uneasy Partnership* (London: Anthem).

Gower, J. and G. Timmins (2008b) 'Russia and Europe: An Uneasy Partnership', in J. Gower and G. Timmins (eds) *Russia and Europe in the Twenty-First Century: An Uneasy Partnership* (London: Anthem).

Graham, L. (2013) *Lonely Ideas: Can Russia Compete?* (Cambridge, MA: MIT Press).

Granholm, N., J. Malminen and G. Persson (eds) (2014) *A Rude Awakening: Ramifications of Russian Aggression Towards Ukraine* (Stockholm: FOI), http://www.foi.se/sv/Sok/Sammanfattningssida/?rNo¼FO I-R–3892–SE, accessed 10 November 2015.

Grant, C. (1999) 'European Defence Post-Kosovo?', *CER Working Paper* (London: Centre for European Reform), http://www.cer.org.uk/sites/ default/files/publications/attachments/pdf/2012/cerwp3-5671.pdf, accessed 30 June 2015.

Greene, J. (2012) 'Russian Responses to NATO and EU Enlargement and Outreach', *Chatham House Briefing Paper*, June 2012, http://www.chathamhouse.org/publications/papers/view/184061, accessed 10 December 2015.

Gretskiy, I., E. Treshchenkov and K. Golubev (2014) 'Russia's Perceptions and Misperceptions of the EU Eastern Partnership', *Communist and Post-Communist Studies*, 47(3–4): 375–83.

Groenleer, M.L.P. and L. G.Van Schaik (2007) 'United We Stand? The European Union's International Actorness in the Cases of the International Criminal Court and the Kyoto Protocol', *Journal of Common Market Studies*, 45(5): 969–98.

Gröne, K. and F. Hett (eds) (2015) *The Russian Crisis and its Fallout: The Impact on the Eastern Partnership States and Central Asia* (Berlin: Friedrich-Ebert-Stiftung).

Grushko, A. (2007) 'Speech by Alexander Grushko at the Conference on Nordic Cooperation and the Northern Dimension', Helsinki, 17 January 2007, Norden2007, http://213214149030.edelkey.net/public/default.aspx?contentid=85850&nodeid=36240&contentlan=2&culture=en-US, accessed 10 December 2015.

Grushko, A. (2010) 'Russia–EU: Fine-Tuning the Relationship', *International Affairs* (Moscow), 56(4): 44–8.

Grynaviski, E. (2013) 'Contrasts, Counterfactuals and Causes', *European Journal of International Relations*, 19(4): 823–46.

Gustafson, T. (2012) *Wheel of Fortune: The Battle for Oil and Power in Russia* (Cambridge, MA: Harvard University Press).

Gutnik, V. (2006) Remarks in the 'European Union: What Lies Ahead?', *International Affairs* (Moscow), 52(3): 116–30.

Gevorkyan N., N. Timakova, A. Kolesnikov and C. Fitzpatrick (2001) *First Person: An Astonishingly Frank Self-Portrait by Russia's President Vladimir Putin* (New York: PublicAffairs).

Haglund, A. (2005) 'The "Northern Dimension": North-Western Russia in Focus', in D. Johnson and P. Robinson (eds) *Perspectives on EU – Russia Relations* (London: Routledge).

Haglund-Morrissey, A. (2008) 'Conceptualizing the "New" Northern Dimension: A Common Policy Based on Sectoral Partnerships', *Journal of Contemporary European Studies*, 16(2): 203–17.

Hale, H. E. (2015) *Patronal Politics. Eurasian Regime Dynamics in Comparative Perspective* (Cambridge and New York: Cambridge University Press).

Hanson, P. (2013) 'Fear of the Future: Russia in the Global Economy in the Next Few Years', *The International Spectator*, 48(3): 34–49.

Hanson, P. (2014) 'The Current State of the Russian Economy', *Russian Analytical Digest*, No. 149, 25 May 2014: 2–5, http://www.css.ethz.ch/publications/pdfs/RAD-149-2-5.pdf, accessed 9 July 2015.

Hanson, P. (2015) 'An Enfeebled Economy', in Keir Giles et al., *The Russian Challenge*, Chatham House Report (London: The Royal Institute of International Affairs).

Hanson, S. (2007) 'The WTO and Russian Politics', *NBR Special Report – Russia and the WTO: A Progress Report,* No 12, March (Seattle: National Bureau of Asian Research).

Hare, P. (2002) *Russia and the World Trade Organization,* Russian-European Centre for Economic Policy, Working Paper Series, July (Moscow: Russian-European Centre for Economic Policy, RECEP).

Hartog, E. (2015) 'Russians Want Better Ties With West, But No Change in Policy – Poll', *Moscow Times,* December 2, http://www.themoscowtimes.com/article/551462.html, accessed 13 December 2015.

Haukkala, H. (2001)' The Making of the European Union's Common Strategy on Russia', in H. Haukkala and S. Medvedev (eds) *The EU Common Strategy on Russia: Learning the Grammar of the CFSP.* Programme on the Northern Dimension of the CFSP No. 11 (Helsinki and Berlin: Finnish Institute of International Affairs and Institut für Europäische Politik.

Haukkala, H. (2003) 'What Went Right with the EU's Common Strategy on Russia', in A. Moshes (ed.) *Rethinking the Respective Strategies of Russia and the European Union,* Special FIIA-Carnegie Moscow Center Report (Helsinki: Finnish Institute of International Affairs; Moscow: Carnegie Moscow Center).

Haukkala, H. (2005) 'The Northern Dimension of EU Foreign Policy', in O. Antonenko and K. Pinnick (eds) *Russia and the European Union: Prospects for a New Relationship* (London and New York: Routledge and IISS).

Haukkala, H. (2006) 'The Role of Solidarity and Coherence in EU's Russia Policy', *Studia Diplomatica – Brussels Journal of International Relations,* 49(2): 35–50.

Haukkala, H. (2008) 'The European Union as a Regional Normative Hegemon: The Case of European Neighbourhood Policy', *Europe-Asia Studies,* 60(9): 1601–22.

Haukkala, H. (2009a) 'From Zero-Sum to Win–Win? The Russian Challenge to the EU's Eastern Neighbourhood Policies', *SIEPS European Policy Analysis,* November, http://www.sieps.se/sites/default/files/581-epa_2009_12.pdf, accessed 26 April 2016.

Haukkala, H. (2009b) 'Lost in Translation? Why the EU Has Failed to Influence Russia's Development', *Europe-Asia Studies,* 61(10): 1757–75.

Haukkala, H. (2010) *The EU–Russia Strategic Partnership: The Limits of Post-Sovereignty in International Relations* (Oxford and New York: Routledge).

Haukkala, H. (2013) 'The Three Paradigms of European Security in Eastern Europe: Co-operation, Competition and Conflict', in S. Biscop and R. Whitman (eds) *The Routledge Handbook of European Security* (London and New York: Routledge).

Haukkala, H. (2014) 'Towards a Pan-European Energy Order: Energy as an Object of Contention in EU–Russia Relations', *Oil, Gas & Energy Law Intelligence,* 12(4): 1–26.

Headley, J. (2008) *Russia and the Balkans: Foreign Policy from Yeltsin to Putin* (London: Hurst).

Headley, J. (2015a). Challenging the EU's Claim to Moral Authority: Russian Talk of 'Double Standards', *Asia Europe Journal*, 13(3): 297–307.

Headley, J. (2015b). 'Russia's Complex Engagement with European Union Norms: Sovereign Democracy versus Post-Westphalianism?', in A. Björkdahl, N. Chaban, J. Leslie, and A. Masselot (eds) *Importing EU Norms: Conceptual Framework and Empirical Findings* (Berlin: Springer).

Heininen, L. (1999) *Euroopan pohjoinen 1990-luvulla: moniulotteisten ja ristiriitaisten intressien alue*. Acta Universitatis Lapponiensis 21/Arctic Centre Reports 30 (Rovaniemi: University of Lapland).

Helm, D. (2015) *The EU Energy Union. More Than the Sum of Its Parts?* CER Policy Brief, November 2015 (London: Centre for European Reform), http://www.cer.org.uk/sites/default/files/publications/attachments/pdf/2015/pb_helm_energy_9nov15-12259.pdf, accessed 12 November 2015.

Helwig, N. and C. Rüger (2014) 'The Legacy of Catherine Ashton', *The International Spectator*, 49(4): 1–17.

Henderson, J. (2015) *Key Determinants for the Future of Russian Oil Production and Exports*. OIES Paper: Wpm 58, April 2015 (Oxford: Oxford Institute for Energy Studies).

Henökl, T. E. (2015) *Inside the External Action Service: 'Unpacking' the EU Foreign Policy Bureaucracy*, PhD dissertation, University of Agder 102, Kristiansand.

Herd, G. (2003) 'Russia and the European Union', in C. Jenkins and J. Smith (eds) *Through the Paper Curtain: Insiders and Outsiders in the New Europe* (London and Oxford: Royal Institute of International Affairs and Blackwell).

Herd, G. (2009) 'Russia's Sovereign Democracy: Instrumentalization, Interests and Identity', in R. Kanet (ed.) *A Resurgent Russia and the West: The European Union, NATO and Beyond* (Dordrecht: Republic of Letters).

Herd, G. and P. Dunay (2011) 'The European Security Treaty (EST): Collective Security or Collective Inaction?', *OSCE Yearbook 2010* (Hamburg: The Institute for Peace Research and Security Policy).

Hernández i Sagrera, R. and O. Potemkina (2013) *Russia and the Common Space on Freedom, Security and Justice*, CEPS Paper in Liberty and Security in Europe, No. 54/February 2013 (Brussels: CEPS).

Herrberg, A. (1998) 'The European Union and Russia: Toward a New Ostpolitik?', in C. Rhodes (ed.) *The European Union in the World Community* (Boulder, CO: Lynne Rienner).

Hill, C. (1993) 'Capability Expectations Gap or Conceptualising Europe's International Role', *Journal of Common Market Studies*, 31(3): 305–28.

Hill, C. (2006) 'The Directoire and the Problem of a Coherent EU Foreign Policy', *CFSP Forum*, 4(6): 1–4.

Hill, C. and W. Wallace (1996) 'Introduction: Actors and Actions', in C. Hill (ed.) *The Actors in Europe's Foreign Policy* (London: Routledge).

Hill, F. and C. Gaddy (2003) *Siberian Curse: How Communist Planners Left Russia Out in the Cold* (Washington, DC: Brookings).

Hill, F. and C. Gaddy (2015) *Mr. Putin – Operative in Kremlin*, 2nd edn (Washington, DC: Brookings Institution Press).

Hill, W. (2012) *Russia, the Near Abroad and the West: Lessons from the Moldova-Transdniestria Conflict* (Washington, DC, and Baltimore: Woodrow Wilson Center Press and Johns Hopkins University Press).

Hille, K. and C. Oliver (2014) 'Russia Takes EU to Court over Ukraine Sanctions', *Financial Times*, 26 October, http://www.ft.com/intl/cms/s/0/8e460fe4-5547-11e4-b750-00144feab7de.html, accessed 2 April 2015.

Hillion, C. (1998) 'Partnership and Cooperation Agreements between the European Union and the New Independent States of the Ex-Soviet Union', *European Foreign Affairs Review*, 3(3): 399–420.

Hillion, C. (2009) *The European Union and its East-European Neighbours – A Laboratory for the Organisation of EU External Relations* (Oxford: Hart Publishing).

Hindess, B. (1989) *Political Choice and Social Structure: An Analysis of Actors, Interests and Rationality* (Aldershot: Edward Elgar).

Höhmann, H., C. Meier and H. Timmermann (1993) 'The European Community and the Countries of the CIS: Political and Economic Relations', *Journal of Communist Studies*, 9(3): 151–76.

Holsti, K. (1992) *International Politics: A Framework for Analysis*, 6th edn (Englewood Cliffs: Prentice-Hall).

Hønneland, G. (2003) *Russia and the West: Environmental Co-operation and Conflict* (London and New York: Routledge).

Hopf, T. (2002) *Social Construction of International Politics: Identities and Foreign Policies, Moscow 1955 and 1999* (Ithaca, NY: Cornell University Press).

Hopf, T. (ed.) (2008) *Russia's European Choice* (Basingstoke: Palgrave Macmillan).

Hough, P. (2012) 'Worth the Energy? The Geopolitics of Arctic Oil and Gas', *Central European Journal of International and Security Studies*, 6(1): 65–80.

House of Lords (2008a) 'After Georgia. The EU and Russia: Follow-Up Report – European Union Committee', 10 October (London: House of Lords).

House of Lords (2008b) 'Managing the EU's Strategy towards Russia', in European Union – Fourteenth Report, 13 May (London: House of Lords).

House of Lords (2015) 'The EU and Russia: Before and Beyond the Crisis in Ukraine', 6th Report of Session 2014–15, 10 February (London: House of Lords).

Howorth, J. and Menon, A. (2015) 'Wake up Europe!' *Global Affairs*, 1(1): 11–20.

Hughes, J. (2013) 'Russia and the Secession of Kosovo: Power, Norms and the Failure of Multilateralism', *Europe-Asia Studies*, 65(5): 992–1016.

Huisman, S. (2002) 'A New European Union Policy for Kaliningrad', Occasional Paper no. 33 (Paris: European Union Institute for Security Studies).

Huntington, S. (1996) *Clash of Civilizations and the Remaking of World Order* (New York: Simon & Schuster).

Hutcheson, D. (2006) 'Democratic Values in the New Europe', *Contemporary Politics*, 12(2): 157–74.

Hutcheson, D. (2011) 'Elections, International Observers and the Politicisation of Democratic Values', *Europe-Asia Studies*, 63(4): 685–702.

Ikenberry, G. J. (2001) *After Victory: Institutions, Strategic Restraint, and the Rebuilding of Order After Major Wars* (Princeton, NJ: Princeton University Press).

Independent International Fact-Finding Mission on the Conflict in Georgia (2009) *Report*, http://news.bbc.co.uk/2/shared/bsp/hi/pdfs/30_09_09_iiffmgc_report.pdf, accessed 13 December 2015.

Interfax (2013) 'Moscow Slams European Parliament Resolution Criticizing Human Rights in Russia', June 14 (*Johnson's Russia List*, 17 June).

Ivanov, I. (2001a) 'The New Russian Identity: Innovation and Continuity in Russian Foreign Policy', *Washington Quarterly*, 24(3): 7–13.

Ivanov, I. (2001b) Speech made by Minister of Foreign Affairs of the Russian Federation Igor Ivanov at a meeting with the leadership of the Republic of Karelia in Petrozavodks, 10 May 2001.

Ivanov, I. S. (2000) 'Russia, Europe at the Turn of the Century', *International Affairs* (Moscow), 46(2): 104–10.

Ivanov, I. S. (2002) *The New Russian Diplomacy* (Washington, DC: The Nixon Center & Brookings Institution Press).

Joenniemi, P. and Sergounin, A. (2003) *Russia and the European Union's Northern Dimension: Encounter or Clash of Civilisations?* (Nizhny Novgorod: Nizhny Novgorod Linguistic University Press).

John, I. G. (1975) 'The Soviet Response to Western European Integration', in I. John (ed.) *EEC Policy Towards Eastern Europe* (Westmead and Lexington, Mass: Saxon House & Lexington Books).

Johnston, C. (2015) 'Sanctions against Russia: Evasion, compensation and overcompliance', *EUISS Brief*, 13.

Johnstone, D. (2014) 'Washington's Frozen War Against Russia', Counterpunch, 9 December, http://www.counterpunch.org/2014/12/09/washingtons-frozen-war-against-russia/, accessed 22 February 2016.

Jokisipilä, M. (2014) 'East or West – or Both at the Same Time? Higher Education as a Battleground for the Russian Soul', in K. Liuhto (ed.) *Baltic Sea Policy Briefing*, 1/2014, 2 June, http://www.centrumbalticum.org/sites/default/files/raportit/bsr_policy_briefing_1_2014_netti.pdf, accessed 6 November 2015.

Jones, A. and G. Fallon (2003) 'The Political Economy of Co-operation, Trade and Aid Between the European Union and Russia', *Journal of Contemporary European Studies*, 11(2): 253–77.

Jones, E., A. Menon and S. Weatherill (eds) (2012) *The Oxford Handbook of the European Union* (London and New York: Oxford University Press).

Jones, S. (2007) *The Rise of European Security Cooperation* (Cambridge: Cambridge University Press).

Jonsson, O. and R. Seely (2015) 'Russian Full-Spectrum Conflict: An Appraisal after Ukraine', *The Journal of Slavic Military Studies*, 28(1): 1–22.

Jørgensen, K.E. (2015) 'The Study of European Foreign Policy: Trends and Advances', in K. E. Jørgensen, Å. Kalland, E. Drieskens, K. Laatikainen and B. Tonra (eds) *The Sage Handbook of European Foreign Policy* (London: Sage).

Jouyet, J. and S. Coignard (2009) *Une presidence de crises. Les six mois qui ont bousculé l'Europe* (Paris: Albin Michel).

Jozwiak, R. (2008) 'Russia to Help EU in Chad', *European Voice,* 29 September.

Jukic, E. (2014) 'Russia Flexes Muscles on EU Bosnia Mission', *Balkan Insight*, 17 November, http://www.balkaninsight.com/en/article/russia-flexes-muscles-on-eu-bosnia-mission, accessed 13 December 2015.

Juncos, A. and R. Whitman (2015) 'Europe as a Regional Actor: Neighbourhood Lost?', *Journal of Common Market Studies*, 53(Annual Review): 200–15.

Jutila, M. (2016) 'European Politics of Double Genocide: Constructing Marxist Genocide in The Soviet Story', submitted manuscript.

Kaczmarski, M. (2014) "Domestic Power Relations and Russia's Foreign Policy, *Demokratizatsiya*, 22(3): 383–410.

Kahneman, D. and J. Renshon (2009) 'Hawkish Biases', in A. T. Thrall and J. K. Cramer (eds) *American Foreign Policy and the Politics of Fear: Threat Inflation Since 9/11* (Abingdon and New York: Routledge).

Kanet, R. (2015) 'The Failed Western Challenge to Russia's Revival in Eurasia?', *International Politics*, 52(5): 503–22.

Karaganov, S. (2003) 'Russia, Europe, and New Challenges', *Russia in Global Affairs*, 1(1): 19–30.

Karaganov, S. (2004) Remarks in 'Why Invent a New Model? Review of the Discussion at the Russian Economic Forum', *Russia in Global Affairs*, 2(3): 179–82.

Karaganov, S. (2005) 'Russia and the International Order', in D. Lynch (ed.) *What Russia Sees*, Chaillot Paper no. 74, January (Paris: European Union Institute for Security Studies).

Karaganov, S. (2007) 'A New Epoch of Confrontation', *Russia in Global Affairs*, 5(4): 23–36.

Karaganov, S. (2013) 'Russia Right to Refuse Cyprus Bail Out but Should Back Strong EU', *Financial Times,* 29 March.

Karaganov, S. (2014) 'Western Delusions Triggered this Conflict and Russians Will Not Yield', *Financial Times*, 15 September.

Karaganov, S. et al. (2005) 'Russia's European Strategy: A New Start', *Russia in Global Affairs*, 3(3): 72–85.

Karagiannis, E. (2015) 'Greece and Russia: The Myths and the Reality', *Moscow Times*, April 7, 2015.

Kaveshnikov, N. (2010) 'The Issue of Energy Security in Relations between Russia and the European Union', *European Security*, 19(4): 585–605.

Kazantsev, A. (2012) 'Policy Networks in European–Russian Gas Relations: Function and Dysfunction from a Perspective of EU Energy Security', *Communist and Post-Communist Studies*, 45(3–4): 305–13.

Kearns, I., L. Kulesa and T. Frear (2015) 'Russia–West Dangerous Brinkmanship Continues', European Leadership Network Policy Brief (London: European Leadership Network).

Kelly, E. (2015) 'EU Will Maintain Scientific Ties with Russia Despite Escalating Tensions', *Science Business*, 3 June, http://www.sciencebusiness.net/news/77056/EU-will-maintain-scientific-ties-with-Russia-despiteescalating-tensions, accessed 23 June 2015.

Kelley, J. (2006) 'New Wine in Old Wineskins: Promoting Political Reforms through the New European Neighbourhood Policy', *Journal of Common Market Studies*, 44(1): 29–55.

Kelley, M. B. (2014) 'Here's Why the EU Isn't Going to Approve Tough Sanctions on Russia Right Now', *Business Insider*, April 23, http://www.businessinsider.com/eu-and-sanctions-on-russia-2014-4, accessed 10 November 2015.

Kennan, G. (X) (1947) 'The Sources of Soviet Conduct', *Foreign Affairs*, July.

Ker-Lindsay, J. (2011) 'Between "Pragmatism" and "Constitutionalism": EU–Russian Dynamics and Differences during the Kosovo Status Process', *Journal of Contemporary European Research*, 7(2): 175–94.

Keukeleire, S. (2003) 'The European Union as a Diplomatic Actor: Internal, Traditional, and Structural Diplomacy', *Diplomacy and Statecraft*, 14(3): 31–56.

Keukeleire, S. and T. Delreux (2014) *The Foreign Policy of the European Union*, 2nd edn (Basingstoke: Palgrave Macmillan).

Khudoley, K. (2003) 'Russia and the European Union: New Opportunities, New Challenges', in A. Moshes (ed.) *Rethinking the Respective Strategies of Russia and the European Union* (Moscow: Carnegie Moscow Center).

Kissinger, H. (1957) *A World Restored: Metternich, Castlereagh and the Problems of Peace* (Boston, MA: Houghton Mifflin).

Klinke, I. (2012) 'Postmodern Geopolitics? The European Union Eyes Russia', *Europe-Asia Studies*, 64(5): 929–47.

Klitsounova, E. (2008) 'Promoting Human Rights in Russia by Supporting NGOs: How to Improve EU Strategies', *CEPS Working Document No. 287*, April (Brussels: CEPS).

Kononenko, V. (2005) 'A Road Map to Nowhere', *Moscow Times*, 14 May.

Konoplyanik, A. A. (2012) 'Russian Gas at European Energy Market: Why Adaptation Is Inevitable', *Energy Strategy Reviews*, 1(1): 42–56.

Konstantinov, G. and S. Filonovich (2008) 'The Transformation of the Russian System of Higher Education', in D. W. Blum (ed.) *Russia and Globalization: Identity, Security and Society in an Era of Change* (Washington, DC: Woodrow Wilson Center Press and Baltimore: The John Hopkins University Press).

Koposov, N. (2011) *Pamiat' strogogo rezhima: istoriia i politika v Rossii* (Moscow: Novoe literaturnoe obozrenie).

Korneev, O. (2012) 'Deeper and Wider Than a Common Space: European Union-Russia Cooperation on Migration Management', *European Foreign Affairs Review*, 17(4): 605–24.

Korppoo, A., J. Karas and M. Grubb (eds) (2006) *Russia and the Kyoto Protocol: Opportunities and Challenges* (London: Chatham House).

Kramer, M. (2008) 'Russian Policy Toward the Commonwealth of Independent States: Recent Trends and Future Prospects', *Problems of Post-Communism*, 55(6): 3–19.

Krastev, I., and M. Leonard (2014) 'The New European Disorder', European Council on Foreign Relations Essay, November 2014 (London: ECFR), http://www.ecfr.eu/page/-/ECFR117_TheNewEuropeanDisorder_ESSAY.pdf, accessed 26 April 2016.

Kratochvil, P. (2008) 'The Discursive Resistance to EU-Enticement: The Russian Elite and (the Lack of) Europeanisation', *Europe-Asia Studies*, 60(3): 397–422.

Kravtsova, Y. (2014) 'EU Links Easing of Visas to Russia's Rights Record', *Moscow Times*, 19 January 2014.

Kremlin (2010) *Verbatim Record of the Meeting of the Commission for Modernization and Technological Development of Russian Economy*, 29 April 2010, http://kremlin.ru/events/president/transcripts/7585, accessed 6 July 2015.

Kremlin (2013) *News conference of Vladimir Putin*, Moscow, December 19, http://en.kremlin.ru/events/president/news/19859, accessed 28 May 2015.

Krickovic, A. (2015) 'When Interdependence Produces Conflict: EU–Russia Energy Relations as a Security Dilemma', *Contemporary Security Policy*, 36(1): 3–26.

Krizhanskaya, Y. (2011) 'Россия сказала "нет" десоветизации', Rosbalt. ru *Rosbalt.ru*, http://www.rosbalt.ru/main/2011/05/06/846408.html, accessed 26 April 2016.

Kropatcheva, E. (2012a) 'Russia and the Role of the OSCE in European Security: A "Forum" for Dialog or a "Battlefield" of Interests?', *European Security*, 21(3): 370–94.

Kropatcheva, E. (2012b) 'Russian Foreign Policy in the Realm of European Security through the Lens of Neoclassical Realism', *Journal of Eurasian Studies*, 3(1): 30–40.

Kryshtanovskaya, O. (2008) 'The Russian Elite in Transition', *Journal of Communist Studies and Transition Politics*, 24(4): 585–603.

Kryshtanovskaya, O. and S. White (1996) 'From Soviet Nomenklatura to Russian Elite', *Europe-Asia Studies*, 48(5): 711–33.

Kryshtanovskaya, O. and S. White (2005) 'Inside the Putin Court: A Research Note', *Europe-Asia Studies*, 57(7): 1065–75.

Kuchins, A. (2015) 'Russia and the CIS in 2014: A Rather Bad Year', *Asian Survey*, 55(1): 148–56.

Kudrin, A. and E. Gurvich (2015) 'A New Growth Model for the Russian Economy', *BOFIT Policy Brief No. 1* (Helsinki: The Bank of Finland).

Kulikov, A. (2015) 'Russia Eyes New Peace Conference without USA to Avoid WWIII', *Pravda* 5 February http://www.pravdareport.com/russia/politics/05-02-2015/129709-russia_usa_third_world_war-0/#sthash.Zv1N5ctM.dpuf, accessed 16 February 2016.

Kupchinsky, R. (2009) *Gazprom's European Web* (Washington, DC: Jamestown Foundation).

Kurowska, X. and B. Tallis (2009) 'EU Border Assistance Mission: Beyond Border Monitoring?', *European Foreign Affairs Review*, 14(1): 47–64.

Kuzemko, C. (2014) 'Ideas, Power and Change: Explaining EU–Russia Energy Relations', *Journal of European Public Policy*, 21(1): 58–75.

Kuzio, T. (2011) 'Political Culture and Democracy: Ukraine as an Immobile State', *East European Politics and Societies*, 25(1): 88–113.

Kuzmin, A. (2015) 'Russian Media Take Climate Cue from Skeptical Putin', *Reuters*, 29 October, http://www.reuters.com/article/2015/10/29/us-climatechange-summit-russia-media-idUSKCN0SN1GI20151029 - xx8ESsAK5rEVzXFO.97, accessed 12 November 2015.

Kyiv Post (2013) 'Official Passport Matter Is Delaying Russia-EU Visa Relaxation, Says EU Diplomat', *KyivPost.com*, 8 October, http://www.kyivpost.com/content/russia-and-former-soviet-union/official-passport-matter-is-delaying-russia-eu-visa-relaxation-says-eu-diplomat-330248.html, accessed 13 November 2015.

Laffan, B., R. O'Donnell and M. Smith (1999) *Europe's Experimental Union. Rethinking Integration* (London and New York: Routledge).

Laird, R. F. (1989) 'Soviet Strategy Toward Western Europe: Implications for the Post-INF Environment', in S. L. Clark (ed.) *Gorbachev's Agenda: Changes in Soviet Domestic and Foreign Policy* (Boulder, CO: Westview Press).

Lally, K. (2014) 'Putin's Remarks Raise Fears of Future Moves Against Ukraine.' *The Washington Post*, April 17, http://www.washingtonpost.com/world/putin-changes-course-admits-russian-troops-were-incrimea-before-vote/2014/04/17/b3300a54-c617-11e3-bf7a-be01a9b69cf1_story.html, accessed 10 November 2015.

Lamy, P. (2002) 'The EU Supports Russia's WTO Bid', in K. Barysch, R. Cottrell, F. Frattini, P. Hare, P. Lamy, M. Medvedkov and Y. Yasin, *Russia and the WTO* (London: Centre for European Reform).

Laqueur, W. (2015) *Putinism: Russia and Its Future with the West* (New York: St Martin's Press).

Larionova, M. (2015) 'Can the Partnership for Modernisation Help Promote the EU–Russia Strategic Partnership?', *European Politics and Society*, 16(1): 62–79.

Laqueur, W. (2015) *Putinism: Russia and Its Future with the West* (New York: St Martin's Press).

Larson, D. and A. Shevchenko (2010) 'Status Seekers Chinese and Russian Responses to U.S. Primacy', *International Security*, 34(4): 63–95.

Lavrov, S. (2005) Speech by Minister of Foreign Affairs of the Russian Federation Sergey Lavrov at the Ministerial Meeting on the Northern Dimension, Brussels, 21 November 2005.

Lavrov, S. (2007) Speech by Minister of Foreign Affairs at MGIMO University on the Occasion of the Start of a New Academic Year, Moscow, 3 September, http://www.mid.ru/brp_4.nsf/e78a48070f128a7b4325699 9005bcbb3/d2ca87d862a0db6dc32574b9001d9be5?OpenDocument, accessed 13 December 2015.

Lavrov, S. (2008a) 'The Responsibility of Russia in World Politics', speech at the International Conference of the Bergedorf Forum, Moscow, October 25.

Lavrov, S. (2008b) Transcript of Remarks and Response to Media Questions by Minister of Foreign Affairs of the Russian Federation Sergey Lavrov at Press Conference Following the First Ministerial Meeting of the Renewed Northern Dimension, St Petersburg, 29 October.

Lavrov, S. (2008c) 'Transcript of Introductory Remarks and Comments by Russian Minister of Foreign Affairs Sergey Lavrov at the Opening Ceremony of the First Ministerial Meeting of the Renewed Northern Dimension', St Petersburg, 29 October, http://www.mid.ru/fr_FR/ press_service/minister_speeches/-/asset_publisher/7OvQR5KJWVmR/ content/id/319118?p_p_id=101_INSTANCE_7OvQR5KJWVmR&_101_ INSTANCE_7OvQR5KJWVmR_languageId=en_GB, accessed 10 December 2015.

Lavrov, S. (2011) 'Russia in a Multipolar World: Implications for Russia-EU-U.S.', speech at the Center for Strategic and International Studies, July 11, http://www.rusembassy.ca/ru/node/589, accessed 13 December 2015.

Lavrov, S. (2013) 'Russia-EU: Prospects for Partnership in the Changing World', *Journal of Common Market Studies*, 51(Annual Review): 6–12.

Lavrov, S (2014a) 'Interview of the Russian Foreign Minister Sergey Lavrov to ITAR-TASS', *The Ministry of Foreign Affairs of the Russian Federation*, 10 September, http://archive.mid.ru//bdomp/brp_4.nsf/e78a48070 f128a7b43256999005bcbb3/d8c4dd75d09c784844257d5000374f29! OpenDocument, accessed 11 December 2015.

Lavrov, S. (2014b) 'Remarks by Foreign Minister Sergey Lavrov at the XXII Assembly of the Council on Foreign and Defence Policy', *Moscow*, 22 November, http://archive.mid.ru//brp_4.nsf/0/24454A08D48F695E C3257D9A004BA32E, accessed 4 December 2015.

Layton, S. (2014) 'Reframing European Security: Russia's Proposal for a New European Security Architecture', *International Relations*, 28(1): 25–45.

Ledeneva, A. (2013) *Can Russia Modernise? Sistema, Power Networks and Informal Governance* (Cambridge: Cambridge University Press).

Legvold, R. (2014) 'Managing the New Cold War: What Moscow and Washington Can Learn from the Last One Foreign Affairs,' *Foreign Affairs*, 93(4): 74–84.

Leichtova, M. (2014) *Misunderstanding Russia: Russian Foreign Policy and the West* (Farnham: Ashgate).

Leino-Sandberg, P. (2005) *Particularity as Universality: The Politics of Human Rights in the European Union*, The Erik Castrén Institute Research Reports 15/2005 (Helsinki: Erik Castrén Institute of International Law and Human Rights).

Lenin, A. (2015) 'RF gotova vozobnovit? Dialog ob otmene viz s ES?', *Rossiiskaya Gazeta*, 15 January, http://www.rg.ru/2015/01/15/dialog-site.html, accessed 8 July 2015.

Lewington, R. (2013) 'Keeping the Peace in the South Caucasus: The EU Monitoring Mission in Georgia', *Asian Affairs*, 44(1): 51–69.

Leonard, M. and N. Popescu (2007) 'A Power Audit of EU–Russia Relations', policy paper, November, (London: European Council on Foreign Relations), http://www.ecfr.eu/page/-/ECFR-02_A_POWER_AUDIT_OF_EU-RUSSIA_RELATIONS.pdf, accessed 8 July 2015.

Leshukov, I. (2001) 'Can the Northern Dimension Break the Vicious Circle of Russia–EU Relations?', in H. Ojanen (ed.) *The Northern Dimension: Fuel for the EU?* Programme on the Northern Dimension of the CFSP No. 12 (Helsinki and Berlin: Finnish Institute of International Affairs and Institut für Europäische Politik).

Levada-Center (2015) 'International Relations', press release, 16 October, http://www.levada.ru/eng/international-relations-0, accessed 13 December 2015.

Lewington, R. (2013) 'Keeping the Peace in the South Caucasus: The EU Monitoring Mission in Georgia', *Asian Affairs*, 44(1): 51–69.

Light, M. (2008) 'Russia and the EU: Strategic Partners or Strategic Rivals?', *Journal of Common Market Studies*, 46 (Annual Review): 7–27.

Light, M. and D. Cadier (2015) 'Introduction', in D. Cadier and M. Light (eds) *Russia's Foreign Policy: Ideas, Domestic Politics and External Relations* (Basingstoke: Palgrave Macmillan).

Likhachev, V. (2003) 'Russia and the European Union', *International Affairs* (Moscow), 49(1): 55–63.

Likhachev, V. (2004) 'Russia and EU: Proficiency Essential', *Russia in Global Affairs*, 2(2): 103–7.

Likhachev, V. (2006) 'Russia and the European Union', *International Affairs* (Moscow), 52(2): 102–14.

Lintonen, R. (2004) 'Understanding EU Crisis Decision-making: The Case of Chechnya and the Finnish Presidency', *Journal of Contingencies and Crisis Management*, 12(1): 29–38.

Lipman, M. (2016) *What Russia Thinks of Europe*. ECFR Commentary, 2 February 2016 (London: ECFR), http://www.ecfr.eu/article/commentary_what_russia_thinks_of_europe5084, accessed 20 February 2016.

Lipponen, P. (1997) 'The European Union Needs a Policy for the Northern Dimension', speech at the 'Barents Region Today' conference, Rovaniemi, Finland, 15 September 1997.

Liuhto, K. (2015) 'The Economic Dependence of EU Member States on Russia', in A. Pabriks and A. Kudors (eds) *The War in Ukraine: Lessons for Europe* (Riga: University of Latvia Press).

Liuhto, K. and Majuri, S. (2014) 'Outward Foreign Direct Investment from Russia: A Literature Review', *Journal of East-West Business*, 20(4): 198–224.

Lo, B. (2003a) 'The Securitization of Russian Foreign Policy under Putin', in G. Gorodetsky (ed.) *Russia Between East and West: Russian Foreign Policy on the Threshold of the Twenty-first Century* (London: Frank Cass).

Lo, B. (2003b) *Vladimir Putin and the Evolution of Russian Foreign Policy* (London: Royal Institute of International Affairs and Blackwell).

Lo, B. (2009) 'Medvedev and the new European Security Architecture', *policy brief paper* (London: Center for European Reform).

Lo, B. (2015) *Russia and the New World Disorder* (London and Washington, DC: Chatham House and Brookings).

Lukyanov, F. (2013) 'The Only Reasonable "Third Way" for Russia', in Bertelsmann Stiftung (ed.) *From Cooperation to Partnership: Moving Beyond the Russia-EU Deadlock*, Europe in Dialogue 1/2013 (Berlin: Bertelsmann Stiftung).

Lynch, D. (2003) ' *Russia Faces Europe*, Chaillot Paper no. 60 European Union Institute for Security Studies.

Lynch, D. (2005) 'Misperceptions and Divergences', in D. Lynch (ed.) *What Russia Sees*, Chaillot Paper No 74, January (Paris: EU Institute for Security Studies).

Maass, A.-S. (2016) *EU–Russia Relations (1999–2015): From Courtship to Confrontation* (London and New York: Routledge).

MacFarlane N. and A. Menon (2014) 'The EU and Ukraine', *Survival*, 56(3): 95–101.

Mahnke, D. (2001) 'Russia's Attitude towards European Security and Defence Policy', *European Foreign Affairs Review*, 6(4): 427–36.

Makarkin, A. (2011) 'The Russian Social Contract and Regime Legitimacy', *International Affairs* (London), 87(6): 1459–75.

Makarychev, A. (2014) *Russia and the EU in a Multipolar World: Discourses, Identities, Norms* (Stuttgart: Ibidem).

Makarychev, A. and S. Meister (2015) 'The Modernisation Debate and Russian–German Normative Cleavages', *European Politics and Society*, 16(1): 80–94.

Mäkinen, S. (2011) 'Surkovian Narrative on the Future of Russia: Making Russia a World Leader', *Journal of Communist Studies and Transition Politics*, 27(2): 143–65.

Mäkinen, S. (2016) 'In Search of the Status of an Educational Great Power? Analysis of Russia's Educational Diplomacy Discourse', Problems of Post-communism, forthcoming.

Mäkinen, S., H. Smith and T. Forsberg, (2016) '"With a Little Help from My Friends": Russia's Modernisation and the Visa Regime with the European Union', *Europe-Asia Studies*, 68(1): 164–81.

Malcolm, N. (1991) 'The Soviet Concept of a Common European House', in J. Iivonen (ed.) *The Changing Soviet Union in the New Europe* (Aldershot: Edward Elgar).

Maltby, T. (2013) 'European Union Energy Policy Integration: A Case of European Commission Policy Entrepreneurship and Increasing Supranationalism', *Energy Policy*, 55: 435–44.

Mané-Estrada, A. (2006) 'European Energy Security: Towards the Creation of the Geo-energy Space', *Energy Policy*, 34(18): 3773–86.

Mankoff, J. (2009) *Russian Foreign Policy. The Return of Great Power Politics* (Lanham: Rowman & Littlefield).

Manners, I. (2002) 'Normative Power Europe: A Contradiction in Terms?', *Journal of Common Market Studies*, 40(2): 235–58.

Manners, I. and R. Whitman (eds) (2000) *The Foreign Policies of European Union Member States* (Manchester: Manchester University Press).

Maresceau, M. (2004) 'EU Enlargement and EU Common Strategies on Russia and Ukraine: An Ambiguous Yet Unavoidable Connection', in C. Hillion (ed.) *EU Enlargement – A Legal Approach: Essays in European Law* (Oxford: Hart).

Marsh, S. (2008) 'EU–Russia Security Relations and the Survey of Russian Federation Foreign Policy: One Year On', *European Security*, 17(2): 185–208.

Marszal, A. (2013) 'EU Will Not Accept Russian Veto, Says Barroso', *The Telegraph*, 29 November, http://www.telegraph.co.uk/news/worldnews/europe/ukraine/10482680/EU-will-not-accept-Russian-veto-says-Barroso.html, accessed 13 December 2015.

Mason, J and P. Taylor (2007) 'EU Deal on Siberia Overflights May Need More Talks', *Reuters*, 14 May.

McCormick, J. (2007) *The European Superpower* (Basingstoke: Palgrave Macmillan).

McEvoy, J. (1997) 'Premier Keen on EU Membership', *Moscow Times*, 19 July, http://www.themoscowtimes.com/sitemap/free/1997/7/article/premier-keen-on-eu-membership/303975.html, accessed 13 December 2015.

McFaul, M. (with S. Sestanovich and J. Mearsheimer) (2014) 'Faulty Powers. Who Started the Ukraine Crisis?', *Foreign Affairs Online*, November/December, http://www.foreignaffairs.com/articles/142260/michael-mcfaul-stephen-sestanovich-john-j-mearsheimer/faulty-powers, accessed 11 November 2015.

McNicoll, T. (2008) 'Sarko Tackles the Bear', *Newsweek International Edn*, 28 September.

Mearsheimer, J. (2014) 'Why the Ukraine Crisis Is the West's Fault. The Liberal Delusions That Provoked Putin', *Foreign Affairs Online*, September/October.

Medvedev, D. (2008) 'Speech at World Policy Conference', *Evian*, 8 October.

Medvedev, D. (2016) Speech at the Munich Security Conference , 13 February, http://government.ru/en/news/21784/, accessed 16 February 2016

Medvedev, D. (2009a) *Go Russia!*, September 10, http://en.kremlin.ru/events/president/news/5413, accessed 28 May 2015.

Medvedev, D. (2009b) 'The Draft of the European Security Treaty', *Moscow*, 29 September, http://en.kremlin.ru/events/president/news/6152, accessed 13 December 2015.

Medvedev, S. (2006) *EU–Russian Relations: Alternative Futures* (Helsinki: Finnish Institute of International Affairs).

Medvedev, S. (2007) The Crisis in EU–Russia Relations: Between 'Sovereignty' and 'Europeanization' Working paper WP14/2007/02. Moscow: State University – Higher School of Economics.

Medvedev, S. (2008) 'The Stalemate in EU–Russia Relations: Between 'Sovereignty' and 'Europeanisation'', in T. Hopf (ed.) *Russia's European Choice* (Basingstoke: Palgrave Macmillan).

Medvedev, S. and I. Neumann (2012) 'Identity Issues in EU–Russia Relations', in R. Krumm, S. Medvedev and H. Schröder (eds) *Constructing Identities in Europe: German and Russian Perspectives* (Baden-Baden: Nomos).

Medvedkov, M. (2002) 'Russia's Accession to the WTO: The View from Russia', in K. Barysch, R. Cottrell, F. Frattini, P. Hare, P. Lamy, M. Medvedkov and Y. Yasin, *Russia and the WTO* (London: Centre for European Reform).

Meister, S. (2011) 'A New Start for Russian–EU Security Policy? The Weimar Triangle, Russia and the EU's Eastern Neighbourhood', *Genshagener Papiere*, 7 – July (Genshagen: Stiftung Genshagen), http://www.robert-schuman.eu/doc/actualites/genshagener-papiere-2011-7-eng.pdf, accessed 10 July 2015.

Mendras, M. (2013) *Russian Politics: The Paradox of a Weak State* (New York: Columbia University Press).

Menkiszak, M., R. Sadowski and P. Zochowski (2014) 'The Russian Military Intervention in Eastern Ukraine', *OSW Analyses*, September 23, http://www.osw.waw.pl/en/publikacje/analyses/2014-09-03/russian-military-intervention-eastern-ukraine, accessed 10 November 2015.

Mérand, F. (2008) *European Defence Policy: Beyond the Nation State* (Oxford: Oxford University Press).

Merikallio, K., and Ruokanen, T. (2015) *The Mediator: A Biography of Martti Ahtisaari* (London: Hurst).

Merlingen, M. (2012) *EU Security Policy: What It Is, How It Works, Why It Matters* (Boulder, CO: Lynne Rienner).

Miller, V. (2004) 'The Human Rights Clause in the EU's External Agreements', *House of Commons Research Paper 04/33*, 16 April (London: House of Commons Library).

Ministry of Foreign Affairs of Russia (MID) (2011) 'О ситуации с правами человека в ряде государств мира' [Report on Human Rights in Certain States], 28 December.

Ministry of Foreign Affairs of the Russian Federation (MID) (2014) 'Заявление МИД России в связи с санкциями США против России', [Comment by the Russian Ministry of Foreign Affairs regarding the United States' sanctions against Russia], 17 July, http://archive.mid.ru//brp_4.nsf/0/25A2BD25E3B202BD44257D1800253CCB, accessed 13 December 2015.

Ministry of Foreign Affairs of the Russian Federation (MID) (2015) 'Comment on the EU Action Plan to Counter Russian Propaganda', *The Ministry for Foreign Affairs of the Russian Federation*, 1269-24-06-2015.

Mintz, A. and K. DeRouen Jr. (2010) *Understanding Foreign Policy Decision Making* (Cambridge and New York: Cambridge University Press).

Missiroli, A. (2002) 'EU-NATO Cooperation in Crisis Management: No Turkish Delight for the ESDP', *Security Dialogue*, 33(1): 9–26.

Missiroli, A. (2004) 'The EU and Its Changing Neighbourhood: Stabilization, Integration and Partnership', in R. Dannreuther (ed.) *European Union Foreign and Security Policy. Towards a Neighbourhood Strategy.* (London and New York: Routledge).

Monaghan, A. (2005) 'Russian Perspectives of Russia-EU Security Relations', *Russian series 05/38* (Sandhurst: Conflict Studies Research Centre).

Moroff, H. (ed.) (2002) *European Soft Security Policies: The Northern Dimension* (Helsinki: Finnish Institute of International affairs).

Morozov, V. (2008) 'Energy Dialogue and the Future of Russia: Politics and Economics in the Struggle for Europe', in P. Aalto (ed.) *The EU–Russian Energy Dialogue: Europe's Future Energy Security* (Aldershot: Ashgate).

Moscow Institute of International Relations (University) of the Russian Ministry of Foreign Affairs (MGIMO) (2015) *European Studies Institute*, homepage, http://english.mgimo.ru/european-studies-institute, accessed 6 November 2015.

Moscow Times (2003a) 'Prodi: Russians May Not Need EU Visas in 5 Years', July 18.

Moscow Times (2003b) 'U.S., EU Concerned Over Yukos', October 29.

Moscow Times (2012) 'Kremlin Pressures Ukraine to Join Alliance', 17 September.

Moscow Times (2013) 'Gazprom Plans $4.7Bln Refund to European Customers in 2013', 11 February, http://www.themoscowtimes.com/business/article/gazprom-plans-47bln-refund-to-european-customers-in-2013/475287.html, accessed 12 November 2015.

Moscow Times (2015) 'Slovak Prime Minister Feels "Betrayed" by EU's Nordstream Deal With Russia', 10 September.

Moshes, A. (2009) 'EU–Russia Relations: Unfortunate Continuity', European Issues, Foundation Robert Schuman, 24 February, http://www.robert-schuman.eu/en/doc/questions-d-europe/qe-129-en.pdf, accessed 16 February 2016.

Moshes, A. (2012) 'Russia's European Policy under Medvedev: How Sustainable Is a New Compromise?', *International Affairs* (London), 88(1): 17–30.

Moshes, A. (2013) 'A Marriage of Unequals: Russian-Ukrainian Relations under President Yanukovych', in S. Meister (ed.) *Economization versus Power Ambitions. Rethinking Russia's Policy towards Post-Soviet States* (Berlin: Nomos & DGAP).

Movchan, A. (2015) 'Just an Oil Company? The True Extent of Russia's Dependency on Oil and Gas', *Eurasia Outlook*, September 14 (Moscow: Carnegie Moscow Center).

Mueller, W. (2009) 'The Soviet Union and Early West European Integration, 1947–1957: From the Brussels Treaty to the ECSC and the EEC', *Journal of European Integration History*, 15(2): 67–85.

Myers, S. (2014) 'Russia's Move Into Ukraine Said to Be Born in Shadows,' *The New York Times*, 7 March.

Nechepurenko, I. (2013) 'Russia-EU Values Gap on Display at Summit', *Moscow Times*, 4 June 2013, http://www.themoscowtimes.com/news/article/russia-eu-values-gap-on-display-at-summit/481132.html, accessed 7 July 2015.

Nesvetailova, A. (2015) 'The Offshore Nexus, Sanctions and the Russian Crisis', *IAI Working Papers 15*, 24 July (Rome: IAI).

Neumann, I. and V. Pouliot (2011) 'Untimely Russia: Hysteresis in Russian-Western Relations over the Past Millennium', *Security Studies*, 20(1): 105–37.

Neumann, I. B. (1996) *Russia and the Idea of Europe. A Study in Identity and International Relations* (London: Routledge).

Neumann, I. (1998). *Uses of the Other: the 'East' in European identity formation* (Minneapolis, MN: University of Minnesota Press).

Neumann, I. B. (1999) *Uses of the Other. The 'East' in European Identity Formation* (Minneapolis, MN: University of Minnesota Press).

Neumann, I. B. (2006) From Ch. 9, p. 25.

Neumann, I. B. (2011) 'Entry into International Society Reconceptualised: The Case of Russia', *Review of International Studies*, 37(2): 463–84.

New Europe (2011) 'Russia Seeks Compromise on Transnistrian conflict', *Neurope.eu*, http://neurope.eu/article/russia-seeks-compromise-transnistrian-conflict/, accessed 13 December 2015.

Newnham, R. (2011) 'Oil, Carrots, and Sticks: Russia's Energy Resources as a Foreign Policy Tool', *Journal of Eurasian Studies*, 2(2): 134–43.

News Conference following EU–Russia Summit (2010) Rostov-on-Don, 1 June, http://en.kremlin.ru/events/president/transcripts/7932, accessed 5 November 2015.

Nezavisimia Gazeta (2007) 'Moscow Benefits from EU Decision to Cancel Aviation Summit', 9 November.

Nice, A. (2013) 'Playing Both Sides: Belarus between Russia and the EU', in S. Meister (ed.) *Economization versus Power Ambitions. Rethinking Russia's Policy towards Post-Soviet States.* (Berlin: Nomos & DGAP).

Nikolaev, M. (2007) 'New Northern Dimension', *International Affairs* (Moscow), 53(3): 81–89.

Nitoiu, C. (2014) 'EU–Russian Relations: Between Conflict and Cooperation', *International Politics*, 52(2): 234–53.

Northern Dimension Partnership on Culture (NDPC) (2010) *Memorandum of Understanding setting out the modalities of establishing the Northern Dimension Partnership on Culture*, St Petersburg, 20 May 2010, http://www.ndpculture.org/media/W1siZiIsIjIwMTQvMTAvMTYvOTJuZ2dweXk5eV8xNl8wMl81OV8zNzRfTWVVtb3JhbmR1bV9vZl9VbmRlcn-N0YW5kaW5nLnBkZiJdXQ/16_02_59_374_Memorandum_of_Under-standing.pdf?sha=8adbd6d27814f8e0, accessed 13 December 2015.

Nowak, B. (2010) 'Forging the External Dimension of the Energy Policy of the European Union', *The Electricity Journal*, 23(1): 57–66.

Nye, J. (2013) 'What China and Russia Don't Get About Soft Power', *Foreign Policy Online*, April 29, http://foreignpolicy.com/2013/04/29/what-china-and-russia-dont-get-about-soft-power/, accessed 26 April 2016.

Nygren, B. (2008) 'Putin's Use of Natural Gas to Reintegrate the CIS Region', *Problems of Post-Communism*, 55(4): 3–15.

Ojanen, H. (1999) 'How to Customise Your Union: Finland and the "Northern Dimension of the EU"', *Northern Dimensions: The Yearbook of Finnish Foreign Policy* (Helsinki: The Finnish Institute of International Affairs).

Ojanen, H. (2000) 'The EU and Its "Northern Dimension": An Actor in Search of a Policy, or a Policy in Search of an Actor?', *European Foreign Affairs Review*, 5(3): 359–76.

Oldberg, I. (2004) *Membership or Partnership: The Relations of Russia and Its Neighbours with NATO and the EU in the Enlargement Context*. Scientific Report, FOI-R-1364-SE, October 2004 (Stockholm: Swedish Defence Research Agency).

OMV Group (2015) *Gazprom and OMV Move Forward with Long-Term Business Projects*, press release, 4 September.

Orttung, R. W. (2009) 'Energy and State–Society Relations: Socio-political Aspects of Russia's Energy Wealth', in J. Perovic, R.W. Orttung and A. Wenger (eds) *Russian Energy Power and Foreign Relations: Implications for Conflict and Cooperation* (London and New York: Routledge).

Orttung, R. W. and I. Overland (2011) 'A Limited Toolbox: Explaining the Constraints on Russia's Foreign Energy Policy', *Journal of Eurasian Studies*, 2(1): 74–85.

Osborn, A. (2005) 'Putin Loses his Smile after Lecture from Bush on Democracy', *The Independent*, 25 February, http://www.independent.co.uk/news/world/europe/putin-loses-his-smile-after-lecture-from-bush-on-democracy-12711.html, accessed 23 February 2016.

Panagiotou, R. A. (2011) 'The Centrality of the United Nations in Russian Foreign Policy', *Journal of Communist Studies and Transition Politics*, 27(2): 195–216.

Panin, A. (2013) 'Overflight Fees to Remain After 2014', *Moscow Times*, September 5, 2013, http://www.themoscowtimes.com/business/article/overflight-fees-to-remain-after-2014/485551.html, accessed 9 July 2015.

Pankov, V. (2007) 'Free Trade between Russia and EU: Pros and Cons', *Russia in Global Affairs*, 5(2): 113–23.

Partnership and Cooperation Agreement (PCA) (1997) *Agreement on Partnership and Cooperation: Establishing a Partnership between the European Communities and Their Member States, of One Part, and the Russian Federation, of the Other Part*, Document 21997A1128(01), http://eur-lex.europa.eu/resource.html?uri=cellar:70f7046b-4dca-476f-a80a-8438fe467bbb.0010.02/DOC_1&format=PDF, accessed 13 December 2015.

Paton Walsh, N. (2004) 'Russian Vote Saves Kyoto Protocol', *The Guardian*, 23 October, http://www.theguardian.com/world/2004/oct/23/society.russia, accessed 12 November 2015.

Patten, C. (2001) 'Russia's Hell-Hole Enclave', *The Guardian*, 7 April, http://www.theguardian.com/world/2001/apr/07/russia.politics, accessed 5 November 2015.

Patten, C. (2005) *Not Quite the Diplomat: Home Truths about World Affairs* (London: Penguin Books).

Patten, C. (2009) 'Europe's Vision-Free Leadership', *Moscow Times*, 26 November.

Pavlova, E. (2014) 'The Russian Federation and European Union against Corruption: A Slight Misunderstanding?', *European Politics and Society*, 16(1): 111–25.

Permanent Mission of the Russian Federation to the European Union (2015) *Culture*, http://www.russianmission.eu/en/culture, accessed 25 June 2015.

Perovic, J. (2009) 'Introduction: Russian Energy Power, Domestic And Internatonal Dimensions', in J. Perovic, R. W. Orttung and A. Wenger (eds) *Russian Energy Power and Foreign Relations: Implications for Conflict and Cooperation* (London and New York: Routledge).

Perritt, H. (2010) *The Roadmap to Independence for Kosovo – A Chronicle of the Ahtisaari Plan* (Cambridge: Cambridge University Press).

Petiteville, F. (2003) 'Exporting "Values"? EU External Co-operation as a "Soft Diplomacy"', in M. Knodt and S. Princen (eds) *Understanding the European Union's External Relations* (London: Routledge).

Pew Research Center (2007) 'Global Unease with Major World Powers', The Pew Global Attitudes Project, June 27 (Washington, DC: Pew Research Center).

Pew Research Center (2015) *Russian Public Opinion: Putin Praised, West Panned*, 10 June, http://www.pewglobal.org/2015/06/10/2-russian-public-opinion-putin-praised-west-panned/, accessed 13 December 2015.

Piccardo, L. (2010) 'The European Union and Russia: Past, Present and Future of a Difficult Relationship', in F. Bindi (ed.) *The Foreign Policy of the European Union: Assessing Europe's Role in the* World (Washington, DC: The Brookings Institution).

Pihl, L. (2002) 'Prodi: EU Enlargement Must Stop Somewhere', *euobserver. com*, 27 November.

Piiparinen, T. (2014) 'Is It Time to Transcend Political Realism in the EU–Russia Security Cooperation? Exploring the Critical Realist Model of Emancipatory Windows', *Journal of International Relations and Development*, early view.

Pinder, J. (1991) *The European Community and Eastern Europe* (London: Royal Institute of International Affairs and Pinter Publishers).

Pinder, J. and Y. Shiskov (2002) *The EU and Russia: The Promise of Partnership* (London: The Federal Trust).

Pleines, H. (2005) 'Russian Business Interests and the Enlarged European Union', *Post-Communist Economies*, 17(3): 269–87.

Polikanov, D. and G. Timmins (2004) 'Russian Foreign Policy under Putin', in C. Ross (ed.) *Russian Politics under Putin* (Manchester: Manchester University Press).

Pomerantsev; P. and M. Weiss (2014) 'The Menace of Unreality: How the Kremlin Weaponizes Information, Culture and Money', *The Interpreter*, 22 November, http://www.interpretermag.com/the-menace-of-unreality-how-the-kremlin-weaponizes-information-culture-and-money/, accessed 13 December 2015.

Pop, V. (2009) 'EU Expanding Its "Sphere of Influence," Russia says', *euobserver.com*, 21 March 2009, https://euobserver.com/foreign/27827, accessed 10 July 2015.

Popescu N. (2011) *EU Foreign Policy and the Post-Soviet Conflicts: Stealth Intervention* (Abingdon: Routledge).

Popescu, N. (2015) 'Sanctions and Russia. Lessons from the Cold War', *Issue Brief 10* (Paris: European Union Institute for Security Studies), http://www.iss.europa.eu/uploads/media/Brief_10_sanctions.pdf, accessed 9 July 2015.

Popescu, N. and A. Wilson (2009) *The Limits of Enlargement-lite: European and Russian Power in the Troubled Neighbourhood* (London: European Council on Foreign Relations), http://ecfr.3cdn.net/befa70d12114c3c2b0_hrm6bv2ek.pdf, accessed 10 December 2015.

Potemkina, O. (2003) 'Some Ramifications of Enlargement on the EU–Russia Relations and the Schengen Regime', *European Journal of Migration and Law*, 5(2): 229–47.

Potemkina, O. (2010) 'EU–Russia Cooperation on the Common Space of Freedom, Security and Justice – a Challenge or an Opportunity', *European Security*, 19(4): 551–68.

Potemkina, O. (2015) 'The EU–Russia Cooperation in Fighting Terrorism', Working Paper no 1, Institute of Europe of the Russian Academy of Sciences, http://www.ieras.ru/english/pub/analit/Working paper IE RAS1,2015.pdf, accessed 12 November 2015.

Povalko, A. (2015) 'Push for the Top', *Times Higher Education Supplement*, https://www.timeshighereducation.com/world-university-rankings/2015/brics-and-emerging-economies/analysis/push-for-the-top, accessed 16 February 2016.

Prange-Gstöhl, H. (2009) 'Enlarging the EU's Internal Energy Market: Why Would Third Countries Accept EU Rule Export?', *Energy Policy*, 37(12): 5296–303.

The Preparatory Action 'Culture in EU External Relations' (2015a) 'Engaging the World: Towards Global Cultural Citizenship', *European Union*, http://cultureinexternalrelations.eu/wp-content/uploads/2013/05/Engaging-The-World-Towards-Global-Cultural-Citizenship-eBook-1.5_13.06.2014.pdf, accessed 25 June 2015.

The Preparatory Action 'Culture in EU External Relations' (2015b) *Russia Country Report*, http://cultureinexternalrelations.eu/wp-content/uploads/2014/02/country-report-Russia-26.02.2014.pdf, accessed 25 June 2015.

Preston, C. (1997) *Enlargement and Integration in the European Union* (London and New York: Routledge).

Prikhodina, M. (2013) 'Russia May Trade Overflight Fees for More Access to Europe', *Russia Beyond the Headlines*, November 26, http://rbth.com/business/2013/11/26/russia_may_trade_overflight_fees_for_more_access_to_europe_32053.html, accessed 9 July 2015.

Prodi, R. (2000) 'Moscow's Mandate for Change: Romano Prodi Finds Much to Be Optimistic about in Vladimir Putin's Russia – Given the Right Programme of Reform', *Financial Times*, 26 May.

Prodi, R. (2004) 'Russia and the European Union: Enduring Ties, Widening Horizons', speech at the Tretyakov Gallery, Moscow, 23 April, http://europa.eu/rapid/press-release_SPEECH-04-198_en.htm, accessed 5 November 2015.

Prozorov, S. (2006) *Understanding Conflict Between Russia and the EU: The Limits of Integration* (Basingstoke: Palgrave Macmillan).

Pursiainen, C. (2008) 'Theories of Integration and the Limits of EU–Russian Relations', in T. Hopf (ed.) *Russia's European Choice* (Basingstoke: Palgrave Macmillan): 149–86.

Pursiainen, C. and S. Medvedev (eds) (2005) *The Bologna Process and its Implications for Russia: The European Integration of Higher Education* (Moscow: Russian-European Centre for Economic Policy – RECEP).

Putin, V. (2001) 'Speech in the Bundestag of the Federal Republic of Germany', *Berlin*, 21 September.

Putin, V. (2003) 'Speech at the Meeting with Representatives of the European Round Table of Industrialists and the Round Table of Industrialists of Russia and the EU', Moscow, 2 December, http://2004.kremlin.ru/eng/text/speeches/2003/12/022100_56575.shtml, accessed 26 June 2007.

Putin, V. (2004) 'Address by President Vladimir Putin', Moscow, September 4, http://en.kremlin.ru/events/president/transcripts/statements/22589, accessed 10 December 2015.

Putin, V. (2005) 'Annual Address to the Federal Assembly of the Russian Federation', Moscow, 25 April, http://archive.kremlin.ru/eng/speeches/2005/04/25/2031_type70029type82912_87086.shtml, accessed 13 December 2015.

Putin, V. (2006) 'Europe Has Nothing to Fear from Russia's Aspirations', *Financial Times*, 22 November.

Putin, V. (2007a) 'Speech and the Following Discussion at the Munich Conference on Security Policy, Munich, February 10, http://en.kremlin.ru/events/president/transcripts/24034, accessed 13 December 2015.

Putin, V. (2007b) 'Speech at the XI St Petersburg International Economic Forum', St Petersburg, June 10.

Putin, V. (2008) 'Speech at the Expanded Meeting of the State Council', Moscow, 8 February. Reprinted as 'Thirst for Victory Has Always Been a Part of Our National Character', *International Affairs* (Moscow), 54(2): 1–15.

Putin, V. (2009) 'Speech at the Opening Ceremony of the World Economic Forum', Davos, 28 January.

Putin, V. (2012) 'Russia and the Changing World', *Moskovskiye Novosti*, 27 February.

Putin, V. (2013a) 'Vladimir Putin Meets with Members the Valdai International Discussion Club', Transcript of the speech and beginning of the meeting, 20 September, http://valdaiclub.com/politics/62880.html, accessed 4 June 2015.

Putin, V. (2013b) 'Presidential Address to the Federal Assembly', Moscow, December 12, http://en.kremlin.ru/events/president/news/19825, accessed 7 July 2015.

Putin, V. (2014) 'Address by President of the Russian Federation', Kremlin, March 18, http://en.kremlin.ru/events/president/news/20603, accessed 2 July 2015.

Putin, V. (2015a) 'Vladimir Putin', interview to the Italian newspaper *Il Corriere della Sera*', *Corriere della Sera – English*, interview 7 June, http://www.corriere.it/english/15_giugno_07/vladimir-putin-interview-to-the-italian-newspaper-corriere-sera-44c5a66c-0d12-11e5-8612-1eda5b996824.shtml, accessed 13 December 2015.

Putin, V. (2015b) Speech at the Plenary session of the 19th St Petersburg International Economic Forum, St Petersburg, June 19, http://en.kremlin.ru/events/president/news/49733, accessed 9 July 2015.

Renner, S. (2009) 'The Energy Community of Southeast Europe: A neo-functionalist project of regional integration', *European Integration online Papers*, 13, 25 February, http://eiop.or.at/eiop/pdf/2009-001.pdf, accessed 13 December 2015.

Rettmann, A. (2010) 'EU–Russia Human Rights Talks Making Little Impact,' *euobserver.com*, 18 June.

Rettmann, A. (2015) 'Gazprom Lobbyists Get to Work in EU Capital', *euobserver.com*, 21 April 2015, https://euobserver.com/foreign/128403, accessed 8 July 2015.

RIAC (2014) 'Internationalization of Russian Universities: the Chinese Vector', Report no. 13, Moscow: Russian International Affairs Council, http://russiancouncil.ru/common/upload/Report13-2014en.pdf, accessed 10 November 2015.

RIA Novosti (2008) 'Putin Pledges Measured Response to NATO Warships in Black Sea', *RIA Novosti*, 2 September, http://sputniknews.com/world/20080902/116488911.html, accessed 26 April 2016.

RFE/RL (2015) '"Brussels Was . . . Asleep": Bildt Assesses EU's Mistakes Regarding Russia', Interview with Carl Bildt, *Radio Free Europe / Radio Liberty*, 22 March.

Richardson, J. and S. Mazey (eds) (2015) *The European Union. Power and Policy-making*, 4th edn (London and New York: Routledge).

Riley, A. (2012) 'Commission v Gazprom: The Antitrust Clash of the Decade?', *CEPS Policy Brief No. 285*, 31 October, https://www.ceps.eu/system/files/PB No 285 AR Commission v Gazprom_0.pdf, accessed 13 December 2015.

Roberts, S. P. and A. Moshes (2015) 'The Eurasian Economic Union: A Case of Reproductive Integration?', *Post-Soviet Affairs*, 23 November, published online 23 October.

Rodkiewics, W. and J. Rogoża (2015) 'Potemkin Conservatism. An Ideological Tool of the Kremlin', *OWS Point of View 48*, February (Warsaw: Centre for Eastern Studies).

Rohrich, K. (2015) 'Human Rights Diplomacy Amidst "World War LGBT": Re-examining Western Promotion of LGBT Rights in Light of the "Traditional Values" Discourse', in A. Chase and J. Goldstein (eds) *Transatlantic Perspectives on Diplomacy and Diversity* (Humanity in Action Press).

Roll, G., T. Maximova and E. Mikenberg (2001) 'The External Relations of the Pskov Oblast of the Russian Federation', SHIFFE-texte no. 63 (Kiel: Schleswig-Holstein Institute for Peace Research, Christian-Albrechts-University Kiel).

Romanova, T. (2004) 'New Dimensions of EU–Russian Relations', in K. Khudoley (ed.) *New Security Challenges as Challenges to Peace Research* (St Petersburg: St Petersburg University Press).

Romanova, T. (2005) *Northwestern Russian Perspective on the Northern Dimension*, a presentation at 'Strengthening the EU Agenda for Baltic Sea Cooperation' seminar, Brussels, 29 November 2005.

Romanova, T. (2008) 'The Russian Perspective on the Energy Dialogue', *Journal of Contemporary European Studies*, 16(2): 219–30.

Romanova, T. (2010) 'The Theory and Practice of Reciprocity in EU–Russia Relations', in K. Engelbrekt and B. Nygren (eds) *Russia and Europe. Building Bridges, Digging Trenches* (London and New York: Routledge).

Romanova, T. (2011) 'The Level-of-Analysis Problem in the Past, Present and Future of EU–Russia Relations', *CEURUS Working Paper no. 2* (Tartu: University of Tartu).

Romanova, T. and Pavlova, E. (2014) 'What Modernisation? The Case of Russian Partnerships for Modernisation with the European Union and Its Member States', *Journal of Contemporary European Studies*, 22(4): 499–517.

Rontoyanni, C. (2002) 'So Far, So Good? Russia and the ESDP', *International Affairs* (London), 78(4): 813–30.

Rossi, J. (2014) 'Russia Foreign Minister: Russia Doing Everything It Can to Resolve Ukraine Crisis', *The Wall Street Journal*, June 9, http://online.wsj.com/articles/russia-foreign-minister-russia-doing-everythingit-can-to-resolve-ukraine-crisis-1402341848, accessed 10 November 2015.

Rotfeld A. and A. Torkunov (2015) *White Spots—Black Spots: Difficult Matters in Polish–Russian Relations, 1918–2008* (Pittsburgh: University of Pittsburgh Press).

Roth, M. (2009) *Bilateral Disputes between EU Member States and Russia*, CEPS Working Document No. 319 (Brussels: Centre for European Policy).

RT (2009) '"Nothing Can Be Valued above Human Life" – Medvedev', *rt.com*, transcript of the statement made by Dmitry Medvedev, 30 October, DOI: 10.1080/1060586X.2015.1115198, https://www.rt.com/politics/medvedev-victims-political-repression/, accessed 13 December 2015.

Rurikov, D. (1994) 'How It All Began: An Essay on New Russia's Foreign Policy', in T. P. Johnson and S. E. Miller (eds) *Russian Security After the Cold War: Seven Views from Moscow* (McLean: Brassey's).

Russell, J. (2007) *Chechnya – Russia's 'War on Terror'* (London: Routledge).

Russia Beyond 2000 (2000) *Business Elites and Russian Foreign Policy*, Russia Beyond 2000, No. 5 (Helsinki: Finnish Institute of International Affairs).

Russian Federation (1999) 'The Russian Federation Middle Term Strategy for Development of Relations between the Russian Federation and the European Union', *Diplomatichesky vestnik*, No 11.

Russian Federation (2000) 'The Foreign Policy Concept of the Russian Federation', 28 June.

Russo, F. (2016) 'The Russia Threat in the Eyes of National Parliamentarians: An Opportunity for Foreign Policy Integration', *Journal of European Integration* 38(2): 195–209.

Rutland, P. (2009) 'US Energy Policy and the Former Soviet Union: Parallel Tracks', in J. Perovic, R. W. Orttung and A. Wenger (eds) *Russian Energy Power and Foreign Relations: Implications for Conflict and Cooperation* (London and New York: Routledge).

Rutland, P. (2014) 'The Impact of Sanctions on Russia', *Russian Analytical Digest*, No. 157, 17 December: 1–7.

Rutten, M. (2001) 'From St Malo to Nice. European Defence: Core Documents', Chaillot Papers 47, May (Paris: WEU Institute for Security Studies).

Saari, S. (2010a) *Promoting Democracy and Human Rights in Russia* (New York: Routledge).

Saari, S. (2010b) 'What Went Wrong with the EU's Human Rights Policy in Russia?', in *EU's Human Rights Policy Towards Russia*, 16 (Brussels: The EU–Russia Centre).

Saari, S. (2014) 'Russia's Post-Orange Revolution Strategies to Increase Its Influence in Former Soviet Republics: Public Diplomacy Po Russkii', *Europe–Asia Studies*, 66(1): 50–66.

Sadowski, R. and A. Wierzbowska-Miazga (2014) *Russia Is Blocking a Free Trade Area Between the EU and Ukraine*, OSW Analyses, July 17, http://www.osw.waw.pl/en/publikacje/analyses/2014-09-17/russiablocking-a-free-trade-area-between-eu-and-ukraine, accessed 10 November 2015.

Sakwa, R. (1996) *Russian Politics and Society*, 2nd edn (London and New York: Routledge).

Sakwa, R. (2008) *Putin: Russia's Choice*, 2nd edn (Abingdon and New York: Routledge).

Sakwa, R. (2014) *Frontline Ukraine: Crisis in the Borderlands* (London: I.B. Tauris).

Sakwa, R. (2015) 'The Death of Europe: Continental Fates after Ukraine', *International Affairs*, 91(3): 553–79.

Salminen, M. and A. Moshes (2009) *Practice What You Preach: The Prospects for Visa Freedom in Russia-EU Relations*, FIIA Report 18 (Helsinki: The Finnish Institute of International Affairs), http://www.fiia.fi/assets/events/FIIA_Report_18_2009.pdf, accessed 5 November 2015.

Sartori, N. (2013) 'The European Commission vs. Gazprom: An Issue of Fair Competition or a Foreign Policy Quarrel?', *IAI Working Papers 13/03*, January.

Sasse, G. (2008) 'The European Neighbourhood Policy: Conditionality Revisited for the EU's Eastern Neighbours', *Europe-Asia Studies*, 60(2): 295–316.

Savranskaya, S., T. Blanton and V. Zubok (eds) (2010) *Masterpieces of History: The Peaceful End of the Cold War in Europe, 1989* (Budapest: Central European University Press).

Scenario Group EU + East 2030 (2014) *The EU and the East in 2030: Four Scenarios for Relations between the EU, the Russian Federation, and the Common Neighbourhood* (Berlin: Friedrich Ebert Foundation).

Schiffers, S. (2015) 'A Decade of Othering: Russian Political Leaders' Discourse on Russia-EU Relations 2004–2014', *East European Quarterly*, 43(1): 1–27.

Schlamp, J. (2008) 'EU–Russia Summit: Brussels and Moscow Rediscover Friendship', *Spiegel Online International*, http://www.spiegel.de/international/europe/eu-russia-summit-brussels-and-moscow-rediscover-friendship-a-590673.html, accessed 13 December 2015.

Schleifer, A. and D. Treisman (2011) 'Why Moscow Says No', *Foreign Affairs*, 90(1): 122–38.

Schmidt-Felzmann, A. (2008) 'All for One? EU Member States and the Union's Common Policy Towards the Russian Federation', *Journal of Contemporary European Studies*, 16(2): 169–87.

Schmidt-Felzmann, A. (2015) 'European Foreign Policy Towards Russia: Challenges, Lessons and Future Avenues for Research', in K. E. Jørgensen, Å. Kalland, E. Drieskens, K. Laatikainen and B. Tonra (eds) *The Sage Handbook of European Foreign Policy* (London: Sage).

Schuette, R. (2004) 'E.U. Russia Relations: Interests and Values – A European Perspective', *Carnegie Papers* Number 54, December (Washington, DC: Carnegie Endowment for International Peace), http://carnegieendowment.org/files/cp54.shuette.final.pdf, accessed 27 August 2015.

Schuilenburg, K. A. (2005) 'The ECJ Simutenkov Case: Is Same Level Not Offside after All?', *Policy Papers on Transnational Economic Law*, no. 13 (Halle: Martin-Luther-University Halle-Wittenberg).

Schumacher, T. and D. Bouris (eds) (2016) *The Revised European Neighbourhood Policy. Continuity and Change in EU Foreign Policy* (Basingstoke: Palgrave Macmillan).

Schumacher, T. and C. Nitoiu (2015) 'Russia's Foreign Policy towards North Africa in the Wake of Arab Spring', *Mediterranean Politics*, 20(1): 97–104.

Seibel, W. (2015) 'Arduous Learning or New Uncertainties? German Diplomacy and the Ukrainian Crisis', *Global Policy*, 6(S1): 56–72.

Semenenko, I. (2013) 'The Quest for Identity: Russian Public Opinion on Europe and the European Union and the National Identity Agenda', *Perspectives on European Politics and Society*, 14(1): 102–22.

Sennett, R. (2012) *Together: The Rituals, Pleasures and Politics of Cooperation* (London: Allen Lane).

Sergunin, A. (2008) 'Russian Foreign-Policy Decision Making on Europe', in T. Hopf (ed.) *Russia's European Choice* (Basingstoke & New York: Palgrave Macmillan), 59–93.

Sergunin, A. (2011) *The EU–Russia Common Space On External Security: Prospects for Cooperation* (Nizhny Novgorod: Nizhny Novgorod Linguistic University).

Sergunin, A. (2014) 'Russian Views on the Ukrainian Crisis: From Confrontation to Damage Limitation', in T. Flichy de la Neuville (ed.) *Ukraine regards sur une crise* (Lausanne: L'Age d'Homme).

Sergunin, A. (2016) *Explaining Russian Foreign Policy Behavior: Theory and Practice* (Stuttgart: ibidem).

Shaffer, B. (2009) *Energy Politics* (Philadelphia: University of Pennsylvania Press).

Shemiatenkov, V. (2002) *EU–Russia: The Sociology of Approximation*, paper presented at the 6th ECSA World Conference, Brussels, 5–6 December.

Sherlock, T. (2011) 'Confronting the Stalinist Past: The Politics of Memory in Russia', *The Washington Quarterly*, 34(2): 93–109.

Sherr, J. (2013) *Hard Diplomacy and Soft Coercion: Russia's Influence Abroad* (London: Chatham House).

Shevtsova, L. (2005) *Putin's Russia*, revised and expanded edn (Washington, DC: Carnegie Endowment for International Peace).

Shiskounova, Y. and I. Zhegulev (2002) 'Putin Surrenders Kaliningrad', Gazeta.ru, 21 November.

Shustov, V. (1998) 'Towards a Europe without Dividing Lines', *International Affairs* (Moscow), 44(2): 45–50.

Siniver, A. (2012) 'The EU and the Israeli-Palestinian Conflict', in R. G. Whitman and S. Wolff (eds) *The European Union as a Global Conflict Manager* (New York and London: Routledge).

Sinkkonen, T. (2011) 'A Security Dilemma on the Boundary Line: An EU Perspective to Georgian-Russin Confrontation after the 2008 War', *Southeast European and Black Sea Studies*, 11(3): 265–78.

Smith, G. (2014) 'Russia may hit back at E.U. with Siberia overflight ban', *fortune.com*, August 5, http://fortune.com/2014/08/05/russia-may-hit-back-at-e-u-with-siberia-overflight-ban/, accessed 9 July 2015.

Smith, H. (2002) *European Union Foreign Policy: What It Is and What It Does* (London: Pluto Press).

Smith, H. (2005) 'The Russian Federation and the European Union – the Shadow of Chechnya', in D. Johnson and P. Robinson (eds) *Perspectives on EU–Russia Relations* (London: Routledge).

Smith, K. E. (2003) *European Union Foreign Policy in a Changing World* (Cambridge: Polity Press).

Smith, M. A. (2013) 'Russia and Multipolarity since the End of the Cold War', *East European Politics*, 29(1): 36–51.

Smith, M. E. (2000) 'Conforming to Europe: The Domestic Impact of EU Foreign Policy Co-operation', *Journal of European Public Policy*, 7(4): 613–31.

Smith, M. E. (2004) 'Institutionalization, Policy Adaptation and European Foreign Policy Cooperation', *European Journal of International Relations*, 10(1): 95–136.

Smith, N. R. (2015) 'The EU and Russia's Conflicting Regime Preferences in Ukraine', *European Security*, 24(4): 525–40.

Smith Stegen, K. (2011) 'Deconstructing the "Energy Weapon": Russia's Threat to Europe as Case Study', *Energy Policy*, 39(10): 6505–13.

Snegovaya, M. (2015) 'Putin's Information Warfare in Ukraine. Soviet Origins of Russia's Hybrid Warfare', *Russia Report 1*, September (Washington, DC: The Institute for the Study of War).

Socor, V. (1993) 'Russia's Army in Moldova: There to Stay', RFE/RL, 2(25): 42–9.

Socor, V. (2010) 'Meseberg Process: Germany Testing EU–Russia Security Cooperation Potential', *Eurasia Daily Monitor*, 7(191), October 22, http://www.jamestown.org/single/?tx_ttnews%5Btt_news%5D=37065&no_cache=1 - .VZNs5CGqrzI, accessed 1 July 2015.

Sokolov, A., K. Haegeman, M. Spiesberger and M. Boden (2014) 'Facilitating EU–Russian Scientific and Societal Engagement' *Science & Diplomacy*, December, http://www.sciencediplomacy.org/article/2014/facilitating-eu-russian-scientific-and-societal-engagement, accessed 13 December 2015.

Solana, J. (1999) 'The EU–Russia Strategic Partnership', speech in Stockholm, 13 October.

Solana, J. (2000) 'The EU–Russia Relationship at the Start of the New Millennium', *Kommersant*, 14 January.

Solana, J. (2008) 'Discours du Haut Représentant de l'Union européenne pour la Politique étrangère et de sécurité commune', speech at the Annual Conference of the European Union Institute of Security Studies, Paris, 30 October.

Spence, D. (1999) 'Foreign Ministries in National and European Context', in B. Hocking (ed.) *Foreign Ministries: Change and Adaptation* (Basingstoke: Palgrave Macmillan).

Spiegel (2008) 'Diplomacy With Russia: EU Civilian Mission Could Monitor Georgian Peace', *Spiegel Online International*, 5 September, http://www.spiegel.de/international/world/diplomacy-with-russia-eu-civilian-mission-could-monitor-georgian-peace-a-576475.html, accessed 13 December 2015.

Spiegel, P. (2014) 'José Manuel Barroso: "Not Everything I Did Was Right"', *Financial Times*, 4 November.

Spiegel Staff (2014) 'Summit of Failure: How the EU Lost Russia over Ukraine', *Spiegel Online* 24 November, http://www.spiegel.de/international/europe/war-in-ukraine-a-result-of-misunderstandings-between-europe-and-russia-a-1004706.html, accessed 13 December 2015.

De Spiegeleire, S. (2003) 'Recoupling Russia to Europe: Staying the Course', *The International Spectator*, 38(3): 79–97.

Splidsboel-Hansen, F. (2002a) 'Explaining Russia's Endorsement of the CFSP and ESDP', *Security Dialogue*, 33(4): 443–56.

Splidsboel-Hansen, F. (2002b) 'Russia's Relations with the European Union: A Constructivist Cut', *International Politics*, 39(4): 399–421.

Staar, R. F. (1987) *USSR Foreign Policies after Détente*, rev. edn (Stanford: Hoover Institution Press).

Stent, A. (1991) 'Gorbachev and Europe: An Accelerated Learning Curve', in H. D. Balzer (ed.) *Five Years That Shook the World: Gorbachev's Unfinished Revolution* (Boulder, San Francisco and Oxford: Westview Press).

Stent, A. (2014) *The Limits of Partnership. U.S.-Russian Relations in the Twenty-First Century* (Princeton and Oxford: Princeton University Press).

Stetter, S. (2004) 'Cross-pillar Politics: Functional Unity and Institutional Fragmentation of EU Foreign Policies', *Journal of European Public Policy*, 11(4): 720–39.

Stokke, O. (1995) 'Aid and Political Conditionality: Core Issues and State of the Art', in O. Stokke (ed.) *Aid and Political Conditionality* (London and Geneva: Frank Cass in association with the European Association of Development Research and Training Institutes EADI).

Stowe, R. (2001) 'Foreign Policy Preferences of the New Russian Business Elite', *Problems of Post-Communism*, 48(3): 49–58.

Stulberg, A. N. (2012) 'Strategic Bargaining and Pipeline Politics: Confronting the Credible Commitment Problem in Eurasian Energy Transit', *Review of International Political Economy*, 19(5): 808–36.

Suganami, H. (1997) 'Stories of War Origins: A Narrativist Theory of the Causes of War', *Review of International Studies*, 23(4): 401–18.

Sullivan, P. (2014) 'The Energy-Insurgency Revolution Nexus: An Introduction to Issues and Policy Options', *Journal of International Affairs*, 68(1): 117–46.

Sutela, P. (2005) 'EU, Russia and Common Economic Space', *BOFIT Online No. 3/2005*, (Helsinki: Bank of Finland), http://www.suomenpankki.fi/bofit_en/tutkimus/tutkimusjulkaisut/policy_brief/Documents/bon0305.pdf, accessed 13 December 2015.

SVOP (2007) *The World around Russia: 2017: An Outlook for the Midterm Future* (Moscow: Council on Foreign and Defence Policy).

Sycheva, V. (2002) 'The Axis of Good', *Itogi*, 26 November (WPS Monitoring Service).

Szabo, S. (2015) *Germany, Russia and the Rise of Geo-Economics* (London: Bloomsbury).

Tallberg, J. (2008) 'Bargaining Power in the European Council', *Journal of Common Market Studies*, 46(3): 685–708.

Talus, K. (2011) 'Long-term Natural Gas Contracts and Antitrust Law in the European Union and the United States', *Journal of World Energy Law and Business*, 4(3): 260–315.

TASS (2014) 'Lavrov Predicts Historians May Coin New Term: The Primakov Doctrine', *TASS*, 28 October, http://tass.ru/en/russia/756973, accessed 13 December 2015.

Tassinari, F. (2004) *Mare Europaeum: Baltic Sea Region Security and Cooperation from post-Wall to post-Enlargement Europe* (Copenhagen: Copenhagen University Press).

Telegina, G. and H. Schwengel (2012) 'The Bologna Process: Perspectives and Implications for the Russian University', *European Journal of Education*, 47(1): 37–49.

The Telegraph (2014) 'EU Needs Long-Term Russia Strategy, Donald Tusk States', *The Telegraph*, 19 December.

Telo, M. (2013) 'Introduction', in M. Telo and F. Ponjaert (eds) *The EU's Foreign Policy: What Kind of Power and Diplomatic Action?* (Farnham: Ashgate).

Thomas, D. C. (2001) *The Helsinki Effect: International Norms, Human Rights, and the Demise of Communism* (Princeton and Oxford: Princeton University Press).

Thorun, C. (2009) *Explaining Change in Russian Foreign Policy: The Role of Ideas in Post-Soviet Russia's Conduct Towards the West* (Basingstoke: Palgrave Macmillan).

Tigner, B. (2015) 'EU Sets Up "Rapid Respond" Unit to Counter Russian Disinformation', *IHS Jane's Defence Weekly*, 2 September 2015: 4.

Times Higher Education (2003) 'EU and Russia Strengthen Cooperation in Space', *The Times Higher Education*, 20 March, https://www.timeshighereducation.co.uk/news/eu-and-russia-strengthen-cooperation-in-space/175452.article, accessed 13 December 2015.

Timmermann, H. (1990) 'The Soviet Union and Western Europe: Conceptual Change and Political Reorientation', in V. Harle and J. Iivonen (eds) *Gorbachev and Europe* (London: Pinter Publishers).

Timmermann, H. (1991) 'The Soviet Union and West European Integration', in J. Iivonen (ed.) *The Changing Soviet Union in the New Europe* (Aldershot: Edward Elgar).

Timmermann, H. (1992) 'Russian Foreign Policy Under Yeltsin: Priority for Intergration into the "Community of Civilized States"', *Journal of Communist Studies and Transition Politics*, 8(4): 163–85.

Timmermann, H. (1996) 'Relations Between the EU and Russia: The Agreement on Partnership and Co-operation', *Journal of Communist Studies and Transition Politics*, 12(3): 196–223.

Timmermann, H. (2001) 'Kaliningrad: Eine Pilotregion für die Gestaltung der Partnerschaft EU-Rußland?', SWP-Studien 23, September (Berlin: Stiftung Wissenschaft und Politik).

Timmins, G. (2002) 'Strategic or Pragmatic Partnership? The European Union's Policy Towards Russia Since the End of the Cold War', *European Security* 11(4): 78–95.

Tisdall, S. (2006) 'West's Muted Response Speaks Volumes', *The Guardian*, 10 October, http://www.theguardian.com/world/2006/oct/10/tisdallbriefing.eu, accessed 11 December 2015.

Tkachenko, S. L. (2008) 'Actors in Russia's Energy Policy towards the EU', in P. Aalto (ed.) *The EU–Russian Energy Dialogue: Europe's Future Energy Security* (Aldershot: Ashgate).

Tocci, N. (2007) *The EU and Conflict Resolution: Promoting Peace in the Backyard* (London and New York: Routledge).

Toje, Asle (2008) 'The European Union as a Small Power, or Conceptualizing Europe's Strategic Actorness', *European Integration*, 30(2): 199–215.

Tolstrup, J. (2013) *Russia vs. the EU: The Competition for Influence in Post-Soviet States* (Boulder, CO: Lynne Rienner).

Tolstrup, J. (2014) 'Gatekeepers and Linkages', *Journal of Democracy*, 25(4): 126–38.

Tonra, B. (1997) 'The Impact of Political Cooperation', in K. E. Jorgensen (ed.) *Reflective Approaches to European Governance* (Basingstoke: Palgrave Macmillan).

Torbakov, I. (2011) "What Does Russia Want?', Investigating the Inter-relationship between Moscow's Domestic and Foreign Policy', *DGA-Panalyse No 1*, May (Berlin: DGAP), https://dgap.org/de/article/getFullPDF/17753, accessed 19 November 2015.

Traub-Merz, R. (2015) *Oil or Cars: The Prospects of Russia's Reindusriali-sation* (Moscow: Study FES).

Trauner, F. and I. Kruse, (2008) 'EC Visa Facilitation and Readmission Agreements: A New Standard EU Foreign Policy Tool?', *European Journal of Migration and Law*, 10(4): 411–38.

Traynor, I. (2002) 'EU and Russia Clash over Baltic Enclave', *The Guardian*, 30 May 2002, http://www.theguardian.com/world/2002/may/30/eu.russia, accessed 3 November 2015.

Traynor, I. (2015) 'Donald Tusk: Putin's Policy Is to Have Enemies and to Be in Conflict', *The Guardian*, 15 March, http://www.theguardian.com/world/2015/mar/15/donald-tusk-putins-policy-enemies-conflict-european-council-sanctions-russia, accessed 13 December 2015.

Traynor, I. and M. White (2000) 'Blair Courts Outrage with Putin Visit', *The Guardian*, 11 March 2000, http://www.theguardian.com/world/2000/mar/11/russia.ethicalforeignpolicy, accessed 9 July 2015.

Trenin, D. (2006) 'Russia Leaves the West', *Foreign Affairs*, 85(4): 87–96.

Trenin, D. (2007) 'Russia Redefines Itself and Its Relations with the West', *The Washington Quarterly*, 30(2): 95–105.

Trenin, D. (2009) 'Russia's Spheres of Interest, not Influence', *The Washington Quarterly*, 32(4): 3–22.

Trenin, D. (2011a) *Post-Imperium: A Eurasian Story* (Washington, DC: Carnegie Endowment for International Peace).

Trenin, D. (2011b) 'Modernizing Russian Foreign Policy', *Russian Politics and Law*, 49(6): 8–37.

Trenin, D. and B. Lo (2005) *The Landscape of Russian Foreign Policy Decision-Making* (Moscow: Moscow Center of the Carnegie Endowment for International Peace).

Tsygankov, A. (2006) 'If Not by Tanks, then by Banks? The Role of Soft Power in Putin's Foreign Policy', *Europe-Asia Studies*, 58(7): 1079–99.

Tsygankov, A. (2012a) *Russia and the West from Alexander to Putin: Honour in International Relations* (Cambridge: Cambridge University Press).

Tsygankov, A. (2012b) 'The Heartland No More: Russia's Weakness and Eurasia's Meltdown', *Journal of Eurasian Studies*, 3(1): 1–9.

Tsygankov A. and F. Fominykh (2010) 'The Anti-Russian Discourse of the European Union', *Russian Politics & Law*, 48(6): 19–34.

Tsygankov, A. and D. Parker (2015) 'The Securitization of Democracy: Freedom House Ratings of Russia', *European Security*, 24(1): 77–100.

Tudoroiu, T. (2012) 'The European Union, Russia, and the Future of the Transnistrian Frozen Conflict' *East European Politics & Societies*, 26(1): 135–61.

Tumanov, S., A. Gasparishvili and E. Romanova (2011) 'Russia–EU Relations, or How the Russians Really View the EU', *Journal of Communist Studies and Transition Politics*, 27(1): 120–41.

Tuomioja, E. (2007) 'Minister Tuomioja's speech at the Conference on The Northern Dimension and Nordic Cooperation in Hanasaari', 17 January, http://213214149030.edelkey.net/public/default.aspx?content id=85888&nodeid=36240&contentlan=2&culture=en-US, accessed 13 December 2015.

Tuomioja, E. (2015) 'Yhteistyöstä on pidettävä kiinni', *Ulkopolitiikka*, 52(3): 38–43.

Tyazhov, A. (2006) 'The Four Common Spaces Between Russia and the EU: Erasing Old of Building New Divides?', *EU–Russia: The Four Common Spaces – Research Bulletin*, 1: 11–19 (Nizhny Novgorod: Nizhny Novgorod Linguistic University).

Tynkkynen, N. (2014) *Russia and Global Climate Governance*, Russie. Nei.Visions No. 80 (Paris: IFRI), http://www.ifri.org/sites/default/files/atoms/files/ifri_rnv_80_eng_tynkkynen_russiaclimatepolitics_september_2014_2.pdf, accessed 12 November 2015.

Tynkkynen, V.-P. (2008) 'The Environment', in *Russia of Challenges* (Helsinki: The Ministry of Defence), http://www.defmin.fi/files/1298/Russia_of_Challenges_nettiversio.pdf, accessed 12 November 2015.

United Nations Security Council (2008) 'Security Council Steps Back from French-Led Draft Resolution, as Russian Delegate Says It Re-Interprets "Moscow Peace Plan" for Propaganda Purposes', press release *SC/9429*, New York, 19 August.

U.S. Energy Information Administration (EIA) (2014) *Russia*. March 12, 2014, http://www.eia.gov/beta/international/analysis_includes/countries_long/Russia/russia.pdf, accessed 4 June 2015.

Utkin, A. I. (1995) 'Russia and the West: The Day After', *PSIS Occasional Paper 3* (Geneva: Programme for Strategic and International Security Studies).

Vahl, M. (2004) 'Whiter the Common European Economic Space? Political and Institutional Aspects of Closer Economic Integration between the EU and Russia', in T. Wilde d'Estmael and L. Spetschinsky (eds) *La Politique étrangère de la Russie et l'Europe. Enjeux d'une proximité* (Brussels: P.I.E.-Peter Lang).

Van Elsuwege, P. (2007) 'The Comon Spaces in EU–Russia and the Future of Northern Dimension', in C. Archer (ed.) *The Northern Dimension of the European Union: Glancing Back, Looking Forward. Proceedings from the Northern Dimensions Network* (Kaunas: Technologija).

Van Elsuwege, P. (2008) 'The Four Common Spaces: New Impetus to the EU–Russia Strategic Partnership', in A. Dashwood and M. Maresceau (eds) *Law and Practice of EU External Relations: Salient Features of a Changing Landscape* (Cambridge: Cambridge Univesity Press).

Van Elsuwege, P. (ed.) (2013) *EU–Russia Visa Facilitation and Liberalization: State of Play and Prospects for the Future*. EU–Russia Civil Society Forum Report, September 2013, http://eu-russia-csf.org/fileadmin/Docs/Visa/Draft_Visa_Report.pdf, accessed 5 November 2015.

van Ham, P. (2015) 'The EU, Russia and the Quest for a New European Security Bargain', Clingendael Report (The Hague: Clingendael).

van Hecke, S. and W. Wolfs (2015) 'The European Parliament and European Foreign Policy', in K. E. Jørgensen, Å. Kalland, E. Drieskens, K. Laatikainen and B. Tonra (eds) *The Sage Handbook of European Foreign Policy* (London: Sage).

Van Rompuy, H. (2012) 'A Letter to the President Medvedev', Brussels, 18 April, 8G812/004302, https://s3.eu-central-1.amazonaws.com/euobs-media/9e404add713f2af808b65302b1dc83ee.pdf, accessed 5 November 2015.

Van Rompuy, H. (2013) 'Russia and Europe Today', lecture at the European University in St Petersburg, 5 September 2013, http://www.consilium.europa.eu/en/press/press-releases/2013/09/pdf/europe-and-russia-today---lecture-by-president-herman-van-rompuy-at-the-european-university-at-saint-petersburg/, accessed 20 February 2016.

VCIOM (2014) 'Russia's Friends and Enemies in Time of Sanctions', press release, No. 1681, (Moscow: Vserossijski Centr Izuchenija Obshchestvennogo Mnenija) http://www.wciom.com/index.php?id=61&uid=1008, accessed 13 December 2015.

VCIOM (2015) 'Russia and Germany: From Partnership to Confrontation', September 18, (Moscow: Vserossijskij Centr Izuchenija Obshchestvennogo Mnenija), http://www.wciom.com/index.php?id=61&uid=1181, accessed 16 February 2016.

Vendil, C. (2001) 'The Russian Security Council', *European Security*, 10(2): 67–94.

Verheugen, G. (2005) 'Working Together to Boost Trade', speech, London, 3 October, europa.eu/rapid/press-release_SPEECH-05-569_en.htm, accessed 14 December 2015.

Volchkova, N. (2007) 'Russia and the WTO: A Russian View', *Russian Analytical Digest*, 24, July, www.res.ethz.ch/analysis/rad, accessed September 2007.

Volk, Y. (2004) *Russian Views of the Northern Dimension after EU enlargement*, remarks at a Jean Monnest seminar, 'New Frontiers or New Borders, Northern Dimension in the Enlarged European Union', Tallinn, 23 November 2004.

Voronov, K. V. (2003) '"Severnoe izmerenie": zatyanuvschiisya debiut', *Mirovaya ekonomika i mezdunarodnye otnoseniya*, No. 2: 76–86.

Wæver, O. (1990) 'Three Competing Europes: German, French, Russian', *International Affairs* (London), 66(3): 477–93.

Wæver, O. (1996) 'European Security Identities', *Journal of Common Market Studies*, 34(1): 103–32.

Walker, S. (2013) 'Ukraine's EU Trade Deal Will Be Catastrophic, Says Russia', *The Guardian*, 22 September, http://www.theguardian.com/world/2013/sep/22/ukraine-european-union-trade-russia, accessed 13 December 2015.

Wallander, C. A. (2007) 'Russian Transimperialism and Its Implications', *The Washington Quarterly*, 30(2): 107–22.

Wallander, C. A. and J. E. Prokop (1993) 'Soviet Security Strategies toward Europe: After the Wall, with Their Backs up against It', in R. O. Keohane, J. S. Nye and S. Hoffmann (eds) *After the Cold War: International Institutions and State Strategies in Europe, 1989–1991* (Cambridge, MA and London: Harvard University Press).

Waltz, K. (1979/2010) *Theory of International Politics* (Long Grove: Waveland Press).

Webber, M. (2000) 'Introduction', in M. Webber (ed.) *Russia and Europe: Conflict and Cooperation?* (Basingstoke: Palgrave Macmillan).

Webber, M. (2001) 'Third-Party Inclusion in European Security and Defence Policy: A Case Study of Russia', *European Foreign Affairs Review*, 6(4): 407–26.

Webber, M. (2002) 'The Former Soviet Union: Russia and Ukraine', in M. Webber and M. Smith with D. Allen, A. Collins, D. Morgan and A. Ehterhami, *Foreign Policy in a Transformed World* (Harlow: Prentice Hall).

Wegren, S. K. (2014) 'Russia's Food Embargo', *Russian Analytical Digest*, 157, 17 December: 8–12.

Weiss, T. G. (2000) 'Governance, Good Governance and Global Governance: Conceptual and Actual Challenges', *Third World Quarterly*, 21(5): 795–814.

Weitz R. (2012) 'The Rise and Fall of Medvedev's European Security Treaty', the German Marshall Fund of the United States, Wider Europe Program.

Weller, M. (2008) *Negotiating the Final Status of Kosovo*, Chaillot Paper No. 114 (Paris: European Union Institute for Security Studies).

Weltschinski, C. (2014) *Cooperation between European and Russian Police Forces*, 21 July (Twente: Faculty of Management and Governance, University of Twente).

Wendt, A. (1999) *Social Theory of International Politics* (Cambridge: Cambridge University Press).

Wessel, R. A. (2000) 'The Inside Looking Out: Consistency and Delimitation in EU External Relations', *Common Market Law Review*, 37(5): 1135–71.

Wessels, W. (2016) *The European Council* (Basingstoke: Palgrave Macmillan).

Westphal, K. (2008) 'Germany and the EU–Russia Energy Dialogue', in P. Aalto (ed.) *The EU–Russian Energy Dialogue: Europe's Future Energy Security* (Aldershot: Ashgate).

Wettig, G. (1991) *Changes in Soviet Policy towards the West* (London, Boulder and San Francisco: Pinter Publishers & Westview Press).

White, B. (2001) *Understanding European Foreign Policy* (Basingstoke: Palgrave Macmillan).

White, S. (2006) 'The Domestic Management of Russia's Foreign and Security Policy', in R. Allison, M. Light and S. White (eds) *Putin's Russia and the Enlarged Europe* (London and Oxford: RIIA and Blackwell Publishing).

White, S., and V. Feklyunina (2015) *Identities and Foreign Policies in Russia, Ukraine and Belarus: The Other Europes* (Basingstoke: Palgrave Macmillan).

Whitman, R. G. and S. Wolff (2010) 'The EU as a Conflict Manager? The Case of Georgia and its Implications', *International Affairs* (London), 86(1): 87–107.

Wiegand, G. and E. Schulz (2014) 'The EU and Its Eastern Partnership: Political Association and Economic Integration in a Rough Neighbourhood', in C. Hermann, B. Simma and R. Streinz (eds) *Trade Policy between Law, Diplomacy and Scholarship*, Liber Amicorum in Memoriam Horst G. Krenzler, EYIEL Special Issue (Berlin: Springer).

Wierzbowska-Miazga, A. (2012) 'Russia's Energy Ultimatum to Moldova', *OSW EastWeek*, 9 September (Warsaw: Centre for Eastern Studies).

Wierzbowska-Miazga, A. (2013) 'Russia Goes on the Offensive Ahead of the Eastern Partnership Summit in Vilnius', *OSW Commentary*, October 1, http://www.osw.waw.pl/en/publikacje/osw-commentary/2013-10-01/russia-goes-offensive-ahead-eastern-partnership-summit-vilnius, accessed 10 November 2015.

Wierzbowska-Miazga, A. and A. Sarna (2013) 'Moscow Deals: Russia Offers Yanukovych Conditional Support', *OSW Analyses*, December 18, http://www.osw.waw.pl/en/publikacje/analyses/2013-12-18/moscow-deals-russia-offers-yanukovych-conditional-support, accessed 10 November 2015.

Wight, C. (2006) *Agents, Structures and International Relations* (Cambridge: Cambridge University Press).

Wilson, A. (2014) *Ukraine Crisis: What It Means for the West* (New Haven: Yale University Press).

Wilson Rowe, E. and H. Blakkisrud (2014) 'A New Kind of Arctic Power? Russia's Policy Dircourses and Diplomatic Practices in the Circumpolar North', *Geopolitics*, 19(1): 66–85.

Wong, R. and C. Hill (eds) (2011) *National and European Foreign Policies: Towards Europeanization* (London and New York: Routledge).

Wright, R. (2002) 'No State Has Ever Been Ruined by Commerce', Remarks in 'The European Economic Area: Round Table Discussion', *International Affairs* (Moscow), 48(4): 180–2.

Wright, T. (2014) 'Mogherini Is the Wrong Choice for Europe' *Brookings Up Front*, 14 August, http://www.brookings.edu/blogs/up-front/posts/2014/08/italian-foreign-minister-mogherini-europe-wright, accessed 2 December 2015.

Yasin, Y. (2002) 'Russia and the WTO: What Is the Alternative?', in K. Barysch, R. Cottrell, F. Frattini, P. Hare, P. Lamy, M. Medvedkov and Y. Yasin, *Russia and the WTO* (London: Centre for European Reform).

Yastrzhembsky, S. (2008) *Russian Envoy to the EU Speaking in Moscow*, 19 February 2008.

Year of Science 2014 (2013) 'Launch Events of the EU–Russia Year of Science 2014', *Moscow*, 25 November.

Year of Science 2014 (2014) 'Closing Conference "EU–Russia STI Collaboration: Good Practice Examples from the Year of Science and Beyond"', *Brussels*, 25 November.

Ylikoski, P. (2007) 'The Idea of Contrastive Explanandum', in J. Persson and P. Ylikoski (eds) *Rethinking Explanation* (Dordrecht: Springer).

Youngs, R. (2001) 'European Union Democracy Promotion Policies: Ten Years On', *European Foreign Affairs Review*, 6(3): 355–73.

Yurgens, I. (2013) 'The EU–Russia Strategic Partnership: Finding a Way Forward', in Bertelsmann Stiftung (ed.) *From Cooperation to Partnership: Moving Beyond the Russia-EU Deadlock*, Europe in Dialogue 1/2013 (Berlin: Verlag Bertelsmann Stiftung).

Zagorski, A. (1997) 'Russia and European Institutions', in V. Baranovsky (ed.) *Russia and Europe: The Emerging Security Agenda* (Stockholm and Oxford: SIPRI and Oxford University Press).

Zagorski, A. (2009) 'The Russian Proposal for a Treaty on European Security: From the Medvedev Intiative to the Corfu Process', in *The OSCE Yearbook 2009* (Hamburg: CORE), http://ifsh.de/file-CORE/documents/yearbook/english/09/Zagorski-en.pdf, accessed 1 July 2015.

Zagorski, A. (2012) 'Russia's Neighbourhood Policy', in S. Fischer (ed.) *Russia: Insights from a Changing Country*, EUISS Report No 11 (Paris: EU Institute for Security Studies), http://www.iss.europa.eu/publications/detail/article/russia-insights-from-a-changing-country/, accessed 13 December 2015.

Zagorski, A. (2013) 'Russia and the European Union: Looking Back and Looking Ahead', in Bertelsmann Stiftung (ed.) *From Cooperation to Partnership: Moving Beyond the Russia-EU Deadlock*, Europe in Dialogue 1/2013 (Berlin: Verlag Bertelsmann Stiftung).

Zakharova, O. (2013) 'Linguistic Look at Russia's Human Rights Record', *Moscow Times*, 8 April.

Die Zeit (1999) 'Das Neue Tandem', interview with Joschka Fischer and Hubert Védrine, *Die Zeit*, 28 October.

Zhurkin, V. (ed.) (2001) *Between the Past and the Future: Russia in the Transatlantic Context* (Moscow: SIBIR).

Zhurkin, V. (2003) 'European Security and Defense Policy: Past Present and Probable Future', International Institute for Peace, http://www.iip.at/publications/ps/0303zhurkin.htm, accessed 13 December 2015.

Zielonka, J. (2006) *Europe as Empire: The Nature of the Enlarged European Union* (Oxford: Oxford University Press).

Zielonka, J. (2011) 'The EU as an International Actor: Unique or Ordinary?', *European Foreign Affairs Review*, 16(3): 281–301.

Zielonka, J. (2014) *Is the EU Doomed?* (Cambridge: Polity Press).

Zonova, T. (2013) 'Cultural Diplomacy as a Soft Power Tool in EU–Russia Relations', article based on presentation at OSCE Talks seminar Cultural diplomacy in a global digital age, Istanbul, 2 May, http://www.osce.org/secretariat/103745?download=true, accessed 26 June 2015.

Zweynert, J. (2010) 'Conflicting Patterns of Thought in the Russian Debate on Transition: 2003–2007', *Europe-Asia Studies*, 62(4): 547–69.

Zysk, K. (2011) 'Military Aspects of Russia's Arctic Policy: Hard Power and Natural Resources', in J. Kraska (ed.) *Arctic Security in an Age of Climate Change* (Cambridge and New York: Cambridge University Press).

Index